Television Production

Phillip L. Harris

*Instructor of Television Production
Fairfax High School Academy for
Communications and the Arts
Fairfax, Virginia*

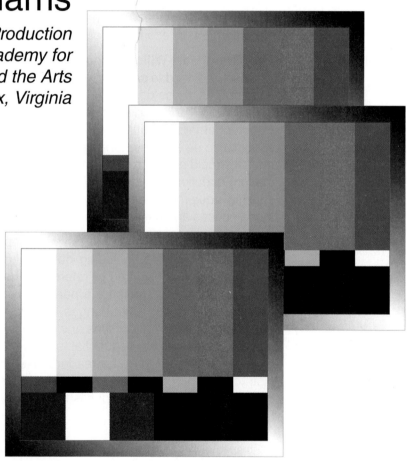

Publisher
The Goodheart-Willcox Company, Inc.
Tinley Park, Illinois
www.g-w.com

Library of Congress Catalog Card Number 2004060789

ISBN-13: 978-1-59070-454-7
ISBN-10: 1-59070-454-1

3 4 5 6 7 8 9 – 06 – 09 08 07

Library of Congress Cataloging-in-Publication Data

Harris, Phillip L.
    Television Production/ by Phillip L. Harris
      p. cm.
    Includes index.
    ISBN-10: 1-59070-454-1
    1. Television–Production and direction. I. Title.

PN1992.75.H37 2006
791.4502′32—dc22   2004060789

Introduction

Television Production introduces the basic skills you need to enter the television production industry. This text provides an overview of the equipment, job responsibilities, and techniques involved in both traditional studio production and remote location work.

This text strongly emphasizes the importance of vocabulary and the correct use of industry terms. When a term is presented, it is set in ***bold italic*** type, is immediately defined, and is then used consistently throughout the chapters that follow. *Talk the Talk* features explain the difference between common consumer terms and professional terms. These features also provide examples of the industry's use of terms. Knowing the use and meaning of the terms presented in each chapter is a significant requirement when beginning a career in the television production industry. Oftentimes, the respect you receive from industry professionals is based greatly on the way you speak. Correctly using professional terms is required at all times in our industry.

Principles involved in camera operation, picture composition, script-writing, lighting, remote shooting, directing, and many other areas are discussed with illustrated examples and explanations. *Production Note* features are found within each chapter and provide additional information or tips that expand on or reinforce a particular topic. *Visualize This* features also reinforce concepts by providing examples intended to help you create a mental picture of a concept or scenario. These features provide examples you can relate to, helping to ensure that you gain the knowledge and skills necessary to be successful.

Even though the technology involved in television and television production is evolving, the basic knowledge and skills required to enter this field remain consistent. **Television Production** is designed to provide a foundation of information and skills on which a rewarding career can be built.

From the Author

Television Production grew out of a need to provide my students with an up-to-date high school textbook on the subject of television production. After trying unsuccessfully for several years to find such a textbook, I finally decided to write one myself. This text is fundamentally a written version of my lecture notes, combined with information from trade magazines, over 30 years of my experiences as a videographer and instructor, and, more recently, interaction with other Broadcasting, Communications, and Television Production instructors as a consultant.

This book could not have been written without considerable help from many people. I must thank my good friend Dick Blocher for his patient willingness to answer any question I put to him. I must thank all of my students for their ideas, consideration, and suggestions, as they were the guinea pigs with the first draft of the text. My good friend, Janet Kerby (Broadcasting instructor at Roane County High School in Spencer, West Virginia) was the initial editor of the first draft. Her impact on this book has been profound and I can't thank her enough. Pete Datoc (a colleague at Fairfax Academy) provided valuable suggestions regarding content and consistency. Randy Jacobson (Digital Photography instructor at Fairfax Academy) and his students provided most of the photography work, and Edward Kim provided the first rough illustrations.

Phillip L. Harris

About the Author

Mr. Harris received a Bachelor of Science degree from East Carolina University and a Master of Arts in Technology Education from George Mason University. He is also a graduate of Imero Fiorintino Lighting Seminars. Mr. Harris's professional work experience includes a wide range of freelance videography (from weddings to commercials), over 25 years as a freelance theatrical makeup designer and artist, and experience directing more than 25 plays and musicals for community theater since 1979.

Mr. Harris brings over 30 years of teaching Television Production to this book. He has provided instruction at Fairfax Academy for Communication and the Arts since the inception of their Television Production program in 2000. As part of the program, Mr. Harris created Digital Wave Productions, a school-based enterprise that allows students to gain professional work experience and earn money while producing video projects for clients. The client list for Digital Wave Productions includes various school and community groups, as well as ExxonMobil Corporation, the National Institutes of Health, and the United States House of Representatives.

In addition to teaching at the academy, Mr. Harris provides consultation services for television and video educational programs. He assists schools and school districts design, develop, and implement these programs and provides related training for teachers of television and video courses. Mr. Harris can be contacted at pharris11@cox.net.

Brief Contents

Contents

Chapter 7

Scriptwriting...147

Chapter 8

Image Display...169

Chapter 9

Lighting...187

Television Production Chapter Components

Important Terms. Each chapter begins with a list of terms that are introduced and defined in that chapter. The terms in this list appear in *blue bold-italic type* when first presented within the chapter.

Objectives. A list of learning objectives is included at the beginning of each chapter. The objectives provide an overview of the chapter topics and explain what each student should know or be able to do upon completion of the chapter.

Chapter 20
Getting Technical– The Video Signal

Important Terms

Field
Frame
Genlock
Horizontal Blanking
Horizontal Retrace
Horizontal Sync Pulse
Interlace
Letterbox
Progressive Scan Technology
Sync Generator
Vectorscope
Vertical Blanking
Vertical Retrace
Vertical Sync Pulse
Waveform Monitor

Objectives

After completing this chapter, you will be able to:

● Describe how the television picture is produced.
● Name and define each of the cathode ray signals.
● Explain the importance of sync to video equipment during production.
● Describe how the imminent changes in video technology will affect both current and new video equipment.

Introduction

Even though current television technology is being tremendously impacted by the digital revolution, the television system most common throughout the country is analog. This chapter provides a rather simple overview of the technical aspects of the analog video signal and is designed as a general perspective for the average production personnel. A basic understanding of the video signal is helpful when troubleshooting problems during a program shoot.

This chapter is not intended to be an introduction to video engineering. A video engineer is intimately acquainted with the intricacies of the television signal from an electronics perspective. Students with an aptitude for electronics may find a rewarding career as a video engineer.

379

---

170   *Television Production*

Graphics: All of the "artwork" seen in a program, including the paintings that hang on the walls of a set, the opening and closing program titles, computer graphics, charts, graphs, and any other electronic representation that may be part of a visual presentation.

Talk the Talk

In some facilities, the terms "visuals" and "graphics" are used interchangeably.

Copyright

Any picture taken from a magazine or book, or a motion picture still frame is almost always copyrighted. This means that these images may not be used in a video program without the copyright owner's permission. The simplest way to obtain images for a production is to create your own; take original photographs or make unique paintings. If existing copyrighted works must be used, find the copyright holder and get permission.

Still Photos

Still photography, if used sparingly, works well in a video program. Excessive use of still photography makes a television program look like a slide show. To make interesting use of still photos, move the camera around on the picture to create a sense of motion.

Assistant Activity

Watch a few documentaries to see this "roaming the camera on a still photo" technique. Notice, also, that sound effects and music are added while the camera is roaming across a still image. The net result is quite effective.

Photos taken with a consumer 35mm camera may be used in a video production, if certain precautions are taken.

● Always take the picture holding the camera horizontally. A picture taken in the horizontal orientation is more closely shaped to the television screen than a vertically oriented picture, **Figure 8-1**. A horizontal picture is a rectangle with the long side on the top and bottom just like a television screen.
● If printing the photo, request a satin finish. A glossy finish poses lighting problems, because glossy paper reflects the glare of lights into the lens of the video camera.
● Photographic slides may be used instead of printed photos. This avoids the lighting glare issue entirely. A photographic slide must be oriented in the slide projector horizontally, rather than vertically.

Talk the Talk. These features explain the difference between consumer and professional terms and provide examples of appropriate use of industry terms.

Assistant Activity. These features contain activities students can complete independently, outside the classroom. The activities enhance the understanding of chapter content and concepts through experience.

Production Note

Some lighting designers prefer to generally light the set, turn off all the general lighting, and then position spot lighting in specific areas where talent will be moving or standing. The general lighting is then turned back on and final adjustments can be made. Other lighting designers prefer to start with the areas specific to the talent and then set up the general lighting. Both techniques work well.

Techniques of Television Lighting

Each of the following basic lighting techniques may be used on any size production studio. Knowing the use and setup of each is crucial to creating quality shots for the program.

Three-Point Lighting

Three-point lighting is the most commonly used photographic lighting technique in television. This technique is designed to make a person look attractive and, at the same time, create the appearance of three-dimensionality on the flat, two-dimensional television screen. Three-point lighting makes use of three instruments for each person/object being photographed, **Figure 9-22**. Each of the three instruments performs a specific function:

- Key Light
- Fill Light
- Back Light

Three point lighting: A common lighting technique that uses three lighting instruments for each person or object photographed: a key light, a fill light, and a back light.

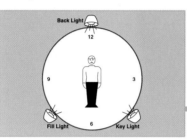

Figure 9-22
This illustrat...
the general...
instruments...
point lighting...

Production Note. The information included in these text features may provide additional, general information that relates to a chapter topic or may provide professional production tips.

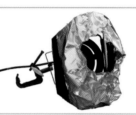

Figure 9-8
Heavy aluminum foil can be used to shape the light projected from an instrument.

Safety Note

Do not use transparent tape, masking tape, or duct tape to attach foil to the instrument. The tape may ignite! This poses a serious safety risk to every person on the set and in the building. Also, water emitted from the sprinkler system will damage every piece of video equipment, the set, costumes, props, and all other valuable items in the studio.

Brightly polished objects, like a silver ashtray or brass lamp, may be part of the set. Highly reflective surfaces create a white spot or star shaped reflection of a lighting instrument or sunlight that is reflected into the lens of the camera. This reflection is called a *light hit* and is generally considered to be an undesired effect. The simplest solution is to remove the object from the set. If this is not an option, a *flag* needs to be placed between the lighting instrument and the object, **Figure 9-**

Light hit: A white spot or star shaped reflection of a lighting instrument or sunlight off a highly reflective surface on the set.

Flag: A flexible metal rod with a clip and a flat piece of metal attached to the end. A flag is positioned between a light source and a reflective surface on the set to avoid light hits.

Safety Note. The information contained in these features provides important cautions related to equipment, environment, and ensuring the well being of all individuals involved in the production.

Control track: A series of inaudible pulses recorded onto a tape that regulates the speed of the tape in playback.

Control Track

The *control track* is a series of inaudible pulses recorded onto a tape that regulates the speed of the tape in playback. The control track is the result of a circuit that puts a little pulse signal, or blip, 30 times per second onto the tape when recording. If the machine is set for 2-hour speed (SP), the blips are spaced further apart because the tape moves relatively quickly through the machine. If the machine is set for the 6-hour speed (EP), the blips are much closer together because the tape moves more slowly through the machine. The blip is placed on the tape every 1/30th of a second, without regard to how fast the tape is moving, **Figure 5-9**.

Figure...
A flag...
reflect...
reflecti...

Visualize This

Imagine you are driving a car on a flat, straight stretch of deserted highway. You are driving down the center of the road and the white line appears as a series of white dashes that disappear under the hood of the car. It would take some practice, but you could regulate the accelerator so that 1 dash goes under the hood every 2 seconds. The white dashes may come in too fast at first, but you slow the car down until exactly 1 dash goes under the hood every 2 seconds. The control track circuit operates the same way. It speeds up and slows the tape down until the pulses occur at 1/30th of a second intervals.

Common recording speeds are:

- SP (Standard Play) records one 2-hour program onto a T-120 tape. The "T-120" designation indicates the tape's run time on a VCR's highest speed setting. The vast majority of VHS movies rented at local video stores are recorded at SP speed.
- LP (Long Play) is a 4-hour speed, twice that of SP, that is being phased out.

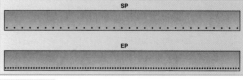

Figure 5-9
The control track pulses are placed further apart when recording in SP mode compared to EP mode.

Visualize This. These text features provide additional explanation for a topic or concept. Visualize This features help students create a vivid picture in their mind, which assists in fully understanding the material.

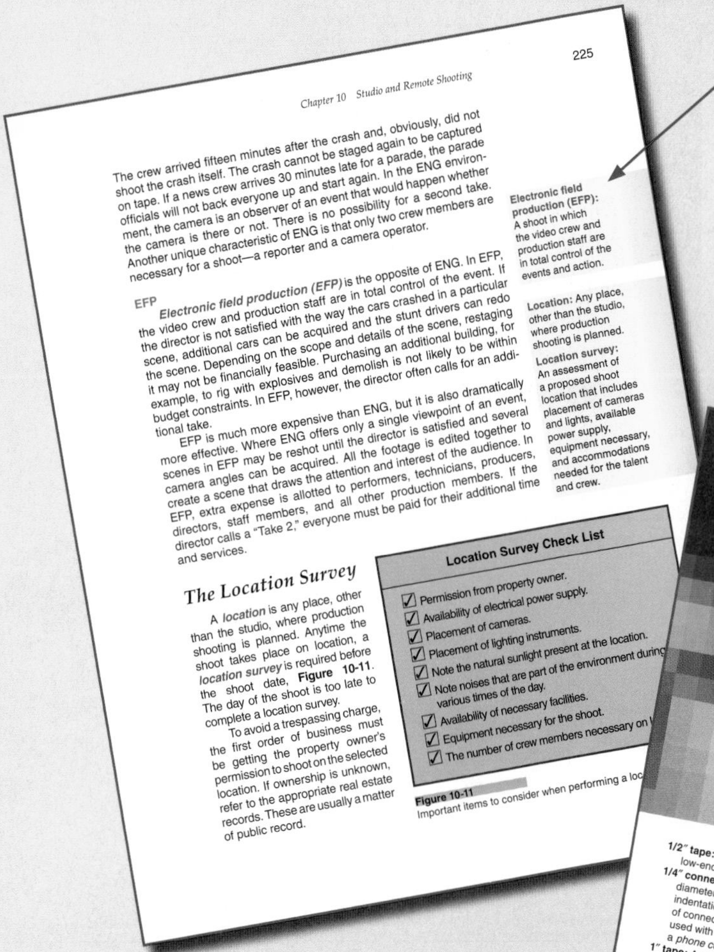

Running Glossary. A feature in the margin of chapter pages that provides definitions of the Important Terms found on each page.

The crew arrived fifteen minutes after the crash and, obviously, did not shoot the crash itself. The crash cannot be staged again to be captured on tape. If a news crew arrives 30 minutes late for a parade, the parade officials will not back everyone up and start again. In the ENG environment, the camera is an observer of an event that would happen whether the camera is there or not. There is no possibility for a second take. Another unique characteristic of ENG is that only two crew members are necessary for a shoot—a reporter and a camera operator.

EFP

Electronic field production (EFP) is the opposite of ENG. In EFP, the video crew and production staff are in total control of the event. If the director is not satisfied with the way the cars crashed in a particular scene, additional cars can be acquired and details of the scene, restaging the scene. Depending on the scope and details of the scene can redo it may not be financially feasible. Purchasing an additional building, for example, to rig with explosives and demolish is not likely to be within budget constraints. In EFP, however, the director often calls for an additional take.

EFP is much more expensive than ENG, but it is also dramatically more effective. Where ENG offers only a single viewpoint of an event, scenes in EFP may be reshot until the director is satisfied and several camera angles can be acquired. All the footage is edited together to create a scene that draws the attention and interest of the audience. In EFP, extra expense is allotted to performers, technicians, producers, directors, staff members, and all other production members. If the director calls a "Take 2," everyone must be paid for their additional time and services.

The Location Survey

A *location* is any place, other than the studio, where production shooting is planned. Anytime the shoot takes place on location, a *location survey* is required before the shoot date, **Figure 10-11**. The day of the shoot is too late to complete a location survey.

To avoid a trespassing charge, the first order of business must be getting the property owner's permission to shoot on the selected location. If ownership is unknown, refer to the appropriate real estate records. These are usually a matter of public record.

Electronic field production (EFP): A shoot in which the video crew and production staff are in total control of the events and action.

Location: Any place, other than the studio, where production shooting is planned.

Location survey: An assessment of a proposed shoot location that includes placement of cameras and lights, available power supply, equipment necessary, and accommodations needed for the talent and crew.

Location Survey Check List

☑ Permission from property owner.
☑ Availability of electrical power supply.
☑ Placement of cameras.
☑ Placement of lighting instruments.
☑ Note the natural sunlight present at the location.
☑ Note noises that are part of the environment during various times of the day.
☑ Availability of necessary facilities.
☑ Equipment necessary for the shoot.
☑ The number of crew members necessary on

Figure 10-11
Important items to consider when performing a loc

Glossary. Each term defined in the Running Glossary throughout the text is contained in the Glossary at the end of the book.

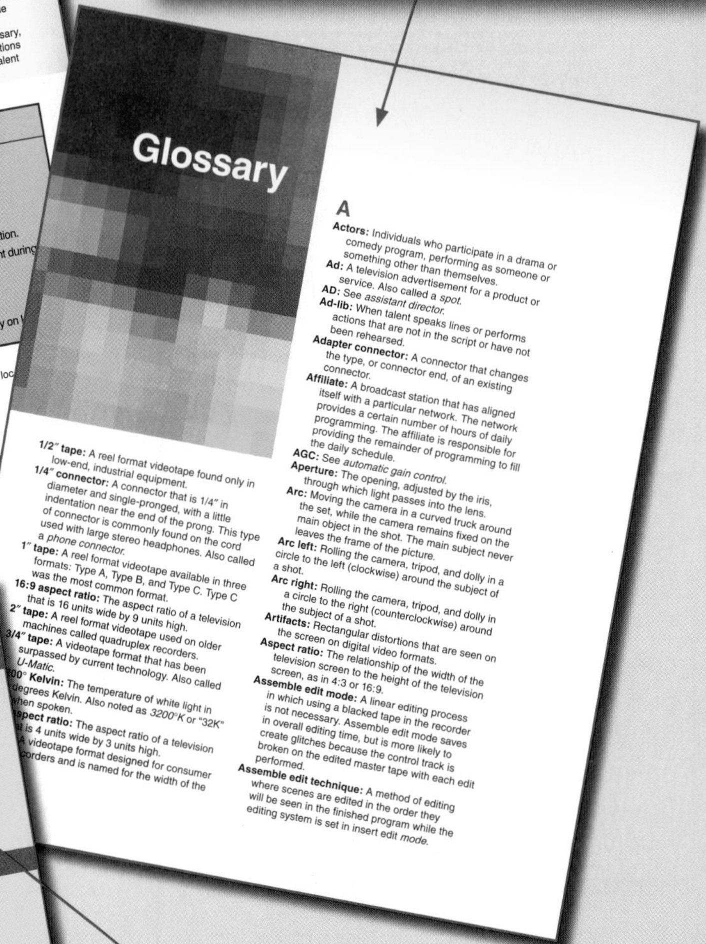

Glossary

A

Actors: Individuals who participate in a drama or comedy program, performing as someone or something other than themselves.
Ad: A television advertisement for a product or service. Also called a *spot*.
AD: See *assistant director*.
Ad-lib: When talent speaks lines or performs actions that are not in the script or have not been rehearsed.
Adapter connector: A connector that changes the type, or connector end, of an existing connector.
Affiliate: A broadcast station that has aligned itself with a particular network. The network provides a certain number of hours of daily programming. The affiliate is responsible for providing the remainder of programming to fill the daily schedule.
AGC: See *automatic gain control.*
Aperture: The opening, adjusted by the iris, through which light passes into the lens.
Arc: Moving the camera in a curved truck around the set, while the camera remains fixed on the main object in the shot. The main subject never leaves the frame of the picture.
Arc left: Rolling the camera, tripod, and dolly in a circle to the left (clockwise) around the subject of a shot.
Arc right: Rolling the camera, tripod, and dolly in a circle to the right (counterclockwise) around the subject of a shot.
Artifacts: Rectangular distortions that are seen on the screen on digital video formats.
Aspect ratio: The relationship of the width of the television screen to the height of the television screen, as in a 4:3 or 16:9.
Assemble edit mode: A linear editing process in which using a blacked tape in the recorder is not necessary. Assemble edit mode saves in overall editing time, but is more likely to create glitches because the control track is broken on the edited master tape with each edit performed.
Assemble edit technique: A method of editing where scenes are edited in the order they will be seen in the finished program while the editing system is set in insert edit *mode*.

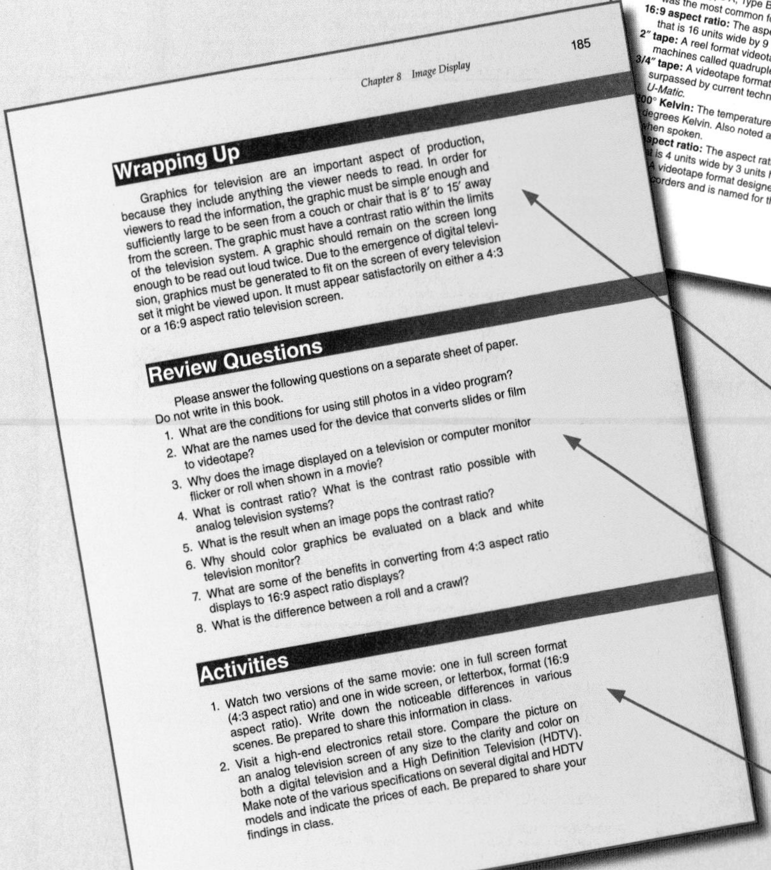

1/2″ tape: A reel format videotape found only in low-end, industrial equipment.
1/4″ connector: A connector that is 1/4″ in diameter and single-pronged, with a little indentation near the end of the prong. This type of connector is commonly found on the cord used with large stereo headphones. Also called a *phone connector.*
1″ tape: A reel format videotape available in three formats: Type A, Type B, and Type C. Type C was the most common format.
16:9 aspect ratio: The aspect ratio of a television that is 16 units wide by 9 units high.
2″ tape: A reel format videotape used on older machines called quadruplex recorders.
3/4″ tape: A videotape format that has been surpassed by current technology. Also called *U-Matic.*
3200° Kelvin: The temperature of white light in degrees Kelvin. Also noted as *3200°K* or *"32K"* when spoken.
4:3 aspect ratio: The aspect ratio of a television that is 4 units wide by 3 units high.
8mm: A videotape format designed for consumer camcorders and is named for the width of the

Wrapping Up

Graphics for television are an important aspect of production, because they include anything the viewer needs to read. In order for viewers to read the information, the graphic must be simple enough and sufficiently large to be seen from a couch or chair that is 8′ to 15′ away from the screen. The graphic must have a contrast ratio within the limits of the television system. A graphic should remain on the screen long enough to be read out loud twice. Due to the emergence of digital television, graphics must be generated to fit on the screen of every television set it might be viewed upon. It must appear satisfactorily on either a 4:3 or a 16:9 aspect ratio television screen.

Review Questions

Please answer the following questions on a separate sheet of paper. Do not write in this book.

1. What are the conditions for using still photos in a video program?
2. What are the names used for the device that converts slides or film to videotape?
3. Why does the image displayed on a television or computer monitor flicker or roll when shown in a movie?
4. What is contrast ratio? What is the contrast ratio possible with analog television systems?
5. What is the result when an image pops the contrast ratio?
6. Why should color graphics be evaluated on a black and white television monitor?
7. What are some of the benefits in converting from 4:3 aspect ratio displays to 16:9 aspect ratio displays?
8. What is the difference between a roll and a crawl?

Activities

1. Watch two versions of the same movie: one in full screen format (4:3 aspect ratio) and one in wide screen, or letterbox, format (16:9 aspect ratio). Write down the noticeable differences in various scenes. Be prepared to share this information in class.
2. Visit a high-end electronics retail store. Compare the picture on an analog television screen of any size to the clarity and color on both a digital television and a High Definition Television (HDTV). Make note of the various specifications on several digital and HDTV models and indicate the prices of each. Be prepared to share your findings in class.

Wrapping Up. Each chapter concludes with a summary of the topics presented.

Review Questions. Questions designed to reinforce the chapter material for the student.

Activities. End-of-chapter activities provide the student with an opportunity for additional experience with the chapter concepts presented.

Chapter 1
The Television Production Industry

Important Terms

Ad
Affiliate
Broadcast
Closed Circuit Television (CCTV)
Commercial Broadcast Television
Educational Television
Home Video
Industrial Television
Large-Scale Video Production Companies
Local Origination
Network
Small-Scale Video Production Companies
Spot
Subscriber Television
Surveillance Television
Syndication

Objectives

After completing this chapter, you will be able to:

● Identify the various areas within the television production industry and cite the unique characteristics of each.

● Describe the roles of networks and affiliates in the process of scheduling programming.

● Explain how the cost of an ad is determined.

Introduction

There are many different types of television production companies and more forming all the time. Because the future of television will undoubtedly be heavily impacted by digital technology, no one can predict how much more the industry will explode. We know that the television production industry is growing incredibly fast and that jobs are plentiful. You do not need to decide which specific area of the industry to go into right now. The topics presented in this chapter are intended to provide a brief idea of the various areas within the industry.

The Growth of Television Technology

The idea of sending a picture over a wire or through the air is an old one. As early as 1862, a still picture was transmitted through a wire. Moving images were not successfully sent for another 65 years. On April 9, 1927, the first moving images were transmitted via television between Washington, DC and New York City. The next year, Charles Jenkins of Maryland was issued a license for the first television station, W3XK. In 1930, Jenkins broadcast the first television commercial.

By 1936, there were 200 television sets in the United States. At the 1939 World's Fair in New York City, the Radio Corporation of America (RCA) sponsored the first televised Presidential speech, delivered by Franklin Delano Roosevelt. This was the viewing public's introduction to RCA's line of television sets. Seven years later, in 1946, the first practical color television system was demonstrated. Color broadcasts became increasingly common by the mid-1950s, **Figure 1-1**.

The number of television sets in use in the U.S. passed the one million mark in 1948. In the same year, Community Antenna Television (CATV) was introduced in mountainous rural areas of Pennsylvania where broadcast television signals could not normally be received. This system would become what we know to be cable TV.

For the first forty years of its life, television was mostly "live." Programs were broadcast as they were being performed. Programs recorded onto film were very poor in quality. In 1948, however, the Ampex Corporation introduced the first broadcast-quality magnetic tape recording system, the Video Tape Recorder (VTR). A practical videotape recording system for home use was not available until 1976.

Satellite broadcasting was introduced in 1962. This development made it possible to send and receive television signals anywhere in the world. In 1969, satellite broadcasting allowed the world to watch

Figure 1-1
In 1954, RCA introduced its first all-electronic color television. The CT-100 had a 12″ screen and sold for $1,000.00. (RCA)

live television pictures being transmitted from the moon. By 1983, consumers could subscribe to direct satellite systems for delivery of programming to their homes, instead of cable systems or conventional broadcast programming.

In 1995, the number of television sets in use worldwide passed the one billion mark. One year later, the Federal Communications Commission (FCC) approved the broadcast standards for high-definition television (HDTV). With the vast changes and improvements that digital technology offers, the FCC decided that standardization was necessary. In 2002, the FCC mandated that television manufacturers must equip all new televisions with tuners capable of receiving digital signals by the year 2007.

Evolution of the Industry

Television production became a thriving industry in the 1950s. The first generation of television production professionals learned the processes, techniques, and technology as they went. The learning process was natural and everyone was learning together.

The second generation of TV production personnel came into the field as it transitioned from black and white to color. This was a huge shift for the consumer, but many of the same production processes applied both to color and to black and white television. Both the early black and white television and the first generation of color television used an analog television process.

The third generation entered the television production industry during the 70s and 80s. These professionals are now confronted with drastic changes in their fields. The television industry, all over the world, is in the process of changing from analog to digital technology. The professionals of this generation have many years experience and are earning sizeable salaries. Their years of experience, however, lie solely in analog technology.

Because today's students have grown up with computers and technology, the digital technology taking over the industry will be easier to learn and use every day, **Figure 1-2**. Computer software production tools, Internet media productions, and digital recording

Figure 1-2
Today's students are very knowledgeable with computers and current technology.

and editing processes require that production personnel working in the current industry environment be informed and proficient with the changing technologies. Employers are eager to hire knowledgeable and ambitious staff members who demonstrate competency with new equipment and resources.

Areas of Television Production

There are many different kinds of television production companies within the industry as a whole. Most consumers are familiar only with broadcast, satellite, and cable television. These forms of television comprise only a small portion of all the television produced. All the broadcast, satellite, and cable television produced in a year represents only about 5% of all the television made annually.

Production Note

Which part of an iceberg is bigger, the part above the water or the portion below the water? The part of an iceberg that lies below the surface is vastly greater in size than the visible peaks above water. Following this example, understand that commercial broadcast/cablecast television is only the proverbial tip of the iceberg in the television production industry, **Figure 1-3**.

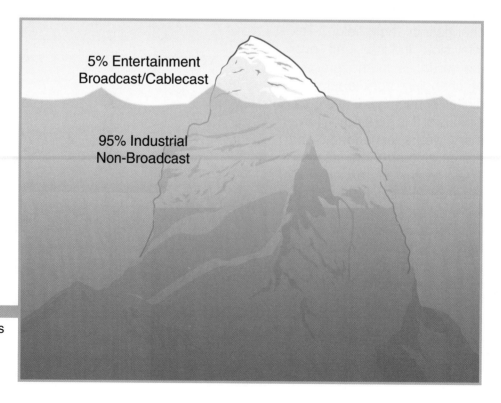

Figure 1-3
The vast majority of jobs available in television production are in non-broadcast television.

Commercial Broadcast Television

Consumers define a "commercial" as a television advertisement for a product. In the television production industry, an advertisement is an *ad* or *spot*, not a "commercial." The industry definition of "commercial" merely refers to a business that is profit generating in nature. *Broadcast* means that the signal travels through the air from one antenna to another antenna.

A *commercial broadcast television* facility is one that is "for-profit" and sends its signal via a transmitter tower through the air. This signal is free and anyone with an antenna may pick it up. The signal is radiated out in a pattern that crosses city, county, state, and national boundaries, **Figure 1-4**.

Talk the Talk

Do not get confused by the term "commercial." Industry professionals call television advertisements "ads" or "spots," not "commercials."

Ad: A television advertisement for a product or service. Also commonly called a *spot*.

Broadcast: The television signal travels through the air from one antenna to another antenna.

Commercial broadcast television: This type of television production facility is "for-profit." The television signal is sent via a transmitter tower through the air and is free for anyone with an antenna to receive it.

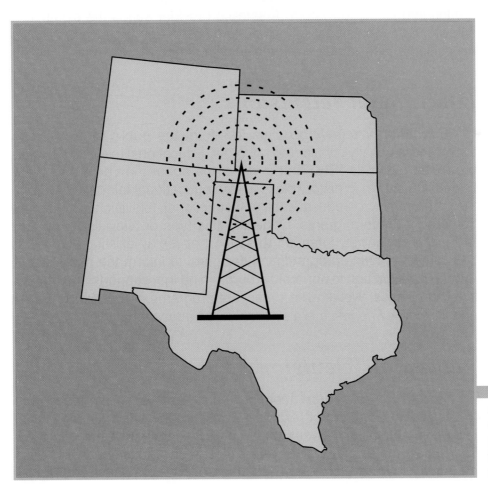

Figure 1-4
A commercial broadcast station sends its signal from an antenna, through the air, to the viewer's antenna.

Subscriber Television

Subscriber television: Fee-for-service programming where customers pay scheduled fees based on the selected programming package. The television signals are transported by satellite transmission or by underground cables.

Subscriber television is fee-for-service programming where customers pay scheduled fees based on the selected programming package. The signals for subscriber television are transported by satellite transmission or by underground cables.

To receive a satellite television signal, special equipment must be installed both inside and outside the home. The available channels and networks vary among the programming packages available and the satellite providers in each area. Most satellite packages now include local programming, such as the local morning and evening news and talk shows.

The signal for each cable television system is available only to a particular region. The cable programming that your home receives is likely different from the programming available to a neighboring town or county. Cable franchises are set up by local governments. Therefore, the available recipients of the programming package are predetermined.

How, then, can a broadcast station's signal be received through an antenna, a cable system, and a satellite system? The broadcast signal starts from a transmission tower, is sent through the air, and is grabbed by either the local cable company's receiving satellite dish or a transmission tower. Most often, the cable company sends the signal underground into its cable system. A satellite provider sends the signal to a satellite. Since the signal is first and foremost a free broadcast signal, it may also be received by anyone else with a receiver antenna.

Educational Television

Educational television: Television that aims to inform the public about various topics. This includes television programming that supports classroom studies and replay's classroom sessions.

Educational television aims to inform the public about various topics and is usually considered nonprofit. Educational television is often broadcast (such as PBS), but a videotape about the Lewis and Clark Expedition shown in history class is also educational television. Most of the programming on educational, or instructional, television is funded by corporate or federal grants. Originally, this type of television programming was exclusively intended to support or replay existing classes. It has come to include programming designed to inform the public about any topic, in addition to nonprofit programming that supports and replays existing classes. Well-known preschool programs, like *Sesame Street* and *Barney & Friends*, are also considered educational television.

Industrial Television

Industrial television: Television that communicates relevant information to a specific audience, such as job training videos.

Industrial television communicates relevant information to a specific audience. For example, a company may use industrial television to train employees or to communicate within the company. Training examples may include tapes that teach workers how to operate machinery, help travelers learn a language, or instruct soldiers on strategy.

A manufacturer of photocopying machines may show a training video to its repairmen, teaching them how to repair a specific copier model. Auto dealers may show a tape informing the mechanics of a specific repair issue. Rather than sending employees to an off-site training class, retail businesses can contract with a production facility to produce a training video. This tape can be viewed on the store premises and be reviewed as often as necessary, **Figure 1-5**. A college may send an informational or promotional video to prospective students, showcasing the particular benefits and offerings of that college.

Closed Circuit Television

Closed circuit television (CCTV) is sent through wires and serves only an extremely small, private predetermined area. For example, your neighbor cannot pick up a signal from your VCR or DVD player and watch the movie playing in it. This is because you have a closed circuit television system. Theoretically, you could string a connecting cable from your VCR or DVD player across the yard to their TV. Both televisions show the movie, but no one else in the neighborhood can receive the signal. Therefore, the person who creates the closed circuit also determines the size of the circuit. The movie channels available in some hotels are configured in a closed circuit. One room of the hotel has perhaps ten VCRs or DVD players, all playing various movies. The signal from each machine is fed into a CCTV system within the hotel, and guests can choose a movie from those playing.

Closed circuit television (CCTV): Television where the signal is sent through wires and serves only extremely small, private, predetermined area.

Figure 1-5
A recorded program provides a more economical and efficient option for training, compared to taking an employee off the job to attend or teach a class.

Surveillance television: A form of CCTV that is usually, but not always, used for security purposes. The cameras used in the system are always interconnected to a closed circuit television system.

Surveillance television is a form of CCTV that is usually, but not always, used for security purposes. Surveillance television is not really television production in the strictest sense of the word. It simply involves setting up a camera to watch an area, **Figure 1-6**. The surveillance cameras are always interconnected to a CCTV system. Surveillance television employs very few people, other than installers. After the system is installed, only a guard is necessary to monitor activity. Surveillance television systems help in protecting and securing banks, prisons, office buildings, apartment buildings, construction sites, and many other public and private locations. Recently, surveillance television has been used at traffic lights to take pictures of traffic violators and as dashboard cameras in police cruisers.

Home Video

Home video: Video-taped records of family events and activities taken by someone using a consumer camcorder.

Home video refers to someone using their consumer camcorder to videotape family events and activities, like a birthday party, **Figure 1-7**. While home video provides an archive for important family events, there is no realistic opportunity for financial gain. One in many thousands of home videos may be awarded a prize on a "silliest home videos" television program. Another possible source of financial gain for a home videographer is the unlikely event of recording something newsworthy while videotaping a family activity. One of the most famous examples of

Figure 1-6
Surveillance cameras are primarily used for security purposes.

Figure 1-7
The main purpose of home video is to archive memorable family events.

this is the Zapruder film of President Kennedy's assassination in Dallas, Texas. News agencies have been known to pay a great deal of money for newsworthy videos shot by enterprising consumers.

Video Production Companies

Large-scale video production companies are facilities with sufficient staff and equipment to produce multi-camera, large-budget programming for broadcast networks or cable networks. Many of the programs you watch on CBS or other networks are not actually produced by network employees. Most networks produce only their own news, news magazines, and sports programming. Most of what is seen on network television is actually produced by another company and sold to the networks for airing.

Small-scale video production companies are businesses with limited staff and equipment resources. They exist by the hundreds across the country. These companies thrive on producing videos of private events (**Figure 1-8**), commercials for local businesses, home inventories for insurance purposes, seminars, legal depositions, and real estate videos. A company of this type has a staff that rarely exceeds five people.

Large-scale video production companies: Facilities with sufficient staff and equipment to produce multi-camera, large-budget programming for broadcast networks or cable networks.

Small-scale video production companies: Businesses with limited staff and equipment resources. They thrive on producing videos of private events, commercials for local businesses, home inventories for insurance purposes, seminars, legal depositions, and real estate videos.

Television Program Origination

A *network* is a corporation that bundles a collection of programs (sports, news, and entertainment) and makes the program bundles available exclusively to its affiliates. The networks generally produce some of their own programming, but do not produce all of their own programs. Networks may produce sports and news oriented programming and some entertainment programming through a production division of the corporation. However, most of the dramatic programming (both dramas and comedies) is produced by large-scale production companies and sold to the networks.

An *affiliate* is a broadcast station that has aligned itself with a particular network. A typical contract between an affiliate station and the network stipulates that the network provides a certain number of

Figure 1-8
Wedding videography is a growing market.

hours of daily programming. The affiliate is responsible for providing the remainder of programming to fill the daily schedule. **Figure 1-9** is an example of a typical day at the fictitious Television Production Network (TPN).

During the 21½ hour broadcast day, the TPN network provides 4 hours of national news and 7½ hours of other entertainment programming. The local affiliate station must provide the remaining 10 hours of programming. It is not likely that a local station can produce that amount of programming on a daily basis. The schedule displayed in **Figure 1-9** indicates that the affiliate station produces local news for 5 of the 10 hours. The affiliate must either create its own programming or buy programming to fill the remaining 5 hours of scheduled broadcast time.

TPN Weekday Schedule			
Time	**Program**	**Affiliate**	**Network**
5:30 a.m.–7:00 a.m.	Local News, Traffic, Weather, Sports	✔	
7:00 a.m.–8:00 a.m.	National Network News		✔
8:00 a.m.–10:00 a.m.	*Good Morning, USA*		✔
10:00 a.m.–11:00 a.m.	Syndicated Talk Show	✔	
11:00 a.m.–12:00 p.m.	Syndicated Reruns of *MASH* and *Gilligan's Island*	✔	
12:00 p.m.–12:30 p.m.	Local News at Noon	✔	
12:30 p.m.–1:00 p.m.	Syndicated Rerun of *I Love Lucy*	✔	
1:00 p.m.–4:00 p.m.	Soap Operas		✔
4:00 p.m.–5:00 p.m.	Syndicated Talk Show	✔	
5:00 p.m.–6:00 p.m.	Local Evening News	✔	
6:00 p.m.–7:00 p.m.	National Network News		✔
7:00 p.m.–8:00 p.m.	Syndicated Game Shows	✔	
8:00 p.m.–11:00 p.m.	Network Entertainment		✔
11:00 p.m.–11:30 p.m.	Local News	✔	
11:30 p.m.–1:00 a.m.	Late Night Network Show		✔
1:00 a.m.–3:00 a.m.	Late, Late Movie	✔	

Figure 1-9
An example of TPN's daily program schedule. Notice that both the network and the affiliate provide programming.

Syndication

Episodes of former network programs that have been purchased and released for syndication are available to affiliate stations. These television programs are sold in blocks of a specified number of episodes or in blocks of time. For example, purchasing a particular program may provide one episode per week for 52 weeks.

If a network program ran for at least 3 years, there are enough episodes (26 episodes per year for a total of 78 episodes over three years) to make it available for syndication. *Syndication* is the process of making a specified number of program episodes available for "lease" to other networks or individual broadcast stations, after the current network's contract for the program expires. Syndicated programs not only include those seen in primetime on major networks, but also some programs that were never picked up by a major broadcast network.

Usually, the production company that made the program "leases" the right to air that program to a network. It is commonly stipulated that the network may air that program a maximum of three times during the broadcast year (September through the following August). After that, the rights to the program revert back to the production company. The production company may then offer a "lease" of the program rights to any customer. Customers may include broadcast networks, subscriber networks, affiliates, or distribution companies that bundle the program with others to create a programming package. For example, a program bundle might include: *I Love Lucy*, *Hogan's Heroes*, *McHale's Navy*, and *Gilligan's Island*. This provides a two-hour, daily package of four shows and the rights to air these programs an unlimited number of times during the broadcast year.

The contract terms for syndicated programs vary greatly. Most contracts depend, to a certain extent, on the program itself and its marketability. A highly marketable show, such as *I Love Lucy*, may be placed in a package and be made available only with the lease of the other three shows included. A bundle of this arrangement allows the distribution company to make more money than with just the one show alone. Another highly marketable show, such as *Law and Order*, may be leased directly from the production company as a multi-episode contract of a single series.

Various types of programs are available for syndication, including:

- Talk Shows
- Game Shows
- Cooking Shows
- Animated Programs
- Children's Shows
- Movies

Syndication: The process of making a specified number of program episodes available for "lease" to other networks or individual broadcast stations, after the current network's contract for the program expires.

Shopping for Programming

Shopping for programming is usually done in person, over the phone, via fax, or on the Internet. When a local affiliate decides to purchase programming, a budget is set. Someone from the affiliate station must negotiate with the vendors to get the highest quality program for the allotted money. A program's popularity and the population size of the broadcast area are among the factors to consider when shopping for programming. These factors directly relate to purchase price of a program. For example, obtaining the talk show *The Oprah Winfrey Show* for Dead Gulch, Nevada with a population of 350 is not nearly as expensive as getting the same program for New York City.

Competition

There is some urgency in the programming decision-making process. If another station in your broadcast area contracts with a vendor for a particular program before you do, they obtain exclusive rights to air the program in your broadcast area.

Many television stations in a single area compete for viewers. Each tries to choose programming that pulls viewers away from the competition, while the competition is doing the exact same thing. To develop the best programming, you must examine the potential audience. Determine who is likely to be watching television at each particular time of day in the area. Knowing the demographics of your audience helps to develop programming that appeals to that audience. Statistics that are considered in demographics include age, gender, race, education, and economic level.

The reason networks run soap operas in the afternoon is that a large number of people home watching TV at that time of day are women caring for young children. The children are down for a nap and the adults are taking a break from a busy morning keeping up with the kids. Many stations run children's programming early in the morning, because children are likely to be watching at that time. Stations usually run programming that appeals to young school-age children later in the afternoon. Ultimately, stations must pay for the programs they buy and must consider the audience when deciding on these purchases.

Local Origination

Local origination is programming made in a specific geographic area, to be shown to the public in that same geographic area. For example, the evening news in New York City reports that traffic is backed up in the Lincoln Tunnel. Do the people watching the evening news in Mayberry, North Carolina hear about the Lincoln Tunnel traffic in New York? Of course not. Viewers in both areas are watching the local news. Local origination comes in many forms. The local evening news is an example of local origination programming. The local station may also produce a program about a local sports team or televise "town hall" meetings and local telethons. These are other examples of local origination programming for a specific community.

Local origination: Programming made in a specific geographic area, to be shown to the public in that same geographic area.

Financing the Programming Decisions

The ads that run during programs pay for the purchase price of those programs. Advertising on the radio or in print is always an option, but television ads are very effective.

The company must first contract with a video production company to produce a television ad. Once the ad is made, the company approaches the television station or network and asks that the ad be aired. The station charges a fee each time the ad is aired. The fee is not a set amount, but changes based on the time of day and the day of the week that the ad airs. If the company wants the ad to air during an extremely popular program that is seen by the largest audience of the week, a substantially higher fee is charged than if the ad runs at 2:00 a.m. during the Late, Late Movie.

Production Note

Companies clamor to purchase coveted ad time during the annually televised Super Bowl. The cost of a 30-second spot fluctuates depending on when the commercial airs during the event. Ads that air before half-time may be charged differently from those airing in the third and fourth quarters. In the span of a decade, the average price tag for a 30-second commercial during the Super Bowl has risen from $1.2 million to $2.25 million.

Television stations or networks cannot rely on individual companies to approach them with product ads. Funding is required to buy programming. Assume that a station's research shows that the majority of the potential audience for programs airing from 11:00 a.m.–12:00 p.m. is either people with impaired health or people who are retired. Programming of interest to this particular audience needs to be purchased. Once the programs are obtained, the sales staff is sent out to find organizations or companies to advertise their products or services during that program. If the station cannot find anyone to advertise during the program, they cannot afford to air the program.

Through a rating system called the Nielsen Ratings, a figure is determined that represents approximately how many people watch a program. If the numbers are too low, advertisers will insist that the advertising rates be lowered to reflect the smaller audience reached. If rates are lowered to the point that the program costs the network more than the ads bring in, the network must either continue to run the program at a financial loss or cancel the program outright. Sometimes a cancelled network program can find an extended life, with new episodes, in the cable industry. A competing network may even pick up a cancelled program and may be able to breathe new life into it.

Production Note

Nielsen Media Research has developed a system that estimates the size and demographics of the viewing audience for almost every program seen on television. To gather this information, the company distributes television diaries to selected Nielsen TV families and installs electronic television monitoring equipment in certain homes. These methods, along with random phone surveying, contribute to generating the ratings that are referenced for both advertising and programming decisions.

The Business of the Industry

Money is the driving force of the television industry. Remove any preconceived ideas that television is an art form. While art may sometimes occur, television is a business, first and foremost. The success and failure of a business hinges on money. Every business decision made considers profits and losses.

Follow the trail of profit motivation in the following scenario:

- Widgets, Inc. has created the "Snapper," a device that opens the flue of a fireplace with the snap of a finger. Advertising on the radio or in print is an option, but the company has decided that the best way to reach their intended customer base is to advertise on television.

- Widgets, Inc. contracts with AdsRUs, a video production company, to produce a television ad. Once the ad is made, Widgets, Inc. writes a check to AdsRUs for their services.

- Widgets, Inc. now approaches a television station or network to ask if they would air the ad for their product.

- The station assigns a fee that Widgets, Inc. will pay each time the ad is aired. The fee depends on the time of day that ad is aired, the day of the week, and during which programs the ad is aired.

- The station uses the fee assessed for the airing of the ad to pay for the purchase of the scheduled programming.

- If no one advertises during a particular block of time or programming, the station cannot afford to continue airing the program(s).

Perhaps this helps you understand the logic behind the cancellation of a television program.

Wrapping Up

Very few people begin their careers in the entertainment, news broadcast, or cable television arenas. Most begin in non-broadcast television, perfect their knowledge and skills, and eventually move into the broadcast arena. Non-broadcast television has many more jobs available than broadcast or cable television, and the jobs are more secure than those in the entertainment industry. The television industry is extremely competitive. To be successful, you must work your way up from the bottom, through the ranks, and prove your worth the whole way.

Review Questions

Please answer the following questions on a separate sheet of paper. Do not write in this book.

1. How can a broadcast station be received through cable and satellite systems?
2. What are the differences between educational television and industrial television productions?
3. List six examples of closed circuit television systems.
4. Explain the relationship between a network and an affiliate station when scheduling daily programming.
5. What is local origination programming? Provide an example of local origination on a broadcast station and an example on a cable channel.
6. How do stations pay for original programming and syndicated programs that they purchase?

Activities

1. Select a 3-hour block of time from the television schedule listing section of a local newspaper or other publication. List the types of television programs aired during the selected block of time and determine the viewing audience for each program type. Make a list of the products that are best suited to advertise during each program.
2. Create your own dictionary of chapter terms. Your instructor will provide an alphabetical list of all the terms defined in this book. Copy the entire list of terms into a separate notebook, leaving two or three lines after each for the definition. Update your dictionary with the corresponding definitions as you complete each chapter. This custom-made dictionary will serve as a reference tool for you throughout this course, future television production courses, and when working in the television production industry.

Important Terms

Assistant Director (AD)	Maintenance Engineer
Audio	Makeup
Audio Engineer	Makeup Artist
Camera Operator	Post-Production
Cast	Pre-Production
CG Operator	Producer
Content Specialist	Production
Crew	Production
Cue	Assistant (PA)
Director	Production Manager
Editing	Production Switching
Editor	Production Team
Executive	Production Values
Producer (EP)	Scenery
Floor Manager	Scriptwriter
Frame	Special Effects
Framing	Staff
Gaffer	Talent
Graphic Artist	Video
Grip	Video Engineer
Lighting Director	VTR Operator

Objectives

After completing this chapter, you will be able to:

- Explain how the responsibilities of each production staff position are dependent on the functions of other production staff positions.

- List the primary responsibilities of each production staff position.

- Describe the activities in each step of a production workflow.

Introduction

To understand an individual role in television production, you must be familiar with all aspects of the production process. Each area of television production is interconnected to many others. The interrelationships resemble a spider web, **Figure 2-1**. To learn proper camerawork, you must understand proper lighting technique. Proper lighting technique is dictated by the colors on the set and the costumes. The colors of the set and costumes directly affect the kind of special effects used in the program. Special effects are created in the special effects generator, but must be edited. Knowing the tools and techniques of editing is also required. To learn television production, you must have a solid understanding of each of the contributing roles.

Figure 2-1
In order to do your job properly, you must know the jobs of others on your production staff. This illustration depicts the spider web of interrelationships between jobs on the production staff.

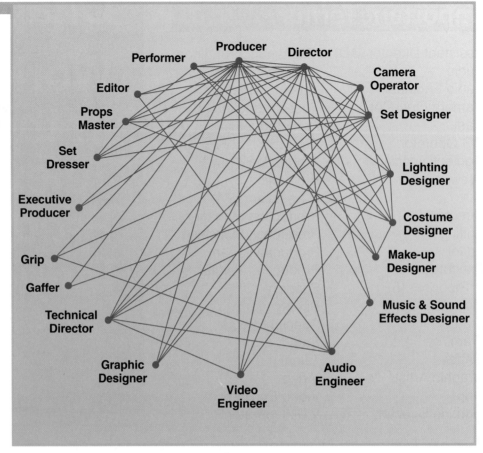

Dividing Up the Work

Staff: Production personnel that work behind the scenes and generally includes management and designers.

Crew: Production personnel that are normally not seen by the camera and generally includes equipment operators.

Talent: Anyone seen by the camera, whether or not they have a speaking or any other significant role in the program, as well as individuals who provide only their vocal skills to the production.

All television production organizations, from the largest to the smallest, divide the production workload among the company's employees. In large production companies, a different individual may be assigned to each of the job titles. In smaller production companies, however, it is not unusual for a single person to fill multiple jobs on the same production. Some jobs are easier to combine than others. For example, it is difficult to imagine acting in front of a camera when you must also fill the role of the camera operator. On the other hand, the person who painted the set could certainly be an actor. These two jobs do not take place at the same time.

The following sections address many of the main jobs included in the collective term "production staff." All production personnel can be divided into three categories:

● The *staff* works behind the scenes. These individuals work in the more creative levels of production management.

● The *crew* are generally equipment operators. They are not normally seen by the camera, but are integral to the production.

● Anyone seen by the camera, whether or not they have a speaking or any other significant role in the program, is *talent*.

Production Note

There are exceptions to the "not seen by the camera" portion of the definitions of staff and crew. For example, at the opening or closing of many newscasts, there is a long shot of the studio. The audience may see a shot that includes the studio's camera operators. Camera operators and technicians are regularly seen on sports programs, such as on the sidelines of a football field. Just because production personnel are shown on television, they are not considered on-screen talent.

The talent hired for a production also includes the individuals who provide only their vocal skills to the production. These positions include the on-screen actors, cast of extras, the narrator, voiceover talent, and announcers. *Cast* is the collective name given to all the talent participating in a production. It is important to remember that a program's talent includes more than actors and on-screen personalities.

Cast: The collective name given to all the talent participating in a production.

Talk the Talk

When referring to multiple individuals hired as talent for a production, the correct plural form of the term is "talent." To say "talents" is incorrect and unprofessional.

Executive Producer

The *executive producer (EP)* provides the funding necessary to produce the program. The EP rarely steps foot on the set. There are times, however, when the EP is involved in every aspect of the production. The level of involvement varies from production to production. A single production may have several executive producers. The more expensive a program is to produce, the more likely it is to have multiple EPs. In some cases, an EP is merely an individual who invests a large sum of money in the program and, in return, is given a credit at the beginning of the program and portion of the profits generated by the sale of the program. The executive producer essentially places the money in the bank and hires a producer.

Executive producer (EP): The person, or people, who provides the funding necessary to produce the program.

Producer

The *producer* purchases materials and services in the creation of a finished program. The producer hires a director, designers, camera operators, a lighting director, sound engineer, and the talent. Materials purchased for the production include set construction items, costumes, and props. The producer also arranges travel plans, if necessary, for

Producer: The person who purchases materials and services in the creation of a finished program.

Production team: Everyone involved in the production, both staff and talent.

Pre-production: Any activity on a program that occurs prior to the time that the cameras begin rolling. This includes production meetings, set construction, costume design, music composition, scriptwriting, and location surveys.

Production: The actual shooting of the program.

Post-production: Any of the activities performed after a program has been shot. This includes music beds, editing, audio overdubs, titles, and duplication.

the staff and talent, including transportation, lodging, and catering of food. Because of the many facets of a producer's job, being successful requires extreme attention to detail and strong organizational skills. The producer is ultimately responsible for the program's successful completion.

The amount of input the producer has on creative decisions varies. Ideally, the producer hires a director with whom he works well. Together the producer and director make the hiring decisions regarding the rest of the production team. The *production team* includes everyone involved in the production, both staff and talent. As decisions are made, the producer and director must constantly be aware of the budget. Compromise is necessary to balance and successfully complete all aspects of the program production.

The producer interacts with the majority of the production staff during pre-production on day-to-day matters. *Pre-production* refers to any activity on the program that occurs prior to the time that the cameras begin rolling. This includes production meetings, set construction, costume design, music composition (**Figure 2-2**), scriptwriting, and location surveys. *Production* refers to the actual shooting of the program. *Post-production* involves anything done after the program has been shot. This includes music beds, editing, audio overdubs, titles, and duplication.

Figure 2-2
Using a Musical Instrument Digital Interface (MIDI) program, a composer sends notes directly from the keyboard to the computer. The notes are placed on sheet music and can be printed, so the music can be performed, recorded, and placed into the soundtrack of the production.

Director

The *director* is in charge of the creative aspects of the program and interacts with the entire staff. While directors are responsible for casting the program's talent, sometimes they must concede to the EP or producer's decisions.

Director: The person who is in charge of the creative aspects of the program and interacts with the entire staff.

Production Note

The director must be conscious of the budget, as well. Casting Tom Cruise in a leading role and insisting on an elaborate set may exhaust the entire production budget on just those two items. The director must compromise for the sake of the production's existence!

The director reviews the program's script and visualizes the entire production, **Figure 2-3**. Those ideas must then be communicated to the staff and talent. The director guides their performances to create an acceptable representation of his vision. During production, the director must coordinate and manage the staff and cast to keep to the production schedule and to ensure that all of the program's elements are properly incorporated.

Figure 2-3
The director reads a script and envisions the way the program's scenes should appear.

Most directors have worked their way up from a production assistant and, therefore, know each job on the staff quite well. That knowledge is key to communication with the staff.

Production Manager

The *production manager* handles the business portion of the production by negotiating the fees for goods, services, and other contracts and by determining the staffing requirements based on the needs of each production. An additional responsibility is to ensure that programs and scripts conform to established broadcast standards. The production manager contributes to the successful completion of a production by managing the budget and available resources.

Production Assistant

In many television production companies, the titles *production assistant (PA)* and *assistant director (AD)* are interchangeable. This duality of terms does not apply to the film industry–only the television industry. The PA serves as a jack-of-all-trades, but a master of none. In some facilities, the PA is merely a "gofer." In most facilities, however, the PA is hired to fill a variety of positions when key personnel are sick, out of town, working on another project, or otherwise unavailable. Most people begin their career as a PA. From the PA position, motivated individuals can rise through the ranks of a facility until reaching the position they want.

On a daily basis, the PA provides general assistance around the studio or production facility. On the occasion that a staff position needs to be temporarily filled, an aggressive and ambitious PA should offer to perform the tasks of that job. If, for example, the studio's audio engineer is temporarily unavailable, take an active part in the advancement of your career and volunteer to fill-in. The competent performance of the position's duties will be noticed by the production team and will undoubtedly be noted for subsequent opportunities.

Production manager: The person who handles the business portion of the production by negotiating the fees for goods, services, and other contracts and by determining the staffing requirements based on the needs of each production.

Production assistant (PA): The person who provides general assistance around the studio or production facility. The PA is commonly hired to fill a variety of positions when key personnel are sick, out of town, working on another project, or otherwise unavailable. In many facilities, the production assistant position is synonymous with the *assistant director (AD)* position.

Production Note

If there are several PAs in the company, it is vital that you volunteer before someone else. A passive individual does not last long in a PA position. You must be active and aggressive. When a qualified person is in front of an employer eagerly saying, "I am qualified. I want to do the work. Give me a chance to prove it," why would the employer offer the position to a wallflower who is too shy to speak up? Aggressive, energetic, and enthusiastic go-getters populate this industry.

Instead of waiting long periods of time for a promotion at a company, it is very common for PAs who have acquired significant skills and experience to move from company to company. This is the only way to move up the ranks within production teams in the industry. Because of this, most professionals in this industry change companies 7 or 8 times within their first 10 years of working. Choosing to stay with one company comes with the risk of waiting years for someone above you to retire, transfer to another company, or otherwise leave the position. Although promotions do occur within companies, it is more likely to happen when moving laterally from one company to another. In addition to proven knowledge and skills, an important key to employment in this industry is networking. Job openings in television production are rarely found in the want ads of the local newspaper.

Production Note

Because changing companies is so common in the television production industry, it is strongly recommended that you maintain your own investment/retirement accounts. Starting a retirement account right out of college is one of the smartest and least expensive things you can do for your own future.

Floor Manager

The *floor manager*, or stage manager, is the director's "eyes and ears" in the studio. The floor manager wears a headset and relays the director's commands to all studio personnel, except the camera operators. The camera operators are usually in direct communication with the director. The floor manager is the only person in the studio that may say, "Cut," other than the director. When the floor manager says, "Cut," it is usually because the director has instructed them to do so.

Floor manager: The person who is the director's "eyes and ears" in the studio. The floor manager relays the director's commands to the studio personnel.

Cue: A signal that implies something specific is to happen.

Production Note

In larger studios, the headset communication system has two channels so that the director can speak just to the camera operators, just to the floor manager, or to everyone at once.

The floor manager is responsible for making sure that the set is ready for production, for initiating the program countdown, and for giving various cues to the talent. A *cue* is a signal that implies something specific is to happen. One familiar cue is the "cut" signal. The floor manager makes a cutting motion with his hand across his neck.

There are many other hand signals and cues that are standard within the industry. The signals can be any action that the team agrees upon and understands, **Figure 2-4**.

Camera Operator

The *camera operator* runs the piece of equipment that captures the video images of the program, **Figure 2-5**. Camera operators are responsible for framing shots that are visually pleasing to the viewers. The director may often call for a particular shot. The camera operator must not only provide the shot requested, but must frame the shot so that annoying or inappropriate background information does not detract from the image.

Figure 2-4
The floor manager gives silent signals to the talent.

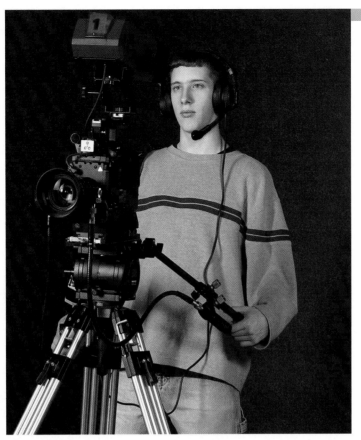

Figure 2-5
The camera operator captures the shots that the director requires. Camera operators never sit down when operating a camera on a tripod and never let go of the tripod pan handles without making certain they are stable and the camera is secured.

Video Engineer

The **video engineer** is the individual ultimately responsible for the technical quality of the video signal, **Figure 2-6**. A video engineer has extensive schooling in the electronics of video production and is

Video engineer: The person who manages the video equipment and is ultimately responsible for the technical quality of the video signal.

Figure 2-6
The video engineer uses specialized test equipment to examine and maintain consistent picture quality.

highly skilled. This member of the production team is greatly valued and highly compensated in any production facility. In the studio environment, one of the video engineer's responsibilities is to ensure that the images captured by each of the studio cameras match exactly. This consistency is important when, for example, the director cuts from one camera to another. The video engineer's skills ensure that an actor's skin color does not change from normal, to pinkish, to greenish when cutting between cameras.

Production Note

Video engineering is an entire science unto itself. This text provides only general information on the topic. The video engineer's job description and responsibilities are in the midst of change with the growing prominence of digital technology in the current video industry.

Audio Engineer

Audio engineer: The person responsible for the audio/sound quality on the production and related equipment.

The ***audio engineer*** is responsible for the audio/sound quality on the production. The audio engineer often operates the microphone mixer, as well as the music and sound effects recorders/players, **Figure 2-7**. The audio engineer mics the talent and is responsible for maintaining the overall audio levels on the studio's master recorder.

Figure 2-7
The audio engineer maintains the quality and volume of the sound, so that viewers never have to adjust the volume on their television sets.

Lighting Director

The *lighting director* decides the placement of lighting instruments, the appropriate color of light to use, and which lamps should be used in the instruments. In a television studio, as on the stage in a high school auditorium, there are an amazing number of lights hanging overhead from pipes on the ceiling. The lights are purposefully aimed in various directions with varying degrees of brightness and color. Determining the placement of the lighting instruments is the lighting director's job. The lighting director's assistant, a *gaffer,* often does the actual hauling of heavy instruments up and down ladders, **Figure 2-8**.

Lighting director: The person who decides the placement of lighting instruments, the appropriate color of light to use, and which lamps should be used in the instruments.

Gaffer: The lighting director's assistant who often does the actual hauling of heavy instruments up and down ladders.

Figure 2-8
The lighting designer tells the gaffer (on ladder) where to aim the lighting instruments.

Scriptwriter

The *scriptwriter* is the person responsible for placing the entire production on paper. The script must meet the objectives of the producer and the message to the viewer must be clear. The scriptwriter is not often an acknowledged expert in the program's subject matter. Because of this, a *content specialist* is usually hired to work with the scriptwriter. The content specialist is a person considered to be an expert in the program's subject.

Content specialists from the military are commonly hired to help scriptwriters and directors create authentic action scenes in movies with military action or plot lines. A content specialist would also, for example, assist a scriptwriter in writing the script for an instructional program that details techniques of a new and innovative heart transplant technique. To ensure accurate information, the content specialist in this scenario would be the doctor who invented the technique. The content specialist reviews the entire script before production begins and is, ideally, present for the shooting to keep everything accurate.

Graphic Artist

The *graphic artist* is responsible for all the artwork required for the production. This includes computer graphics, traditional works of art, charts, and graphs. The graphic artist is usually very well versed in computer graphics applications, from the amazing animations seen in modern films to the charts and graphs included in an economics program.

VTR Operator

The *VTR operator* is in charge of recording the program onto videotape by correctly operating the VTR equipment, **Figure 2-9**. Producing a recording of the program with quality video and audio is an immense responsibility. The VTR operator must take every precaution to ensure that each piece of equipment is functioning properly to produce a quality recording of every scene.

Editor

The *editor* is responsible for putting the various pieces of the entire program together. The individual scenes are rearranged into the proper order with all the mistakes and bad takes removed, leaving only the best version of each scene. The editor must be aware of the psychological effects involved with the theory of movement and passage of time, as different angles of the same person or scene are cut together. A skilled editor, for example, makes two sides of a conversation, shot on two different tapes at different times and locations, flow together into a natural sounding conversation on one tape.

Figure 2-9
The VTR operator places the entire program on the master videotape.

Talk the Talk

"Editor" is a television production term with dual definitions. This chapter addresses the person, called an editor, who arranges the individual pieces of a program to produce a complete product. To do this, the editor uses a machine that is also called an editor. Variations of this machine are discussed in Chapter 19, *Video Editing*.

Makeup Artist

The *makeup artist* is responsible for applying cosmetics to the talent's face and body, giving them the intended appearance in front of the camera, **Figure 2-10**. The cosmetics may enhance facial features or actually change the appearance entirely, as necessary in portraying a particular character convincingly.

Makeup artist: The person responsible for applying cosmetics to the talent's face and body, giving them the intended appearance in front of the camera.

Figure 2-10
The makeup artist ensures that performers look natural under the bright studio lights.

CG Operator

The *CG operator* creates the titles for the program using a character generator, **Figure 2-11**. Titles include the credits that appear before and after a movie or television show, as well as the news flash that crawls across the bottom of the television screen. The titles may be a single page, scrolling, or have animated letters. The CG operator must create titles that are accurate and appropriate for the program and ensure that they are legible to viewers.

Grip

The *grip* is a person who moves the equipment, scenery, and props on a studio set. In the theater world, a grip is called a stagehand. Perhaps the job title comes from the fact that one must have a good grip in order to move anything large!

Maintenance Engineer

The *maintenance engineer* keeps all the production equipment working according to "factory specifications." The maintenance engineer is not a repairman, but may assist in troubleshooting if problems arise. His primary responsibility is to ensure that each piece of production equipment functions at its optimum performance level, **Figure 2-12**.

Figure 2-11
The CG operator types the titles for the program.

Figure 2-12
The maintenance engineer keeps equipment running in top performance.

Program Production Workflow

The following is a general overview of the steps in producing a program. The amount of time involved in completing each step depends on the type of production. Completing most of the steps when producing a public service announcement, for example, would likely take considerably less time than when producing a one-hour, prime-time drama. One of the best ways to create a successful program is to have excellent production values in the program. *Production values* are the general aesthetics of the show. Most of this book is aimed at showing you how to attain these high production values.

Production values: The general aesthetics of the show.

Various terms are presented in the sections that follow, as well as in the proceeding chapters. Many of the terms have commonly known "consumer" definitions. Additionally, some words used in this business, just as in the English language, have multiple definitions. Memorize the professional definitions of terms and learn the difference between those with multiple meanings. Use the terms appropriately during class to help you use them correctly when working in the television production industry.

Program Proposals

The first step in producing a program is to develop a program proposal (discussed in Chapter 7, *Scriptwriting*). This essentially is a plan that includes the basic idea of the program, the program's format, intended audience, budget considerations, location information, and a rough shooting schedule. The program proposal is reviewed by investors and production companies for financing considerations and overall project approval.

Scriptwriting

Before a script is written for the program, a script outline is created. This outline contains comments noting the direction of the program and varies depending on the program format (drama, panel discussion, interview, or music video). Television scripts are written in a two-column format. The left column contains video/technical information and the right column presents audio and stage direction.

Producing

The day-to-day activities involved in actually producing a program ensure that the production process runs as smoothly as possible:

● Coordinate schedules.
● Acquire the necessary resources.
● Monitor the activity and progress of various production teams.
● Weigh budgetary considerations.

Important decisions that affect the program's ultimate success are made throughout the production process.

Directing

Directing involves shaping the creative aspects of the program and interacting with the entire staff and cast to realize the director's visualization of the production. In addition to verbally providing direction during production, many important pre- and post-production directing activities contribute to a program's success.

Lighting

When planning the lighting for a production, there should be sufficient light to meet the technical requirements of the camera. Enough light should be installed to produce an acceptable picture on the screen. Various lighting techniques are also used to meet the aesthetic requirements of the director. Accurate lighting in a program is necessary to create the desired mood, appearance, and setting. Most importantly, placement of lighting instruments contributes to creating three-dimensionality on a flat television screen.

Scenery, Set Dressing, and Props

Scenery: Anything placed on a set that stops the distant view of the camera. Outside the studio, scenery may be a building or the horizon.

Careful planning and consideration when choosing scenery, set dressings, and props helps to create a believable environment for the program. The placement of these items on a set contributes to producing the illusion of three-dimensionality in a program. *Scenery* is something that stops the distant view of the camera. In a studio, the scenery may be fake walls, set furniture, or a curtain. Outside the studio, it may be a tree, building, or the horizon. The scenery is nearly everything behind the main object of the shot, **Figure 2-13**. Set dressing includes all the visual and design elements of a set, such as rugs, lamps, wall coverings, curtains, and room accent accessories (discussed in Chapter 12, *Props, Set Dressing, and Scenery*). Props are any of the items handled by the performers, excluding furniture, **Figure 2-14** (discussed in Chapter 12, *Props, Set Dressing, and Scenery*). Furniture may be a prop if used for something other than its intended use.

Figure 2-13
Scenery is anything, other than people, that appears behind the main object of the picture.

Figure 2-14
Props are items, other than furniture, that are handled by performers.

Costumes and Makeup

Costumes and makeup enable actors to look like the characters they portray. Even news anchors and other on-screen personalities who are not "acting" wear makeup and have their wardrobe selected to ensure the best possible appearance on the television screen.

Costume selection is dependent on many existing factors, including plot, setting, set dressing, program format, and lighting arrangement. *Makeup* is any of the cosmetics applied to a performer's skin to change or enhance their appearance. The makeup may create a drastic change, such as aging, aliens, or injuries, or it may simply enhance the talent's features while in front of a camera.

Graphics

Graphics are any and all of the "artwork" seen in a program, including computer graphics, traditional works of art, charts, and graphs (discussed in Chapter 8, *Image Display*). When choosing or creating graphics for use on television, particular attention must be paid to the degree of detail in the graphic. Losing the fine detail in images is natural in the process of creating an analog television picture (digital technology is continually evolving and changing this limitation). A beautifully detailed title font of medieval style writing, for example, may look wonderful on a computer screen, but will likely dissolve into mush on a television screen. Currently, the television screen requires bolder images than a computer screen. If the audience is unable to read what is written on the screen, or cannot clearly see the information presented in a chart, then you are not effectively communicating.

Camera Operation

The portion of the program that you can see is called *video*. The camera operator is responsible for capturing the program images with a video camera.

Makeup: Any of the cosmetics applied to a performer's skin to change or enhance their appearance.

Video: The portion of the program that you can see.

Frame: The actual edge of the video picture; the edge of the picture on all four sides.

Framing: Involves placing items in the camera's frame by operating the camera and tripod.

Talk the Talk

The term "video" has differing consumer and professional definitions. "Video" is often used to refer to the tape or the DVD you rent or purchase for viewing at home. Television production professionals use "video" to refer to the visual portion of a program, the part that is seen by the audience.

A *frame* is the actual edge of the video picture; the edge of the picture on all four sides, **Figure 2-15**. *Framing* a shot is the camera operator's responsibility and involves placing items in the picture by operating the camera and tripod. Shooting a vase of flowers sitting on a table seems simple until you realize there are an infinite number of ways to shoot it (long shot, close-up, from a side angle, from below, from above, zoom in, or zoom out). A good camera operator has the ability to frame shots effectively for the audience.

We have all seen home movies taken of someone else's family. Home movies are usually not tolerable to watch for long periods of time. One reason is camerawork; it is generally shaky and out of focus, **Figure 2-16**.

Figure 2-15
The edge of a picture on all four sides is the frame. An operator frames a shot by determining exactly what to include in the frame.

Figure 2-16
An out of focus shot has poor production value.

An important production value is quality camerawork. Put the camera on a tripod for stability and frame the shots correctly. Make sure that people in the video do not have oddly cut off body parts, **Figure 2-17**.

Audio Recording

Audio: The portion of a program that you can hear. Audio includes narration, spoken lines, sound effects, and background music.

Audio is the portion of a program that you can hear. Audio includes narration, spoken lines of talent, sound effects, background music, and all other aspects of a program that are heard by the audience.

Video Engineering

When shooting in a studio, there may be three cameras shooting the scene from three different angles. Each camera has a different picture:

- Camera 1 is on one news anchor in a close-up.
- Camera 2 has a two-shot of both anchors.
- Camera 3 is on the other news anchor in a close-up.

Production switching: The process of cutting between cameras.

All three of these cameras connect to a production switcher, **Figure 2-18**. A cable coming from the switcher connects to a videotape recorder. By pressing buttons marked "1," "2," and "3," the picture from different cameras can be sent to the recorder. The process of cutting between cameras (from Camera 1, to Camera 3, to Camera 2, and back to Camera 1) is called *production switching*.

Special Effects

Special effects: Anything the audience sees in a video picture that did not really happen in the way it appears on the screen.

An entire book could be written on special effects alone. In simplest terms, *special effects* are anything the audience sees in a video picture

Figure 2-17

A shot of a person "missing" important parts of the body is considered a poor production value.

that did not really happen in the way it appears on the screen. Special effects alter the reality perceived by the viewer.

Production Note

One of the cardinal rules of television production and filmmaking: "It does not have to be, it only has to appear to be!"

Editing

Placing the individual scenes in logical order on another tape is called editing (discussed in Chapter 19, *Video Editing*). When writing a research paper, you make notes on note cards. One of the next tasks in the process is to arrange the note cards in an order that makes the paper flow logically. This process of arranging corresponds to editing a video program.

A program is not usually shot in the order it is eventually seen in. All the scenes that take place in one location are shot at the same time, even if they appear at different times in the finished project.

In a professional movie, imagine that scenes 25, 41, and 97 all take place in Egypt at the Sphinx. Scenes 24, 40, and 98 take place at the Eiffel Tower in Paris, France. Consider the increased production cost if all the people and equipment went back and forth three times to these distant locations. Setting up once at each location and shooting all the necessary scenes requires that the completed scenes be edited back together in the proper order.

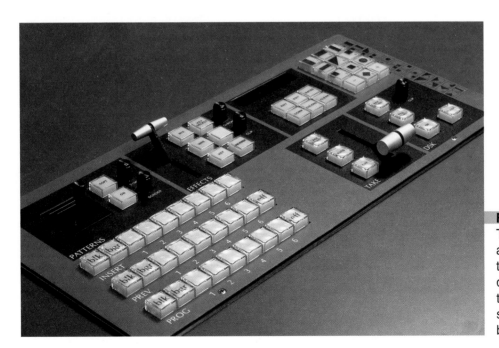

Figure 2-18
The production switcher allows the operator to send pictures from different cameras to the videotape recorder, simply by pushing a button or pulling a lever.

Duplication and Distribution

A master program is copied to multiple media formats, such as tape or DVD, for distribution and viewing. The programs may be individually sold by a retailer, used as informational material for a specific workforce or company, or be broadcast and viewed on televisions in millions of homes.

Assistant Activity

Be prepared to discuss your experience with each of the three following scenarios.

- Watch 20 minutes of the local or national news tonight with the sound turned off. Can you still follow what the newscasters are communicating? Why?

- Watch 10 minutes of a sitcom with the sound turned off. Can you still follow the storyline?

- Try watching a commercial that you have never seen before with the sound turned off. Obviously, the product name appears on screen at some point. What is the commercial trying to tell you about the product? Can you figure it out without the audio?

Wrapping Up

The academic aspects of TV production must be learned to understand how all the elements of production fit together. Everyone needs to understand everyone else's job in order to fit into the matrix of production.

There are hundreds of factors to consider when producing a television program. Since this course is career-oriented, these factors are grouped loosely around job clusters. This chapter presented only a few of the main jobs involved in producing a television program. An enormous number of people are involved in producing a television program from beginning to end. Remember that this text is an introduction to television production. It is not intended to be the end of your learning, rather just the beginning.

Review Questions

Please answer the following questions on a separate sheet of paper. Do not write in this book.

1. Explain the difference between the talent and the staff of a production.
2. What are the three phases of program production?
3. Describe how the director interacts with the program's producer.
4. What information is included in a program proposal?
5. Define the frame of a video picture.
6. Explain the process of production switching.
7. Why is it usually impractical to shoot all of the scenes of a program in sequential order?

Activities

1. Videotape the final credits of your favorite television show. Play the credits back slowly and notice all the job titles listed. List any of the titles that are unfamiliar to you and research the responsibilities of each job. Be prepared to present this information in class.
2. Make an illustrated poster of the basic hand signals used by floor managers on a production set.

Careerpage.org.
A Web site sponsored by the National Alliance of State Broadcasters Associations that provides broadcasting industry professionals with a job information and search tool.

Important Terms

Aperture
Auto-Focus
Auto-Iris Circuit
Camcorder
Camera Control
  Unit (CCU)
Camera Head
Charge Coupled
  Device (CCD)
Convertible Camera
Docking
Dolly
Fluid Head
Focal Length
Focal Point
Focus
Friction Head
F-Stop
Gain
Hot
Iris

Lens
Optical Center
Pan Handle
Pedestal Column
Pedestal Control
Remote Control Unit
  (RCU)
Studio Camera
Studio Pedestal
Subjective Camera
Target
Tripod
Tripod Head
Variable Focal Length
  Lens
Viewfinder
Zebra Stripes
Zoom In
Zoom Lens
Zoom Lenses
Zoom Out

Chapter 3
The Video Camera and Support Equipment

Objectives

After completing this chapter, you will be able to:

- Explain the differences between the various video cameras available.

- Identify each part of a video camera and note the corresponding function.

- Differentiate between the focal length and the focal point related to a zoom lens.

- Explain the interrelationship between f-stops, the iris, and aperture in controlling light.

- List the challenges and benefits involved in using hand-held camera shooting.

- Identify the types of tripod heads available and cite the unique characteristics of each.

Introduction

The camera is one of the first pieces of equipment that new students gravitate toward because it appears to be the most central item in a television production studio. Good camera operators must first learn the capabilities of their equipment. This chapter presents parts of the video camera, related support equipment, and basic operation procedures.

Types of Video Cameras

Several types of video cameras are available for professional use. Each camera type offers unique benefits and restrictions.

Studio Cameras

Studio camera: A television camera placed on a tripod or studio pedestal for exclusive use within the studio.

Tripod: A three-legged stand that supports a camera.

Dolly: A three-wheeled cart onto which the feet of a tripod are mounted. A dolly allows smooth camera movements to be performed.

Studio pedestal: A large, single column on wheels that supports the camera and is pneumatically or hydraulically controlled.

The *studio camera* is usually very large and too heavy to be used as a remote camera in the field. Because of its size, studio cameras may be placed on a three-legged stand, called a *tripod*, for support. To allow smooth camera movement, the feet of the tripod are placed into a three-wheeled cart called a *dolly*, **Figure 3-1**. A *studio pedestal* is another common type of camera support. The camera is attached to a large, single column on wheels that is pneumatically or hydraulically controlled, **Figure 3-2**. The size, weight, and mount of the studio camera dictate that it not be taken out of the studio.

Talk the Talk

When referring to multiple camera dollys, the correct spelling of the term is "dollys." This rule applies only when making reference to this particular piece of equipment.

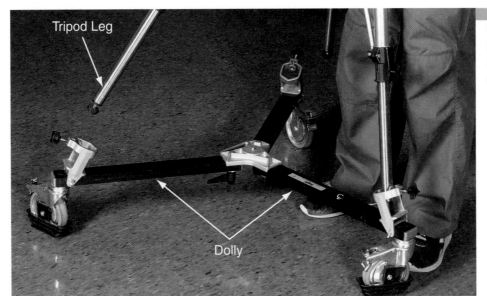

Tripod Leg

Dolly

Figure 3-1
When a tripod is secured into a dolly, the camera may be moved smoothly across the studio floor.

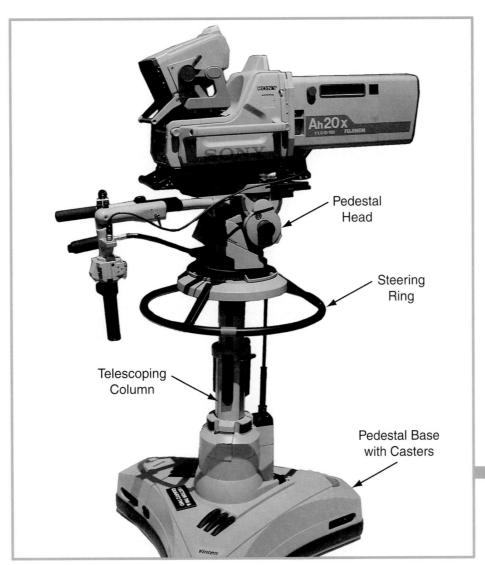

Pedestal Head

Steering Ring

Telescoping Column

Pedestal Base with Casters

Figure 3-2
Placing the camera on a pedestal provides a steady and smooth shot while in the studio. (Vinten Broadcast Ltd.)

Camera control unit (CCU): A piece of equipment that controls various attributes of the video signal sent from the camera and is usually placed in the control room or the master control room. Also commonly called a *remote control unit (RCU)*.

Each studio camera comes with a *camera control unit (CCU)*, sometimes referred to as a *remote control unit (RCU)*, **Figure 3-3**. The CCU is a piece of equipment that controls the video signal sent from the camera and is usually placed in the control room or the master control room. The CCU controls many signals from the camera, including the color, tint, contrast, and brightness. The video engineer manipulates the CCU controls to match the signal from each camera involved in the shoot, **Figure 3-4**.

Visualize This

The video engineer adjusts the settings on CCUs to match the signal from each camera to the others in the studio. The following scenario is likely to occur when cameras are not matched:

The on-screen talent is wearing a red dress and three cameras are shooting her. Every time the switcher cuts from one camera to another, the color of the dress changes from a shade of purple to orange to pink. This creates problems in the editing room during post-production.

Camcorders

Camcorder: A portable camera/recorder combination.

Professional *camcorders* are lightweight, portable cameras, **Figure 3-5**, but are not quite as small as consumer camcorders. Professional models have many more internal components. The professional camcorder is a television camera and recorder in one unit and is relatively simple to take into the field. While in use, it is placed on the operator's right shoulder or on a field tripod.

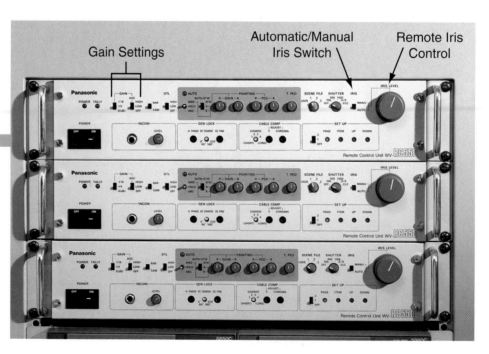

Figure 3-3
The video engineer uses the camera control units (CCU) to adjust the attributes of studio cameras from the control room. This provides a central location for one person to control all the cameras, rather than adjusting the settings on each camera itself on the studio floor.

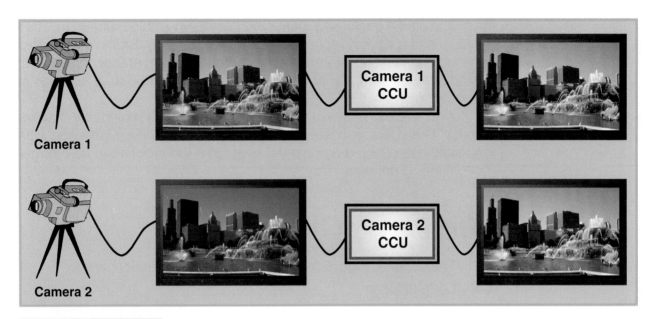

Figure 3-4
A CCU matches the video signals when shooting with multiple video cameras.
(Jack Klasey)

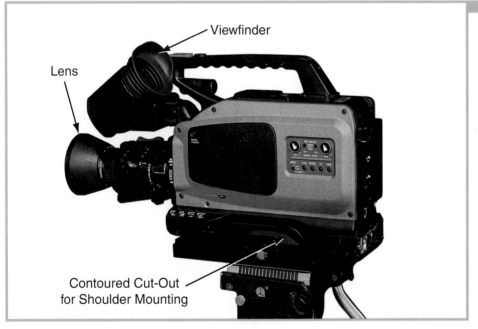

Figure 3-5
A professional camcorder can produce high-quality pictures outside of the studio.

Convertible Cameras

A *convertible camera* may be purchased with a variety of accessory packages that make it operational in a studio, as a portable field camera, or both. Many small-scale studios purchase convertible cameras because they are adaptable to a variety of situations and are often less expensive than larger studio cameras.

Convertible camera:
A camera with a variety of accessory packages available to make it operational in a studio, as a portable field camera, or both.

The studio package configuration of a convertible camera includes a CCU and a viewfinder (a small television monitor). Studio viewfinders measure at least 5″ diagonally. The camera operator stands several feet behind the camera, so the image must be large enough to be seen at that distance.

A remote camera package configuration usually includes a 1″ viewfinder. The operator is likely to have the camera on his shoulder with his right eye pressed against the eyecup of the viewfinder, so a larger viewfinder is not necessary.

The Parts of the Camera

The camera, **Figure 3-6**, is comprised of four major parts:
- Camera Head
- Viewfinder
- Camera Lens
- Recorder

Camera Head

Camera head: The portion of the video camera that contains all the electronics needed to convert the reflection of light from the subject into an electronic signal.

The *camera head* is the actual camera portion of the equipment, **Figure 3-6**. It contains all the electronics needed to convert the reflection of light from the subject into an electronic signal. The incoming light

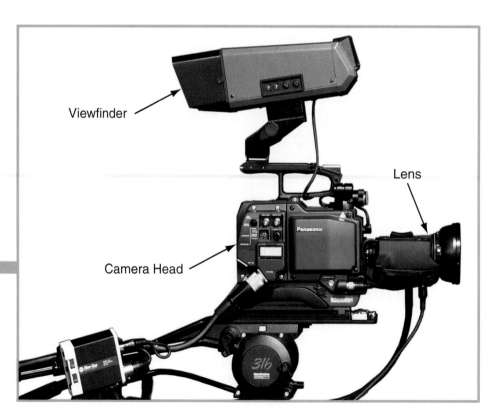

Viewfinder

Lens

Camera Head

Figure 3-6
Even a convertible camera, which may be configured either as a studio camera or a remote camera, has the same basic four components as other types of video cameras.

is split, usually by a prism, into individual red, green, and blue beams. Each beam hits the photosensitive surface, or the *target*, of the corresponding *charge coupled device (CCD)*. The photosensitive elements on one side of the dime-sized CCD convert the light into an electronic, or video, signal. The video signal exits on the opposite side of the CCD and enters the rest of the camera. The charge coupled device is more commonly referred to as the "CCD" or "chip." Professional cameras contain three CCDs, one for each colored light beam.

Gain Control

Gain is the strength of the video signal. Some cameras have a "gain select" or "gain switch," while others may have the feature available through a menu option. On a studio camera, the control may be located on the CCU. If this function is available, you should be aware of its effect on the recorded image. Improper use of the gain switch can result in unusable footage. Adjusting this control allows the strength of the signal going from the camera to the recorder to be increased or decreased. The white level, black level, color, and tint are all equally affected when the gain setting is changed.

Target: Photosensitive surface of a charge coupled device (CCD).

Charge coupled device (CCD): A dime-sized component of the camera head into which light enters and is converted into an electronic, or video, signal. The video signal exits on the opposite side of the CCD and enters the rest of the camera.

Gain: The strength of the video signal.

Production Note

The average consumer would say that the gain control adjusts the picture's brightness. In reality, gain is to brightness as a cubic zirconia is to a diamond. They look similar to an untrained eye, but there are vast differences between them. Adjusting the gain control changes the strength of the actual video signal. In the realm of audio, gain is synonymous with volume. When the brightness is adjusted, the amount of "white" in a picture is increased or decreased.

When shooting something that is dimly lit, the picture will be dark. In this respect, the camera is no different from your eye. It is difficult, sometimes impossible, for the human eye to see in the dark. A soldier on night maneuvers, for example, absolutely must be able to see in the dark. In this situation, night vision goggles are used. In recent years, news programs have commonly shown images of night vision from war zones. However, these images are not very clear. When a camera is shooting in the dark, increasing the gain may artificially brighten the picture.

As the gain is increased, the resulting image becomes increasingly grainy. This kind of picture is unusable in most professional productions. It is recommended that the gain switch never be moved from the "0" (zero) position. If an image is too dark, a light source should be added.

Assistant Activity

Manipulate the gain control while the camera is attached to a monitor to see the effects on the picture.

Viewfinder

A *viewfinder* is a small video monitor that allows the camera operator to view the images in the shot, **Figure 3-6**. Some viewfinders have a special feature that displays *zebra stripes*, black and white diagonal stripes, on any object that is too brightly lit. This is an extremely useful feature that should be engaged, if it is available.

Camera Lens

In the early days of television, the imaging device on cameras was not a CCD, but a vacuum tube. Early cameras had several different lenses attached to a wheel called a "lens turret," **Figure 3-7**. Zoom lenses were not available on these early pieces of equipment. Technology has brought great changes and improvements to the imaging processes of television production.

Viewfinder: A small video monitor attached to the camera that allows the camera operator to view the images in the shot.

Zebra stripes: A special function of some viewfinders that displays black and white diagonal stripes on any object in a shot that is too brightly lit.

Talk the Talk

Both the individual pieces of glass and the casing that houses the glass discs are called lenses. To differentiate these terms within this chapter, note that "lens" refers to the individual pieces of glass and "lens assembly" refers to the piece of equipment that houses the entire assembly of lenses. When working in the industry, both are referred to as a "lens" and are differentiated only by the context of the sentence.

The *lens* is an assembly of several glass discs placed in a tube on the front of a camera. Its primary purpose is to concentrate, or *focus*, the incoming light rays on the surface of the imaging device, or the target. A picture is considered to be "in focus" when the adjoining lines of contrast are as sharp as possible.

Lens: An assembly of several glass discs placed in a tube attached to the front of a camera.

Focus: The act of rotating the focus ring on a camera lens until the lines of contrast in the image are as sharp as possible.

Auto-focus: A common feature on consumer cameras that keeps only the center of the picture in focus.

Production Note

If something is shot out of focus, it cannot be fixed later during editing. It must be re-shot. After shooting a scene, always rewind the tape and check for any errors before moving on.

Auto-focus is a common feature on consumer cameras that keeps only the center of the picture in focus. Most consumers enjoy this feature because they do not need to adjust any of the camera settings to get an image that is in focus. Because the average consumer usually places the most important portion of a picture in the center, the camera feature is quite satisfactory.

Auto-focus is not used on many professional cameras, because focus is a creative tool and professionals prefer to have creative control over the images. As the next chapter explains, the most important items in a shot should never be placed in the center of a frame. Therefore, the auto-focus feature keeps the wrong items in focus. Professionals should always turn the auto-focus option off.

Figure 3-7
This camera was used in the 1950s for both studio and field production. The attached lens turret rotates to allow the lenses to be changed from one size to another. (Chuck Pharis Video)

Production Note

Many people misuse the word "focus;" they incorrectly use it instead of "zoom." For example, "focus in on the apple on the kitchen counter." The word "focus" used in this context actually communicates that the camera should zoom in on the apple on the counter. Use "focus" only when dealing with a picture that is blurry and in need of focus.

Zoom Lenses

Most television lenses are ***zoom lenses***, in that they are capable of magnifying an image merely by twisting one of the rings on the lens. For example, a camera that is 15′ away from a person can capture a very tight shot of their eyes. The zoom lens may be operated at any speed, from extremely fast to so slowly the audience barely perceives that something is getting larger or smaller. Rotating the zoom lens so that the center of the picture appears to be moving toward the camera is called a ***zoom in***. Rotating the zoom lens so that the center of the picture appears to be moving away from the camera is called a ***zoom out***.

It is very important to understand that a zoom shot does not produce the same effect for the audience as a shot where the camera physically moves toward the subject, or a dolly shot. A dolly shot, discussed further in the next chapter, takes the audience into the set in the same way a person moves through his environment. A dolly actually changes the perspective. The natural picture from a dolly shot, without a zoom, is three-dimensional and more realistic. When zooming in, the center of the picture gets larger; it is magnified. It does not appear as though the camera moves closer to the object, only that the center of the picture is larger. The zoom makes it possible to get a close-up of an object without physically moving the camera over uneven terrain. With a zoom shot, however, the image takes on a flat appearance.

Zoom lenses: A camera lens assembly that is capable of magnifying an image merely by twisting one of the rings on the outside of the lens housing. Also called a ***variable focal length lens***.

Zoom in: The act of rotating a ring on the zoom lens so that the center of the picture appears to be moving toward the camera.

Zoom Out: The act of rotating a ring on the zoom lens so that the center of the picture appears to be moving away from the camera.

Visualize This

Imagine that you are standing in the front of the classroom, facing the students. From this vantage point, some of the students in the third row of desks, positioned horizontal to you, are not completely visible. Parts of their bodies, such as arms or hands, are blocked by students in the first and second rows. From your perspective, Rachel's left arm and hand are hidden. If you take a few steps down the aisle to stand even with the second row, you can see Rachel's arm on her desktop without a problem. As the camera (your eyes) moves into the set, the viewing perspective changes. Your body's movement is a dolly move. Another result of the dolly move is that Rachel gets larger in the picture because you are closer to her.

Move back to the front of the class to examine this situation with a camera zoom. Rachel's left arm is blocked from view again because Bill, in the second row, is obstructing your view. Do not take a single step toward Rachel. Instead, pick up a pair of binoculars and view Rachel through them. She is larger in the picture, just like in the dolly, but you are still unable to see her arm. This is because Bill is larger now as well, and is still blocking your view. This movement is like a zoom shot with a video camera because it does not change the visual perspective. You will not see Rachel's left arm until either you move, Bill moves, or Rachel moves.

Optical center: The physical location within the lens assembly where an image is inverted. Also called the *focal point*.

Zoom lens: The particular piece of glass within the lens assembly that moves forward and back, magnifying or shrinking the image accordingly. This individual lens is the focal point, or optical center, of the zoom lens assembly.

Focal length: The distance (measured in millimeters) from the optical center, or focal point, of the lens assembly to the back of the lens assembly.

When an image passes through a zoom lens, it is turned upside down, or is inverted. The physical location within the lens assembly where the inversion occurs is called the *optical center*. Another name for the optical center of the lens is the *focal point*. The optical center, or focal point, may not be in the center of the lens assembly as measured in inches, **Figure 3-8**. For example, the center is 3″ on a lens that measures 6″ long from front to back. The optical center is the point where the image is inverted, regardless of the physical location inside the lens assembly or the distance from the front or back of the lens assembly.

As the outside ring of a zoom lens assembly is rotated, one of the individual lenses inside the lens assembly moves backward or forward. You can see this movement by looking into a zoom lens as it is manipulated. As this piece of glass moves forward and back, the image is magnified or shrinks accordingly. This particular moving piece of glass within the lens assembly is called the *zoom lens*. This individual zoom lens is the focal point, or optical center, of the zoom lens assembly. The image is inverted wherever the zoom lens is positioned, within the range of the lens assembly, **Figure 3-9**.

Focal length is the distance (measured in millimeters) from the optical center (focal point) of the lens assembly to the back of the lens assembly, **Figure 3-10**. The "back" of the lens is the end of the lens assembly that attaches to the camera. The "front" of the lens assembly is the part closest to the subject being photographed or filmed. Camera

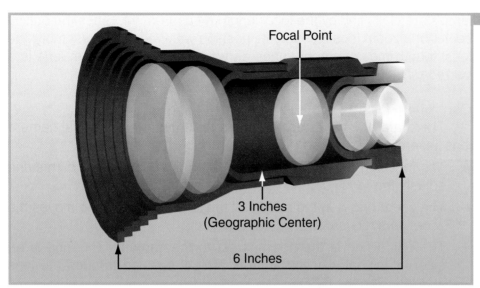

Figure 3-8
The optical center of a lens is not always in the physical center of the lens.

Focal Point

3 Inches
(Geographic Center)

6 Inches

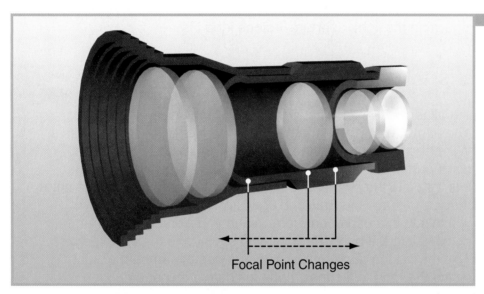

Figure 3-9
The individual zoom lens slides forward and backward within the zoom lens assembly. The focal point is located wherever the zoom lens is positioned.

Focal Point Changes

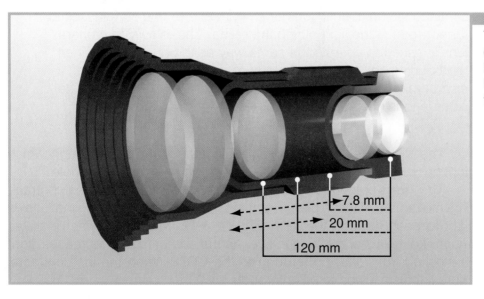

Figure 3-10
The focal length is the distance (in millimeters) between the back of the lens assembly and the focal point.

7.8 mm

20 mm

120 mm

Variable focal length lens: A lens in which the optical center can vary its position within the lens assembly, varying the focal length measurement as well. Also called a *zoom lens*.

lenses are classified by the focal length measurement. Since the optical center of a zoom lens can vary its position within the lens assembly, the focal length measurement varies as well. Therefore, a zoom lens is a *variable focal length lens*.

Controlling Light

There are at least three moveable rings on a professional camera lens assembly, **Figure 3-11**:

- The focusing ring is furthest away from the camera body. This ring adjusts the focus of the image in the frame of the picture.
- The zoom ring is in the middle of the lens assembly and moves the zoom lens forward and backward.
- The f-stop ring is the ring nearest to the camera. This ring is an external indicator of the amount of light passing through the lens and reaching the CCD.

Three specific components of a lens assembly work together in regulating the light: aperture, f-stops, and iris.

Visualize This

When you enter a dark movie theater, your eyes dilate. The part of your eye that determines eye color, the iris, contracts. When the iris contracts, the pupil gets larger. The pupil is the black part in the center of the eye that is essentially a hole that lets light into the eye. With the pupil enlarged, more light can enter the eye to reach the rods and cones of the retina. This allows you to see in a darkened room. When you exit the theater and go back into the bright daylight, you squint and the iris expands. This makes the pupil smaller and reduces the amount of light hitting the rods and cones. If the iris cannot expand enough to sufficiently reduce the amount of light hitting the retina, you continue to squint until you get a headache or find sunglasses to further reduce the light hitting the retina. The television camera lens is asked to operate the same way as the human eye when reproducing colors and tones and reacting to changes in the environment's light. It valiantly tries, but does not succeed. The camera lens needs a human to help it operate.

Aperture: The opening, adjusted by the iris, through which light passes into the lens.

Iris: A component of a lens that is comprised of blades that physically expand and contract, adjusting the aperture size.

The *aperture* is the opening, adjusted by the iris, through which light passes. Aperture is nothing that can be touched; it is a hole.

The *iris* is comprised of blades that physically expand and contract. The movement of these blades adjusts the size of the opening that allows light to pass through the lens, **Figure 3-12**. A camera's iris operates much like the iris of the human eye. As the size of the iris increases, light is blocked from passing through to the CCD. When the iris contracts, more light is allowed to pass through.

Figure 3-11
A professional lens has at least three moveable rings: the focus ring, the zoom ring, and the f-stop ring.

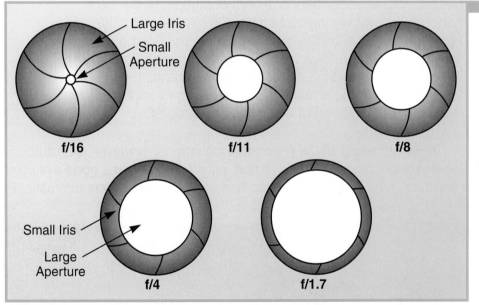

Figure 3-12
The size of the iris determines the size of the aperture. A large iris creates a small aperture; reducing the size of the iris produces a larger aperture.

Auto-iris circuit: A feature on many consumer and professional cameras that automatically examines the light levels coming into the camera and adjusts the iris according to generic standards of a "good" picture.

F-stop: A camera setting that determines the amount of light passing through the lens by controlling the size of the iris.

Many consumer and professional cameras have an auto-iris circuit, as well as a manual iris control. The *auto-iris circuit* examines the light levels coming into the camera and opens or closes the iris according to the generic definition of a "good" picture. The auto-iris is a useful feature for most circumstances in television production.

Many cameras offer a manual iris control in addition to the automatic circuit. Adjusting the iris manually is accomplished by moving the f-stop ring. The *f-stop* setting determines the amount of light that passes through the lens by controlling the size of the iris. If the camera lens has a manual f-stop ring (some consumer cameras do not), numeric values are written on the corresponding moveable ring, **Figure 3-13**. When the f-stop ring is manually turned, the operator hears or feels a series of clicks or bumps that indicate movement from one f-stop to another. Lower f-stop settings (numbers) allow a greater amount of light to pass through the lens. Higher f-stop numbers indicate that smaller amounts of light can pass through. The appropriate f-stop setting varies per situation, based on the lighting in the environment and the brightness of the object(s) in the shot.

Visualize This

To understand the purpose and function of f-stops, consider the speedometer of a car. While driving a car, you look at the dash and see that the speedometer indicates you are traveling at 40 miles per hour. You want to accelerate to 55 miles per hour. To accomplish this, you reach your hand forward and push the needle of the speedometer with your finger up to 55, right? Of course not. Moving the needle of the speedometer does not increase the speed of the vehicle because the speedometer does not contribute to the car's performance. It only indicates what the car is doing. The accelerator increases the gasoline flow to the engine, which then works faster and causes the car to increase its speed. On a camera, the f-stop ring is the speedometer, the iris is the accelerator, and the amount of light passing through the lens (aperture) is the speed at which the car is traveling.

When shooting in high contrast situations, however, the auto-iris essentially becomes confused. It first adjusts to produce a good picture of the darker items, but the light items then begin to glow. When automatically

Figure 3-13
The f-stop ring is labeled with a series of numbers.

F-stop Numbers

adjusting for the light objects in the frame, the dark items lose all detail. The auto-iris should be disengaged in this type of situation. If this feature can be disengaged, manually adjust the f-stop ring to produce the best quality picture.

Production Note

It is important to remember how the aperture, f-stops, and the iris relate to each other. The f-stop *indicates* the size of the iris, which *creates* the size of the aperture.

Recorder

On many camera systems, the recorder is a separate part that is directly connected to the camera head. This allows a variety of video recorders to be used with a single camera head. Attaching the recorder to the camera head is not necessarily done with a cable. A short cable may run from the back of the camera and down to a recorder hanging off the camera operator's shoulder. Most recorders, however, attach directly to the camera head by sliding into a notch on the back of the head. The two parts lock together making one larger "camcorder." The process of attaching the camera head and recorder is called ***docking***. Cameras and recorders that are designed to dock to each other are called "dockable."

Docking: The process of attaching the camera head and recorder together to make one larger "camcorder."

Mounting the Camera

There are two basic ways to support a camera while in use:
- Hand-Held Shooting
- Tripod Shooting

Hand-Held Shooting

Many consumer cameras are literally held in the operator's hands. The size and weight of most professional cameras make it difficult to be held in the operator's hands for any extended amount of time. Professional cameras usually rest on the right shoulder of the operator, with both hands holding the camera lens steady. The right hand is positioned inside a strap holding it to the zoom lens control. The left hand holds the focus ring of the lens. See **Figure 3-14**.

At first glance, the hand-held camera technique appears easy. The operator does not need to be concerned with carrying and setting up a heavy tripod. However, hand-held camera operation quickly loses its appeal when gravity takes its toll. The camera operator's arms tire quickly, and the heavier the camera is, the faster this happens. The result is very poor camerawork. An unsteady camera shakes, wiggles, tilts sideways, and eventually begins to point at the ground. Even if the camera is hand-held for a short time, the shot moves with every rise and fall of the camera operator's chest while breathing.

Production Note

Professionals do not operate a camera with only one hand! The right shoulder bears the brunt of the weight of the camera. The right hand is positioned inside a strap holding it to the zoom lens control. The left hand holds the focus ring of the lens. Both hands should be on the camera when operating with the hand-held technique. A stable picture is virtually impossible if only one hand is used. Additionally, a $15,000 to $60,000 camera is very unlikely to fall off your shoulder when held with both hands.

If the lens is zoomed in on a person or object, the slightest shake or wobble is amplified. The resulting image is annoying to the audience. The further the lens is zoomed out, the less noticeable any shaking

Figure 3-14
The camera operator can make use of items in the field to help steady a hand-held camera. A—One technique is to lean against a wall. This essentially makes the operator two legs of a tripod, with the wall as the third. B—An open car door can provide tripod-like support to the camera operator. The open door is one leg, the roof is another leg, and the operator's legs are the third leg of the makeshift tripod.

becomes. Therefore, always operate in the "zoomed out" position when hand-holding a camera. To get a close-up, move closer to the object; do not use the zoom.

If it is absolutely necessary to hand-hold a camera, brace yourself against a wall or tree, lean against a car door, or lie on the ground, **Figure 3-14**. Hold your breath to get the shot while steady, but realize that nothing will be usable beyond 5–10 seconds. There are many hand-held shots in the news, but the image cuts from one shot to another in the stories from the "field." Anyone can hold a steady shot for a few seconds. The editor cuts out all the shaking shots.

The Glidecam™ is a device that attaches to a harness worn by the camera operator, **Figure 3-15**. This harness is similar to that worn by a bass drummer in a marching band. A spring-loaded and shock absorbing arm is attached to the harness. The camera attaches to the arm using the same kind of mounting plate found on tripods. Using the Glidecam, the weight of the camera is taken by the harness and, therefore, by the operator's entire torso. Because the arm is spring-loaded, the camera shot is kept steady even while the operator climbs steps, runs, or walks.

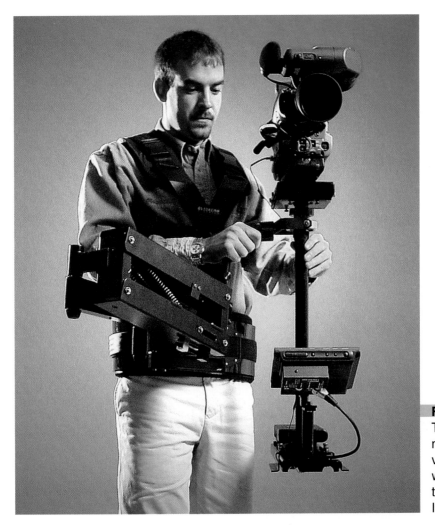

Figure 3-15
The Glidecam is a body mount that facilitates very smooth camera-work without using a tripod. (Glidecam Industries, Inc.)

Assistant Activity

To help you understand how a Glidecam type assembly works:

1. Fill a 16 oz. drinking glass with water to ½″ from the top.
2. Hold the glass in your hand with your arm curved as it would be if you were holding the pole of a carousel horse.
3. Keep your arm in this position and walk, run, go up and down stairs, or dance without spilling a drop of the water.

How is it possible that the water does not spill? The muscles in your wrist, arm, elbow, and shoulder act as spring-loaded shock absorbers. If you hold the glass to your chest, with the knuckle of your thumb actually touching your chest, the water will spill almost immediately upon moving. The shock absorption has been removed and the glass is directly attached to the motion of your body.

The Glidecam arm absorbs the shock of motion in very much the same way as your arm does in this activity.

Subjective Camera

Subjective camera:
A hand-held camera technique, in which the camera itself becomes the eye of one cast member. The viewers see the world through the eyes of that character.

Subjective camera is a special hand-held camera technique, **Figure 3-16**. The camera itself becomes the eye of one cast member. The viewer sees the world through the eyes of that character. Examples of this technique include:

● A camera is mounted in a stunt driver's car. As the car is driven up and down hills at high speeds, the audience's stomachs lurch as if they were actually riding in that vehicle.

Figure 3-16
In a subjective camera shot, the camera becomes the eyes of one character in the program.

● In a suspense film, the camera is positioned outside a house in the middle of the dark woods. "We" are looking through the branches of a bush into a window of the home. "Our hand" reaches up into the field of view of the camera and pushes away leaves on the bush to clear our view into the house.

Tripod Shooting

A tripod is the three-legged stand to which the camera is attached. The telescoping legs on most tripods allow the operator to position the camera at varying heights. The legs on all tripods spread out from the center. On most tripods, each leg operates independently. This is useful if the camera needs to be set up on a sloped terrain, such as the side of a hill. Each leg can be extended and spread out at different angles, which facilitates level mounting of the camera head on an uneven surface. Most tripods and tripod heads are made with a leveling bubble that assists the operator in ensuring that the camera head is level when mounted.

Tripods often have a column in the center, called a *pedestal column*, to raise or lower the camera. On the side of the pedestal column is the *pedestal control*, which is a crank that twists a gear to raise and lower the column. Turning the pedestal control to raise the column is to pedestal up and lowering the column is to pedestal down (discussed in Chapter 4, *Video Camera Operations*). This action does, however, cause considerable shaking of the camera. The audience sees every wiggle and shake of the camera if it is *hot*. A camera is hot when the image captured by the camera is being recorded. Pedestal up and down only when the camera is not hot. A camera mounted on a studio pedestal, on the other hand, may pedestal up and down with great smoothness.

Mounting Heads

The *tripod head* is the assembly at the top of the pedestal column to which the camera attaches, **Figure 3-17**. The tripod head has several handles and knobs. The handles and knobs allow the operator to pan and tilt the camera attached to the tripod head. The tripod head moves on the tripod in much the same way as your head moves on your neck. It can be tilted to point at the ceiling or the floor, or from side to side. One or two *pan handles* may be attached to the back of the tripod head,

Pedestal column: A column in the center of a tripod used to raise or lower the camera.

Pedestal control: A crank on the side of the pedestal column that twists a gear to raise and lower the pedestal column.

Hot: The state of a video camera when the image captured by the camera is being recorded.

Tripod head: The assembly at the top of the pedestal column to which the camera attaches.

Pan handle: A device attached to the back of the tripod head that allows the camera operator to move the tripod head while standing behind the tripod.

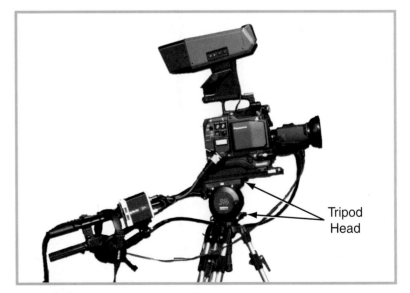

Tripod Head

Figure 3-17
The tripod head is located on top of the legs and pedestal column of the tripod, and includes the mounting plate or wedge.

Friction head: A mounting assembly on some tripods that stabilizes the camera using the pressure created when two pieces of metal are squeezed together by a screw.

Fluid head: A mounting assembly on some tripods that stabilizes the camera using the pressure between two pieces of metal and a thick fluid that provides additional resistance to movement.

Figure 3-18. The pan handles allow the camera operator to move the tripod head while standing behind the tripod. There are two types of tripod heads available: the friction head and the fluid head.

A *friction head* is found on less expensive tripods and on almost all consumer tripods. The camera is stabilized by the pressure created when two pieces of metal are squeezed together by a screw. Releasing the pressure (loosening the screw) reduces resistance between the pieces of metal and the parts slide easily against each other. The camera can then be tilted up and down using the handle. This type of tripod head is not usually found in a professional television setup.

The *fluid head* is similar to the friction head, in that pressure between two pieces of metal restricts movement of the head. However, the fluid head has a thick fluid, such as oil or grease, between the two pieces of metal. This provides additional resistance to movement. The tripod head can be loosened, but is never completely free to move without resistance.

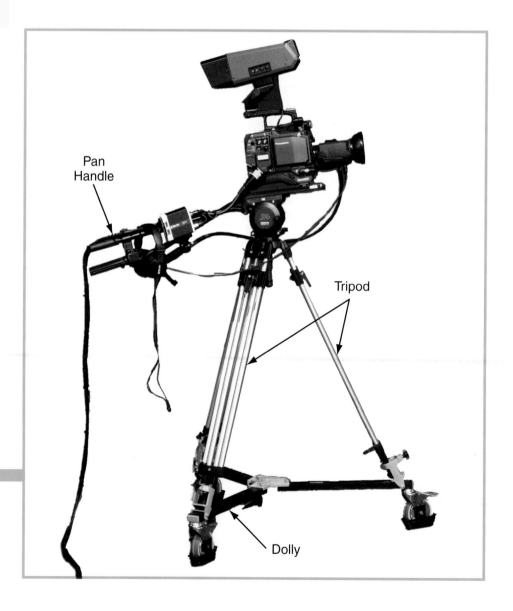

Figure 3-18

Pan handles allow the operator to perform camera movements while the camera is mounted to the tripod head.

Camera operators prefer more resistance to create smooth and stable camera movements. If the head were completely resistance free, the camera would move with the slightest twitch or breath of the operator. The fluid head allows the camera operator to place fluctuating levels of pressure on the head, without moving the head until enough force is intentionally exerted. This prevents camera movement caused by slight touches on the pan handles.

Visualize This

To help you understand how a fluid head provides greater resistance:

1. Swing one of your arms while standing in a room. Notice the free movement of your arm.

2. Imagine that you are standing in water up to your neck moving your arm the same way. The fluid (water) provides some resistance to movement and you have to work a bit harder to create the same motion.

3. Imagine standing in a pool of oil swinging your arm. It would be even more difficult to move.

Increasingly thicker fluids provide greater resistance to movement.

Camera Care and Maintenance

To help ensure the highest quality images, proper care and maintenance of video equipment is necessary. The recommended handling includes both appropriate cleaning and storage of equipment.

Cleaning a Dirty Lens

As with other pieces of video production equipment, the camera lens is delicate and requires special care when cleaning. Commonly used cleaning solutions and materials are not appropriate for use on a camera lens.

Seeing little spots on a camera's viewfinder is not necessarily an indication that the lens is dirty. Perhaps the dirt is on the front of the viewfinder. Clean the viewfinder with a soft cloth. If this does not remove the spots, the lens should be cleaned. The following are some firm rules about cleaning lenses:

● Never touch a lens with your bare fingers.

● Never use a cloth or tissue moistened with saliva to wipe a lens clean. Saliva ruins the lens.

- Wipe dirt away using photographic lens paper only.
- Use compressed air from a can to blow dirt off a lens. Never try to blow the dirt off with your breath.

Post-Production Camera Care

While not in use, both studio cameras and camcorders should be stored in a protected and temperature-controlled location. All the related cables should be coiled and stored with the camera or camcorder.

Guidelines for care of a studio camera:

- Lock the pedestal and camera mounting head to prevent movement while not in use.
- Close the iris and attach the lens cap.
- Move the camera to a safe location within the studio.

Guidelines for care of a camcorder:

- Remove the videotape from the camcorder.
- Close the iris and attach the lens cap.
- Power-off all the camera functions (light, microphone, recorder).
- Detach the camera from the tripod when transporting the equipment.
- Place the camera in its case for storage and transport, **Figure 3-19**.

Figure 3-19
Place the video camera in its case for safe transport and storage.

Wrapping Up

The television production industry is labor and skill intensive. Careers in this industry require long hours of work. On the other hand, it is difficult to find anyone working in the television production industry who does not like his or her job.

Think about high school football players. Every August, before the school year even starts, they go to school and practice outside in the summer heat for hours on end. To them, it is not work. Most people in the television production industry do not refer to their job responsibilities as work. They say things like:

- "I have a shoot today."
- "I'm going to the studio."
- "I'm starting to edit now."

The word "work" is not used in normal conversation with production people, because most consider it fun.

Review Questions

Please answer the following questions on a separate sheet of paper. Do not write in this book.

1. List the parts of a studio camera and note the function of each part.
2. How does the appearance of an image change when the gain is adjusted?
3. What is the optical center of a zoom lens?
4. Explain the significance of the numbers printed on the f-stop ring of a camera lens.
5. What challenges are presented when hand-held shooting with a professional camera?
6. List the benefits of using a tripod when shooting outside of the studio.
7. What is the difference between a friction head and a fluid head?
8. What are the appropriate materials to use when cleaning a camera lens?

Activities

1. To illustrate the proper result of focusing a camera lens, perform the following:
    1. Place a piece of white paper on the right side of a piece of black paper.
    2. Point a camera at both pieces of paper.
    3. Move the lens so that the camera is out of focus.
    4. Notice that the left edge of the picture is clearly black and the right edge is clearly white. It is difficult to determine where the image turns from black to white, as the center of the picture is gray.
    5. Twist the focus ring of the lens, slowly bringing the picture into focus.
    6. The center of the picture becomes less and less gray and the image becomes sharper. When the picture is completely "in focus," the separation between black and white is as sharp as possible.
2. Create an analogy (a written paragraph or an illustration) that effectively explains the relationship between f-stops, the iris, and aperture.

Important Terms

Arc
Arc Left
Arc Right
Close-Up (CU)
Depth of Field (DOF)
Dolly
Dolly In
Dolly Out
Establishing Shot
Extreme Close-Up
 (ECU/XCU)
Extreme Long Shot
 (ELS/XLS)
Four Shot
Great Depth of Field
Group Shot
Head Room
High Angle Shot
Long Shot (LS)
Low Angle Shot
Macro
Medium Close-Up
 (MCU)
Medium Long Shot
 (MLS)
Medium Shot (MS)
Mid Shot
Minimum Object
 Distance (MOD)
Narrow Angle Shot

Nose Room
Over-the-Shoulder
 Shot (OSS)
Pan
Pan Left
Pan Right
Pedestal
Pedestal Down
Pedestal Up
Pre-Focus
Profile Shot
Pull Focus
Rack Focus
Reaction Shot
Rule of Thirds
Selective Depth
 of Field
Shallow Depth of Field
Shot
Shot Sheet
Three Shot
Tilt
Tilt Down
Tilt Up
Truck
Truck Left
Truck Right
Two Shot
Wide Angle Shot (WA)

Objectives

After completing this chapter, you will be able to:

- Explain how depth of field contributes to composing a good picture.
- Describe the composition of each type of camera shot.
- List and define a variety of camera movements.
- Explain how a videographer can psychologically and physically affect the audience.

Introduction

While learning to operate a camera is not complex, becoming a talented camera operator requires dedication and skill. Great camera operators:

- Know the basic rules of composition.
- Know the basic process of production methodology.
- Know the capabilities of their equipment.

Composing Good Pictures

Composing good pictures begins with learning some basic principles. This basic information is the foundation on which experience is built and only experience can perfect camera composition skills.

Pre-Focusing Zoom Lenses

A zoom lens cannot be focused while it is in the "zoomed out" position. Focusing a zoom lens is a three-step process called *pre-focus*. To pre-focus a zoom lens:

1. Zoom in on the furthest object on the set that must be in focus in the shot. The furthest object that must be in focus might not be the background. For example, picture a cowboy on a horse in a prairie with the Rocky Mountains in the background. The furthest object in this shot that must be in focus is most likely the cowboy, not the mountains.
2. Focus the camera on that object.
3. Zoom the lens back out.

Following these three steps, everything from about 6′ in front of the camera to the furthest object focused on (in step 2) will be in focus. Everything remains in focus until the camera is moved toward or away from the object focused on, or until the lighting on the set is changed.

Many cameras offer a *macro* setting for the lens. The macro feature allows the operator to focus on an object that is very close to the camera, almost touching the lens.

Depth of Field

The closest an object can be to the camera and still be in focus is the *minimum object distance (MOD)*. Minimum object distance contributes to depth of field. *Depth of field (DOF)* is the distance between the MOD and the furthest point from the camera that the subject can be positioned and still remain in focus, **Figure 4-1**.

Pre-focus: A three-step process to focus a zoom lens. 1) Zoom in on the furthest object on the set that must be in focus in the shot. 2) Focus the camera on that object. 3) Zoom the lens back out.

Macro: A lens setting that allows the operator to focus on an object that is very close to the camera, almost touching the lens.

Minimum object distance (MOD): The closest an object can be to the camera and still be in focus.

Depth of field (DOF): The distance between the minimum object distance and the furthest point from the camera that a subject can be positioned while remaining in focus.

Assistant Activity

To help clarify this concept, find the MOD of your eyes.
1. Hold up your index finger about 12″ away from your face.
2. Look at your fingerprint; you should be able to clearly see it.
3. Slowly move your finger in toward your face.

As you move your finger, there comes a point when your eyes can no longer focus on your finger and you are unable to clearly see the fingerprint. This point is the minimum object distance (MOD) of your eyes.

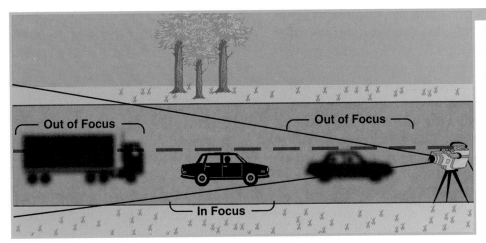

Figure 4-1
The depth of field is
the area in front of the
camera, regardless of
the distance, in which
objects are in focus.

Most of the time, a camera's depth of field should be as large as possible. This is called *great depth of field*. When using a great depth of field, zooming and some camera movements (such as a truck or arc) do not cause the image to go in and out of focus. However, when every element in the picture is in focus, no one particular item stands out for emphasis.

The use of *shallow depth of field* moves the audience's attention to the one portion of the picture that is in focus. By using shallow depth of field, the program's director can control exactly what the viewer looks at within the frame of the picture. For example, scenes on television and in movies where the foreground is in focus and the background is out of focus direct the viewer's attention to the item or action in the foreground, **Figure 4-2**. The reverse is commonly used as well; the background is in

Great depth of field:
When a camera's depth
of field is as large as
possible, but also keeps
all the items in the image
in focus while zooming.

Shallow depth of field:
A depth of field tech-
nique that moves the
audience's attention to
the one portion of the
picture that is in focus.

Figure 4-2
The pain this young
woman feels is more
powerful with the back-
ground out of focus. A
shallow depth of field
complements this image.

Selective depth of field: A technique of *choosing* to have a shallow depth of field in a shot or scene.

Rack focus: The process of changing focus on a camera while that camera is hot. Also called **pull focus**.

focus and the foreground is out of focus. When using a shallow depth of field, the camera operator must refocus the camera if the talent moves, even slightly, toward or away from the camera, or if any camera movements are performed.

Selective depth of field is the technique of *choosing* to have a shallow depth of field in a shot or scene. One dramatic effect that results from this technique is changing the camera's focus from the foreground to the background (or the reverse) while the camera is hot. The attention of the audience may be intently concentrated on a foreground image, but the camera gradually brings something unexpected from the background into focus. The process of changing focus on a camera while that camera is hot is called **rack focus**, or **pull focus**. Selective DOF loses its impact when overused in the course of a program.

Visualize This

The following is a powerful example of the use of selective depth of field. The scene described is an anti-war spot that was used during a Presidential campaign in the 1960s.

A little girl wearing a yellow dress chases a butterfly around a beautiful field of flowers. She giggles and is obviously having a grand, happy time. The background is an out of focus greenish color. The viewer simply assumes that the background contains vegetation of some kind. The camera moves toward a shot of the girl's smiling face, with the palms of her two small hands upraised and reaching toward the butterfly a bit closer in the foreground. Right before the viewer's eyes, the camera's focus shifts and brings the background of the shot into focus. When in focus, the background vegetation becomes a line of fifty or more soldiers with rifles ready to fire, stealthily moving out of the trees and toward the camera.

The use of selective depth of field makes the line of soldiers surprising background material and increases the impact of the scene.

Three factors affect depth of field:
- Aperture—the size of the opening in the lens that allows light into the camera.
- Subject to Camera Distance—the distance between the camera and the subject of the shot.
- Focal Length—the amount the lens is zoomed in or out.

Production Note

Remember: the f-stop *indicates* the size of the iris, which *creates* the size of the aperture.

More movement in each of these three areas creates a more pronounced effect for either shallow or great DOF, **Figure 4-3**. For example, the effect on DOF produced by zooming in and increasing the aperture is not as great as when the camera moves closer to the subject in addition to the zoom and aperture adjustment.

Camera lenses are operated by camera operators. Even though depth of field involves manipulating light, the lighting designer does not have a part in this process. The camera operator creates depth of field by manipulating the lens. Set lighting does not affect depth of field. Depth of field is affected by subject to camera distance, focal length, and aperture (not light).

Since the majority of scenes in programs are shot using a great depth of field, a smaller aperture is more commonly used. A smaller aperture requires higher light levels to capture a good quality picture. This explains why there are so many bright lights on the ceiling of a TV studio. Studio sets are saturated with light, allowing the camera apertures to be reduced when necessary without affecting the picture quality.

Depth of Field			
Director's Goal	**Zoom Technique**	**Dolly Technique**	**F-Stop Setting**
Obtain a shallow depth of field.	Zoom In	Dolly In	Use a lower f-stop value: • Reduces the iris • Increases the aperture; more light passes through the lens
Obtain a great depth of field.	Zoom Out	Dolly Out	Use a higher f-stop value: • Enlarges the iris • Decreases the aperture; less light passes through the lens

Figure 4-3
Depth of field chart.

Lines of Interest

Rule of thirds: A composition rule that divides the screen into thirds horizontally and vertically, like a tic-tac-toe grid placed over the picture on a television set. Almost all of the important information included in every shot is located at one of the four intersections of the horizontal and vertical lines.

The *rule of thirds* for television production divides the screen into thirds horizontally and vertically; like a tic-tac-toe grid placed over the picture on a television set, **Figure 4-4**. Almost all of the important information included in every shot is located at one of the four intersections of the horizontal and vertical lines. Studies have shown that the human eye is drawn to those four points of any picture first and not to the center of the screen, as is commonly assumed.

To follow the rule of thirds when shooting, the talent should be positioned so that their eyes are ⅓ of the way down from the top of the screen. In broadcast television, important people and objects in a shot are slightly left or right of the center. The center of the tic-tac-toe box rarely contains the main subject or important object of the shot.

Action

Nearly every shot in broadcast television includes some kind of action. Either the main subject matter (objects or talent) in the picture provide action or movement, the camera moves to provide a moving shot, or both the camera and subject matter move. There is rarely a shot without some type of action. Audiences today have become accustomed to seeing one action shot after another and quickly lose interest if this is not the case.

Assistant Activity

Rent a movie you have recently seen and thought was boring. Watch it again and notice the percentage of shots having little or no action.

Figure 4-4
The rule of thirds states that the most interesting aspects of a picture should be positioned near the four intersecting points on a tic-tac-toe grid.

Head Room

The space from the top of a person's head to the top of the screen is called *head room*, **Figure 4-5**. This space should be kept to a minimum, unless something important is going to happen above the head of the talent.

Head room: The space from the top of a person's head to the top of the television screen.

Figure 4-5
Head room is an important consideration when framing a shot. A—Excessive head room usually indicates that something is about to happen above the subject's head. B—Correct head room spacing ensures that the audience's attention is not diverted from the main subject of the shot.

Nose Room

Nose room is the space from the tip of a person's nose to the side edge of the frame. Novice videographers often make errors in framing with respect to nose room. The natural tendency is to place the talent in the center of the screen with equal space on either side. That is acceptable only if the talent is facing the camera. The more the talent looks to the right or the left, the more room should be placed between their nose and that same edge of the screen, **Figure 4-6**. If the talent is walking parallel to the camera, sufficient space should be placed in front of the person as they walk. If the scene is shot without enough nose room in this scenario, the talent appears to be pushing the frame of the picture with their nose as they walk. Additionally, if the person is moving laterally, the shot should be enlarged to at least a mid shot. Otherwise, the talent is likely to walk right out of camera view.

Visualize This

Imagine a scene in a horror movie. One of the characters is about to be attacked by a vampire approaching from behind. It would be appropriate to leave space behind the talent in the frame so the vampire could enter the picture. In a horror movie, however, any time space is left behind someone, the audience expects a monster to jump in behind the talent. To mislead the audience, place the space behind the talent in the frame and either:

● Make sure nothing happens from *that* direction, or
● Have action occur on the unexpected opposite side of the screen.

Doing this once or twice is effective and increases the reaction of the audience. Using this technique more often reduces its effect and will be laughed at by the audience.

Calling the Shots

A *shot* is an individual picture taken by a camera during the process of shooting the program footage. In a typical studio shoot with three cameras, the output from each camera runs into a switcher in the control room. The director must decide which image to place on the master tape and which camera to pull the image from. To do this, buttons on the switcher are selected to cut from one camera to another. For example, close-up shots of individual characters may be needed at various times in the program. To capture the shots necessary, the director must know what is going to be said and what actions are going to happen before they occur on the set. This way, the camera operators can be directed into position to capture the necessary shot when it happens. This kind of planning requires that the director be 5–10 seconds mentally ahead of the performers at all times.

Figure 4-6
Nose room is another
consideration when
shooting. A—Correct
nose room framing
leaves sufficient space
between the talent and
the edge of the shot.
B—With too little nose
room in a shot, the audi-
ence expects something
to happen behind the
subject.

Far less stress would be placed on the director if he did not have to think far enough ahead in the program to tell the camera operators to move. It would also be more efficient if the camera operators knew in advance what their next shot is supposed to be. This would allow them to execute the camera move before the moment arrives for their camera to be hot. Using a *shot sheet* relieves some of this stress and makes directing a three-camera shoot easier. A shot sheet lists each shot numerically and separates each per camera.

Shot sheet: A numer-
ical listing of each shot
to be captured by each
camera in a multi-
camera shoot. Shot
sheets are developed
specifically for each
camera.

To use a shot sheet, the director reviews the script before the shoot and plans each of the camera shots. Each shot is assigned a sequential number. The numbered shots, with corresponding brief descriptions, are divided per camera and written on sheets of paper, **Figure 4-7**. On the day of the shoot, the shot sheets are taped to the side of the appropriate camera. During the shoot the director can merely say, "Take shot 4" instead of, "Camera 2, I want you to have a close-up of Mary next so get your shot ready while I'm still on camera 3."

As soon as the director cuts from camera 3 (shot 3) to the shot of Mary on camera 2 (shot 4), the camera 3 operator looks at his shot sheet and sees that he does not have shot 5. He does, however, have shot 8. The operator reviews the brief description and readies the shot without being told to do so. Camera 1 was assigned shot 5 and had the shot set-up and ready to go. Using shot sheets makes a multi-camera shoot much more efficient.

There are many different types and sizes of camera shots that can be taken of a person standing in a studio. It is imperative to learn the names of individual shots and what each shot incorporates. Unfortunately, all professional television facilities do not use exactly the same terms. While working in the industry, it is important to know how your facility defines its terms. The sections that follow present the most common definitions of various "person" shots, but the terms are not universal.

Camera 1	Camera 2	Camera 3
2–Mid shot John/Mary	4–Close-up Mary	1–Close-up John
5–Close-up John	6–Three shot John, Mary, Bill	3–Wide shot entire set
7–Close-up of phone	9–Close-up on fireplace	8–Mid shot Mary

Figure 4-7
Shot sheets are developed for each camera involved in a shoot.

Wide Shots

The ***extreme long shot (ELS/XLS)*** is also known as a ***wide angle shot (WA)***. This is generally considered to be the biggest shot a camera can capture of the subject matter, **Figure 4-8**. This shot includes a person's entire body from head to toe, and as much surrounding information as the camera can capture by dollying and zooming out.

Overusing the extreme long shot can prove ineffective. An extreme long shot of a crowd that is viewed on a small 13″ television screen appears to be an image of a multicolored wheat field waving in the breeze. A shot that is too "long" creates a picture without detail.

An ***establishing shot*** is a very specific type of extreme long shot. The establishing shot is used to tell the audience where and when the program takes place. For example, if the opening shot is of a dusty town with dirt roads, cowboys riding horses, and a stagecoach approaching,

Extreme long shot (ELS/XLS): The biggest shot a camera can capture of the subject matter. Also called a *wide angle (WA) shot*.

Establishing shot: A specific type of extreme long shot used to tell the audience where and when the program takes place.

the audience can assume that the program is set in the Old West. Directors periodically return to an establishing shot during a scene to reinforce the location and to prevent confusion.

A *long shot (LS)* captures a person from the top of the head to the bottom of the feet, **Figure 4-9**. Much less of the surrounding details are included, compared to the extreme long shot.

Long shot (LS): A shot that captures a subject from the top of the head to the bottom of the feet and does not include many of the surrounding details.

Figure 4-8
An extreme long shot is the largest shot the camera can get. The ELS is usually a shot of a person from head to toe and also includes as much detail of the subject's surroundings as possible.

Figure 4-9
A long shot includes the subject from head to toe only.

Medium long shot (MLS): A shot that includes the top of a subject's head to a line just above or just below the knee.

Individual Subject Shots

A *medium long shot (MLS)* includes the top of a person's head to a line just above or just below the knee, **Figure 4-10**.

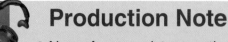

Production Note

Never frame a picture so that the edge of the picture cuts a joint of the human body (ankles, knees, waist, wrists, elbows, or neck). The person appears to have amputated body parts, **Figure 4-11**.

Figure 4-10
The bottom edge of a medium long shot is just below or just above the subject's knee.

Figure 4-11
Never frame a shot that cuts off a person at a natural joint of the body.

The *medium shot (MS)* is also referred to as a *mid shot*, **Figure 4-12**. This shot captures a person from the top of the head to a line just above or below the belt or waistline.

A *medium close-up (MCU)* frames a person from the top of the head to a line just below the chest, **Figure 4-13**. This is the type of shot usually seen of newscasters on daily news programs.

Medium shot (MS): A shot that captures a subject from the top of the head to a line just above or below the belt or waistline. Also called a *mid shot*.

Medium close-up (MCU): A shot that frames a subject from the top of the head to a line just below the chest.

Figure 4-12
The medium shot, or mid shot, includes the subject's head to just above or below the waistline.

Figure 4-13
A medium close-up captures a person from head to just below the chest.

Figure 4-14
The close-up shot includes a subject's head and neck, and must also include the top of their shoulders.

Figure 4-15
A close-up shot that does not include the subject's shoulders leaves a "floating" head in the frame.

A *close-up (CU)* shot is also known as a *narrow angle* shot. When shooting a person, this shot captures the top of the head to just below the shoulders, **Figure 4-14**. When framing a close-up shot, it is important to include the top of the shoulders. If the shoulders are not included, the resulting image is a disembodied head at the bottom of the screen, **Figure 4-15**.

An *extreme close-up (ECU/XCU)* is a shot of a specific body part, **Figure 4-16**. This may be used, for example, in a makeup ad showing how mascara enhances the appearance of the eyes.

Multiple Subject Shots

- A *two shot* includes two items of primary importance. A shot of two news anchors sitting at the news desk is an example of a two shot.
- A *three shot* frames three items. For example, the sportscaster joins the two news anchors at the news desk.
- A *four shot* captures four items. Picture the meteorologist joining the news anchors and sportscaster at the news desk.
- A *group shot* incorporates any number of items above four. The shot of a basketball team after winning a game is an example of a group shot.

Close-up (CU): A shot that captures a subject from the top of the head to just below the shoulders. Also called a *narrow angle shot*.

Extreme close-up (ECU/XCU): A shot of an object that is so magnified that only a specific part of the object fills the screen.

Two shot: A shot that includes two items of primary importance.

Three shot: A shot that frames three items.

Four shot: A shot that captures four items.

Group shot: A shot that incorporates any number of items above four.

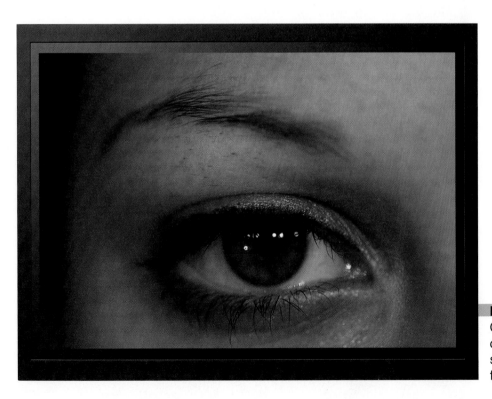

Figure 4-16
On a person, an extreme close-up is a shot of a specific body part or feature.

Reaction shot: A shot that captures one person's face reacting to what another person is saying or doing.

Profile shot: A shot in which the talent's face is displayed in profile.

Specific View Shots

A *reaction shot* captures one person's face reacting to what another person is saying or doing. This is a very powerful type of shot.

A *profile shot* is considered to be a bad shot, **Figure 4-17**. The talent's face in profile appears completely flat on the screen and creates an unflattering picture.

Production Note

The television screen is flat. A videographer must arrange shots in a way that creates the illusion of three dimensions and depth when displayed on a flat screen. When framing an individual shot of an object, whether it's as small as a person or as large as a building, try to shoot it at an angle. For example, a straight-on shot of a person with their nose pointed at the camera lens appears very flat. Likewise, a profile shot also appears flat. If the shot is taken at an angle, somewhere between a profile and a straight-on shot, three dimensionality and depth are achieved. The most common shot is an angle that includes all of one side of the face and enough of the other side to see the cheekbone or eyebrow. When shooting a building, try to shoot it from a corner that includes two sides of the building instead of just one side.

Figure 4-17
The profile shot produces a very flat appearance.

The *over-the-shoulder shot (OSS)* is an extremely common shot on any program, **Figure 4-18**. The backside of one person's head and top of their shoulder is in the foreground of the shot. A full-face shot of the other person in the conversation is in the background of the shot. One OSS is usually followed by another OSS from the other side of the conversation. It is a more interesting shot than just a close-up of each person speaking or listening.

Over-the-shoulder shot (OSS): A shot in which the backside of one person's head and shoulder are in the foreground of the shot, while a full-face shot of the other person in the conversation is in the background.

Figure 4-18
An over-the-shoulder shot adds three dimensions to an otherwise flat two-person conversation.

Camera Movement

There is a specific term to indicate every type of camera movement possible. Being familiar with these terms is important to effectively communicate within the industry. Camera directions are always given in respect to the camera operator's point of view, not the talent's point of view. Unlike theatrical stage directions, camera movement commands in television production are intended for the camera operators. Illustrations of each camera movement defined are presented in **Figure 4-19**. The camera operator may use these camera movements in conjunction with zooming to create the director's intended effects.

Dolly: Physically moving the camera, its tripod, and dolly perpendicularly toward or away from the set.

Dolly in: Smoothly pushing the camera directly forward toward the set.

Dolly out: Pulling the camera backward while facing the set.

Truck: Moving the camera, its tripod, and dolly to the left or right in a motion that is parallel to the set.

Truck right: To move the camera, its tripod, and dolly sideways and to the right while continuing to face the set.

Truck left: To move the camera, its tripod, and dolly sideways and to the left while continuing to face the set.

Pan: Moving only the camera to scan the set horizontally, while the dolly and tripod remain stationary.

Pan left: Moving the camera to the left to scan the set, while the dolly and tripod remain stationary.

Pan right: Moving the camera to the right to scan the set, while the dolly and tripod remain stationary.

● ***Dolly.*** Physically moving the camera, its tripod, and dolly perpendicularly toward or away from the set. Smoothly pushing the camera directly forward toward the set is ***dollying in***. ***Dollying out*** involves pulling the camera backward while facing the set.

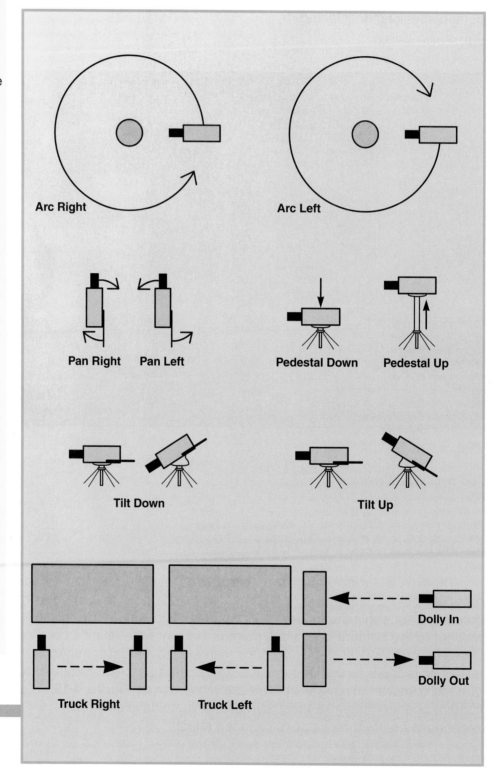

Figure 4-19
Illustrations of the camera movements defined.

🎤 Talk the Talk

The word "dolly" has two meanings in the television production industry:

- **Noun:** It is the three-wheeled cart in which the tripod sits, enabling the tripod to be smoothly rolled around the studio.
- **Verb:** It is a camera movement in which the camera tripod, and dolly move perpendicularly toward or away from the set.

- *Truck.* Moving the camera, its tripod, and dolly to the left or right in a motion that is parallel to the set. To *truck right*, move sideways and to the right while continuing to face the set. This image is much like looking at people standing on a station platform while on a train pulling away. Moving sideways and to the left, while continuing to face the set, is to *truck left*.

- *Pan.* Moving only the camera to scan the set horizontally; the dolly and tripod remain stationary. *Pan left* is when the camera scans to the left, and *pan right* is when the camera scans to the right.

🎧 Production Note

Never follow a pan left with an immediate pan right, or vice versa. The movement in the resulting image is not pleasing to the viewer. You can cut to a different camera between a pan left and a pan right without ill effects.

- *Tilt.* Pointing only the front of the camera (lens) vertically up or down; the dolly and tripod remain stationary. *Tilting up* is pointing the lens up toward the ceiling. *Tilt down* by pointing the lens of the camera down toward the ground.

- *Pedestal.* Raising or lowering the camera on the pedestal or tripod, while facing the set. The tripod and dolly remain stationary. *Pedestal up* is raising the camera height. *Pedestal down* is lowering the height of the camera.

- *Arc.* Moving the camera in a curved truck around the set, while the camera remains fixed on the main object in the shot. The main subject never leaves the frame of the picture. An *arc right* involves rolling the camera, tripod, and dolly in a circle to the right (counterclockwise) around the subject of the scene. Rolling the camera, tripod, and dolly in a circle to the left (clockwise) around the subject is an *arc left*.

Tilt: Pointing only the front of the camera (lens) vertically up or down while the dolly and tripod remain stationary.

Tilt up: Pointing the camera lens up toward the ceiling, while the dolly and tripod remain stationary.

Tilt down: Pointing the camera lens down toward the ground, while the dolly and tripod remain stationary.

Pedestal: Raising or lowering the camera on the pedestal of a tripod, while facing the set. The tripod and dolly remain stationary.

Pedestal up: Raising the camera on the pedestal of a tripod, while facing the set. The tripod and dolly remain stationary.

Pedestal down: Lowering the camera on the pedestal of a tripod, while facing the set. The tripod and dolly remain stationary.

Arc: Moving the camera in a curved truck around the set, while the camera remains fixed on the main object in the shot. The main subject never leaves the frame of the picture.

Arc right: Rolling the camera, tripod, and dolly in a circle to the right (counterclockwise) around the subject of a shot.

Arc left: Rolling the camera, tripod, and dolly in a circle to the left (clockwise) around the subject of a shot.

Psychology of Presentation

Some television production techniques, if used properly, can actually cause the audience to physically "feel" something. An example of this is subjective camera, described in the previous chapter. The audience sees images from a camera mounted in a stunt driver's car as he drives up and down large hills at high speeds. The audience can feel their stomachs turn as the car rockets down a steep hill. The videographer can also plant attitudes in the minds of viewers merely by the way a picture is framed. A program has the power to shape the viewers' perception of someone or something without expressly verbalizing an opinion. This is a significant power to have over a large number of people. An experienced and talented camera operator can influence an audience without the majority of individuals even realizing their opinion has been manipulated. This kind of talent comes with great responsibility as well.

A *low angle shot* is created by placing the camera anywhere from slightly to greatly below the eye level of the talent and pointing it upward, **Figure 4-20**. The talent appears to be above the audience. Tilting the

Low angle shot: A shot created by placing the camera anywhere from slightly to greatly below the eye level of the talent and pointing it upward.

Figure 4-20
In a low angle shot, the camera is placed low to the ground and looks up at the subject.

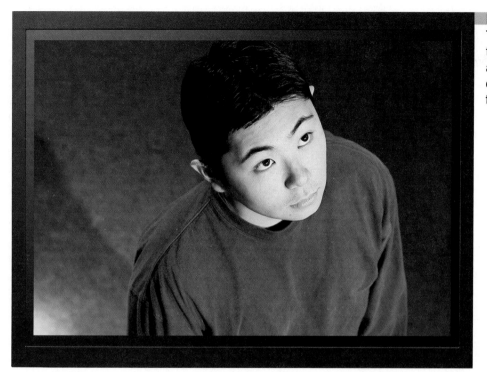

Figure 4-21
The camera is high off the ground in a high angle shot and looks down on the object in the shot.

camera up while shooting a character makes the audience feel respect for the character, as well as inferiority to the character and possibly even fear of the character.

On the other hand, tilting the camera down causes the audience to feel superior to the character. The character is perceived as weak and insignificant. Shooting talent with the camera high in the air, pointing down at an angle is called a ***high angle shot***, **Figure 4-21**.

High angle shot:
Shooting talent with the camera high in the air, pointing down at an angle.

The greater the degree of tilting up or down heightens or lessens the degree of these emotions as felt by the audience. Making the audience feel inferior or superior only occurs with consistent use of low or high angle shots. Randomly using low or high angle shots on a character does not evoke the same emotions from the audience. If this technique is performed with extreme degrees of tilting, the entire effect is obvious to the point of being comedic. Always experiment before putting the final image on tape.

To impart a neutral feeling, the camera should be placed at the talent's eye level. News sets in professional television studios are on raised platforms. The goal of news programming is to have newscasters relate to the audience and be believable as they report. Since newscasters sit in chairs, the cameras would be looking down on them as they report. It is not practical to have the cameras pedestal down to the eye level of the talent. Camera operators would have to bend over to see through the camera's viewfinder for the entire duration of the shoot. Building platforms for the newscasters is much less expensive than the medical care required for camera operators with back ailments from being bent over lowered cameras for extended periods of time.

Wrapping Up

Ultimately, the camera operator is responsible for framing each shot that is recorded for a program. In addition to camera focus and zooming, the camera operator must consider camera movements, specific shots and angles, and following the impromptu instructions of the director. An important section of this chapter addresses selective depth of field and the factors, controlled by the camera operator, that create selective depth of field. Only the camera operator can affect depth of field by manipulating the lens. Remember that the camera's aperture affects depth of field, not lighting. If the camera operator closes the iris down some, for example, the depth of field increases, but the picture is dark. In this case, the lighting designer may be asked to add additional lighting to the set. The set design and lighting contribute to the production goals, but the camera operator must capture all the program elements to realize the director's vision.

Review Questions

Please answer the following questions on a separate sheet of paper. Do not write in this book.

1. List the steps in pre-focusing a zoom lens.
2. Explain why a camera's depth of field should most often be as large as possible.
3. Why is shallow depth of field used in a program?
4. How does the rule of thirds affect picture composition?
5. What is nose room?
6. How is a shot sheet created and used during production?
7. What is the purpose of an establishing shot in a program?
8. Describe a scene in which an over-the-shoulder shot would likely be used.
9. Explain the difference between a dolly camera movement and a truck camera movement.
10. How does the camera angle affect the audience's perception of a character?

Activities

1. Create a shot sheet for a three-camera production instructing viewers on how to make a peanut butter and jelly sandwich. The shots must vary. No single shot should last more than three seconds.

2. Choose one category of camera shots discussed in this chapter (wide shots, individual subject shots, multiple subject shots, or specific view shots). Create a display that illustrates each of the shots included in the selected category.

3. Use your own body to demonstrate the camera movements described in this chapter.

   ● *Pan Left:* Stand perfectly still and turn your head to your left.

   ● *Pan Right:* Stand perfectly still and turn your head to your right.

   ● *Tilt Up:* Stand perfectly still and point your nose to the ceiling of the room.

   ● *Tilt Down:* Stand perfectly still and point your nose to the ground between your feet.

   ● *Pedestal Up:* Rise up on your tiptoes while facing forward (toward the set).

   ● *Pedestal Down*: Squat down while facing forward (toward the set).

   ● *Dolly In*: Smoothly walk forward, directly toward the set.

   ● *Dolly Out*: Smoothly walk backward while facing the set.

   ● *Truck Right*: Walk sideways to the right while facing the set.

   ● *Truck Left*: Walk sideways to the left while facing the set.

   ● *Arc*: Walk in a circle around an object, keeping your eyes fixed on that object. Walking to your right (counterclockwise) is an arc right. Walking to your left (clockwise) is an arc left.

Establishing shot.
This establishing shot tells the audience that the program takes place in a
busy convention center. (National Association of Broadcasters)

Important Terms

½" Tape
¾" Tape
1" Tape
2" Tape
8mm
Artifacts
Betacam
Betacam SP
Betamax
Beta SX
Control Track
D-9
Digital Betacam
  (Digi-Beta)
Digital S
Dropout
Dubbing
DVCam
DVCPRO
DVCPRO50
Head
Helical Scan

Hi8
Input
Mini-DV
Monitor
Monitor/Receiver
Output
Quadruplex (Quad)
Receiver
RF
RF Converter
Slant Track
Super VHS (S-VHS)
Tail
Test Record
Tracking Control
U-Matic
VHS
VHS-C
Video Heads
Video Noise
VTR Interchange
Y/C Signal

Objectives

After completing this chapter, you will be able to:

● Explain the process of cleaning video heads.

● Identify professional quality videotape formats among all the types available.

● Describe the function of the control track in regulating the playback speed of videotape.

● Explain the role of an RF converter in a television's use of audio and video signals.

Introduction

There are many formats of videotape and videotape recorders. "Format" refers to the size of the tape in terms of width, the materials used to make the tape, and the way the signal is placed on the tape by the recorder. This chapter discusses many of the most common formats and related issues that apply to professional video recorders.

Videotape Quality

The quality of videotape is directly related to how the videotape is made, **Figure 5-1**. General steps in the manufacturing process include:

1. Adhesive is placed on a long strip of plastic.
2. An oxide material capable of holding a magnetic signal is sprinkled on the adhesive.
3. The oxide is pressed into the adhesive and the tape is rolled up on a spool.

Both the plastic and the oxide material are relatively standard on consumer VHS tapes. The most common area for variances in quality is the grade of adhesive used on the tape. This is also the reason there is such a wide range of retail prices with consumer VHS videotapes.

"Gold" and "Platinum" designations on videotape packaging are not indicators of the videotape's quality. Several trade magazines regularly rate these products. Research the various brands and types available. An inexpensive tape often has low-cost, low-grade adhesive holding the magnetic recording medium to the plastic base. Once the adhesive fails, the magnetic medium comes loose from the plastic. Pieces then stick to the video heads of the VCR or fall into the bottom of the VCR. So, either the tape heads need to be cleaned or the circuit boards are littered with magnetic material.

Production Note

The magnetic recording medium that comes loose from the plastic base may fall on the circuit board inside the VCR. These pieces of magnetic material can actually bridge tiny electrical contacts on the circuit board and cause a short-circuit or malfunction of the machine.

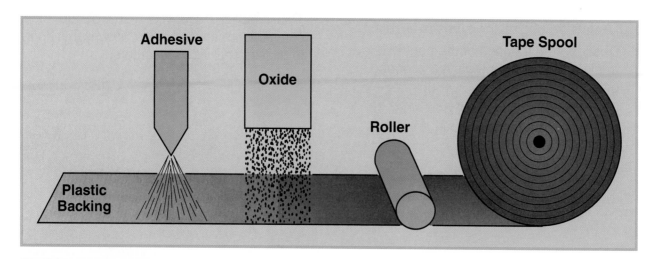

Figure 5-1
All videotape is manufactured using relatively similar processes. The one variable is the quality of the adhesive.

Once the medium falls off the videotape, a tiny white dot is seen on the television screen when the video head passes over the "empty spot" on the tape. This dot is called *dropout*. Once a tape starts showing dropouts, it should be discarded. Dropouts are often confused with dirty heads. When the heads of a VCR are dirty, the whole screen is affected by hundreds of white spots. Dropouts are individual, randomly appearing white spots.

Dropout: A tiny white dot seen on the television screen when the medium has fallen off an analog videotape and the video head passes over an "empty spot" on the tape.

Video Heads and Helical Scan

Video heads are the mechanisms inside a VCR that lay down the video signal onto a tape when in record mode. When the VCR is in playback mode, video heads pick up the video signal from a tape. Consumer VCRs typically have 2, 3, or 4 video heads located around the head drum. Professional VCRs may have several more video heads depending on the format and quality of the machine. The video head drum assembly inside the VCR casing is tilted, while the tape transport system is horizontal. As the video heads spin, they place a video signal on the videotape in a slanted pattern, **Figure 5-2**. This slanted video track allows much more information to be placed on the tape than if the heads were horizontal. All videocassette tape formats utilize this *slant track* method of placing the signal on a tape. Another name for the slant track system is *helical scan*. The word "helical" comes from the Greek form of the word "helix," which means something in a spiral shape. The videotape is wrapped around the video head and, because the head is slanted, a spiral effect is created.

Video heads: The components inside a VCR that lay down the video signal onto a tape when in record mode. When a VCR is in playback mode, the video heads pick up the video signal from a tape.

Helical scan: The pattern in which a video signal is placed onto a videotape. The videotape is wrapped around the video head and, because the head is slanted, the video signal is recorded diagonally on the tape. Also called *slant track*.

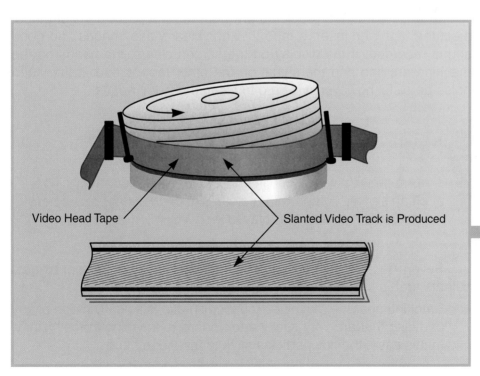

Video Head Tape   Slanted Video Track is Produced

Figure 5-2
The video head drum is tilted, yet the tape moves across it horizontally. This causes the signal to be placed on the entire width of the videotape in a series of "slant tracks."

Dirty Video Heads

Video heads should be cleaned only when they are dirty, and not necessarily according to the manufacturer's schedule. The very process of cleaning the heads has an effect on their life span. Do not clean a VCR's heads unnecessarily.

Usually, only two of the video heads around the head drum are used for normal recording and playback. The others are used for still-frame and/or slow-motion playback. Dirty video heads do not pick up the signal well and, therefore, produce many white spots on the television screen commonly referred to as "snow," **Figure 5-3**. The black and white dots seen on a screen if the videotape is blank or if the heads are dirty is professionally referred to as *video noise*. The quantity of white dots is related to how dirty the heads are. The entire screen is noisy if both heads are dirty, but the audio can still be heard. If the audio is muffled or wavering, the audio head is dirty.

Video noise: The black and white dots seen on a screen if the videotape is blank or if the heads are dirty.

Talk the Talk

The correct use of industry terminology is considered an initiation test when working in the television production industry. For example, using the term "snow" to describe the black and white dots displayed on a screen is not appropriate. This incorrect usage may cause peers and superiors to question your knowledge. The correct term is "video noise," or simply "noise."

To ensure that the problems are not due to a particular videotape, eject the tape and insert a tape that has clear video images and good sound recorded. If the display on the screen clears, the heads on the machine are fine and the signal on the other tape is bad. If the video noise persists, however, it is time to clean the video heads.

Talk the Talk

A tape with clear video images and good quality sound has a "clean signal." A tape with a clean signal does not produce any video or audio noise when played on a VCR.

Several factors can cause the heads to get dirty, but the four biggest culprits are:

● Smoking near the machine. Tobacco smoke is actually made of tiny particles that are very sticky and adhere to anything in the vicinity. In this case, the tiny particles stick to the video heads.

- Using poor quality videotape. Once low-cost, low-grade adhesive fails, the magnetic medium comes loose from the plastic tape. Pieces may then stick to the video heads of the VCR.
- A family pet resting on top of the warm VCR. Pet hair and dander fall into the machine.
- Touching the surface of the videotape. Never touch the surface of videotape. Skin has oils on the surface that transfer to the tape. From the tape, the oils are almost instantly transferred to the video heads.

Cleaning Video Heads

Some head-cleaning kits are safe and effective. However, some head-cleaning cassettes damage the heads in the process of cleaning them. Video heads are very thin and fragile. The best way to clean video heads is by hand. Professionals in a production facility are very unlikely to use head-cleaning cassettes; they manually clean the video heads. The sections that follow present this cleaning process, step by step.

Production Note

Suppose a friend's eyeglasses were dirty and you offer to clean them. The friend gratefully hands them to you to clean and you pull out a piece of sandpaper to clean the eyeglass lenses. What do you think your friend would say? "Stop!" Of course! There is no doubt that the dirt could be removed from the lenses by using the sandpaper, but the lenses would be scratched horribly in the process. This scenario illustrates the potential problem that exists when using some head-cleaning kits available in the marketplace. Some head-cleaning cassettes surely will clean the heads, but may also damage them in the process.

Remove the Top Casing

All VCRs are designed to be opened quickly by technicians. Perform the following to remove the top casing from a VCR:

1. Unplug the unit from the wall.
2. Remove the screws in the top, sides, and back of the VCR that hold the top onto the machine, **Figure 5-4**. Some manufacturers may engrave the chassis with small arrows pointing to these particular screws. Do not unscrew every screw on the outside case. This will cause the internal parts to fall away from the chassis.
3. Remove the top casing.
4. Place the screws in a secure place.

If you encounter any resistance while removing the top, STOP. The top is designed to be easily removed. Check to make sure each of the screws that secure the top have been unscrewed. Some tops do not lift directly off. Some may slide back a little and then lift up.

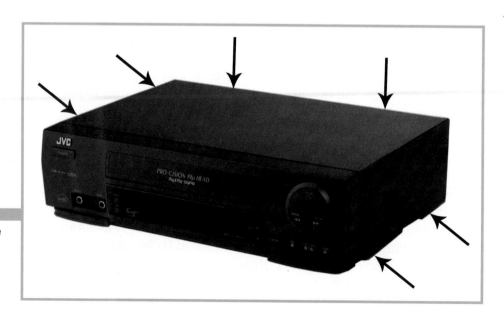

Figure 5-4
The arrows indicate the most common places where the top casing is secured with screws onto a VCR.

Locating the Video Heads

With the cover off, the bright silver video head drum should be visible. The drum looks like two drums placed on top of each other with a tiny crack between them. The bottom drum is stationary, but the top drum spins. Gently turn the upper drum and look for a little protrusion, about the size of the tip of a ballpoint pen, in the space between the drums, **Figure 5-5**. This protrusion is a video head. There is another video head 180° on the other side of the drum. If the machine has more than two heads, look for the others around the circumference of the drum.

Video Head

Figure 5-5
The video heads are located on the head drum assembly. This assembly rotates at a very high rate of speed.

Cleaning Supplies and Steps

Video head cleaning fluid can be purchased at most electronic specialty supply stores. "Wood" alcohol or "denatured" alcohol may also be used, but never use isopropyl (rubbing) alcohol. Do not use cotton swabs to clean video heads. The fibers stick to the corners of the heads and can cause problems worse than before cleaning began. Use foam swabs, with a foam rubber tip, instead of cotton swabs, **Figure 5-6**. Swabs with a small piece of chamois on the tip are also available for video head cleaning.

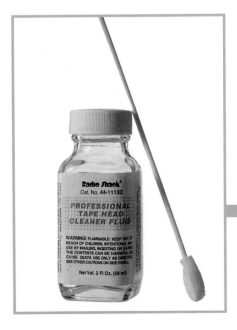

Figure 5-6
Use only video head cleaning fluid or "denatured" or "wood" alcohol and foam or chamois swabs to clean video heads.

To clean the video heads:

1. Dip the foam swab into the cleaning fluid.
2. Rub the swab on each video head in a *sideways* motion, **Figure 5-7**. Rubbing the swab up and down will cause the head to break.

After heads are cleaned, replace the outside cover of the VCR and secure each screw that was removed. Plug the machine into the electrical socket and insert a tape with a clean signal on it. If the image is clean when displayed, the video heads have been successfully cleaned. If the picture is still noisy, repeat each step. This process applies to both consumer and professional machines.

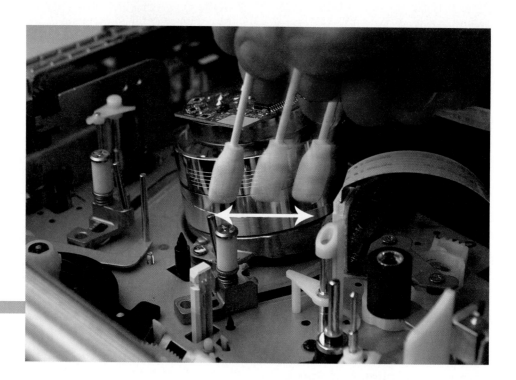

Figure 5-7
Rub the swab over the video heads in a horizontal direction only.

Videotape Widths and Formats

Several videotape formats are available; each is best suited for certain applications or effects. Videotape formats are further categorized by the actual width of the tape. There are definite differences between the consumer and professional varieties of videotape.

Videotape Reels

2″ tape: A reel format videotape used on older machines called quadruplex recorders.

Quadruplex (Quad): A very large, older videotape recorder that uses 2″ tape.

In the early days of video recording, videotape was not packaged in tidy cassettes, as it is today. Videotape was on reels, much like film reels. The tape on reels came in three widths:

● *2″ tape* is used on machines called *quadruplex*, or *quad*, recorders. These older machines are between the size of an oven and a refrigerator. Quad recorders are rapidly being phased out and replaced with newer, smaller machines of much higher quality.

● *1″ tape* comes in three formats: Type A, Type B, and Type C. Type C was the most common format.

● *½″ tape* is found only in low-end, industrial equipment and is relatively inexpensive. This type of videotape has been almost totally phased out.

> **1″ tape:** A reel format videotape available in three formats: Type A, Type B, and Type C. Type C was the most common format.
>
> **½″ tape:** A reel format videotape found only in low-end, industrial equipment.

🎤 Talk the Talk

When referring to these reel formats, only the size designation is used: 2″, 1″, or ½″. "That program was recorded on 1″." The words "videotape" or "reel tape" are understood and, therefore, not actually spoken when industry professionals use these videotape format terms.

Videocassettes

Videocassettes are now the industry standard. There are, however, many types of videocassettes available. Several of the types discussed are pictured in **Figure 5-8**.

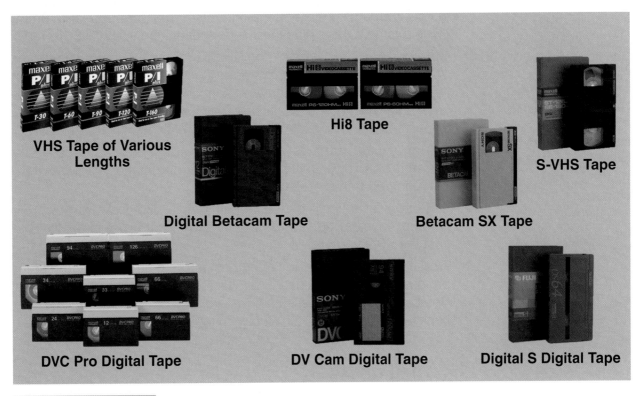

Figure 5-8

Pictured are some of the most common types of videotapes.

Betamax: A ½″ videotape format developed as a consumer medium. It is, for the most part, extinct.

VHS (Video Home System): A ½″ videotape format that emerged as the preferred standard for consumer VCRs.

VHS-C: A ½″ videotape format that is shorter than regular VHS and is, therefore, packaged in a compact cassette.

8mm: A videotape format designed for consumer camcorders and is named for the width of the tape.

Hi8: An 8mm videotape that is higher in quality and uses a different recording system than 8mm.

Super VHS (S-VHS): A low-end, industrial ½″ videotape format that is superior to VHS.

U-Matic: A ¾″ videotape format that has been surpassed by current technology. Also known as ¾″ **tape**.

Betacam: A ½″ format, broadcast-quality videotape.

Betacam SP: A ½″ videotape format that used to be the best format for professional television use, but digital video formats are challenging this format in professional markets.

Artifacts: Rectangular distortions that are seen on the screen on digital video formats.

Many of the videotapes discussed are "upwardly compatible." This means that a lower-end tape may be played in a higher-end machine, but a higher-end tape may not necessarily play in a lower-end machine.

- *Betamax* is a ½″ format developed as a consumer medium. This format is, for the most part, extinct. Terms like "Beta," "Betacam," and "Betacam SP" refer to formats still in use professionally. While the names are similar, the professional variety is an entirely different format from the consumer Betamax format.

- *VHS (Video Home System)* is a ½″ format that emerged as the preferred standard for consumer VCRs. VHS tape labeled with a "T" and a number, such as T-120, indicates the tape's run time on a VCR's highest speed setting. In the example "T-120," the tape lasts for 120 minutes at the highest speed setting. VHS tape can be purchased in a variety of lengths, including T-160, T-120, T-90, T-60, and T-30. Other formats of videotape also use this method to indicate tape length.

- *VHS-C* is the same tape format as VHS, but the tape is shorter and packaged in a smaller cassette. The smaller cassette fits into some newer consumer camcorders that are too small to handle a full-sized VHS cassette. The "C" stands for "Compact."

- *8mm* is a videotape format designed for consumer camcorders and is named for the width of the tape. This format is upwardly compatible with Hi8, but a Hi8 tape does not play on an 8mm deck.

- *Hi8* is also an 8mm videotape. It is higher in quality and uses a different recording system, making this format far superior to 8mm. Hi8 equipment does play 8mm tape, in addition to the Hi8.

- *Super VHS (S-VHS)* is a ½″ videotape format that is far superior to VHS. Many professionals consistently use this low-end, industrial format. *Y/C* is the professional name for the signal placed on S-VHS tape. An S-VHS videocassette does fit into a VHS recorder, but the Y/C signal recorded on it does not necessarily play on a consumer VCR.

- *U-Matic*, or *¾″ tape*, is a ¾″ format that has been surpassed by current technology. Decks for ¾″ tape are no longer manufactured, but many ¾″ decks are still in service.

- *Betacam* is a ½″, broadcast-quality tape. Betacam is upwardly compatible with Betacam SP, but is somewhat lower in quality and cost than Betacam SP.

- *Betacam SP* was, at one time, considered to be the best format for professional television use. Digital video formats currently challenge Betacam SP in professional markets. A Betacam SP deck is backward compatible with Betacam tapes.

Digital Formats

Digital videotape formats do suffer degradation problems similar to dropout on analog tapes. *Artifacts* on digital video formats are rectangular distortions that are seen on the screen.

- *Digital Betacam (Digi-Beta)* is a ½" tape with higher quality than Betacam SP. The cassette is the same size as Betacam SP, but allows quality recording of digital signals, instead of analog signals.
- *Beta SX* is a ½" tape that uses digital MPEG compression. The Beta SX equipment also plays Beta SP tapes.
- *Mini-DV* is a 6mm digital video format used by many industrial video producers. The mini-DV tape is metal evaporated tape. Mini-DV tape is upwardly compatible with DVCPRO and DVCPRO50.
- *DVCPRO* is an excellent 6mm professional digital video format. The DVCPRO tape is metal particle tape. DVCPRO is upwardly compatible with DVCPRO50. A DVCPRO deck also plays mini-DV tapes.

Production Note

Mini-DV tape is the size of a box of matches found at many restaurants and costs about $7 per tape. This tape format may be reused a maximum of nine times before artifacts begin to appear. A DVCPRO tape costs between $32 and $50 and fits snugly into the front pocket of a man's dress shirt. It may be reused up to 100 times. DVCPRO tape is more economical in the long run than mini-DV. Most importantly, the metal particle tape of DVCPRO holds a much stronger signal than metal evaporated tape used in mini-DV tape.

- *DVCPRO50* is a 6mm digital format with even higher quality than DVCPRO. A DVCPRO50 deck plays both DV and DVCPRO tapes.
- *DVCam* is a 6mm digital format that is proprietary for Sony Corporation.
- *Digital S* is a ½" digital format tape that is broadcast quality. This format is also known as *D-9*.

Compatibility

VTR interchange refers to the ability of a tape recorded on one machine to be played back on another machine. As long as both machines are the same format, regardless of brand or model, the tapes can be successfully played on both machines.

At present, the VHS format is the most popular distribution format for industrial and commercial programming. While VHS tape does not provide a very robust signal, the quality is sufficient on any television screen. Because of this, nearly all videotape duplication begins with a high-quality master and is then *dubbed*, or copied, down to VHS.

Digital Betacam (Digi-Beta): A ½" videotape with higher quality than Betacam SP and the capability of recording of digital signals instead of analog signals.

Beta SX: A ½" videotape that uses digital MPEG compression.

Mini-DV: A metal evaporated tape, 6mm digital video format used by many industrial video producers.

DVCPRO: A 6mm, metal particle tape used as a professional digital video format.

DVCPRO50: A 6mm digital format with even higher quality than DVCPRO.

DVCam: A 6mm digital format that is proprietary for Sony Corporation.

Digital S: A ½" digital videotape format that is broadcast quality. Also known as *D-9*.

VTR interchange: The ability of a tape that was recorded on one machine to be played back on another machine.

Dubbing: The process of copying the recorded material on a videotape.

Control Track

Control track: A series of inaudible pulses recorded onto a tape that regulates the speed of the tape in playback.

The ***control track*** is a series of inaudible pulses recorded onto a tape that regulates the speed of the tape in playback. The control track is the result of a circuit that puts a little pulse signal, or blip, 30 times per second onto the tape when recording. If the machine is set for 2-hour speed (SP), the blips are spaced further apart because the tape moves relatively quickly through the machine. If the machine is set for the 6-hour speed (EP), the blips are much closer together because the tape moves more slowly through the machine. The blip is placed on the tape every 1/30th of a second, without regard to how fast the tape is moving, **Figure 5-9**.

Visualize This

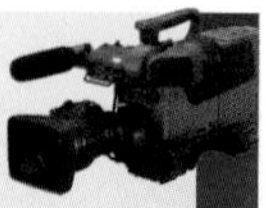

Imagine you are driving a car on a flat, straight stretch of deserted highway. You are driving down the center of the road and the white line appears as a series of white dashes that disappear under the hood of the car. It would take some practice, but you could regulate the accelerator so that 1 dash goes under the hood every 2 seconds. The white dashes may come in too fast at first, but you slow the car down until exactly 1 dash goes under the hood every 2 seconds. The control track circuit operates the same way. It speeds up and slows the tape down until the pulses occur at 1/30th of a second intervals.

Common recording speeds are:

- **SP** (Standard Play) records one 2-hour program onto a T-120 tape. The "T-120" designation indicates the tape's run time on a VCR's highest speed setting. The vast majority of VHS movies rented at local video stores are recorded at SP speed.
- **LP** (Long Play) is a 4-hour speed, twice that of SP, that is being phased out.

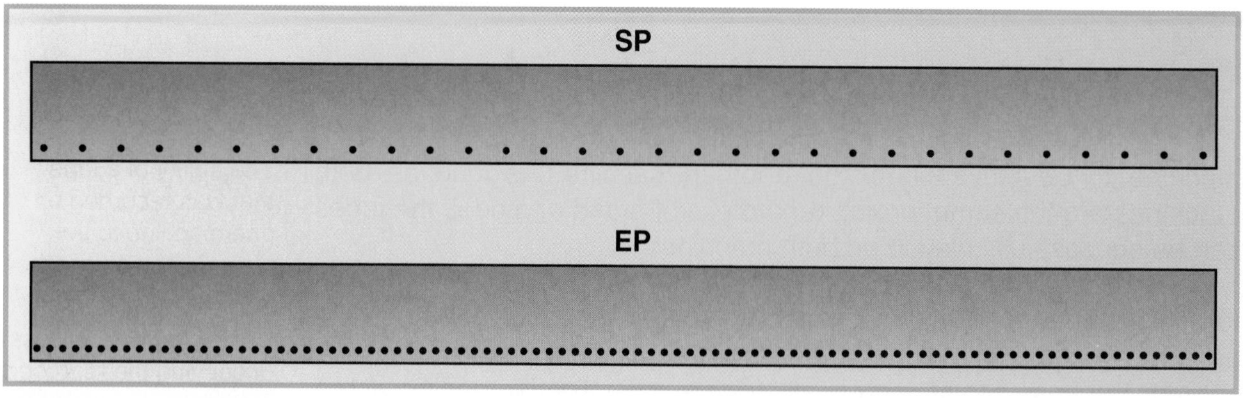

Figure 5-9
The control track pulses are placed further apart when recording in SP mode compared to EP mode.

- **EP** (Extended Play) records 6 hours of programs onto a T-120 tape, three times that of SP. The quality of an EP recording is noticeably less than an SP recording.

When a machine is in playback mode, the same circuit that placed the pulses on the tape now "listens" for the blips or pulses. The tape is sped up or slowed down accordingly, timing the pulses to appear every 1/30th of a second. For example, a VCR that is manually set to EP speed plays an SP tape perfectly because the circuit monitors the control track. The tape speed is adjusted to correctly play the tape. Depending on the VCR, the audio may cease and the screen may turn blue while this adjustment is made.

When watching a tape on a machine other than the one the tape was recorded on, a series of horizontal white lines may sometimes appear on a portion of the screen, **Figure 5-10**. The white lines may even pulse, or rapidly appear and disappear. In this case, the control track circuit is not able to compensate enough to correct the display. The circuit only has a certain range in which it can speed up or slow down the tape. If using a professional VCR the *tracking control* knob must be manually adjusted until the lines disappear. The tracking control should be adjusted back to its normal position when finished watching the tape, otherwise every subsequent tape will display the white lines. Newer consumer VCRs have a built-in, automatic tracking control function that cannot be manually adjusted.

Tracking control: A knob on a professional VCR that is used to manually adjust the tape tracking speed.

Figure 5-10
If horizontal white lines persistently appear on the screen, manually adjust the tracking control.

Input: A port or connection on a VCR through which a signal enters the VCR, such as the "audio in."

Output: A port or connection on a VCR through which the signal leaves the deck and travels to another piece of equipment, such as the "video out."

The control track circuit is extremely important. Some compare the importance of the control track pulses to the sprocket holes found on motion picture film. Each is vital to viewing a program.

Inputs and Outputs

A signal comes into the VCR through an *input* on the back of the deck, such as the "audio in." The signal leaves the deck and travels to another piece of equipment through an *output*, such as the "video out." This may seem obvious, but it is very easy to be careless and accidentally attach a CD player to the "Audio Out" connector on an amplifier.

Test Recordings

Test record: The process of using the VTR to record audio and video signals before the session taping begins to ensure the equipment is functioning properly and to indicate any necessary adjustments.

A *test record* is the process of using the VTR to record audio and video signals before the session taping begins. Many recording sessions are lost and must be reshot because the test recording step was omitted. For the technician, a test record indicates if the equipment is functioning properly and if any adjustments are necessary. For example, a test record lets the technician know if the video heads are dirty before program taping begins.

To make a test record once all the equipment is connected and powered on:

1. Press "Record" and "Play" on the machine.
2. Record any available signal for one minute.
3. Rewind the tape and play it back.
4. Listen for appropriate audio and watch for appropriate video.
5. Make any necessary adjustments before beginning the taping session.

Production Note

Before a scene begins, the VCR operator places the machine in record mode and presses "Play" to begin recording. Unfortunately, operators commonly forget to hit "Play" after setting the record mode. As a result, the record circuit is open, but the tape does not move. The staff and crew watch the monitors during the shoot and see the scenes as they should be. However, the tape in the recorder never moves. To complicate the situation further, some novice directors skip reviewing the scene they just shot before moving on. In the editing room weeks later, the director realizes there is no taped footage of that particular scene!

It is important to be certain that the recording machine is properly set to tape each scene. The footage should be immediately reviewed to ensure that the scene has been recorded and is of acceptable quality.

Radio Frequency

VCRs create pure video and pure audio. Many consumer television sets, however, cannot receive pure video and pure audio on two separate cables. The video and audio must be combined into one cable and converted into an *RF* (Radio Frequency) signal by a small box inside the VCR called an *RF converter*, **Figure 5-11**. The RF converter takes the pure video and audio and combines them into one radio frequency. The radio frequency is either Channel 3 or Channel 4, depending on how the switch on the back of the VCR is set, **Figure 5-12**. Most people have

RF: Radio frequency signal that is a combination of both audio and video.

RF converter: A small module inside the VCR that combines pure video and audio into one radio frequency.

Figure 5-11
The RF converter changes pure video and pure audio signals into one radio frequency.

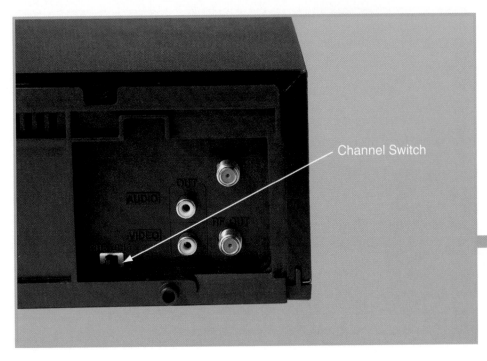

Channel Switch

Figure 5-12
The signal coming from a VCR's "Antenna Out" connector can be received on either Channel 3 or 4 on a television set.

their television set tuned to Channel 3 or Channel 4 to watch videotapes. Once combined as a radio frequency, a cable carries the signal from the "Antenna Out" on the VCR to the "Antenna In" on the television set.

A television set that can receive only RF signals is a ***receiver***. A television set that can receive only pure video and audio signals is a ***monitor***. A ***monitor/receiver*** is a hybrid television that can receive both pure video and audio and a RF signal. The types of connectors on the back of the television indicate the television type, **Figure 5-13**. A monitor television has RCA and/or BNC connectors. Connectors are discussed in Chapter 6, *Audio Basics*. An F-connector for coaxial antenna cable or two screws for a flat-lead antenna are found on receiver televisions. Monitor/receiver televisions have both RCA and/or BNC connectors and an F-connector or the two screws.

Some newer, higher-end consumer televisions are equipped with multiple inputs. A signal can be connected to the RF connector and to "Video In" and "Audio In" connectors. These multiple inputs may be used for video games, additional VCRs, and DVD players. Television sets with multiple inputs have a button or a menu option that enables the user to switch from one input to another.

Recording Audio and Video

Before a taping session begins, the VTR operator must perform a test record. This step avoids certain disasters that are discovered weeks later in the editing room. While the VTR is in record mode, you are usually not able to determine if it is recording good audio and video. A monitor displays only what is going *into* the machine, not what

Receiver: A television set that can receive only RF signals.

Monitor: A television set that can receive only pure video and audio signals.

Monitor/Receiver: A hybrid television that can receive pure video and audio signals, as well as RF signals.

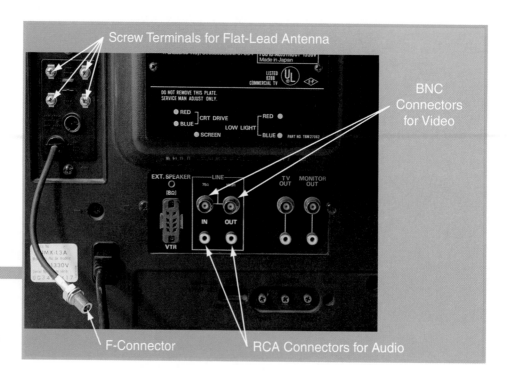

Figure 5-13
A monitor/receiver has connectors capable of receiving RF, as well as pure video and pure audio.

is actually *being recorded*. Performing a test record before each taping session verifies that the audio and video signals are not only reaching the VTR, but are also being properly recorded.

Most recorders have a video AGC (automatic gain control), **Figure 5-14**. This control automatically adjusts the video signal coming into the machine to the best levels for recording. Inexperienced operators should leave the video AGC circuit active.

Heads and Tails

The beginning of every take has a "lead-in" of at least 15 seconds, called a *head*. The head usually consists of the display of the slate and the countdown. Each scene should have a minimum of a 10-second "lead-out" at the end, called a *tail*. During this lead-out, the performers simply continue their action without dialog for an additional 10–15 seconds until the director calls, "Cut." The talent does not ad lib lines during the tail, but continues the mood of the scene through silent body language. The recorded head and tail on each take is very important in the editing process, **Figure 5-15**.

Head: A 15-second "lead-in" recorded onto tape at the beginning of every take.

Tail: A 10-second "lead-out" recorded onto videotape at the end of each scene.

Figure 5-14
The video AGC should remain active most of the time.

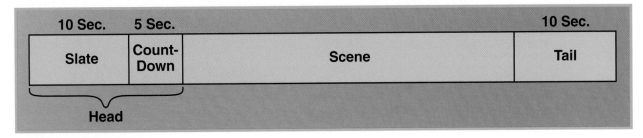

Figure 5-15
Heads and tails must be shot for all scenes.

Production Note

Do not simply fast-forward the tape at the end of a take, instead of recording a tail. The portion of tape that was fast-forwarded does not have control track. This causes problems in the editing room and may prevent a successful edit of the program.

A tail also serves as a safety feature. When a tape is stopped, it retracts slightly into the cassette. If the tape is stopped immediately at the end of a scene, it is quite possible that the beginning slate of the next scene will record over the end of the scene just shot. Additionally, most camcorders and recorders have a feature called automatic back-spacing. This guarantees that the tape is about 3–5 seconds behind the initial stop point. A tail ensures that if any part of the previous scene is recorded over, it is the tail and not the actual scene.

Audio Levels

The VCR operator, or camcorder operator, is in control of the audio levels that are recorded onto the tape. In the studio, the audio engineer mixes the audio signals into a single signal and sends it to the videotape recorder. The videotape recorder displays the recorded audio levels on VU meters. See Chapter 6, *Audio Basics*. The audio levels for an analog recording should fluctuate between −3 and +3 db on the meters. On a digital recorder, the levels should hover near −20. The recorded audio levels are a crucial portion of the program and cannot be fixed in the editing room if they are recorded improperly.

Wrapping Up

Due to the many different formats of videotape and videotape recorders, it is important to remember that tapes created in one format are usually not suited for playback on a machine of another format. Regardless of the tape's format, the control track is central to quality recording. The concept of the control track is the foundation of analog videotape editing.

Review Questions

Please answer the following questions on a separate sheet of paper. Do not write in this book.

1. What are the possible causes of white spots appearing on the screen while viewing a videotape?
2. What are some common causes of dirty video heads?
3. List the appropriate materials to use for cleaning video heads.
4. What is an upwardly compatible videotape?
5. How is the control track related to the playback speed of a videotape?
6. What is the purpose of a test record?
7. What does an RF converter do?
8. How do monitors, receivers, and monitor/receivers differ from each other?
9. What is the purpose of the head and the tail at the beginning of each scene?

Activities

1. Research the evolution of videotape formats and create a timeline that includes important dates, innovations, and events.
2. Inspect the television sets in your home and determine if each is a receiver, a monitor, or a monitor/receiver.

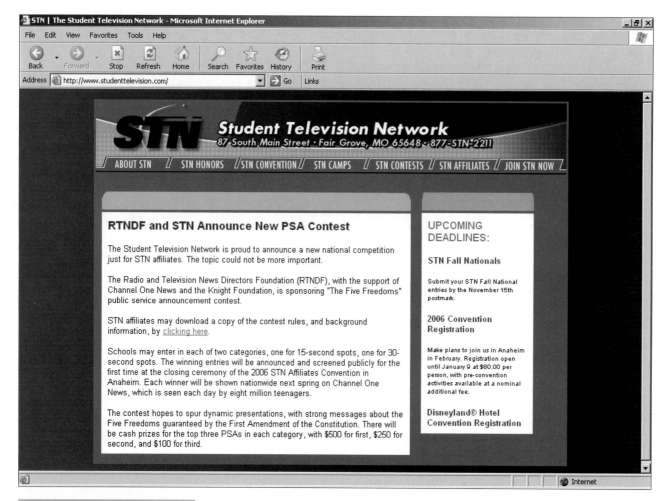

www.studenttelevision.com.
The Student Television Network aims to support and enhance broadcasting and video production education in schools by providing a network of student and instructor resources and activities.

Chapter 6
Audio Basics

Important Terms

Objectives

After completing this chapter, you will be able to:

- Explain the function of audio for television productions.
- List the most common use of each type of microphone presented.
- Describe the importance of the pick-up pattern classification when selecting a microphone.
- Cite the appropriate VU meter readings for both an analog audio system and a digital audio system.
- Identify various connectors and the connector end type of each.

Introduction

Audio is so important to the television production business that it is placed first in the phrase "Audio/Visual (A/V)." Watching television can be very frustrating if the audio is muted. A chase scene in a movie is nowhere near as entertaining without screeching tires and exciting music. The low, muffled sound of footsteps moving closer or a sudden, high-pitched scream adds to the suspense and shock of a horror movie. Audio is vitally important in getting a message across in television and the movies. Unfortunately, most students new to television production tend to think primarily about the video aspect of a program and consider the audio only as an afterthought. This type of thinking is a recipe for disaster.

The Functions of Sound for Television

Without sound, programs become silent movies. All sounds on television serve one or more of the following four functions:

- Voice Track
- Music and Sound Effects
- Background Sound
- Room Tone

Voice track: The audio portion of a program created through dialog or narration.

On-camera narrator: Talent who provides program narration while being seen by the camera.

Off-camera narrator: Talent who provides program narration, but is not seen by the viewer. Also called *voiceover (V.O.)*.

The *voice track* is usually the primary means of getting a message to the viewer's ears and may be considered the most necessary audio of a program. The voice track is the sound created through dialog or narration. Narration takes two forms:

- On-camera narration
- Off-camera narration, also known as Voiceover (V.O.)

Typically, if the viewer sees the narrator speaking, the talent is called an *on-camera narrator*. When viewers hear but do not see the narrator, the program is making use of *off-camera narration*, also called *voiceover (V.O.)*, **Figure 6-1**.

Music and sound effects set the mood and enhance the action of a program. The emotion of a scene is dramatically enhanced with properly selected and timed background music. Sound effects can be purchased on tape or CD, and added where appropriate in a program.

Figure 6-1
The narrator often watches the video portion of a documentary and speaks the narration into a mic attached to an additional recorder. In the editing phase, the narration track is synchronized and recorded onto the same tape with the video.

Background sound is the noise that is normally associated with a particular location. For example, the background sounds for a scene taking place in a school classroom may include the sound of papers rustling, pens tapping, the faint sound of hallway noise, and the hum of fluorescent lighting fixtures.

Room tone is the sound present in a room, or at a location, before human occupation. This is also called *natural sound*, or *nat sound*. The sound of an air conditioner fan, pipes rattling, and, most importantly, the "silence" of a room are examples of room tone.

Background sound: The noise that is normally associated with a particular location.

Room tone: The sound present in a room or at a location before human occupation. Also called *natural sound (nat sound)*.

Assistant Activity

Listen to the silence of a room. Although you have probably never noticed it, the silence of different locations varies greatly. Go to your bedroom; remain perfectly still and listen. Do the same in the family room and in the backyard. You will soon realize that the "silence" is notably different in each location.

Place a good pair of stereo headphones with full earmuffs over your ears and do not turn on any sound. Listen to that kind of "silence." All of these "sounds of silence" are surprisingly unique.

If shooting on location, it is important to clear the set for a few minutes after the equipment is set up. Once all the talent and crew have left the location set, turn on the recorder and record at least three minutes of "silence." The recorded natural sound of each location is useful when editing the program. The natural sound may be used to cover unwanted sounds in the background of a scene that were not noticed while shooting. Using the natural sound of a location creates a much less noticeable audio edit than if true silence were used.

Sound Frequency

Sounds can generally be divided into three basic groups: low-frequency sounds, mid-range sounds, and high-frequency sounds.

Most people are familiar with common band instruments and the sounds they create. Common instruments are used in the following examples of the three frequency categories:

- Low-frequency instruments include the bass guitar, bass drum, and the tuba. A bass vocalist is also categorized in the low-frequency range.

- Mid-range sound frequency instruments are trumpets, clarinets, and French horns. Alto and tenor vocalists fall within the mid-range. The human speaking voice is generally in the mid-range, as well.

- High-frequency sound is created by flutes, piccolos, and soprano vocalists.

Microphone (Mic):
The piece of equipment that picks up sounds in the air and sends them down a wire to the mixer or recorder.

Generating element:
A thin surface inside the mic which vibrates when hit by sound waves in the air. The vibration moves a tiny wire back and forth through a magnetic field creating an electrical signal. Also called a *diaphragm*.

Dynamic mic: A very rugged, virtually indestructible type of mic that has good sound reproduction ability.

Types of Microphones

A *microphone* is the piece of equipment that picks up sounds in the air and sends them down a wire to the recorder. Fundamentally, all microphones work the same way. Sound waves in the air hit a thin surface inside the mic, a *diaphragm* or *generating element*, which then vibrates. The vibration moves a tiny wire back and forth through a magnetic field creating an electrical signal, **Figure 6-2**. This electrical signal is sent down the mic cable to an amplifier or a recorder.

Talk the Talk

The term "microphone" is commonly abbreviated as "mic" or "mike."

Microphones may be classified by the type of generating element each employs:

- Diaphragm that vibrates a coil housed in a magnetic field.
- Thin piece of metal foil or coated film.
- Thin piece of metal surrounded by a magnetic field.

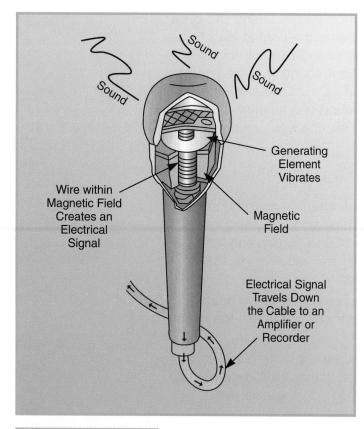

Wire within Magnetic Field Creates an Electrical Signal

Generating Element Vibrates

Magnetic Field

Electrical Signal Travels Down the Cable to an Amplifier or Recorder

Figure 6-2
This illustration provides a general representation of how microphones work.

Dynamic Microphones

The generating element in a *dynamic microphone* is a diaphragm that vibrates a small coil that is housed in a magnetic field. It is a very rugged, virtually indestructible, mic that has good sound reproduction ability, **Figure 6-3**. Dynamic mics are designed to hear different sound frequencies—the pitch of a sound, not its volume or strength. The dynamic mic most commonly found on a television studio is designed to operate only in normal speaking voice frequencies. They are not designed to mic musical instruments or accompanying vocals. The dynamic mics used in a studio setting do not pick up high- and low-frequency sounds as well as they pick up the mid-range sounds of speech. Using a mic that picks up mid-range sounds to mic musical instrument or stage performers would result in music that is lacking in sound quality and reproduction.

Figure 6-3
A dynamic mic is the perfect choice for most applications. It is extremely rugged in design.

Condenser Microphones

The generating element used in *condenser microphones* is a thin piece of metal foil or coated film. This type of mic requires an external power supply (usually a battery) in order to operate, **Figure 6-4**. Condenser microphones are also called *electret condenser microphones*. They can pick up a greater range of sound frequencies than dynamic mics and are usually more expensive.

Condenser mic: A type of mic that requires an external power supply (usually a battery) to operate. Also called an *electret condenser mic*.

Ribbon Microphone

The *ribbon microphone* is the most sensitive of all mic types. A thin ribbon of metal surrounded by a magnetic field serves as the generating element in this type of mic. At one time, ribbon mics were the only type found in commercial radio stations. They are now primarily used in music recording studios. Superb sensitivity is a great advantage of this type of mic. The fragility of the generating element is an expensive disadvantage of the ribbon mic. An accidental bump of the mic itself or the "pop" produced from the rush of air released when pronouncing a

Ribbon mic: The most sensitive type of mic, primarily used in music recording studios. A thin ribbon of metal surrounded by a magnetic field serves as the generating element.

Figure 6-4
The condenser mic requires an external power supply.

"p" sound could break the ribbon inside the microphone. In recording studios, a barrier made of shaped wire covered with a piece of nylon is placed between the ribbon mic and the talent. This *pop filter* protects the mics from explosive "t" and "p" sounds and catches moisture and rushes of air before they hit and damage the diaphragm of the ribbon mic, **Figure 6-5**.

Non-Professional Microphones

Ceramic and crystal microphones are most often found in consumer electronics kits. The generating element is a ceramic compound in ceramic mics and a salt crystal in crystal mics. These types of mics are not appropriate for industrial or broadcast use. Both are usually quite inexpensive, but have poor quality, performance, and fidelity.

The microphone built into a camcorder should not be used in professional recording scenarios. It has a very limited pick-up range and, when inside a room, produces audio that sounds like the person speaking has a bucket over his head. This microphone picks up the grinding sound of the zoom lens motor, the rubbing or knocking sounds of the operator's fingers and hands operating the camera, and the sound of the operator's breathing. These are not components of quality audio.

Specialized Microphones

The *boundary microphone* is most commonly a condenser type, as described in a previous section. Boundary mics are becoming the most common way to mic a stage or large room. These mics do not look

Figure 6-5
Using a pop filter protects the generating element of a microphone. The generating element may be damaged by the sudden rush of air created when speaking or singing "t" and "p" sounds. (Popless Voice Screens)

like any others that most consumers commonly see. They work on the principle that sound is reflected off hard surfaces and are usually placed on a table, floor, or wall, **Figure 6-6**.

The *wireless mic* has a practical advantage over all other mics that connect to the recording unit with a wire. A wireless mic has a short cable that runs from the mic to a radio transmitter with an antenna. The transmitter is sometimes built into the mic itself. The microphone itself may be any one of the types previously discussed. The other half of the wireless system is the receiver, which takes the signal from the transmitter and sends it through a cable to the recorder, **Figure 6-7**. A primary advantage of this wireless system is the freedom of movement it allows the performers. They do not need to be concerned with tripping over mic cables while performing. Additionally, the audio engineer does not need to lay many feet of mic cable, tape it to the floor for safety's sake, and pull up the cable to recoil it at the end of the shoot.

Some may consider wireless mics to be the mic of choice for all applications. This is not the case. Wireless mics transmit and receive signals using a radio frequency. This is very effective, as long as no one else in the vicinity uses the same radio frequency. Wireless mics are prone to interference from walkie-talkies, baby monitors, CB radios, and even heavy machinery. Use wireless mics whenever appropriate and practical, but always keep a backup of "wired" mics and mic cable just in case.

Figure 6-6
The boundary mic is commonly used to mic a stage for a dramatic performance.

Wireless mic: A mic that uses a short cable to connect the mic to a radio transmitter with an antenna, or the transmitter may be built into the mic itself. The transmitter wirelessly sends the signal to the receiver, which sends the mic signal through a cable to the recorder.

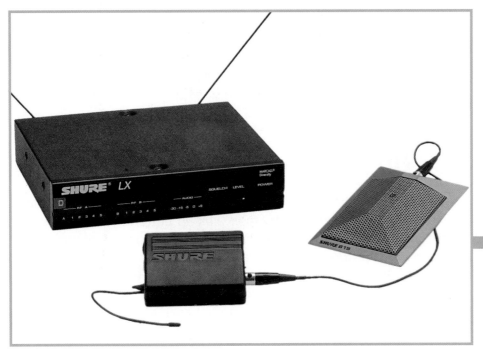

Figure 6-7
The wireless mic allows a performer to have freedom of movement, without the danger of tripping over a mic cable.

Parabolic reflector mic: A very sensitive mic that looks like a satellite dish with handles and is designed to pick up sounds at a distance.

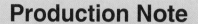

Production Note

When recording a theatrical event, there is an excellent chance that the stage performers or the theater's tech crew will be using their own wireless mics. Always check the frequencies being used by the theater and compare them to the frequencies of your equipment. If the frequencies are close, use wired mics instead.

Figure 6-8
The parabolic reflector mic is capable of clearly picking up sounds from a significant distance.

A *parabolic reflector microphone* is a very sensitive mic that looks like a satellite dish with handles, **Figure 6-8**. This type of mic is designed to pick up sounds at a distance. The operator simply aims the mic at what he wants to hear and the sound is received very clearly. The pick-up range of a parabolic reflector microphone depends on the refinement of the electronics on the inside of the mic. The sensitivity of the electronics inside the mic is directly related to the cost—the more sensitive the electronics, the higher the purchase price.

The parabolic reflector microphone is often seen on the sidelines of professional football games. When using these mics at a professional sporting event, an experienced operator knows when to turn off the audio feed from the mic. Some of the sounds picked up are not likely to be appropriate for prime-time television.

Pick-up pattern: A term that describes how well a mic hears sounds from various directions.

Omni-directional mic: A mic with a pick-up pattern that captures sound from nearly every direction equally well.

Pick-Up Pattern

In addition to the type of generating element they contain, microphones are further classified by their pick-up pattern. *Pick-up pattern* refers to how well the mic hears sounds from various directions.

An *omni-directional mic* has a pick-up pattern that captures sound from nearly every (omni) direction equally well, **Figure 6-9**. The only weak area for this type of mic is the sound coming directly from the rear of the mic.

Figure 6-9
The omni-directional mic picks up sounds from nearly all directions.

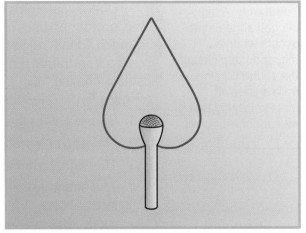

Figure 6-10
A uni-directional mic has a pick-up pattern in the shape of a heart, thus the name "cardioid."

Mics with a *uni-directional* pick-up pattern pick up sound from primarily one (uni) direction, **Figure 6-10**. A uni-directional mic is also known as a *directional mic* or a *cardioid mic*. The term "cardioid" is derived from the shape of the pick-up pattern; it is shaped like a valentine heart. The point of the heart is aimed at the source of the sound. Sounds from the sides and rear of the mic are not heard as well, or not at all. The cost of a uni-directional mic is usually proportionately related to how far away it can pick up sounds and how much sound outside of the pick-up pattern is eliminated. The longer and narrower the pick-up pattern, the more expensive the microphone.

In a noisy environment, a directional mic is a better choice for a narrator than an omni-directional mic. If an omni-directional mic is used, the viewer may have a difficult time separating the talent's voice from the background sounds.

Directional mics are available in various degrees, or grades, of directionality, **Figure 6-11**. A *hypercardioid mic* has a narrower and longer pick-up pattern than a cardioid mic. A *supercardioid mic* has an even narrower pattern. More directional still is the *shotgun mic*. Sometimes, the shotgun mic is literally mounted on a rifle stock and even has a sight to help in aiming it at the sound source. The parabolic reflector mic is a version of a directional mic.

Cardioid mic: A mic with a pick-up pattern that captures sound from primarily one direction. Also called a *uni-directional mic* or *directional mic*.

Hypercardioid mic: A directional mic with a narrower and longer pick-up pattern than a cardioid mic.

Supercardioid mic: A directional mic with a narrower pick-up pattern than a hypercardioid mic.

Shotgun mic: A directional mic with an extremely narrow pick-up pattern.

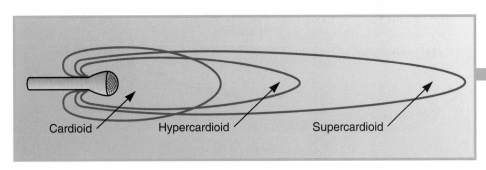

Cardioid   Hypercardioid   Supercardioid

Figure 6-11
The cardioid mic can be purchased with varying degrees of narrowness in its directional pick-up pattern.

Feedback: A high-pitched squeal that occurs when a microphone picks up the sound coming from a speaker that is carrying that microphone's signal.

Directional mics are most important when recording music. If the performer uses an omni-directional mic and steps in front of the band's speakers, a high-pitched squeal is emitted. The squeal is called *feedback*. Feedback occurs when a microphone picks up the sound coming from a speaker that is carrying that microphone's signal. **Figure 6-12**. A feedback loop is created when:

1. Sound enters the microphone.
2. The sound is transmitted to an amplifier.
3. The signal from the amplifier is sent to a speaker.
4. The sound from the speaker goes through the air and back into the microphone.

Each time this circle is made, the pitch gets higher and louder. If the cycle is not stopped, the speakers could be permanently damaged. To prevent feedback, the sound coming from the speakers needs to be blocked from hitting the mic. Using a directional mic decreases the likelihood of feedback because of its narrow pick-up pattern.

Production Note

To stop the high-pitched squeal of feedback:
- Move the mic away from the speaker.
- Bury the mic in your armpit.
- Turn down the amplifier.
- Turn the speaker away from the mic.

Determine what caused the feedback and take precautions to ensure it does not happen again.

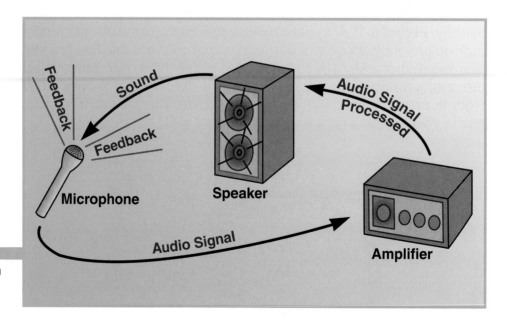

Figure 6-12
Feedback occurs when a mic "hears" its own signal.

Mics on the Set

A mic stand is the most commonly known device designed to hold a microphone in place. In television, however, the mic stand is not often seen. A talk show host may have a microphone on a desk stand, but that mic is often only a prop.

Production Note

Many students ask about a "boom mic" during class discussion. No such piece of equipment exists. If you were to walk into a professional audio store and ask where the boom mics are located, the staff would look at you like you were from another planet. They would have no idea what you are asking for. A microphone boom is, however, commonly used in television production.

Boom: A pole that is held over the set with a microphone attached to the end of the pole. Any type of mic may be attached to the end of the boom.

Hand-held mic: A mic that is designed to be held in the hand, rather than placed on a boom or clipped to clothing.

Mic mouse: A device made of acoustical foam in the shape of a half-cylinder that turns a hand-held microphone into a boundary mic. A mic is placed inside the foam and the entire assembly is placed on the floor or desktop.

A *boom* used in television production is essentially a pole that is held over the set with a microphone attached to the end of the pole. The mic picks up the sound of the talent performing on the set. Any type of mic can be attached to the end of the boom. The goal of the boom operator is to get the mic as close to the talent as possible without dipping the mic into the picture.

The *hand-held microphone* is designed to be held in the hand, rather than placed on a stand or clipped to clothing. A *mic mouse* is a handy device that turns a hand-held microphone into a boundary mic, **Figure 6-13**. In many cases, only two or three are needed to mic an entire stage for a performance. The mic mouse is made of acoustical foam in the shape of a half-cylinder. A mic is placed inside the foam and the entire assembly is placed on the floor or desktop. With the dark gray foam and the black mic cable extending out of the foam, it looks like a large mouse.

Figure 6-13
A mic mouse can convert a hand-held mic into an area mic.

Mics on Talent

Lavaliere (lav) microphone: A small mic that hung from a cord around the talent's neck. A lav mic used to be the only type of mic that could be attached to people.

Lapel mic: The smallest type of mic that can be worn by talent and is attached to clothing at or near the breastbone with a small clip or pin. Sometimes referred to as a "lav."

Figure 6-14
A lapel mic is quite small and can be attached to the talent's clothing.

Years ago, the only small mic that could be attached to people was called a *lavaliere (lav) microphone*. Newscasters in the studio wore a lavaliere mic that hung from a cord around their neck. The mic itself was about the size of an adult's thumb. Technology has made great strides in this particular area. The smallest mic now worn by talent is the *lapel mic*, **Figure 6-14**. It is attached at or near the breastbone of the talent with a small clip or pin. The cord is routed under the clothing to be less obvious. The most common lapel mic is about the size of a pencil eraser. Because the lapel mic evolved from the lav mic, many industry professionals still refer them as "lavs."

Handling and Care of Microphones

Proper microphone etiquette requires reasonable judgment be used to ensure longevity of the audio equipment and the safety of staff and talent. This includes both everyday use and handling and the storage of equipment. Microphones should be handled very carefully.

Production Note

If any noise or action could damage a human eardrum, that action may also damage a microphone. The equivalent of slapping the head of a microphone is being slapped in the ear with a cupped hand. This action could burst the eardrum. Treat a microphone the same way you would treat the ears of someone you care for.

Below are a few general guidelines:

- Never blow into a microphone to see if it is working. A strong burst of air can damage or tear the microphone's diaphragm just as it can damage or permanently impair the human eardrum.

- Do not shout into a microphone. Extreme sound vibrations can stretch the diaphragm out of shape just as these vibrations can stretch the tissue of the eardrum. This causes a mic to receive sound vibrations improperly, if at all. The tissue of the human eardrum can be stretched by the extreme sound vibrations at a loud concert, resulting in temporary hearing difficulty in the hours after such a concert.

- Never let anyone put their lips directly on the mic. Saliva enters the mic which moistens and softens the diaphragm. This obstructs the microphone's ability to receive sound vibrations just as sound vibrations cannot get through to the eardrum when water is trapped in the ear.

- Do not slap the head of the microphone to hear the muffled thump through the speakers. The increased air pressure can tear the microphone's diaphragm, just as being hit with a cupped hand over the ear can burst the eardrum.

- Do not exhale directly into or inhale through the microphone. Exhaling into the mic forces moisture in that softens the diaphragm. Inhaling through the mic transfers all the bacteria inside the mic to you through your mouth. Inhaling through the mic also creates a loud hiss in the sound reproduced.

- Never swing a mic by its cord. The centrifugal force created separates wired connections inside the mic and prevents any sound from being reproduced.

Proper Use of Microphones

Many amateur bands use mics that have a silver ball of mesh on the tip, **Figure 6-15**. Beneath the wire mesh is usually foam that protects the diaphragm of the mic. The foam provides a barrier to moisture and rushing

Figure 6-15
A microphone used for music vocals is designed to handle a wide range of frequencies, while also protecting the diaphragm.

air when a performer places their lips directly on the mic. Speaking or singing with your lips directly on a mic is not necessary for sound reproduction, but it is a style commonly seen in popular music videos. Amateur bands, trying to emulate popular bands, imitate this style while performing. Singing enthusiastically with lips pressed on the mic pushes saliva into the black foam under the surface of the wire mesh mic tip. After a performance, all of the mics are packed up and stored until the next practice or show. The moisture on the foam surface is stored in the dark, at room temperature, and away from any airflow. This is the perfect environment for bacteria growth. From practice to practice, or show to show, it is very unlikely that the same mic will be used consistently by the same person. The next band member to use the mic will place his lips directly on the bacteria-infested mic while singing. In an effort to keep the performers and equipment germ-free and healthy, do not allow talent to place their lips directly on the surface of a microphone.

When holding a mic like a reporter, the mic should be placed firmly in the fist keeping fingers still around the shaft of the mic. Moving or adjusting the fingers produces a very distracting sound that is picked up by the mic. A reporter should place the knuckle of their thumb against the sternum of their chest to properly position the mic while reporting. A common mistake made by novice reporters when interviewing is to point the mic at the subject/guest when asking a question and then pointing the mic at themselves as the guest answers. Even though this is backwards, it is a very easy mistake to make. When interviewing children, do not stand over them. Being on their level creates a much more pleasing picture and the child is not intimidated by an adult standing over him/her.

Never place an audio or mic cable beside an electrical cable. A persistent hum may be heard through the audio system. It is unavoidable that an audio cable will sometimes be near a power cable. Keep the runs of cable apart for as much of the length as possible. Limit the portions that are close in proximity to as few as feasible. If the cables must intersect, make sure it is at a 90° angle.

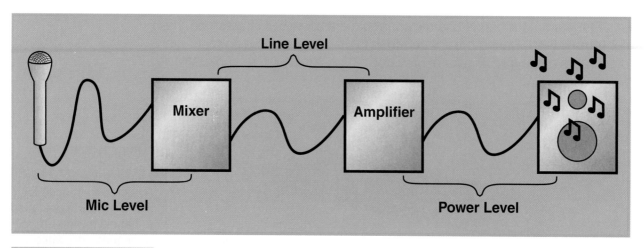

Figure 6-16
Levels illustration.

Impedance

Microphones create a signal that is sent through a cable to be recorded. There are two different kinds of signals that mics can send: high impedance and low impedance. A *high impedance (HiZ)* mic is typically inexpensive, low-quality, and cannot tolerate cable length much longer than 8'. For these reasons alone, high impedance mics are not usually found in TV studios. A *low impedance (LoZ)* mic is typically of high-quality, costly, and can tolerate long cable lengths.

Levels

It is important to know the three levels of audio, because the output of one level cannot be connected into the input of another. The result is either massive distortion or hearing nothing at all. The three levels of audio are, **Figure 6-16**:

● *Mic Level.* The level of audio that comes from a microphone. It is designed to be sent to the "mic in" on a recorder or mixer.

● *Line Level.* The level of audio between pieces of audio equipment. For example, the level of audio going from the output of a CD player to the input on an amplifier.

● *Power Level.* The audio level from the output on an amplifier to the speaker.

Mixers

A *mic mixer* combines only the microphone signals into a single sound signal. An *audio mixer* is designed to take the sounds from a variety of sources, like mics, a CD player, or tape player, and combine them into a single sound signal that is sent to the recorder, **Figure 6-17**.

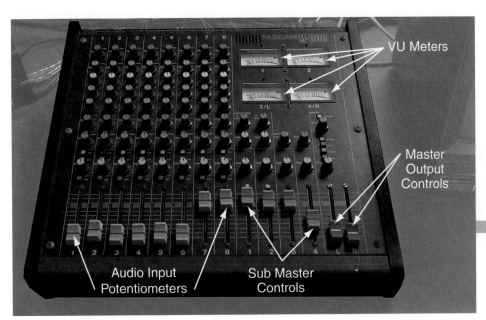

High impedance (HiZ): A type of mic that is typically inexpensive, low-quality, and cannot tolerate cable lengths longer than 8'.

Low impedance (LoZ): A type of mic that is costly, high-quality, and can tolerate long cable lengths.

Mic level: The level of audio that comes from a microphone. It is designed to be sent to the "mic in" on a recorder or mixer.

Line level: The level of audio between pieces of audio equipment. For example, the level of audio going from the output of a CD player to the input on an amplifier.

Power level: The audio level from the output on an amplifier to the speaker.

Mic mixer: A piece of equipment that combines only the microphone signals into a single sound signal.

Audio mixer: A piece of equipment that takes the sounds from a variety of sources, such as mics, a CD player, or tape player, and combines them into a single sound signal that is sent to the recorder.

Figure 6-17
The audio mixer has a different pot for each audio input. The volume unit (VU) meters indicate the level of the audio.

Potentiometer (Pot): A knob or a slider that controls the strength of signals coming into the mixer.

Volume unit meter (VU meter): A meter on either an audio or mic mixer that indicates signal strength.

In both the mic mixer and audio mixer, each signal coming into the mixer can be controlled with a *potentiometer*, or *pot* for short. A pot is usually a knob or a slider. As a knob, it functions like the volume knob on a stereo. The signal coming in gets stronger as the knob is turned to the right. If the control is a slider, it is moved with the operator's finger. The further the slider is moved away from the operator, the stronger the signal coming in.

When using either of the mixers, the operator gauges the signal strength by watching a *VU (volume unit) meter*, **Figure 6-18**. VU meters take two forms:

- One type looks similar to a car's speedometer, with a scale and a needle to indicate the signal strength.
- Another type is a series of LEDs that light as the signal gets stronger.

To operate either mixer type:

1. Activate the sound source. Play a CD or instruct the talent to talk.
2. Bring up a single pot until the sound reaches a desired level on the VU meter.
3. Repeat for each individual microphone or sound source. All the pots are typically not adjusted identically. The pot running a naturally loud voice is set much lower than the pot for a soft-spoken person's microphone. All background music should be relatively low or it drowns out the dialog in the scene.
4. Bring up the pot labeled "master" to send the mixed signal out of the mixer to the recorder.

By adjusting the potentiometer, the audio engineer makes certain that the audio signal is appropriately strong. If the system uses analog technology, the master VU meters should fluctuate between −3 and +3 db. If the system is digital, the VU meters should hover near −20.

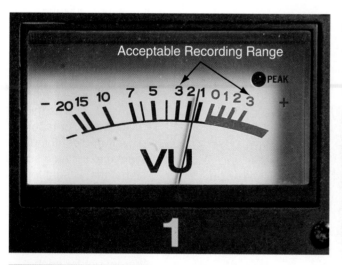
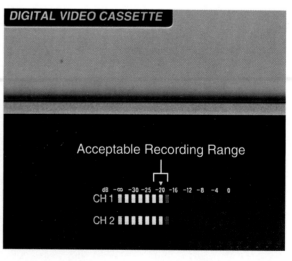

Figure 6-18
In analog recording, the audio meter should fluctuate between −3 and +3. In digital recording, the audio meter should hover in the area of −20.

Production Note

When monitoring the master VU meters, the needle should never touch the far right edge of the meter. This is called "burying the needle," or recording "in the mud." Burying the needle means the audio is being over-recorded. This cannot be fixed in post-production. Over-recording or under-recording the audio when shooting raw footage is an error that a professional usually only makes once. This mistake requires that everyone involved in the production must reconvene to re-shoot the otherwise perfect footage. Reconvening everyone and gathering all the necessary equipment is so incredibly expensive that most people do not make this mistake again.

Automatic Gain Control

The *automatic gain control (AGC)* is a circuit found on most consumer video cameras that controls the audio level during the recording process. If the sound is soft, the AGC turns the recording levels up. If the sound is loud, the AGC turns the recording levels down. While this sounds very helpful, the circuit is always about a second behind "real life." If the recording level is turned up when using analog audio recording because the recorded sound is low, a noticeable and undesired tape hiss can be heard. If possible, this circuit should be disabled on consumer VHS, S-VHS, Hi-8, or 8mm camcorders. There is one exception to this rule. The audio AGC circuit proves quite useful when recording music. This circuit adjusts the audio level for the unpredictable soft and loud portions of a musical piece. This circuit also works well when it is built into a digital camcorder, whether consumer or professional.

Many digital camcorders, both consumer and professional, have built-in AGC circuits. Because the AGC circuit used with digital camera recording technology operates much faster than with analog technology, the undesired tape hiss is not recorded. Therefore, disengaging the AGC circuit on a digital camcorder is not always necessary.

Automatic gain control (AGC): A circuit found on most consumer video cameras that controls the audio level during the recording process.

Connectors

Connectors are the metal devices that attach cables to equipment or to other cables, **Figure 6-19**. Any cable can carry any video or audio signal, as long as the cable is adapted for the necessary connector. A connector can be classified into only one of the following categories:

- *Chassis mount connectors* are built into a piece of equipment.
- *Cable end connectors* are on the end of a length of cable.
- *Adapters* change the type, or connector end, of existing connectors.

Connectors: Metal devices that attach cables to equipment or to other cables.

Chassis mount connector: A connector that is built into a piece of equipment.

Cable end connector: A connector found on the end of a length of cable.

Adapter: A device that changes the type, or connector end, of an existing connector.

Figure 6-19
All connectors are either permanently attached to a piece of equipment (chassis mount), on the end of a cable (cable end), or designed to change one connector type into another type (adapter).

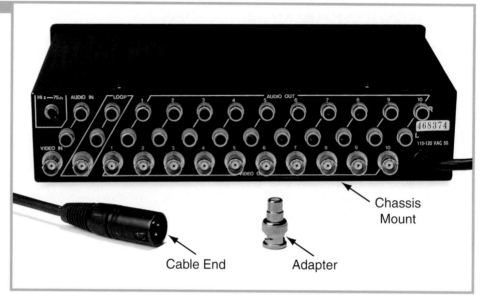

Chassis Mount

Cable End   Adapter

Plug: A connector with one or more pins that are designed to fit into the holes of a jack (female connector). Also called a *male connector*.

Jack: A connector with one or more holes designed to receive the pins of a male (plug) connector. Also called a *female connector*.

One type of connector end is referred to as the *plug*, or the *male connector*. The other connector is a *jack*, or the *female connector*. Male connectors have one or more pins that are designed to fit into the holes of a female connector. Female connectors have one or more holes designed to receive the pins of a male connector. Refer to **Figure 6-20** to see some examples of the connector types defined.

Talk the Talk

When referring to these types of connectors, only the connector name used: BNC, DIN, ¼″, mini, or Y/C. "Please bring a female RCA to male PL259." The words "connector" or "adapter" are understood and, therefore, not actually spoken when industry professionals use these connector terms.

BNC connector: A type of connector commonly used in television production. The female and male versions lock together securely with a simple ¼-turn twist.

BNC Connector

The female and male versions of this connector lock together securely with a simple ¼-turn twist. A *BNC* is the most common connector used in television production.

DIN Connector

DIN connector: A term that refers to any type of connector with 4 or more holes/pins.

This is a generic term that refers to any connector with 4 or more holes/pins. *DIN connectors* are also commonly found on computer equipment cables. In television production, use this term only if there is no other more exact term available.

	Name	Description
	T-Connector	2 female BNCs to male BNC
	Y-Connector	2 female RCAs to male RCA
	Barrel adapter	2 female BNCs
	Barrel adapter	2 female RCAs
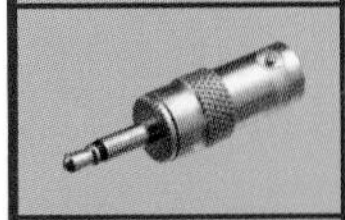	Adapter	Female BNC to male mini
	Adapter	Female BNC to male PL259
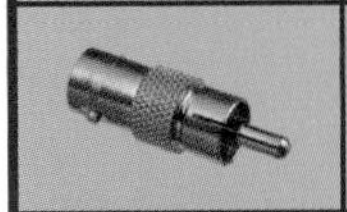	Adapter	Female BNC to male RCA
	Adapter	Female PL259 to male BNC
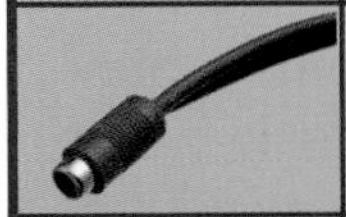	Cable end connector	Female RCA
	Adapter	Female RCA to male BNC
	Adapter	Female RCA to male PL259
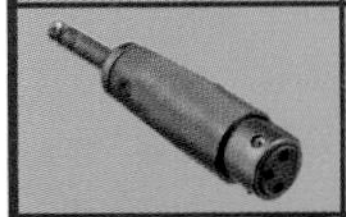	Adapter	Female XLR to male ¼″ phone
	Cable end connector	Male F-connector

Figure 6-20
Various connector types used in the television production industry.

F-Connector

The **F-connector** comes in two styles: push-on and professional. On the push-on style connectors, the male end simply pushes onto the female connector. The professional style F-connectors have a small nut that secures the male and female ends together. The BNC connector has almost completely replaced the F-connector in the industry. While

F-connector: A type of connector that carries an RF signal and is commonly found on the back of consumer VCRs.

Phone connector: A connector that is ¼″ in diameter and single-pronged, with a little indentation near the end of the prong. This type of connector is commonly found on the cord used with large stereo headphones. Also called a *¼″ connector*.

Mini connector: A connector that is ⅛″ in diameter and single-pronged. It is most commonly found on headsets used with portable CD players.

Phono connector: A connector commonly found on the back of quality home entertainment system components. The female phono connector is usually a chasis mounted connector. The male phono connector is usually a cable end connector with a single, center prong surrounded by a shorter crown. Also called *RCA connectors*.

PL259 connector: A connector that is similar to the F-connector, but much larger. The male end has a single prong with a large nut to tighten.

Y/C connector: A video input and output connector that is characterized by four tiny round pins and a rectangular plastic stabilizing pin.

S-VHS connector: The consumer term for a Y/C connector.

the F-connector requires tedious manipulation of a tiny nut to secure it, the BNC requires only a quarter-turn. F-connectors are commonly found on the back of consumer VCRs. The female chassis mount connectors are marked "Ant. In" and "Ant. Out." The male F-connector is on the cable going from the VCR to the cable box or television.

Phone Connector

A *phone connector* is ¼″ in diameter and single-pronged, with a little indentation near the end of the prong. It is also called a *¼″ connector*. Large stereo headphones have a phone connector at the end of the cord to connect with the stereo equipment.

Mini Connector

A *mini connector* is ⅛″ in diameter and is single-pronged. The mini looks similar to the ¼″ connector, but is smaller in size. This type of connector is most commonly found on headsets for portable CD players.

Phono Connector

The components of a quality home entertainment system usually have *phono connectors*, or *RCA connectors*, on the back. They are labeled "audio in," "audio out," "left," and "right." The female phono connector is usually a chassis mount connector, with the male then being a cable end connector. The male has a single center prong surrounded by a shorter crown.

PL259 Connector

The *PL259 connector* is similar to the F-connector, but is much larger. A CB radio is very likely to have a PL259 connector for the antenna. The male end has a single prong with a nut to tighten, like the F-connector. The nut is larger and easier to handle, but still must be twisted many times to achieve a secure connection. The PL259 has also been replaced, for the most part, by BNC connectors.

Y/C Connector

A *Y/C connector* has four tiny round pins and a rectangular plastic stabilizing pin. This connector may be nickel or gold plated. Because of the fine pins, it is a fragile connector for video inputs and outputs. The consumer term for Y/C connectors is *S-VHS connectors*.

XLR Connector

An **XLR connector** is usually a 3-pin connector for microphones, but can be 4-pin, 5-pin, and other pin configurations. When it is a 3-pin connector, it is called an XLR connector. If there are more than 3 pins, it is referred to by the number of pins. For example, "4-pin XLR," or "5-pin XLR." The advantage of an XLR connector is that the male and female ends fit together and a hook automatically locks the two together. The male and female do not separate once locked. A button on the connector disengages the hook, and the ends separate easily.

T-Connector

A **T-connector** is a special kind of connector that takes its name from its shape; it looks like the capital letter *T*. It is made entirely of metal and does not flex. The three ends of a T-connector are used to split one signal into two signals, or to combine two signals into one.

Y-Connector

A **Y-connector** is very similar to the T-connector, except it has three wires with a connector on the end of each. All are tied together in the middle. A Y-connector serves the same function as the T-connector.

Adapters

An adapter is used to change one type of connector into another. For example, a cable that ends in a male BNC needs to plug it into a female RCA chassis mount connector. Using the appropriate adapter, the male BNC can become a male RCA. Most studios have a wide variety of adapters, with almost every conceivable combination available.

Production Note

It is best to have as few adapters as possible in runs of cable. A little bit of the signal is lost at every adapter connection in the run. Think of it as a leaky hose. Each adapter in the run is like poking another hole in the hose.

A **barrel** is a type of adapter that has the same type of connector and connector end on both sides. Connecting a female RCA to a female RCA barrel, for example, allows a crew member to get a necessary 12′ length from two 6′ cables.

XLR connector: A connector that usually has 3-pins, but can have 4-pins, 5-pins, and other pin configurations. The male and female ends lock together with a hook.

T-connector: A connector that is shaped like the capital letter *T* and is made entirely of metal. The three ends of a T-connector are used to split one signal into two signals, or to combine two signals into one.

Y-connector: A connector that has three wires with a connector on the end of each. All the wires are tied together in the middle. The three ends of a Y-connector are used to split one signal into two signals, or to combine two signals into one.

Barrel adapter: A type of adapter that has the same type of connector and connector end on both sides.

Wrapping Up

Knowing the appropriate use of and name given to each of the connectors is an important step in learning how to record quality audio. More advanced audio courses and experience will help develop your audio recording technique.

A confusing situation that a novice audio technician may encounter, however, involves recording a stage performance. Do not take a direct feed off the audio board of the theater, if offered by the theater's audio engineer. Set up your own microphones on the stage. While connecting to the audio board is the easier option, you run the risk of recording very poor quality audio onto the tape. If recording the audio from the theater's audio board:

- The tape has only the sounds picked up by the audio mixer's microphones. Any performers who are not specifically speaking or singing into a microphone are not heard at all. The same holds true for any instruments not playing into a mic. The live audience hears all the instruments, but the tape's audience only hears what is played into a microphone.

- The audio mixer mixes the signals from the mics and sends them to an amplifier to be sent out over the theater's speakers. The purpose of the audio mixer is to reinforce and amplify the sounds, so the live audience hears them well. The live audience hears a blend of live, electronically mixed, and amplified sounds. When recording a performance, your purpose is to record all the sounds in the theater onto the videotape. This is not possible when the mixer sends only some of the sounds—just those picked up by microphones.

- Any mistake made by the audio mixer is clearly evident on your tape, but you will bear the responsibility and blame for the audio quality.

Review Questions

Please answer the following questions on a separate sheet of paper. Do not write in this book.

1. What is the difference between background sound and room tone?
2. Explain how microphones work.
3. List five types of microphones available and the unique characteristics of each.
4. How does feedback occur? How can it be prevented?
5. What is the difference between high impedance and low impedance?

6. What are the acceptable VU meter readings for analog audio systems and for digital audio systems?
7. What is the difference between male and female connector ends?
8. Which connectors combine multiple signals into one?
9. Which connectors are likely to be found on home entertainment equipment?

Activities

1. Create illustrations that demonstrate the pick-up patterns of omni-directional microphones, uni-directional microphones, and cardioid microphones.
2. Inspect the connectors on various pieces of electronic equipment in your home. List several of the items and identify the type of connector(s) used with each.

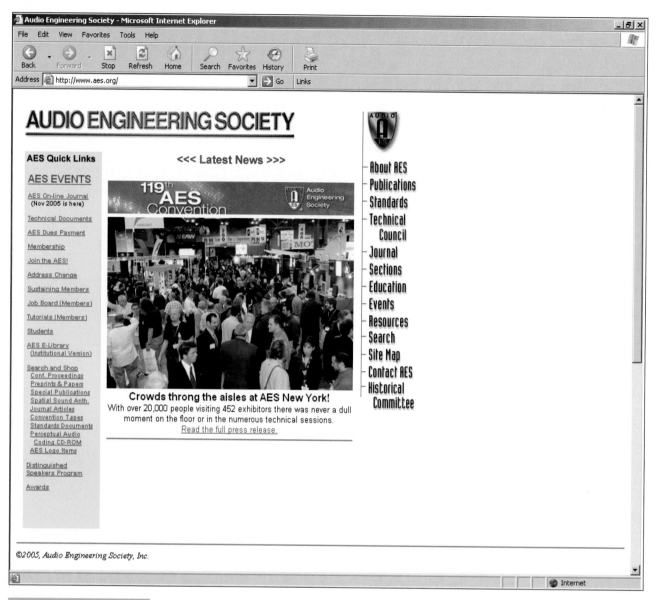

www.aes.org

The Audio Engineering Society is a professional audio technology society whose membership includes engineers, scientists, executives, educators and students involved in every area of the audio industry.

Important Terms

Actors
Big Talking Face (BTF)
Concert Style
Documentary
Drama
Format Script
Interview
Lecture
Lecture/Demonstration
Magazine
Montage
Music Video
Nod Shots
Outline Script
Panel Discussion
Program Proposal
Public Service Announcement (PSA)
Script
Story Style
Storyboards
Talking Head
Visualization
Word-for-Word Script

Objectives

After completing this chapter, you will be able to:

- Name each of the program formats presented and cite the unique characteristics of each.
- List the expected components of a program proposal.
- Identify the elements in each type of script used in television production.

Introduction

Too many students experience anxiety when they hear the word "writing." One of the best things that can be said about television scriptwriting is that it bears little resemblance to the writing style required for academic courses. Although scriptwriting is relatively simple to do, *good* scriptwriting takes talent and skill.

Program Formats

Script: An entire program committed to paper, including dialog, music, camera angles, stage direction, camera direction, and computer graphics (CG) notations.

Lecture: A program format in which the talent speaks and the camera shoots almost entirely in a medium close-up. Also known as *big talking face (BTF)* and *talking head*.

Lecture/ Demonstration: A program format that provides action and makes use of props in addition to lecture. Examples of this format include cooking shows, how-to shows, and infomercials.

Panel discussion: A program format that presents a group of people gathered to discuss topics of interest. Daytime talk shows are an example of this format.

A *script* is an entire program committed to paper. It includes dialog, music, camera angles, stage direction, camera direction, computer graphics (CG) notations, and all other items that the director or scriptwriter feels should be noted.

There are many different kinds of television programs, each with unique requirements of the script. Most programs fit into one of the following categories:

● *Lecture.* The lecture program format is the easiest format to shoot; the talent speaks and the camera shoots almost entirely in a medium close-up. All that is needed for this format is the talent, a camera, and a podium for the talent to stand behind, **Figure 7-1**. Other names for the lecture format are *BTF* (*big talking face*) or *talking head*. This format has the lowest viewer retention and is often the mark of an amateur.

● *Lecture/Demonstration.* The lecture/demonstration format lends itself to the numerous cooking shows, how-to shows, and infomercials seen on television today. This format is more interesting to watch than a lecture alone because of the action and many props used by the performers, **Figure 7-2**.

● *Panel Discussion.* The many Sunday morning network programs that bring a group of professionals together to discuss current news and political topics are examples of the panel discussion format. Also included are the popular daytime talk shows. These programs are not difficult to produce, as long as there is a limited number of

Figure 7-1
A single individual speaking from behind a podium provides little visual interest or action. Because of this, the lecture format has the lowest viewer retention rate of all the programming formats.

Figure 7-2
The lecture/demonstration format adds action that corresponds to the lecture and is more interesting for viewers to watch.

people on the panel, **Figure 7-3**. Panel discussions are driven by the program's content, not action. As more people are added to a panel discussion, the shot to include all members gets rather wide. A wide shot is also a tall shot. This increases the risk of shooting off the top of the set. To keep the top of the set in the shot, the camera may need to tilt down and inadvertently make the studio floor the most prominent item in the picture.

Figure 7-3
The panel discussion format is relatively easy to shoot and provides viewers with interesting information, depending on the talent and the topic.

Interview: A program format that involves a conversation between an interviewer and an interviewee.

Nod shots: A cutaway shot often used in interview programs and usually recorded after the interviewee has left the set. In a nod shot, the interviewer does not say anything, but simply "nods" naturally as if listening to the answer to a question.

Documentary: A program format that is essentially a research paper for television. The audio in the program is on-camera and/or off-camera narration. The video footage used in the program is determined by the topic research and should support the audio of the program.

Drama: A program format that includes both dramas and comedies and requires actors to portray someone or something other than themselves.

Actors: Individuals who participate in a drama or comedy program, performing as someone or something other than themselves.

Magazine: A program format comprised of feature packages, that address a single story.

Music video: A program format that serves to promote a band, a new song, or an album.

- *Interview.* On location or in the studio, the two-person interview can be electrifying. People like Barbara Walters have built entire careers on making a simple conversation a compelling program for the audience. The interview format is often shot with only one camera. To get various camera angle cuts between the interviewer and the interviewee, the interviewee is shot for the entire duration of the interview. The audio picks up the questions asked by the interviewer, but the camera only shoots the interviewee's face. After the interviewee has left the set, the camera shoots the interviewer asking the same questions a second time and records some *nod shots*. Nod shots are a special kind of cutaway (discussed in Chapter 13, *Production Staging and Interacting with Talent*). The interviewer does not say anything, but simply "nods" naturally as if listening to the answer to a question. When collecting nod shots, the interviewer faces the direction where the interviewee was positioned during the interview. In the editing room, the angles and nod shots are cut together to create what looks like a conversation between the two people.

- *Documentary.* A documentary program is essentially a research paper for television; the topic is researched, the information is outlined, and the script is written. See **Figure 7-4**. The audio in a documentary may be either off-camera narration, on-camera narration, or a combination of both. The audio portion of the script should be roughly written out before any shooting begins. In the process of writing, a shot sheet is developed. For a documentary program, a shot sheet is like a grocery list of shots needed to support the audio portion of the script. When shooting, the shots on the list are captured. Additionally, the director watches for other shots that include specific items, people, or anything that adds to the program's content and would be interesting to the viewers. Shot sheets are only a guide and are rarely long enough to provide enough footage to assemble an entire program. Always shoot more footage than is listed on the shot sheet.

- *Drama.* This term includes both dramas and comedies, **Figure 7-5**. The drama format requires a different kind of talent, actors. *Actors* take on a role in a program and perform as someone or something other than themselves.

- *Magazine.* The magazine format originated from programs like "60 Minutes," but has become more than news-oriented programming. A regular news broadcast presents each story in two minutes or less. A magazine format program is comprised of feature packages that address a single story. This allows more interesting detail to be included about each story, but fewer stories to be included in each program.

- *Music Video.* The music video has become a common and influential force in our culture. Items such as clothing, shoes, fashion accessories, and hairstyles gain popularity when seen in a music

Documentary Script	
592a Channel 9 sign	Television
592b Channel 7 sign	Production trains
592c Channel 4 sign	students for
593 DW TV studio sign on door. Door opens on studio in production	entry-level positions in television studios as production assistants.
594 Shot of SEG, tilt up to monitors	It also provides students with a greater
595 Waveform adjustment	hands-on background than most colleges
596 Shoot studio camera viewfinder. ZO rack focus to interview in studio set	offer. Students write, direct, shoot, edit,
597 Operate editors	and deliver their own programs.
598 Focal Point title on CG, run title program	A 30-minute program is produced by students
599 Music video clip	each week for the Fox Cable
600 Passive switcher	System.
601 Dark studio, switch on lights, light board in foreground	We produced the program you are watching right now.
602 A crew shooting a program on location	Location shooting with portable equipment is
603 Loading a car with equipment	a favorite of the students.
604 Drum solo tape	So are music videos.
605 Rayburn music video	Students may work for
606 Channel 10 control room	Channel 10 while taking the class.
607 Wedding	We frequently accept jobs working for the
608 Floor manager gives cue	community as fundraisers. The students
609 Open barn doors	even earn a salary.
610 Operate audio mixer	The class is run like a real video production
611 Director talks into headset. Shot from studio into control room. ZO to see studio camera perform pan to aim at "us"	company, so student responsibility and dependability are strongly emphasized.
613 AFI book	Students in this class are considered to be college-bound.
614 College survey form	The instructor provides considerable help
615 Place lapel mic on student	in matching student interest
616 Move platform	with schools of communications.
617 Hall of fame plaque	If you are interested in the lucrative,
618 "Digital Wave Productions" rolls up on screen. Student stops tape.	glamorous, and demanding field of
619 CU hands taking tape out of machine. Slow ZO. Hands place into case. MS of person smiling at camera and walking out of control room	Television Production, check us out.

Figure 7-4

A documentary script combines research information on a topic and shots that support the information presented.

Concert style: A type of music video in which the audience sees the band perform the music that is heard.

Story style: A type of music video in which the audience hears the music, but does not see the band perform. Instead, actors act out a story line that is supported by the lyrics of the song.

Public service announcement (PSA): A program that is 30 or 60 seconds in length and aims to inform the public or to convince the public to do (or not to do) something in the interest of common good.

video. Music videos also serve to promote a band or a new song or album, in the hopes of increasing the sales of CDs and concert tickets. Most music videos are one of three types:

○ *Concert Style.* The audience sees the band perform the music that is heard. A concert style music video may include a compilation of different concerts the band has performed, a studio performance, or various locations.

○ *Story Style.* The audience hears the music, but never sees the band. Instead, actors act out a story line that is supported by the lyrics of the song.

○ A hybrid of a concert style and a story style music video.

Figure 7-5
A drama requires that talent with acting ability be used in the program.

Production Note

When producing a music video, copyright permission is the first and foremost consideration. Do not break the law!

● *Public Service Announcement/Ad (PSA).* Generally, Public Service Announcements/Ads are 30 or 60 seconds in length. The purpose of a PSA is to inform the public or to convince the public to do (or not to do) something in the interest of common good, **Figure 7-6**. Anti-drug and anti-drinking and driving campaigns are examples of PSAs. A typical television ad, on the other hand, attempts to convince the public to purchase goods or services.

Figure 7-6
A PSA provides the public with information or tries to
persuade the public to do or not to do something.

Visualization

Visualization is the ability to mentally picture the finished program.
Visualizing a program is similar to daydreaming. The visualized details
of a program should be put on paper, so that others can share the vision.
Only when everyone, the crew and cast included, shares the vision for
the program can it become a reality. George Lucas waited to make *The
Phantom Menace*, the fourth *Star Wars* film, until computer graphics
technology was sophisticated enough to realistically reproduce onto the
screen the creatures and worlds he visualized in his mind.

Visualization: The
ability to mentally picture
the finished program.

Storyboards

Some professionals use storyboards to help with visualization,
Figure 7-7. *Storyboards* resemble comic books, in that they present
a sketch of the way the image on television should look. The disadvantage in using storyboards is the considerable time and talent required
to draw each scene. Storyboards do, however, offer an image of the
scriptwriter's vision to everyone who sees them.

Storyboards: Sketches
that portray the way
the image on television
should look in the
finished program.

Figure 7-7
Storyboards assist the crew in creating the director's vision of the program.

The Program Proposal

The *program proposal* is created by the scriptwriter and provides general information about the program, including:

- The basic idea of the program.
- The applicable program format.
- The message to be imparted to the audience.
- The program's intended audience.
- Budget considerations.
- Shooting location considerations.
- A rough program shooting schedule.

The program proposal is presented to an executive producer for approval, either in written form or orally in a meeting. A program proposal is presented before writing a full script, to avoid wasting time and expense on a script that may be completely rejected by the executive producer. The program proposal allows for an initial "green light" on the project.

It is important to think through a script idea during the initial proposal stage. Using visualization, the scriptwriter can get a feel for the program and determine the direction of the script. The executive producer may reject the proposal, accept it, or ask for further details. Depending on the selected program format, the next step may vary.

Research

Both documentaries and interviews require that the program topic be researched. When interviewing someone, it is important to be proficient enough on the topic to hold a conversation that is interesting and informative. When developing a research paper, the research information is often organized on note cards. The notes are then turned into individual paragraphs of the paper. In television, the individual paragraphs become scenes.

The Outline

If a program proposal is accepted, creating an outline is usually the next step. All dramas, lectures, lecture/demonstrations, and documentaries use the same kind of outline. It is very brief, and not at all like the outline written for a research paper in school. An outline includes comments, noting the direction of the program.

Assistant Activity

Find the last research paper you wrote. Reduce the major theme of each paragraph to a single, brief sentence. In doing this, you would create the outline for a documentary on the topic of that research paper.

In any of the formats described, the developed outline is submitted to the executive producer who either:

● Disapproves it.
● Tweaks the outline a bit.
● Gives suggestions to modify it.
● Approves it.

If approved, the next step is writing the actual script.

Drama Outline

An outline for a drama breaks each major event in the story into the fewest number of words possible and places each on a different line. **Figure 7-8** is an example of an outline for a drama called "Little Red Riding Hood." It is a brief, chronological listing of the program's progression. The dialog is either nonexistent or minimal—just enough to relay the main point of each scene.

Figure 7-8
The outline script for a drama is a brief, chronological presentation of a program.

House: Mom gives basket to LRR.
Warns not to stray from path.
Doorstep: Kiss goodbye, wave.
Path: LRR walking.
Path: Wolf sees LRR.
Path: LRR walking.
Path: Wolf running ahead to GM's house.
Path: LRR walking.
GM's house: Wolf breaks in and eats GM.
GM's house: LRR arrives and goes into bedroom.
Bedroom: LRR and Wolf conversation "what big...."
Bedroom: Wolf jumps up and chases LRR.
Bedroom: Woodsman bursts in and kills wolf.
Bedroom: Out pops GM.
The end.

Panel Discussion or Interview Outline

The outline for either an interview or panel discussion does not list major events or show progression. In these outlines, the only necessity is a list of at least 20 questions for the interviewee. Any questions that can be answered in 10 words or less, with a number, or with a "yes/no" response does not count toward the 20 question minimum. Short answers make for an uninteresting program. For example, the question "How long have you been _____?" is widely overused on television. Unless the answer is unusual and sparks interest, viewers do not pay attention to the answer. "How" (not "how long") and "why" are the best kinds of question-starters to use.

Production Note

A 7-year-old child who has just played a piano concerto at a major concert hall is asked how long he has been playing the piano. If the answer is "5 years," the question is worthwhile. However, if a 50-year-old man is asked the same question and responds "30 years," it is not particularly interesting.

Every listed question may not be asked in the course of the interview or panel discussion program. A particularly interesting answer to a question may lead to an impromptu follow-up question. However, if the conversation lags, standby questions can jump-start the conversation.

Music Video Outline

Concert style music videos do not require an outline. Only those with a story line corresponding to the lyrics and music require an outline. The second step in producing a music video may be to obtain copyright permissions or, once obtained, begin outlining and scripting. (Permissions are discussed in Chapter 16, *Music*.) By this point, the executive producer should have heard the music and approved the quality and suitability of the lyrics. The lyrics of some songs are wholly inappropriate to be broadcast to the general public.

Expanding an Outline

Once completed, it may be necessary to expand your outline to include more detail about the program. To do this, take each line of the outline and list details related to that line. Much like the outline you would create for a research paper, list sub-topics and supporting details for each main topic line of the outline. See **Figure 7-9**. Provide five to seven lines of detail for each main topic. When the outline has been sufficiently expanded, it will be ready to go to script form.

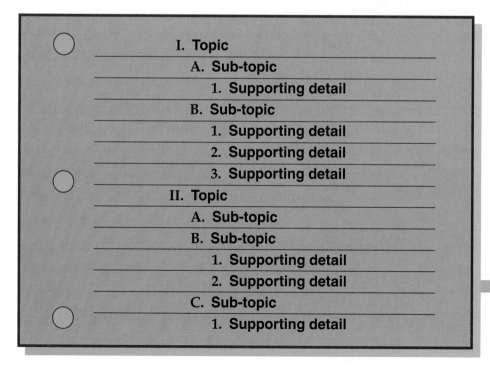

I. **Topic**
   A. **Sub-topic**
      1. **Supporting detail**
   B. **Sub-topic**
      1. **Supporting detail**
      2. **Supporting detail**
      3. **Supporting detail**
II. **Topic**
   A. **Sub-topic**
   B. **Sub-topic**
      1. **Supporting detail**
      2. **Supporting detail**
   C. **Sub-topic**
      1. **Supporting detail**

Figure 7-9
Use Roman numerals, letters, and numbers to create an expanded outline.

Writing the Script

It is recommended that all scripts be written using a computer word processing program. If written with a word-processing program and saved, any alterations and changes requested by the executive producer or client are easily made without rewriting multiple pages of script.

Production Note

Make sure to keep a copy of each revised version of scripts. After your revisions are complete, do not simply press "Save." Choose "Save As" and rename the file to reflect the revision sequence, such as "Scene 4 revision 3." Otherwise, the previous version cannot be retrieved for future review or if a previous version is preferred later in the process.

Unlike film scripts, television scripts are always written in two columns. The left column is reserved for the video and technical information. The right column holds the audio and stage direction. The information in the right-hand column of a television script is exactly what is contained in a "play-style" script for a theatrical performance.

The right and left columns are not the same size. The video column is narrower than the audio column, taking only ⅓ of the page width, **Figure 7-10**. The audio column (right column) occupies ⅔ of the page, because there is always more audio detail to include than video information.

Each line of the video column lines up horizontally with the corresponding line in the audio column. The result may appear to be a lot of wasted space on a page. The empty space makes the page very easy and clear to read. When video and audio events occur simultaneously, they line up together on the script page.

The video portion of the script can make use of many abbreviations, as long as the director and crew all understand the meanings. All camera movements on the script should be abbreviated. There is not enough time to speak full directions over the headsets. For example, "ZO-2S Brian/Mike" is the equivalent of "zoom out to a two shot of Brian and Mike."

Types of Scripts

In television production, there are three types of scripts:
● Word-for-Word
● Outline
● Format

PSA Word-for-Word Script	
Stay in School!	
Video	***Audio***
	Music Note: Rowdy rock instrumental at significant volume in beginning. Slowly lower the volume of the music track to zero when the narrative indicates the band broke up.
WS amateur band performing	**I WAS GONNA BE A ROCK STAR.**
CU wall of beige tile wall very slow pan/tilt. It's ok if the audience is not quite sure what the image is.	
CU of Neil (lead singer) performing	**I HAD MY ACT DOWN.**
CU wall of beige tile wall very slow pan/tilt	**I WROTE A LOT OF STUFF.**
CU Neil writing at a keyboard	**ME AND MY BUDDIES WERE NEGOTIATING A RECORD DEAL.**
CU wall of beige tile wall very slow pan/tilt	**WE HAD A LOT OF IDEAS OF WHAT WE'RE GONNA DO AND WHO WE'RE GONNA BE.**
LS Neil walking out of a school directly toward the camera, ending with a MCU of his smiling face.	(Neil walking out of school in direction of camera) **AND I FIGURED, "HOW IS HISTORY OR SCIENCE GONNA HELP ME IN THE MUSIC INDUSTRY?" SO, I DROPPED OUT OF HIGH SCHOOL.** (Tosses notebook in trash can, looks at camera and gives "thumbs up" sign)
CU wall of beige tile wall very slow pan/tilt	**THEN THE RECORD DEAL FELL THROUGH AND THE BAND BROKE UP**
MLS as Neil watches fellow band member drive off	**CAUSE EVERYONE WENT OFF TO COLLEGE.**
CU wall of beige tile wall very slow pan/tilt	**THAT'S OKAY, WHAT'S RIGHT FOR THEM ISN'T NECESSARILY WHAT'S RIGHT FOR ME.**
Continue CU wall of beige tile wall very slow pan/tilt bringing ECU of 3/4 side view of Neil's face into the picture. He speaks to the camera	(Music Note: Bring in "elevator music" noticeable) **(THAT WAS FOUR YEARS AGO, EVERYONE HAS A JOB NOW. ME, I FINALLY FOUND ONE, TOO.** (Audio: loud Beep)
ZO to MS as Neil turns profile to face a computer screen revealing that he is wearing an intercom headset on the previously hidden side of his face	(startled by the beep) (To camera) **OH!** (Neil turns to computer screen and speaks to the microphone of the headset) **I'M SORRY, DID YOU WANT FRIES WITH THAT? OKAY, PULL UP TO THE SECOND WINDOW.**
Graphic	**STAY IN SCHOOL. GIVE YOURSELF SOME CHOICES.**

Figure 7-10
A television script is always written in two columns, with the video in the left column and the audio and stage direction in the right column.

Word-for-Word Script

In a *word-for-word script*, every word spoken by the talent is written out, **Figures 7-11** and **7-12**. This type of script is used in dramas, music videos, lectures, and documentaries.

When writing a word-for-word script, write the right-hand column material first (audio and stage direction for performers). While writing the audio, visualize how the program will look. When you imagine a camera angle switch, move to the left column of the next line in the script and note "switch" in the video box. A change in camera angle can even occur in the middle of a sentence. Be sure to make a quick note of the visualized switch before moving on with the audio column.

Once the entire right column is complete, allow the content specialist to review the script, if applicable. With the content verified, begin determining the shots needed for each audio box in the script. In the left column, describe each shot needed including the size of the shot, subject of the shot, the camera movements, and all other information pertinent to the video. Remember that a box in the script only contains the video or audio for a single shot. One sentence of audio may include five shots. Therefore, that one sentence spans five boxes in both the audio and video columns.

Outline Script

The *outline script* usually has a word-for-word introduction and conclusion, but an outline for the body of the script. For example, the questions for an interview are all scripted, **Figure 7-13**. For the initial draft, the scriptwriter does not know how the interviewee may respond and the answers cannot be scripted. The interviewee's response is noted in the audio column of the script as "the talent answers," "talent response," or a similar phrase.

For an interview program, it is best to have an informal rehearsal of the questions with the person you are interviewing. Record the audio of the conversation to use as a reference when writing the script. Keep in mind that the interviewee will probably not give exactly the same responses during the actual interview. But, this prepares you for the type of responses to expect and helps you better understand how the entire program will flow. This information is important in developing the video column of the script. Remember that you want to cut to a different image about every 7 seconds. Plan for variety in the video column of your script!

A cooking show is another example of a program that uses an outline script. When writing the script for a cooking show, detail each step involved in the preparation of the dish, including the exact measurement of each ingredient, in the right-hand column of the script. Each step should be placed in a separate box of the audio column. When the script is complete, the chef should review it to ensure every step is included and is accurate. After the audio is verified, determine the shots needed for each step. The credit roll for a cooking program should include the recipe(s) and corresponding ingredients for each dish prepared.

Word-for-Word Music Video Script		
Empire of the Sun		
Seconds	*Video*	*Audio*
1. 0.00-0.05	Intro shot beats 1, 2, 3, 4 PC Walking beats 5, 6 Blaine walking beats 7, 8	Opening music
2. 0.05-0.10	Andy walking beats 9, 10 Phil walking beats 11, 12 PC MCU pose beat 13 Blaine MCU pose beat 14 Andy MCU pose beat 15 Phil MCU pose beat 16	Music
3. 0.11-0.16	Phil hits cymbal-beat 17 shot starts zoomed in on cymbal and zooms out for the rest of bar ends in a LS of whole band	Music
4. 0.16-0.21	New LS of whole band	Music
5. 0.22-0.26	MLS of Chapin and Rachel on bench from front	Now you've left me to die in this forgotten cell
6. 0.26-0.31	LS of Austin and Matt throwing football	You've left me a bitter man or can't you tell
7. 0.31-0.36	LS of Matt throwing ball too high over Austin's hands	Well I'm here now girl and from grace I have fell
8. 0.36-0.41	LS of Chapin and Rachel as ball lands next to them	To you I'd have given up my soul to sell
9. 0.42-0.46	LS of Rachel getting off bench to grab ball	But you rejected my love, told me to stay away
10. 0.47-0.51	Quick shot of Austin walking toward her as she picks ball up and turns into a subjective shot	Well I'm back to offer my love for just one day
11. 0.51-0.55	CU of Rachel's eyes, and then Austin's eyes	So you got this last chance, think about it please
12. 0.56-1.00	MLS Rachel walks over to Austin and they hold hands, quick CU of Chapin looking mad	Don't waste your time on that guy, besides I've heard he's a tease.
13. 1.01-1.04	LS of whole band from front	Music
14. 1.05-1.09	MS of Blaine	Music
15. 1.10-1.14	MS of Andy	Music
16. 1.15-1.18	MS of Phil	Music

Figure 7-11
A word-for-word music video script with time code.

Word-for-Word Drama Script	
Scene 22	
Fade in Cam 2, 2S, ZO for 3S	*(We are inside the apartment. Christine is snuggled up against Lenny. They are watching a movie on TV. A Christmas tree is in the background. Evan comes into the apartment from the theater.)*
	Evan: *(singing)* Hello young lovers, wherever you
Take 1, 2S Christine and Lenny	Evan: are. Lenny and Christine: Hi, Evan! Lenny: How'd it go tonight?
Take 3, MS of Evan	Evan: Knocked'em dead. Watcha watchin'?
Cam 1, 2S C & L	Christine: A Summer Place Lenny: At Christmas! Can you believe it?
Cam 3, MS of Evan	Evan: *(laughs)* Easter Parade would be worse. Hey, *(interrupting as they turn back to watch the movie)* tell me about today.
Cam 2, 2S of C & L Cam 1, move to CU of Lenny	Lenny: Well, we started out by pretending we were rich. Christine: Yeah, dressed up in our finest and walked into Saks. You should have seen the saleslady when Lenny told her he didn't like the $25,000 fur coat I had been fawning over.
	Lenny: I thought she was going to have heart failure. *(laughs)* Then we came back to the apartment for lunch and --
Cam 3, MS Evan	Evan: *(interrupting)* Lunch!
Cam 1, CU Lenny	Lenny: Yeah. And then we --
Cam 3, Begin ZI to MCU Evan	Evan: You didn't do anything else this morning?
Cam 2, 2S L & C	Lenny and Christine: No.
Cam 3, MCU Evan	Evan: Do you know what day this is?
Cam 2, 2S L & C	Lenny: Sure, it's Tuesday.
Cam 3, MCU Evan	Evan: *(evenly)* The audition.
Cam 2, 2S L & C	*(Lenny freezes. Christine slowly looks from Evan to Lenny. Silence. Lenny looks frightened.)*
Cam 3, MCU Evan	*(Evan looks from one to the other.)* Evan: Well, what happened at the audition?
Cam 1, CU Lenny	Lenny: Evan, I...it was an accident. I mean --
Cam 3, CU Evan	Evan: You mean what? What about the audition I set up for you?
Cam 1, CU Lenny	Lenny: *(Unable to face Evan)* I forgot about it. *(silence)*
Cam 3, CU of Evan	Evan: *(Calmly enraged)* Christine, would you excuse us please?
Cam 2, 2S L & C Cam 3, Move to 2S of L & E	Christine: Well, it is getting kinda late. Call me tomorrow? *(Lenny nods and helps her on with her coat.)* *(In a whisper to Lenny)* Are you sure I should leave? *(Lenny nods; Christine exits.)*
Cam 3, 2S L & E	Lenny: Evan, I– Evan: I don't want to hear it, Lenny.
Cam 1, CU Lenny	Lenny: But, I–
Cam 2, CU of Evan	Evan: Lenny, I don't want to hear it now.
Cam 3, 2S E & L	Lenny: But Evan, I want to ex–
	Evan *(With quiet fury. Turning to Lenny)* Lenny, no.
Fade out	

Figure 7-12
A word-for-word drama script.

Outline Format Television Interview Script
Title: Movie Theaters in the 21st century
Page 23

VIDEO	AUDIO
Host walks past the camera. Pan right as he walks into the stairwell and up the stairs.	Host: **Now that you've had some insight on running a theater, I'm going to show you where all the magic happens,**
Host walking from the stairwell into the projection room.	**the projection room. We'll talk to the projectionist.**
Pan right and zoom to MS of Host walking up to the projectionist.	Host: **Hello, (**projectionist's name**). Can we hang with you for a while and see how you do your job?**
Cut ELS left side angle shot of projectionist and host.	Projectionist: **Sure.**
Cut between host and interviewee every time a question is asked.	Host: **What kind of training does a projectionist need?**
	Projectionist answers.
Get many cutaways for editing variety.	Host: **What kind of training does a projectionist get?**
	Answer.
	Host: **How long is the film for most movies?**
	Answer.
	Host: **Do you need to clean the film before loading it?**
	Answer.
	Host: **What can you do if the film is damaged?**
	Answer.

Figure 7-13
An outline script for a television interview with notations for interviewee responses.

Format Script

Format script: A program script that is very brief and used for programs in which the order of events is predetermined and the sequence of each episode is consistent.

The *format script* is very brief and is used for the evening news, panel discussions, talk shows, game shows, and other programs whose format does not change from episode to episode. See **Figure 7-14**. The on-screen talent and lines may change, but the shots are predictable from a production point of view. The order of events in programs of this type is predetermined and the sequence of every episode is consistent.

Assistant Activity

Write a format script for a late night talk show. If everyone in the class writes one for a different episode this week, you will discover that all the scripts are nearly identical. The only variations are the faces on the screen and the dialog. The format/order of events remains constant from episode to episode.

Format Script	
Late Night Talk Show	
Segment 1	*Intro*
LS Walk on MS Host during monologue Cutways of audience reactions	Host welcomes audience to show Lists guests Opening monologue
Segment 2	*Guest 1*
Intercuts between MCU of host, MCU of guest, 2S of both, and cutaways of audience	Host and guest chat/interview
Segment 3	*Guest 2*
Intercuts between MCU of host, MCU of guest, 2S of both, and cutaways of audience	Host and guest chat/interview
Segment 4	*Musical Group*
Variety of MLS, MS, MCU, and CU of performers	Band plays
Segment 4	*Guest 3*
Intercuts between MCU of host, MCU of guest, 2S of both, and cutaways of audience	Host and guest chat/interview
Segment 5	*Wrap-up*
MCU host then WS to include all guests	Host thanks guests and audience all guests

Figure 7-14
A format script for a late night talk show program.

Writing Style

In most academic writing situations, students are encouraged to carefully choose their words, be mindful of the rules of sentence structure, and abide by the rules of composition. In general, students are expected to follow the commonly accepted grammar and usage rules. This type of writing is called "formal." Formal writing is difficult for some people. Nearly all school textbooks are written with a formal writing style. Formal writing is not used in script writing. Scripts are written the way people talk, using contractions and slang. Sometimes scripts do not even have complete sentences.

The television script is written in an informal style to aid in easy understanding. For example, if you are reading a book and find a passage that you do not understand, you go back and reread it. This cannot happen on television. On television, if a concept or sentence is missed, it is gone. Therefore, on television, sentences are short, simple, and easily understood.

For those who have anxiety about writing, try dictating scripts into a tape recorder. After dictation is complete, the tape can be transcribed. Also, there are now computer programs that allow you to speak into a microphone and the computer types what is spoken. These "voice-to-text" programs are so inexpensive that many new computers are shipped with the software already installed.

Production Note

Do not waste words! The audience only sees what you show them. If showing a close-up of a rose, do not waste words by having a narrator state the obvious: "As you can see, here we have a rose." Do not describe what the audience is seeing, unless providing information their own eyes may not acquire. If the visual is complex, on the other hand, some interpretation may be necessary so the audience understands what they are seeing.

Word Processing Programs

Most word processing programs are very similar. The steps listed below to set up a table for script text are comparable from program to program. Before typing a script, insert and format a table:

1. Select the "Table" menu option at the top of the screen.
2. Click "Insert/Table."
3. On the screen presented, specify that the table should have 2 columns.
4. Click "OK" at the bottom of the screen. A table with two equal columns is displayed on the page.
5. Place the cursor over the vertical line that separates the two columns.

6. Click on the vertical line and drag it toward the left margin, until it is about ⅓ of the way across the page.

Once the table is in place and formatted, enter the video instructions in the left column and the audio information in the right column. Use the "Tab" key on the keyboard to move from one column to the next. To add rows to the table, tab out of the last cell on the table to return an empty row beneath. Continue hitting the "Tab" key to move the cursor from one empty cell to the next, adding multiple empty rows onto the table.

While reviewing the script, you may discover that a block contains too much audio in relation to the scripted video angles. To add a new row with empty right (audio) and left (video) blocks:

1. Place the cursor in front of the word to be placed in a new block.
2. Select the "Table" menu option at the top of the screen.
3. Click "Insert" and select "Rows Below" from the menu returned.

Highlight the section of audio text you want to move into the new block and drag it to the blank block. This provides an empty block on the left side of the table to enter new video text and instructions.

The Montage

Montage: A production device that allows a gradual change in a relationship or a lengthy time passage to occur in a very short amount of screen time by showing a series of silent shots accompanied by music.

The *montage* is a script/production device that allows a gradual change in a relationship or a lengthy time passage to occur in a very short amount of screen time. It is usually set to music and does not include any dialog. The following is an example of shots in a montage, presented in shot sheet format:

> Shots of:
> A couple having dinner.
> The couple going to a museum.
> The couple playing in a park.
> The couple coming out of a movie theater.
> The couple swimming at a public pool.
> The couple raking leaves.
> The couple at a Halloween costume party.
> The couple shoveling snow.
> The couple decorating their home for the winter holidays.
> The couple assembling kites in a park for their children.

A love song accompanies the series of shots. As a result, two minutes of real time shows that a year has passed in the couple's lives and depicts how their relationship has grown.

Wrapping Up

Never shoot a program without a script. When this rule is broken, the crew inevitably ends up re-shooting on location because the first shoot lacked a plan. Few people would attempt a cross-country auto trip without planning the trip on a map ahead of time. At the same time, few people strictly adhere to the original plan. Traffic backups, taking side trips on a whim, and road construction are just a few things that may sidetrack a journey. The same is true for a script. Few scripts are shot exactly the way they are written. They do, however, provide the backbone structure to hold the director's creative vision together. Deviations occur in the shooting process, but the basic structure of the program is constant because a script exists.

Review Questions

Please answer the following questions on a separate sheet of paper. Do not write in this book.

1. What are nod shots? How are they used?
2. What items are included in a program proposal?
3. What is a script outline?
4. List the three types of scripts used in television production and the unique characteristics of each.
5. Why are television scripts written using informal language?
6. What is a montage?

Activities

1. For each of the program formats listed below, name a television show that serves as a format example:
   - Lecture
   - Lecture/Demonstration
   - Panel Discussion
   - Interview
   - Drama
   - Magazine
   - Music Video
   - PSA

Be prepared to explain the characteristics of the selected television show that qualify it as an example of the corresponding program format.

2. Record an episode of your favorite sitcom and create an outline for the program. Remember that an outline for this type of program breaks each major event in the story into the fewest number of words possible and progresses chronologically.

Objectives

After completing this chapter, you will be able to:

- Describe the appropriate use of still photos in a video production.
- List guidelines for creating text to display on a television screen.
- Explain how contrast ratio affects television graphics.
- Differentiate between 4:3 and 16:9 aspect ratios.

Introduction

Graphics consist of any artwork required for a production, including the paintings that hang on the walls of a set and the opening and closing program titles. Also included in the graphics for a program are charts, graphs, and any other electronic representation that may be part of a visual presentation. Currently, most graphics are computer-generated. Others are still created with paper or canvas and ink, paint, or any other medium that an artist might use.

Graphics: All of the "artwork" seen in a program, including the paintings that hang on the walls of a set, the opening and closing program titles, computer graphics, charts, graphs, and any other electronic representation that may be part of a visual presentation.

Talk the Talk

In some facilities, the terms "visuals" and "graphics" are used interchangeably.

Copyright

Any picture taken from a magazine or book, or a motion picture still frame is almost always copyrighted. This means that these images may not be used in a video program without the copyright owner's permission. The simplest way to obtain images for a production is to create your own; take original photographs or make unique paintings. If existing copyrighted works must be used, find the copyright holder and get permission.

Still Photos

Still photography, if used sparingly, works well in a video program. Excessive use of still photography makes a television program look like a slide show. To make interesting use of still photos, move the camera around on the picture to create a sense of motion.

Assistant Activity

Watch a few documentaries to see this "roaming the camera on a still photo" technique. Notice, also, that sound effects and music are added while the camera is roaming across a still image. The net result is quite effective.

Photos taken with a consumer 35mm camera may be used in a video production, if certain precautions are taken.

- Always take the picture holding the camera horizontally. A picture taken in the horizontal orientation is more closely shaped to the television screen than a vertically oriented picture, **Figure 8-1**. A horizontal picture is a rectangle with the long side on the top and bottom just like a television screen.
- If printing the photo, request a satin finish. A glossy finish poses lighting problems, because glossy paper reflects the glare of lights into the lens of the video camera.
- Photographic slides may be used instead of printed photos. This avoids the lighting glare issue entirely. A photographic slide must be oriented in the slide projector horizontally, rather than vertically.

Figure 8-1
The horizontally oriented picture is more closely shaped to a
television screen than the vertical image.

With the prominence of digital video, many nonlinear editors
(discussed in Chapter 19, *Video Editing*) accept image files in various
formats, such as .jpg, .tif, and .gif. There are also computer programs
available that allow the user to crop and change a photo in many ways
before sending it to the nonlinear editor, **Figure 8-2**.

Figure 8-2
Some computer programs allow photographs to be cropped and otherwise manipulated before placing them in a program.

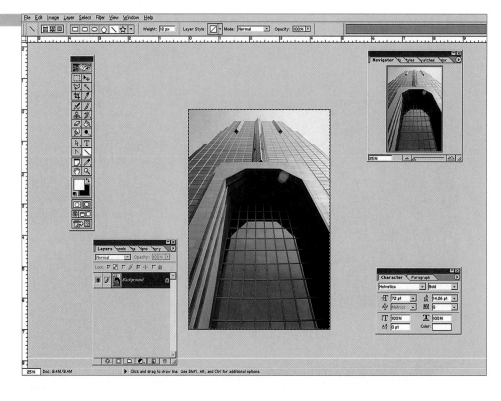

Still images that are not manipulated by a computer must be shot with a video camera. Printed photographs should be placed on an easel to be captured by the video camera. With photographic slides, the camera captures images that are projected onto a screen. Neither of these low-cost scenarios produces the high quality video image output of a *telecine* (pronounced "tell-eh-scene"). A telecine is a device that, in concept, is a slide projector or movie projector pointed directly at the television camera lens. This machine is the size of two refrigerators set side by side. It is quite expensive and many optical maneuvers must be made for the image to actually get onto the videotape. The concept is very simple, but is quite complex to execute. The most advanced telecines take theatrical motion pictures and convert them to videotape for purchase or rental. A telecine is also referred to as a *multiplexer*, *film chain*, or *film island*.

Telecine: A device that facilitates the transfer of film images onto videotape. Telecines are used, for example, to transfer theatrical motion pictures to videotape for purchase or rental. Also called a *multiplexer*, *film chain*, or *film island*.

Motion Picture Film

While the majority of television production involves videotape, a great deal of film is also used. As such, a basic understanding of the medium and how to use film in a video environment is necessary.

A piece of motion picture film is nothing more than a series of still pictures. Each picture is only slightly different from the next. When projected rapidly, one picture after the other, the illusion of motion is created. When you watch a movie, 24 individual pictures are projected per second. This rate is expressed as 24 *fps* (frames per second).

Fps: The rate at which individual pictures are displayed in a motion picture and on television, expressed as frames per second.

Therefore, a picture is projected for a flash, is followed by black while the projector advances one frame, and a new picture is flashed. The pictures are flashing in such rapid succession that the blackness is not perceptible to our conscious mind.

Television also uses the concept of frames. However, individual pictures cannot be seen on a piece of videotape. Videotape appears to simply be a ribbon of brown or black. The television signal is a magnetic signal on the tape, but is essentially recorded one picture at a time. The frame rate for television is 30 fps.

The difference between motion picture frame rate (24 fps) and television frame rate (30 fps) explains why the image on a television or computer monitor often flickers or rolls when pictured in a movie. The difference between the frame rates periodically results in the "black" between motion picture frames, which are followed or preceded by the "black" between frames of the television picture. When this occurs, the image is black long enough for the human eye to detect. Our minds register the blackness that occurs in different places on the picture, as a roll.

High Definition Television (HDTV) technology can use the motion picture frame rate of 24 fps, as well as the television frame rate of 30 fps. This HDTV 24 fps capability is the reason that the image flicker or roll is now rarely seen in a movie theater. The flicker and roll of images remains a problem in home videos, however.

Assistant Activity

Turn on a computer monitor and take a short video of the screen with a consumer video camera. Do the same with a television set. The flicker and roll is visible both on the camera's viewfinder and the tape when played back.

Text

Most of the text seen on the television screen is created on a computer and electronically fed into the video switcher to be recorded with the program onto videotape. When viewing text on a computer screen, relatively small text is easily read because you are less than three feet away from the monitor. When sitting further from the monitor, all the letters are too small and the words seem to run together. When watching television, most viewers sit between eight and fifteen feet away from the screen. Any words that appear on the screen must be large enough to be clearly read at the distance.

Letters on a television screen need to be relatively large, with only a few words on the screen at a time. One of the basic rules of television graphics is that no more than 5 lines of writing and no more than 5 words per line should appear on the screen, **Figure 8-3**. There are exceptions to this rule. The most notable exception is the opening text narrative of the "Star Wars" series of films. Clearly, there are more words per line

Figure 8-3
A basic rule for using text on the television screen.

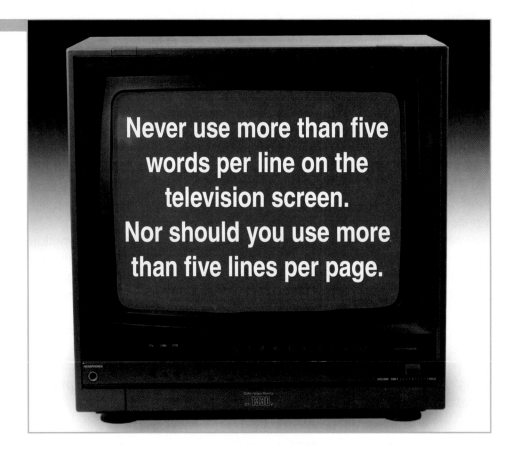

Never use more than five words per line on the television screen.
Nor should you use more than five lines per page.

and more lines per page in the opening sequences than the rule states. However, if the words or lines are revealed to the audience one at a time, more lines and words can be placed on a page. When the videographer forces viewers to look only at a certain place on the screen, he can "feed" viewers the writing at will.

Production Note

A graphic should remain on the screen long enough to be read out loud twice.

If many lines of text are presented on screen at once, the audience finds it very difficult or impossible to read. For example, the "fine print" displayed at the end of a car sale or lease promotional spot on television explains the details of the advertised deal. By law, the advertiser must display this information in the spot. But, the text is created in such a small type and is displayed so briefly on the screen, it is unlikely that many viewers have ever been able to read the contents. The law does not specify that the information must be presented in an easily legible format.

The numerous font styles available in word processing programs are also available for creating television titles. Many of the fonts, however, are unusable. Only bold, simple letters can be clearly read on the television screen. Fancy and elaborate fonts simply do not display well on television, **Figure 8-4**. The clear representation of these fonts on a computer monitor is not an indicator that they will translate well to the poorer quality of the television receiver. Keep in mind that the image quality on a computer monitor is generally twice that of a television monitor. When creating titles on a computer, always view the titles on a television monitor to verify that they are readable. The picture on a television screen is actually a collection of horizontal lines. These horizontal lines distort the fine detail of fancy lettering.

Contrast Ratio

Contrast ratio is the relationship between the brightest object and the darkest object in the television picture. The human eye can see 100% contrast between black and white objects, or a contrast ratio of 100:1. This means that we have no difficulty seeing black objects on a white background or white objects on a black background. The text of this book is black on a white page, for example. Some digital cameras actually have a contrast ratio of 100:1. However, the most commonly used analog television system has a contrast ratio of 40:1. The 40:1 limit cannot be exceeded as long as the majority of the viewing audience has analog television sets. In the future, as more people purchase digital televisions, the 40:1 requirement will be converted to 100:1.

Contrast ratio: The relationship between the brightest object and the darkest object in the television picture.

Figure 8-4
Fancy or thin fonts are not clearly visible on the television screen, even though they appear clear on a computer monitor.

On a scale of 1 to 100, "1" represents no-luminance, or black, and "100" represents total-luminance, or white. As an example, imagine a long board with equal sections numbered 1 to 100 and shorter board with the same sized sections numbered 1 to 40. The board that is 40 units long represents the television scale of 40:1. The 100-unit board represents a realistic scale of 100:1. The first unit on each board is black. Each subsequent unit is a lighter shade of gray, with the last unit on each board being white, **Figure 8-5**. Even though each board begins with black and ends with white, the 40:1 television scale is missing many shades in between.

If number 1 on the television contrast ratio scale is placed even with number 1 on the realistic contrast ratio scale, the difference in the color range becomes obvious, **Figure 8-6**. While the end of the television scale is white, the corresponding realistic color is medium gray. That medium gray color is the lightest object the television can display if there is a substantial amount of black in the picture. In this scenario, any object that truly is a medium gray color is displayed as white on the television screen, because white is the lightest color the television set can produce. Any object lighter than medium gray in this picture begins to glow with an otherworldly light.

If number 40 on the television scale board is placed on top of number 100 on the realistic board, the black end of the television scale corresponds to a lighter medium gray on the realistic board, **Figure 8-7**. The

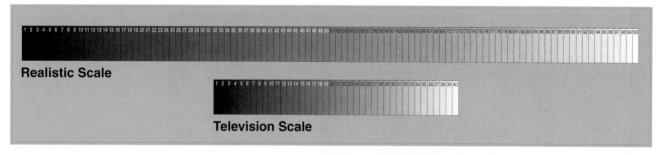

Figure 8-5
With the 40-unit board beside the 100-unit board, the ends of the 40-unit board represent the upper limit of "lightness" and the lower limit of "darkness" possible on the television set.

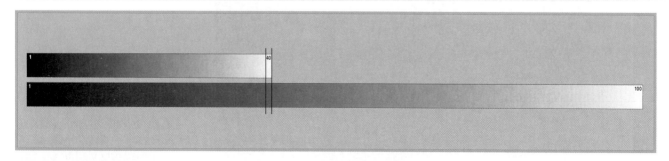

Figure 8-6
The lightest end of the television scale falls in the medium-gray range on the realistic scale.

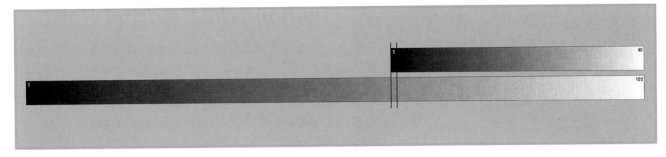

Figure 8-7
The darkest end of the television scale falls in the light-gray
range on the realistic scale.

lighter medium gray is the darkest object that the camera sees when
the majority of the picture is white. Objects of this color appear black on
the television screen. Anything darker than the gray appears black and
without detail. Those objects literally look as if they were cut out of the
TV screen and replaced with pitch-black paint.

Visualize This

A student once decided to produce a program about the
degrees of wear and tear on automobile tires as her class project.
In preparing for the shoot, she painted the backdrop of the set
a relatively bright yellow. Once the tires were arranged on the
set, against the yellow background, she realized that the camera
could not "see" any detail on the tread of the tires. The tires were
solid black shapes on the monitor. The lack of detail was caused
because she had exceeded the contrast ratio in the image.

What this means, in most cases, is that the middle of the 40-unit television scale should be placed in the center of the 100-unit realistic scale.
To produce a quality, realistic picture, make certain that there is nothing
lighter or darker in the picture than the shade of gray that appears on
either end of the stick. If an object is darker, it appears black. If an object is
lighter, it appears white. The further toward either end of the 100-unit stick
an object falls, the more negative black or white attributes it acquires.

Production Note

For scenes that require a greater amount of darkness, like
exploring a cave, remember that the television contrast ratio scale
has been moved down the realistic contrast ratio scale. The talent
should not be dressed in bright white costumes. If shooting in an
extremely light environment, such as Antarctica, the television
contrast ratio scale has been moved to the upper end of the
realistic contrast ratio scale. The actors should not wear dark navy
blue parkas.

Figure 8-8
Popping the contrast ratio of a predominantly dark picture causes light colored items to glow.

Popping the Contrast Ratio

Light colored objects glowing and dark colored objects losing detail are examples of exceeding the contrast ratio limitations, or ***popping the contrast ratio***, of video. See **Figure 8-8**. When the contrast ratio is popped, diagonal zebra stripes appear on the camera's viewfinder indicating that an object in the scene is too brightly lit, **Figure 8-9**. When zebra stripes appear, it is not always necessary to make adjustments. The image is not considered to be "bad" unless the negative effects intrude on the main focus of the picture. The zebra stripes only indicate that there is a problem. Once the camera operator makes the problem known, it is up to the program's director to decide if the problem is worth correcting.

For example, a "glow" that appears on the visible part of the white shirts on a group of men wearing black suits may be dismissed. If this group is considered to be relatively minor characters in the scene, the zebra stripes on the small amount of white underneath the black suits can be ignored to continue shooting.

Pop the contrast ratio:
When the brightness or darkness of objects in a shot exceeds the contrast ratio limitations of video.

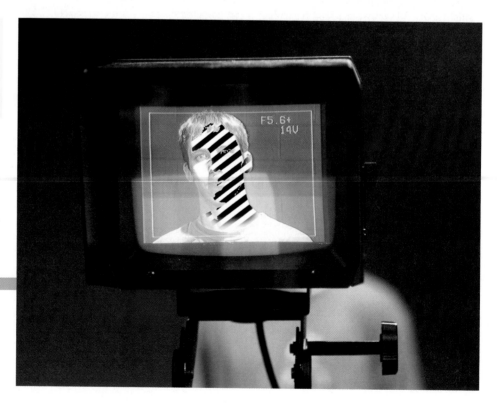

Figure 8-9
The camera operator sees zebra stripes through the camera's viewfinder when something in the shot is too brightly lit.

On the other hand, when shooting something outside a ski lodge, the image is quite *hot*, or very bright, due to all the white snow in the environment. The main character skis into the frame of the camera wearing a dark green outfit. Both the character's face and outfit appear completely black because the outfit has popped the contrast ratio. This is not an acceptable shot. One solution is to paint the snow a gray color, but this is not a sensible or realistic option. Practical solutions to this problem include:

● Shoot the scene at night. This, however, might not work for the scene.

● Close the aperture of the camera or place filters on the camera lens to reduce the amount of light coming in. As the amount of light coming in is reduced, the television scale begins to move lower on the realistic scale. The costume and the talent's face will eventually be visible.

● Change the character's costume.

● Zooming in on the subject of the shot. Zooming in reduces the amount of bright snow in the picture and magnifies the center of the picture. The contrast ratio lessens.

The concept of contrast ratio applies to production graphics, in that white letters should not be used on a black background. High contrast ratios should be avoided for television images. At the same time, colors with a similar luminance value should not be used together in a picture. Luminance refers to the degree of lightness in relation to the degree of darkness in a picture. For example, two colors most associated with the winter holiday season are red and green. These colors are very likely to find their way into a written graphic—red letters on a green background or green letters on a red background. Anyone with a black and white television sees an almost entirely gray screen, **Figure 8-10**.

Hot: A term used to describe an image or shot that is very bright.

Figure 8-10
Different colors with the same luminance value appear to be almost the same shade of gray on a black and white screen.

Colors of contrasting luminance should be used in graphics, but the contrasting colors cannot exceed the 40:1 contrast ratio. Many professional cameras have black and white viewfinders on them, allowing the camera operator to easily evaluate the quality of any graphic shot. However, if the graphics are generated on a computer, they should always be fed into a black and white monitor and reviewed before going to tape.

Television systems reproduce most colors very well. However, red, pink, and orange are very difficult to reproduce accurately for technical engineering reasons. These colors should be avoided as much as possible in television production.

Aspect ratio: The relationship of the width of the television screen to the height of the television screen, as in 4:3 or 16:9.

4:3 aspect ratio: The aspect ratio of a television that is 4 units wide by 3 units high.

Aspect Ratio

Aspect ratio refers to the relationship of the width of the television screen to the height of the television screen. From the early 1950s to the present day, television sets common in most homes have an aspect ratio of 4 units wide by 3 units high, or a *4:3 aspect ratio*, **Figure 8-11**. This ratio applies to any unit of measure that is employed, such as centimeters, inches, feet, miles, or yards.

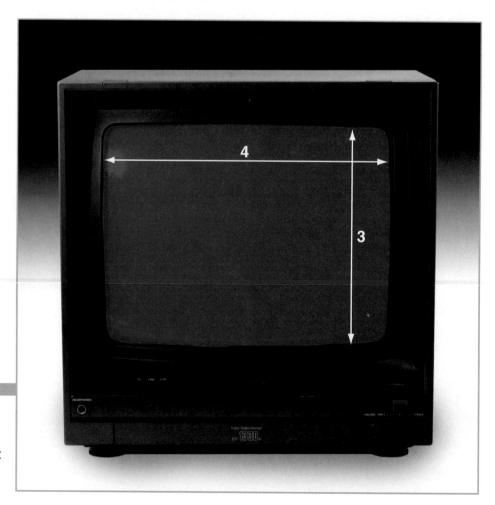

Figure 8-11
Currently, the most common shape of a television screen is a rectangle with an aspect ratio of 4:3 (4 units wide by 3 units high).

The recorded video images of a wide screen motion picture, or an average theatrical release film, are 16 units wide by 9 units high, or in *16:9 aspect ratio*. See **Figure 8-12**. Images this size cannot be entirely viewed on a 4:3 aspect ratio television screen. The original video image is too wide to completely fit on the television screen. Only about three-fourths of the video image actually appears on the television screen, **Figure 8-13**. Currently, the only way to see the entire image on a 4:3 screen is to "letterbox" the image. Letterboxing displays the entire image, from left to right, on the television screen. The top of the image is pushed down and the bottom of the image is pushed up. The result is a narrow horizontal strip on the screen, with a black bar on the top and bottom of the screen, **Figure 8-14**.

16:9 aspect ratio:
The aspect ratio of a television that is 16 units wide by 9 units high.

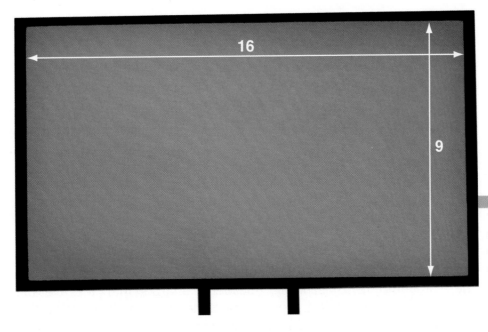

Figure 8-12
The standard television screen format is transitioning from the 4:3 aspect ratio format to 16:9 aspect ratio.

Figure 8-13
About one-quarter of a 16:9 picture does not fit on a 4:3 aspect ratio screen.

Figure 8-14
An entire movie image can be placed on a 4:3 screen by "letterboxing" the picture. Letterboxing requires that the image be shrunk vertically to fit on the television screen.

Production Note

The recorded images on 35mm and 70mm theatrical film are much larger than the available 16:9 aspect ratio. The 16:9 aspect ratio format incorporates as much of the original film image as current technology permits.

The standard television aspect ratio is changing from 4:3 to 16:9. The 16:9 aspect ratio is more closely shaped to a 35mm motion picture or still photo image. On 16:9 format televisions, viewers see much more of the original film images when watching movies at home. In addition to viewing more of the original film, viewers will also be seeing digital images. Digital images displayed on a digital television are strikingly clear. Consider the clarity of images viewed on a computer monitor. These images are, most likely, noticeably sharper than the average picture on a television set. Now, understand that the digital television image is greatly improved from the display on a high-resolution computer monitor.

The Federal Government has organized a digital conversion project that provides a schedule and guidelines and for all broadcast stations in the United States to convert from broadcasting an analog signal to broadcasting in digital video format. The only way to view television after the conversion is complete is either with a new digital television or with a converter box connected to an analog television. The converter equipment takes the superior digital image, changes it into an analog image, and sends that signal to the analog television set.

Production Note

The 16:9 aspect ratio is not synonymous with large, "wide screen" television sets. Many 16:9 screens are large, but they can be rather small as well. The 16:9 ratio refers to the shape of the screen, not the amount of real estate it occupies.

Essential Area

The concept of aspect ratio is very important when generating graphics. All graphics need to be in the 16:9 format. At the same time, the *essential area* of the graphic must be in 4:3 aspect ratio. Essential area is the area that *must* be seen on any television set, regardless of aspect ratio or age, and includes all the words in a graphic. Words cannot be cut off by the limitations of the left and right margins of the television set. For example, a graphic created to advertise a local business does not communicate the correct information if the essential area is not considered, **Figure 8-15**. The background is not included in the essential area. Therefore, the background may be a solid color created in 16:9 aspect ratio.

Essential area: The area of an image or shot that must be seen on any television set, regardless of aspect ratio or age, and must include all the words in a graphic.

Character Generator

The *character generator*, or *CG*, essentially creates letters (generates characters). Think of a CG as a video word processor. The primary function of the CG is to create titles. Titles may be very simple pages that appear on the screen, or they can move across the screen. The titles can move around on the screen in seemingly three-dimensional motions. The letters can be animated or stationary. The degree and style of movement should contribute to the overall effect of the video program, rather than being a display of, "Look at the cool things I can do with this computer program."

Character generator (CG): A device that creates (generates) letters (characters), primarily for titles.

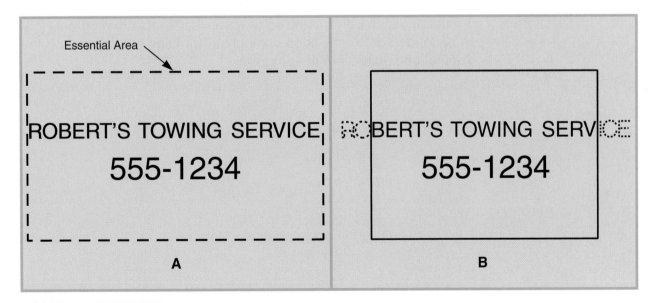

Figure 8-15

The essential area is the region that must be seen by the viewer. A—The essential area does not include a margin or space between the end of words and the edge of the screen. B—Do not allow any of the graphic text to fall outside of the 4:3 aspect ratio essential area.

Production Note

The term "CG" has another definition unrelated to title creation. CG also means "computer generated." When used in this context, CG is usually mentioned with special effects. Many special effects are created on a computer, and when referring to them one might say "the special effects are CG." The context of the sentence provides the key to how "CG" is used in conversation or direction.

Credits: The written material presented before and/or after a program listing the names and job titles of the people involved in the program's production.

Roll: Titles in a program that move up the screen.

Crawl: Words that appear either at the top or the bottom of the screen and move from the right edge of the screen to the left, without interrupting the program in progress.

The simplest and most common types of titles are the credit roll and the crawl. *Credits* are the written material presented before and/or after a program listing the names and job titles of the people involved in the program's production. In a *roll*, titles move up the screen, as if they were printed on a long roll of paper. A credit roll, for example, usually occurs at the end of the program. In order to be read by the audience, the titles must move up the screen. If titles move down the screen, the viewer's eyes are constantly jerked up and down which creates a feeling of discontent with the audience. A *crawl* appears either at the top or bottom of the screen, without interrupting the network programming or footage. Words move from the right edge of the screen to the left edge of the screen. This right to left motion is most pleasing because we read from left to right. Running a crawl from the left to the right also creates a feeling of discontent with the audience. Local news programs use a crawl to display current traffic conditions and weather updates on the bottom or top of the screen.

There are many different CG computer programs available. Some are independent hardware and software units. Others are programs that can be loaded onto a desktop computer. The titles are created on the computer and edited into the program.

Wrapping Up

Graphics for television are an important aspect of production, because they include anything the viewer needs to read. In order for viewers to read the information, the graphic must be simple enough and sufficiently large to be seen from a couch or chair that is 8′ to 15′ away from the screen. The graphic must have a contrast ratio within the limits of the television system. A graphic should remain on the screen long enough to be read out loud twice. Due to the emergence of digital television, graphics must be generated to fit on the screen of every television set it might be viewed upon. It must appear satisfactorily on either a 4:3 or a 16:9 aspect ratio television screen.

Review Questions

Please answer the following questions on a separate sheet of paper. Do not write in this book.

1. What are the conditions for using still photos in a video program?
2. What are the names used for the device that converts slides or film to videotape?
3. Why does the image displayed on a television or computer monitor flicker or roll when shown in a movie?
4. What is contrast ratio? What is the contrast ratio possible with analog television systems?
5. What is the result when an image pops the contrast ratio?
6. Why should color graphics be evaluated on a black and white television monitor?
7. What are some of the benefits in converting from 4:3 aspect ratio displays to 16:9 aspect ratio displays?
8. What is the difference between a roll and a crawl?

Activities

1. Watch two versions of the same movie: one in full screen format (4:3 aspect ratio) and one in wide screen, or letterbox, format (16:9 aspect ratio). Write down the noticeable differences in various scenes. Be prepared to share this information in class.
2. Visit a high-end electronics retail store. Compare the picture on an analog television screen of any size to the clarity and color on both a digital television and a High Definition Television (HDTV). Make note of the various specifications on several digital and HDTV models and indicate the prices of each. Be prepared to share your findings in class.

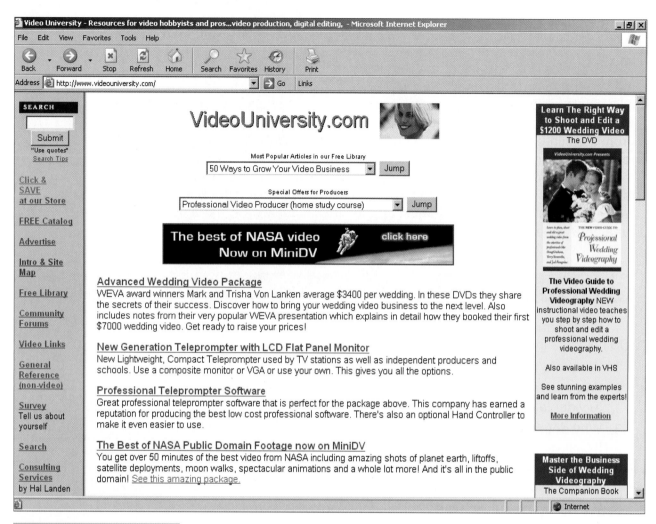

www.videouniversity.com.
A Web site that provides information and resources for film and video
production businesses.

Important Terms

3200° Kelvin (3200°K)
Back Light
Background Light
Barndoors
Bounce Lighting
C-Clamp
Cross-Key Lighting
Diffusion Device
Dimmer
Fill Light
Flag
Flood Light
Floor Stand
Four Point Lighting
Fresnel
Gel
Grid

Hard Light
Kelvin Color
  Temperature Scale
Key Light
Lamp
Light Hit
Light Plot
Lighting Instrument
Limbo Lighting
Raceway
Scoop
Scrim
Soft Light
Spotlight
Three Point Lighting
White Balance

Objectives

After completing this chapter, you will be able to:

- Identify the various types of lighting instruments and cite unique characteristics of each.
- Explain how different colors of light affect a video image.
- List the methods to control lighting intensity.
- Describe the goal and instruments used in each of the television lighting techniques presented.
- Describe the methods recommended to extend the life of lamps.
- Explain how contrast ratio affects the process of lighting a set.

Introduction

There are two main functions of lighting for television production:

- To meet the technical requirements of the camera. There should be enough light to produce an acceptable picture on the screen.
- To meet the aesthetic requirements of the director. Sufficient lighting is necessary to create the desired mood, from an artistic standpoint. A romantic dinner, for example, should have a different lighting design than a football game.

Ultimately, the television screen is a flat piece of glass. Industry professionals try to create the "illusion" of a three-dimensional image by manipulating many objects and aspects of a program. To create three-dimensions:

- Shoot a person in a three-quarter angle, rather than in profile.

- Apply makeup to the talent to create lines of light and shadow (discussed in Chapter 15, *Makeup Application and Costume Considerations*).
- Paint a production set to create the illusion of three dimensions.
- Make certain areas more prominent on the screen through the creative use of light and shadow.

Special lighting is necessary in television production because the lens aperture is closed significantly to accomplish great depth of field. Closing the lens aperture requires that the light level be increased, or our wonderfully focused picture will be a wonderfully focused *dark* picture.

Using Professional Terms

It is imperative that consumer terms not be used in a professional studio environment. Using the correct terminology is considered an entrance exam for a television production technician. The importance of correctly using industry terms cannot be overstated.

Production Note

As a newcomer to the television production industry, using the correct terminology is considered an "entrance exam" of sorts. You risk losing respect and credibility among industry peers and superiors if you use consumer terms in the workplace or misuse professional terms.

Lamp: The part of a lighting instrument that glows when electricity is supplied.

Lighting instrument: The device into which a lamp is installed to provide illumination on a set.

The average consumer calls the fixture on the end table in their living room a "lamp" and the part inside that glows a "lightbulb." Television production industry professionals do not use these terms. In the industry, a *lamp* illuminates a set when installed in a *lighting instrument*.

Talk the Talk

When referring to a lighting instrument, only the word "instrument" is used. "This instrument needs a new lamp." The word "lighting" is understood and, therefore, not actually spoken when industry professionals use this term.

In the television production industry, the word "light" has two definitions:

- "Lights" refer to the collection of all the instruments used in the studio or on location. "Let's turn the lights on now." Most people refer to an "instrument" only when referring to a specific lighting instrument.
- "Light" also refers to the illumination created by turning on a lamp. For example, the lighting engineer may use a light meter to measure the amount of light hitting or reflecting off an object on the set.

Types of Light

The two types of illumination used on a studio are defined by the type of shadows they produce—hard and soft.

Hard light creates a sharp, distinct, and very dark shadow. Hard light is the type necessary to create shadow puppets against a wall. If a hard light instrument is hung from the ceiling of a TV studio and pointed straight down onto an object, there is a perfectly shaped shadow on the floor below the object, **Figure 9-1**. The line on the floor, between the lighted area and shadowed area, is very thin and distinct.

Soft light creates indistinct shadows. Using a soft light instrument in the previous example creates a very indistinct shadow pattern on the floor. There is no definitive line between the lighted areas and shadowed areas, **Figure 9-2**. The lighted area gradually fades into shadowed area.

Hard light: A type of illumination used in the studio that creates sharp, distinct, and very dark shadows.

Soft light: Type of illumination used in a studio that creates indistinct shadows.

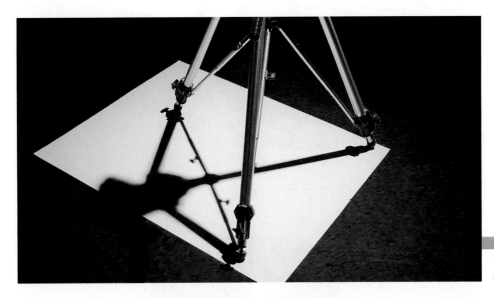

Figure 9-1
Hard light creates sharp, distinct shadows.

Figure 9-2
Soft light creates indistinct shadows.

Types of Lighting Instruments

The most common hard light instrument in the studio is a ***spotlight***, **Figure 9-3**. Spotlights can be fixed to a pipe on the ceiling or wall, placed on a stand, or be very moveable. The moveable spotlights, "spots" for short, are often used in theatrical presentations when the spotlight follows a person around on the stage.

The ***fresnel***, pronounced "fruh-nel" (with the accent on the second syllable), is another hard lighting instrument, **Figure 9-4**. It is a lightweight instrument that is easily focused and can produce a great deal of light.

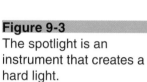

Spotlight: A hard light instrument.

Fresnel: A hard light instrument that is lightweight and easily focused.

Figure 9-3
The spotlight is an instrument that creates a hard light.

Figure 9-4
The fresnel is a lightweight, focusable, hard lighting instrument.

A *flood light* is a soft lighting instrument that provides general lighting in a large area. One of the most common flood lights is a *scoop*, **Figure 9-5**. The scoop is named such because it looks like an ice cream scoop. It is a half-spheroid shaped instrument that creates a great deal of light.

Convertible spotlights have a sliding lever on the body of the instrument, **Figure 9-6**. The instrument is a hard light in one setting and converts to a soft lighting instrument by sliding the lever.

Flood light: A soft light instrument that provides general lighting in a large area.

Scoop: A common type of flood light with a half-spheroid shape that produces a great deal of light.

Figure 9-5
The scoop lighting instrument is named for its domed, or scoop, shape. (Mole-Richardson Co., Hollywood, CA)

Figure 9-6
A convertible spotlight is very versatile because it can create hard or soft light.

Accessories

Even though a spotlight is a hard light, it only creates a circle of light in varying diameters. The need may arise for light to be projected in a specific shape or blocked from hitting one particular object on the set. The most commonly used items to shape and block light are called *barndoors*, **Figure 9-7**. Barndoors are fully moveable metal flaps that attach to the front of the instrument. The operator moves them into the beam of light to block or reshape the light.

> ## ! Safety Note
>
> The barndoors get very hot! If the instrument is on or has recently been turned off, wear gloves when handling the barndoors.

Aluminum foil is commonly used to produce the same effects as barndoors, **Figure 9-8**. It is recommended that heavier foil, designed to line barbecue grills, be used instead of regular foil used in the kitchen. The instruments get very hot and heavier foil lasts longer. Some very interesting and creative shadow patterns can be created using this inexpensive medium. To use aluminum foil to shape or block light:

1. Tear off a sheet several feet long.
2. Shape it into a cylinder.
3. Attach it to the front of the instrument with metal paper clips (not plastic or vinyl coated).
4. Turn the lighting instrument on and shape the foil by hand.

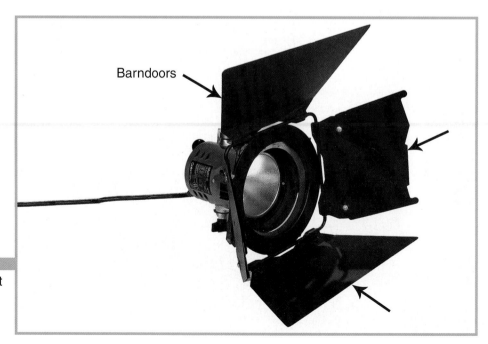

Figure 9-7
Barndoors allow the light to be shaped, rather than merely projecting light in a large circle.

Barndoors

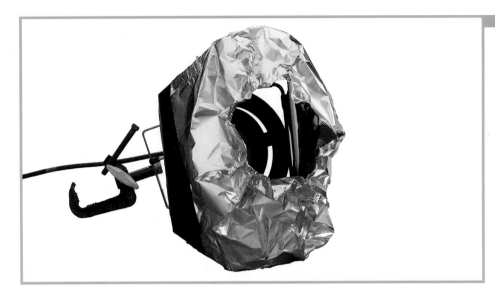

! Safety Note

Do not use transparent tape, masking tape, or duct tape to attach foil to the instrument. The tape may ignite! This poses a serious safety risk to every person on the set and in the building. Also, water emitted from the sprinkler system will damage every piece of video equipment, the set, costumes, props, and all other valuable items in the studio.

Light hit: A white spot or star shaped reflection of a lighting instrument or sunlight off a highly reflective surface on the set.

Flag: A flexible metal rod with a clip and a flat piece of metal attached to the end. A flag is positioned between a light source and a reflective surface on the set to avoid light hits.

Brightly polished objects, like a silver ashtray or brass lamp, may be part of the set. Highly reflective surfaces create a white spot or star shaped reflection of a lighting instrument or sunlight that is reflected into the lens of the camera. This reflection is called a *light hit* and is generally considered to be an undesired effect. The simplest solution is to remove the object from the set. If this is not an option, a *flag* needs to be placed between the lighting instrument and the object, **Figure 9-**

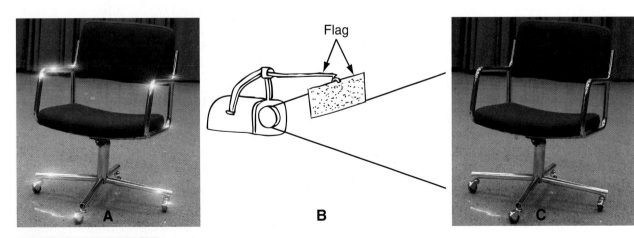

Flag

A   B   C

Figure 9-9
A flag prevents light hits by blocking light from hitting a particular item on a set. A—Shiny surfaces on a set reflect light from the lighting instruments used. B—A flag is placed between the lighting instrument and the reflective surface on the set. C—With the light blocked from the shiny surfaces, light hits are avoided.

9. A flag has two parts. The first part is a flexible metal rod, perhaps 2′–3′ long, with a clip at the end of the rod. This rod is attached to the side of the lighting instrument with the excess length extending in front of the instrument. The second part of the flag is a small flat piece of metal cut into a specific shape. The lighting designer attaches the metal flag to the clip and bends the rod until the flag is positioned between the light source and the reflective surface on the set. The light is blocked from the polished object, but the rest of the set is still illuminated by the lighting instrument.

Safety Note

Do *not* use wooden dowels or cardboard to make a flag. When exposed to the heat of the lighting instruments, these materials become a fire hazard.

Fluorescent Instruments

The types of instruments previously discussed in this chapter all use incandescent lamps. Fluorescent instruments are a recent offering in the market. Fluorescent lamps come in many shapes and sizes, but are similar in appearance to the fluorescent tubes used in fixtures at home or school. There is, however, one major difference. Professional fluorescent lamps are available in various color temperatures. The most important of those color temperatures to the video industry is the 3200° Kelvin lamp. Color temperatures are discussed in detail later in this chapter.

Fluorescent instruments and lamps have several advantages over the incandescent variety. Overall, fluorescent lamps are far less expensive to replace. For example, one type of incandescent lamp may cost $45 and last for about 50 hours before burning out. A fluorescent lamp may cost $20 and last 15,000 hours. Additionally, the fluorescent lamp consumes far less electricity and generates much less heat than an incandescent lamp. A fluorescent lamp can be touched with a bare hand while turned on. It is warm, but usually not warm enough to burn.

To the human eye, a fluorescent lamp actually appears to be considerably less bright than an incandescent lamp. While it is less bright, the images created under fluorescent instruments appear beautifully on video. This is because a fluorescent lamp provides the exact frequency of light required by the camera. An incandescent lamp spreads a wide frequency of light, most of which the camera does not need. Since a fluorescent lamp is not as bright as an incandescent lamp, talent is less likely to squint at the camera while performing due to bright lights on the set. Incandescent instruments are still needed on a set, but using fluorescent instruments can reduce the number needed and, therefore, reduce the cost of operation.

Supports for Lighting Instruments

Lighting instruments may be attached to *floor stands* in the studio. A light stand is a tripod (3 legs) or quadripod (4 legs) with a long vertical pole to which the lighting instrument is clamped. Floor stands have several disadvantages:

- They are very top-heavy when the instrument is attached to the top of the pole and may be tipped over easily.
- The electrical power cable lies on the floor of the shooting area and is a tripping hazard, **Figure 9-10**. To be safe, the power cords should be taped down to the floor.
- They use valuable floor space.
- It is easy for studio personnel to accidentally walk in front of them, casting a shadow on the entire set.

Floor stand: A tripod or quadripod (4 legs) with a long vertical pole to which a lighting instrument is clamped.

Figure 9-10
A floor stand can support small lighting instruments, but there are several precautions the crew must observe.

On a remote shoot, however, floor stands are a necessity. The crew should be conscious of them and be cautious around them. Some smaller portable lighting systems come with large spring-loaded clamps. These clamps allow the instruments to be attached to a flat, steady object, like the edge of an existing door or table, **Figure 9-11**.

In the studio, the best mounting option for lighting is to use a *grid*, **Figure 9-12**. Most studios have a grid hanging about twelve inches below the ceiling. This grid is made of pipe that is at least two inches in diameter. Lighting instruments attach to the grid using the *C-clamp*, **Figure 9-13**, built into the instrument. The bottom of the "C" is attached to the instrument and the top hooks onto the pipe. A large threaded screw is tightened to firmly press against the pipe and secure the instrument safely to the grid.

Grid: A pipe system that hangs from the studio ceiling and supports the lighting instruments.

C-clamp: A clamp in the shape of a *C*, used to attach lighting instruments to the grid.

Figure 9-11
This large clamp allows an instrument to be attached to a sturdy shelf, door, or table.

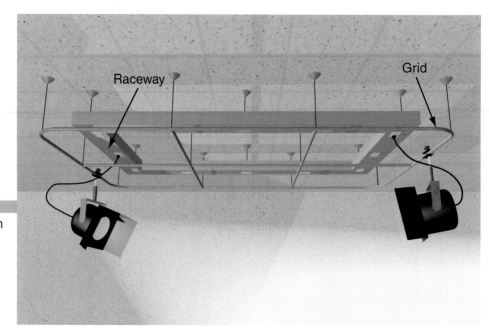

Figure 9-12
A grid is the pipe system that hangs from the ceiling and supports the instruments. The raceway supplies electricity for the instruments.

Raceway

Grid

Figure 9-13
A C-clamp attaches the lighting instrument to the grid.

! Safety Note

Any instrument that hangs on the grid should have an additional safety chain attached. The chain should loop around part of the instrument and around the grid pipe. If the C-clamp comes loose, the safety chain prevents the instrument from falling to the ground and possibly injuring someone standing beneath it.

Hanging beside the grid pipes, or attached to the ceiling above the grid, is the *raceway*. See **Figure 9-12**. The electrical cables and outlets that power the instruments on the grid are part of the raceway. Each of the many outlets on the raceway is numbered and corresponds to a dimmer or switch on the lighting board. The lighting instruments are plugged into the outlets, which are powered selectively by the lighting board. This eliminates the need to climb ladders to turn the lighting instruments on and off. The electrical wiring is not placed within the grid piping because of the puncture or crushing hazard that exists with the use of C-clamps. If a C-clamp is overtightened and punctures a grid pipe, the electrical current running inside the wiring poses a great danger to the lighting director or gaffer on the ladder.

Raceway: The electrical cables and outlets that hang beside the grid pipes or mounted to the ceiling above the grid to power lighting instruments on the grid.

Colors of Light

Colors reflect different frequencies of light. A frequency is measurable and, therefore, can be graphed. In 1848, the scientist Lord Kelvin devised a system to quantify and measure color. At that time, a black carbon rod was considered to be the blackest item available. Using the concept that black is the absence of color, Lord Kelvin applied heat to the black rod. As his eye began to discern a color change, he noted the color and measured the amount of heat that was applied to produce that

Temperature	Color
2000K	Red
2500K	Yellow
3000K	Pale Yellow
3200K	White
4000K	Green
4500K	Greenish Blue
5000K	Blue
6500K	Cobalt Blue
7000K	Violet
10,000K	Black

Figure 9-14
Approximate values of the Kelvin Color Temperature Scale.

color, **Figure 9-14**. Based on the data collected, Lord Kelvin created a scale by which colors could be measured. The *Kelvin Color Temperature Scale* measures color temperatures in degrees Kelvin.

Modern technology allows us to use combinations of materials, such as tungsten, quartz and halogen gas, to produce light of the same color temperature without applying the extreme levels of heat Lord Kelvin used. However, instruments made of these materials still get incredibly hot and will burn the skin if touched after being on for as little as one minute.

Kelvin Color Temperature Scale: A scale developed by the scientist Lord Kelvin that measures color temperatures of light in degrees Kelvin.

Production Note

Understand that we are discussing the colors of light, not colors of paint. The principles that apply to each are different. When dealing with light, the color white is created when all the colors of light are combined. Black is the absence of all colors. A television screen is black until it is turned on. The screen becomes bright white, even though the lights creating the picture are red, green, and blue.

White Light

3200° Kelvin: The temperature of white light in degrees Kelvin. Also noted as *3200°K* or "32K" when spoken.

In television production, the most important result of Lord Kelvin's research is that *3200° Kelvin* (*3200°K*) equals white light. In order to reproduce colors and flesh tones properly on television, the light hitting the object must be white.

Talk the Talk

When temperature is written in degrees Kelvin, the word "Kelvin" is replaced with an upper case "K": 4500°K.

When this same temperature is spoken aloud, the last two zeroes of the temperature reading and the word "degrees" are omitted: "45K."

Most home videos taken indoors have a yellow hue to them, **Figure 9-15A**. This is because the lamps inside the instruments in most homes are considerably cooler than 3200°K and, therefore, produce light that is less than white. The Kelvin temperature of most incandescent light-bulbs for home use is about 2000°K. On the other hand, video taken under regular fluorescent ceiling lights has a greenish hue, **Figure 9-15B**. The fluorescent lights used in classrooms and professional buildings are considerably warmer than 3200°K. These lights are between 4000°K and 4500°K. Light in that temperature range is blue-greenish and produces a gray, unhealthy look on natural flesh tones. Video shot outside under sunlight appears to be tinted with a shade of blue, **Figure 9-15C**. Sunlight is 5000°K and up, which produces various shades of blue.

The only time objects on television appear their actual color is when pure white light, 3200° Kelvin, is used. Most television lamps are rated at 3200°K. This temperature rating refers to the color of light emitted by the lamp, not the brightness of the light emitted. The brightness is indicated by the wattage of the lamp. A 1000-watt 3200°K lamp is much brighter than a 300-watt 3200°K lamp. However, both produce the same white light.

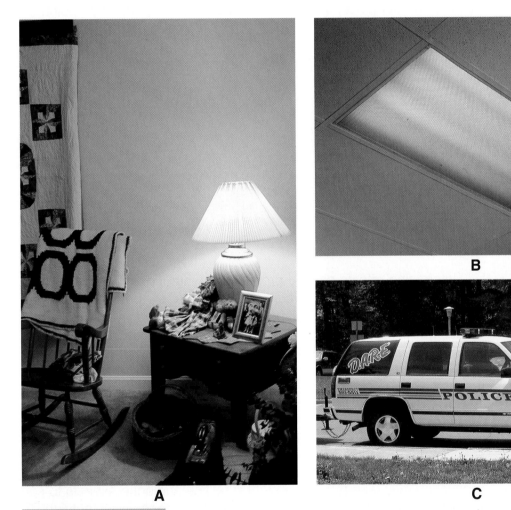

A

B

C

Figure 9-15

A—Color temperatures below 3200°K cause the yellowish tone of pictures taken in consumer house lighting. B—A standard fluorescent light tube emanates a blue-greenish tint due to a color temperature in the 4000°K–4500°K range. C—The camera sees sunlight in a bluish tint.

To get the necessary 3200°K white light at home or when shooting outside, two options are available:

- Bring enough lighting instruments to overcome the natural light of the area and to flood it with white light.
- Trick the camera into thinking it is getting white light, even though it is not.

To "trick" the camera, activate the **white balance** circuit while the camera is pointed at a white object on the set that is under the lighting that you are balancing for (such as sunlight, incandescent light, or studio lights). The camera is forced to see the object as white, without regard to the type of light hitting it. The camera then sees all other colors correctly because it has been balanced to one color (white). Other colors fall neatly into place on the scale. For example, assume that the color orange is two shades up from red and two shades down from yellow on the Kelvin scale. Each color is identified by its relationship to adjoining colors. Accurately identifying one of the colors places all the other colors into their proper place, using the one specified as a reference point.

White balance: A function on cameras that forces the camera to see an object as white, without regard to the type of light hitting it or the actual color of the object.

Assistant Activity

1. Attach a color monitor to the video output of a camera.
2. Point the camera at a white object.
3. Notice that it does not appear white on the monitor. It may appear greenish, grayish, or even pinkish.
4. Press the white balance button on the camera.
5. Watch the monitor carefully to see the object transformed to a true white color.

Interesting effects can be produced by intentionally throwing off a camera's white balancing circuit. For example, try pointing a camera at a red object and white balance on it. The camera then tries to turn anything red into a white color. In the process, every other color of the spectrum is shifted out of kilter as well.

Colored Light

Some types of programs or specific scenes require that colored lights be used on the set. For example, a rock band's concert is likely to have many different colored lights on the set. A scene in a dramatic production may take place in a nightclub. The audience expects to see various mood-enhancing colored lighting instruments in a nightclub. To turn the white light from a lamp into a colored light, a thick, heat-resistant plastic sheet called a *gel* is used. Gels can be purchased from theatrical lighting stores and are available in hundreds of shades and colors. The

Gel: A heat resistant, thick plastic sheet placed in front of a lighting instrument to turn the white light from a lamp into a colored light.

material is cut into a small rectangle that fits into a special gel holder on the front of a lighting instrument, **Figure 9-16**. The white light passes through and becomes the color of the gel.

Because colored lighting instruments are often used to create a specific mood or effect, it is important that the audience be able to view the colored lighting on the screen. In order for the audience to properly perceive the colored lights, perform the white balance with the colored lights turned off, and only the white lighting instruments turned on. When the colored lights come on, the camera sees each as the actual color they are. White balancing on an object that is under a colored light throws the camera's color reproduction circuits out of kilter.

Lighting Intensity

Once the lighting instruments have been set up, either on a set or on location, controlling the intensity of the light becomes an important task. If a person is too brightly lit, they may appear to glow. Depending on the time of day, natural sunlight may cast dark shadows on the talent's eyes, nose, and chin. Several techniques are effective in reducing the amount of light that hits an object on a set.

Move the Instrument

Moving the lighting instrument(s) further away from or closer to the set is the most common solution in controlling the intensity of light. Move a lighting instrument further away from the set to reduce the amount of light hitting the objects on the set, decreasing the lighting intensity. To increase the lighting intensity, move the instrument closer to the set.

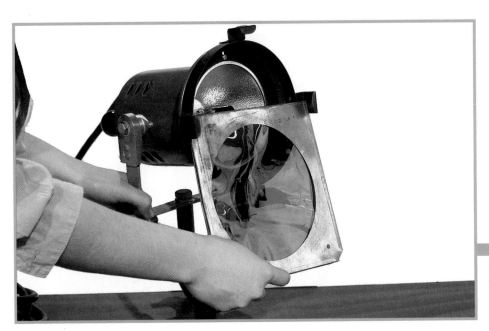

Figure 9-16
A gel can change the color of the white light emitted from an instrument.

Replace the Lamp

Replacing the lamp with one of lower wattage decreases the intensity of the light. For example, remove a 1000-watt lamp from an instrument and replace it with a 400-watt lamp. Make certain that the new lamp is rated at 3200°K. A lower wattage light rated at 3200°K still produces white light, just less of it.

Use a Diffusion Device

A *diffusion device* is placed on the front of the lighting instrument. Diffusion devices soften the light, in addition to reducing its intensity, without reducing the color temperature. A *scrim* is a type of diffusion device that may be purchased from a theatrical supply house. When placed in front of a lighting instrument, it appears transparent or translucent, **Figure 9-17**. These devices are most commonly attached using a gel holder, but metal paper clips may be used, as with the aluminum foil on barndoors.

Diffusion device: A device that is placed in front of a lighting instrument to reduce and soften the intensity of light without altering the color temperature.

Scrim: A type of diffusion device that appears transparent or translucent when placed in front of a lighting instrument.

Production Note

Either metal window screening (not nylon) or a piece of fiberglass may be used as diffusion devices. Metal window screening is available at hardware stores and may be cut to size and inserted into a gel holder. The fiberglass material may be found at an auto parts store and is commonly used to repair body damage on cars with fiberglass bodies. These materials provide effective, inexpensive options to the professional items available.

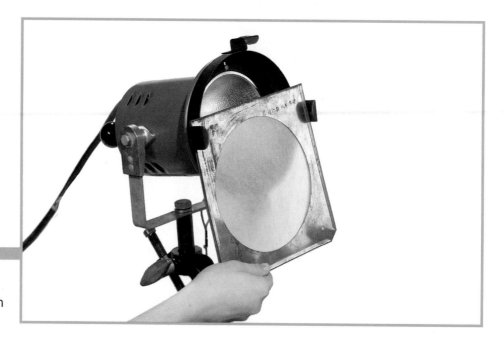

Figure 9-17
Diffusion material reduces and softens the light coming from an instrument.

Use Bounce Lighting

Bounce lighting occurs when the instrument is not directly pointed at the subject of the shot, **Figure 9-18**. Instead, the instrument is pointed at a photographic reflector or at the ceiling, a wall, or even the ground. Two things occur when lighting is bounced off another object:

- The light takes on the color of the object it was bounced off. Always bounce light off a white object.

- The light's intensity is reduced. Bouncing light off a highly reflective surface, such as a mirror, negates both of these problems.

Many videographers pack a white tablecloth or bedsheet in their equipment bag. In addition to its use as a bounce lighting aide, either comes in handy as a source for doing a white balance. For example, placing a white sheet on the ground at the talent's feet reflects light back at the face from below. This effectively fills in dark shadows created by the sunlight.

Bouncing light off a mirror or other highly reflective surface may compensate when it is not possible to place a lighting instrument in a particular spot. Hang a mirror in that spot on the set. Mirrors are very useful with cameras, as well. Remember not to have any writing in a shot when using mirrors. The text of the writing is reversed in a mirror.

Use a Dimmer

Dimming an instrument is the least desirable solution. A *dimmer* is a device attached to the power control of a lighting instrument that can reduce or increase the amount of electricity that flows through the instrument. A lamp glows because electricity flowing through it heats the filament. In television production, that filament must glow white. Using a dimmer to reduce the amount of electricity flowing through the lamp causes the light to dim and cool. A cooling lamp progressively takes on a

Bounce lighting: A lighting technique where a lighting instrument is not pointed directly at the subject of the shot, but the light is bounced off another object, such as a ceiling, wall, or the ground.

Dimmer: A device attached to the power control of a lighting instrument that can reduce or increase the amount of electricity that flows to the lamp.

Key Light Only

Bounce Lighting

Final Image

Figure 9-18
A white surface can bounce light to help fill in a dark shadowed area of the subject.

reddish, cooler tint. This is why many TV studios do not use the dimmer option available on the lighting board. The instruments are simply turned on or off.

Preserving the Life of Incandescent Lamps

Exercise extreme care to ensure that lamps last as long as possible, avoiding costly replacement. Some precautions to take with incandescent lamps include:

- Never turn them on and off in rapid succession. To get a strobe light effect, buy a strobe light. Regular studio lamps burn out in a very short time if they are flashed on and off.
- Never move incandescent instruments while the lamp is hot, whether they are on or have been recently turned off.
- Never completely close the barndoors and then turn on the lamp. The lack of ventilation can cause the lamp to burn out prematurely.
- Never touch an incandescent lamp with your fingers. Handle it by the foam it is packed in, a paper towel, or tissue paper, but never handle it with your hands, **Figure 9-19**.

> **! Safety Note**
>
> An incandescent lamp should never be handled with bare hands. No matter how clean, there is always a certain amount of oil on your skin that is transferred to the surface of the lamp. When the lamp is turned on, it reaches very high operating temperatures and boils the oil to the point of evaporation. This creates a spot on the hot glass of the lamp that is cooler than the rest of the surface. This will cause the glass to shatter.

Figure 9-19
Oils on the skin will ruin a lamp. Never touch a good lamp with your bare fingers.

Planning the Set Lighting

Before the set is built, the lighting designer meets with the program director. In this meeting, the director describes what the set looks like, provides a set diagram, and explains the movement of the talent. The director may also express his particular lighting preferences.

During set construction, the lighting designer (LD) studies the set diagram and determines the placement of lighting instruments, where they will be aimed, and their intensity levels. When the lighting decisions are final, the LD develops the *light plot*, or diagram for instrument placement, **Figure 9-20**.

Light plot: A diagram developed by the lighting designer that indicates the placement of lighting instruments on the set of a program.

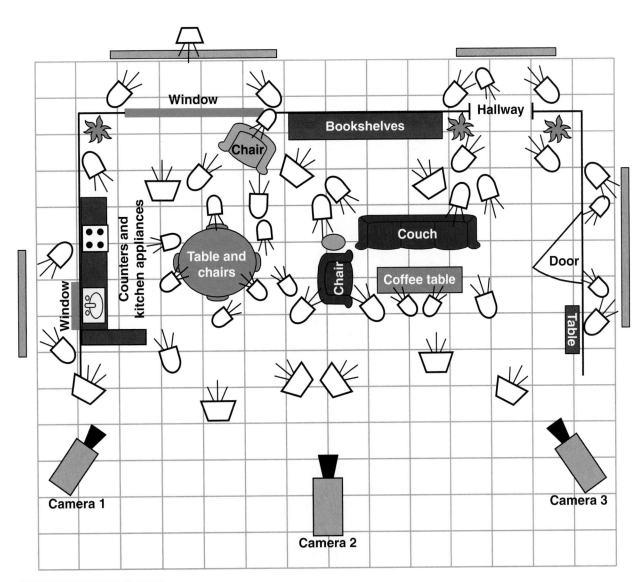

Figure 9-20
A light plot indicates the placement, brilliance, color, and aiming of the lighting instruments.

After the set is built and dressed, the LD begins to light the set. The instruments are hung over the set and plugged into the raceway. The following is a general procedure used in lighting a set:

1. The LD turns out all the lights in the studio after giving the crew sufficient warning. The set must be completely dark so the LD can see the effect of the movement and placement of each instrument.

2. The LD turns on one of the instruments. Either the LD or a gaffer climbs a ladder, puts on heavy work gloves, and manually aims and focuses the instrument on a specific area of the set. Anyone adjusting a lighting instrument while it is turned on should always wear heavy gloves to prevent fingers from being burned, **Figure 9-21**. The instruments are moved very gently when hot. If jarred sharply, the lamp may burn out.

3. Once aimed, the instrument is turned off and the next one is turned on.

4. Repeat this process as many times as necessary with each instrument.

5. When the entire light plot has been aimed and is precisely focused, all of the instruments are turned on at once. There will always be a few final adjustments before the job is complete.

Figure 9-21
Always wear protective gloves when handling hot instruments.

Production Note

Some lighting designers prefer to generally light the set, turn off all the general lighting, and then position spot lighting in specific areas where talent will be moving or standing. The general lighting is then turned back on and final adjustments can be made. Other lighting designers prefer to start with the areas specific to the talent and then set up the general lighting. Both techniques work well.

Techniques of Television Lighting

Each of the following basic lighting techniques may be used on any size production studio. Knowing the use and setup of each is crucial to creating quality shots for the program.

Three-Point Lighting

Three-point lighting is the most commonly used photographic lighting technique in television. This technique is designed to make a person look attractive and, at the same time, create the appearance of three-dimensionality on the flat, two-dimensional television screen. Three-point lighting makes use of three instruments for each person/ object being photographed, **Figure 9-22**. Each of the three instruments performs a specific function:

- Key Light
- Fill Light
- Back Light

Three point lighting: A common lighting technique that uses three lighting instruments for each person or object photographed: a key light, a fill light, and a back light.

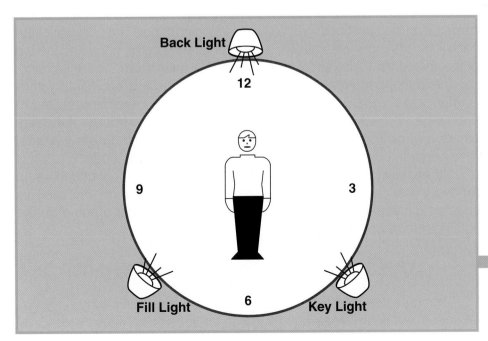

Figure 9-22
This illustration presents the general placement of instruments in a three-point lighting setup.

Key light: The lighting instrument that provides the main source of illumination on the person or object in a shot.

Fill light: The lighting instrument that is placed opposite the key light to provide illumination on the other side of the talent's face or object in the shot.

Back light: The lighting instrument placed above and behind, at the twelve o'clock position, the talent or object in a shot to separate the talent or object from the background.

Background light: A lighting instrument that is pointed at the background of a set.

Key Light

The *key light* provides the main source of illumination on the object, **Figure 9-23A**. It is usually in the front of or above the object and on an angle to the left or right. It is never placed directly above or directly in front of the object. For example, imagine the face of a clock. The key light is located at either four-thirty or five o'clock on the right side of the stage or at seven o'clock or seven-thirty on the left side.

When placing the key light, the location of the primary source of light must be considered. If lighting a living room for a scene that is supposed to take place at noon, the primary source of light would probably be the windows of the room. If the window is on the talent's right side, the key light is placed on the talent's right side to augment the light coming in from the window.

The key light is a hard light; it produces sharp shadows. If a person is lit only with the key light, the eye on the opposite side of their face is completely shadowed. There are also a heavy nose and chin shadows on the side of the face opposite the key light.

Fill Light

The *fill light* is placed opposite the key light to light the other side of the talent's face, **Figure 9-23B**. If the key light is positioned at five o'clock, for example, then the fill light is placed at seven o'clock.

The fill light is a softer light that is lower in intensity. It reduces the dark shadows created by the key light to a certain extent. If the fill light completely reduced the shadows created by the key light, it would be a second key light. This would result in a flat image on the television screen. The fill light must be of lower intensity than the key light to leave some of the shadows that create a three-dimensional appearance.

Back Light

The *back light* is placed above and behind the talent at the twelve o'clock position, **Figure 9-23C**. It must be fairly high to avoid any of the cameras on the set shooting directly into the instrument. The purpose of the back light is to provide some illumination on the top of the head and the top of the shoulders. It also serves to separate the talent from the background.

Inexperienced lighting personnel often confuse a back light with a *background light*. These two instruments are the exact opposites of each other. A background light is pointed at the background of the set, where a back light is pointed at the back of the talent. In other words, they are pointed in exact opposite directions from each other.

When using three-point lighting, there is a three-point lighting setup for every member of the cast, at every spot on the set they move. This should help explain why there are so many lighting instruments on the lighting grid of the TV studio.

Assistant Activity

The areas on a set where talent will be situated for a period of time are lit using three-point lighting. Look back to Figure 9-20. Locate the instruments configured for three-point lighting and determine where talent will most consistently be positioned on the set.

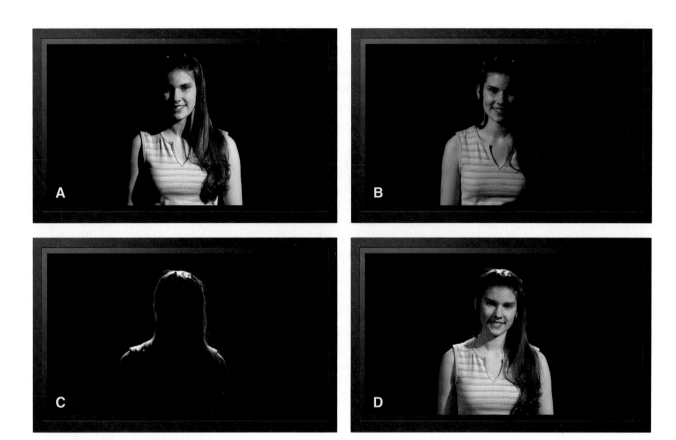

Figure 9-23
A—The key light is a hard light that supplies the primary source of illumination on an object. B—The fill light somewhat reduces the harsh shadows created by the key light. C—The back light illuminates the top of the head and shoulders. D—The proper use and placement of each of the three instruments produces a well-lit, three-dimensional subject.

Four-Point Lighting

Four-point lighting is somewhat easier to accomplish than three-point lighting. Four instruments (two key lights and two fill lights) are placed in a square around the talent, **Figure 9-24**. The two key lights

> **Four point lighting:**
> A lighting technique that uses four lighting instruments for each person or object photographed: two key lights and two fill lights. The two key lights are positioned diagonally opposite each other, and the two fill lights are placed in the remaining two corners.

Key Light   12   Fill Light

9

3

Fill Light   6   Key Light

Figure 9-24
Four-point lighting is easier to set up than three-point lighting, but requires an additional instrument.

are positioned diagonally opposite each other, and the two fill lights are placed in the other two corners. In four-point lighting, the camera can arc all the way around an object and the lighting levels remain sufficient.

An advantage of four-point lighting is that it is very easy to set up. However, this technique requires more instruments, electricity, and lamps, which results in increased cost.

Cross-Key Lighting

Cross-key lighting is a hybrid of three-point and four-point lighting, with the added ability to cover more than one person/object in the lighting spread, **Figure 9-25**. As an example, picture two people sitting in chairs on the set. Both chairs are angled slightly toward each other, but are generally facing six o'clock. In cross-key lighting, a fill light is placed directly at six o'clock. A key light is placed at four o'clock and another is placed at eight o'clock. A back light is positioned at ten o'clock and another at two o'clock. The cross-key lighting technique essentially moves the instruments away from an object. The key light nearest the person on the right is the fill light for the person on the left. The key light for the person on the left becomes the fill for the person on the right.

A few more instruments may be necessary when using cross-key lighting, but the final number of instruments is significantly lower than if using multiple three-point lighting setups. Cross-key lighting reduces energy costs, as well as the heat produced in a studio.

Cross-key lighting: A lighting technique that combines aspects of both three-point and four-point lighting, with the added ability to cover more than one person or object in the lighting spread.

Contrast Ratio

The two extremes of light are black (the absence of all light) and white (the presence of all light). Contrast ratio, as discussed in Chapter 8, *Image Display*, is the relationship of the amount of darkness to the amount of lightness in a picture. The television camera and the television set have extreme difficulty in reproducing both black and white at the same time. Therefore, large quantities of these colors are rarely seen in the same picture.

Some television studios have black curtains that surround the sides of the studio. A completely black background can be very useful. A completely white background may also be useful. If, for example, the talent is staged with a black, white, or any solid color background, the viewer considers the talent to be removed from reality. A solid colored background gives no visual clues as to where or when the action is taking place. Lighting with this kind of background is called *limbo lighting*. Limbo lighting causes the background to be a solid and indistinct color. Many car commercials are shot on a white floor with an indistinct white background. Singers often perform in front of a solid black background, **Figure 9-26**. The solid background concentrates the viewer's attention on the performance.

Limbo lighting: A lighting technique in which the background of the set is lit to create the illusion of a solid-colored, indistinct background.

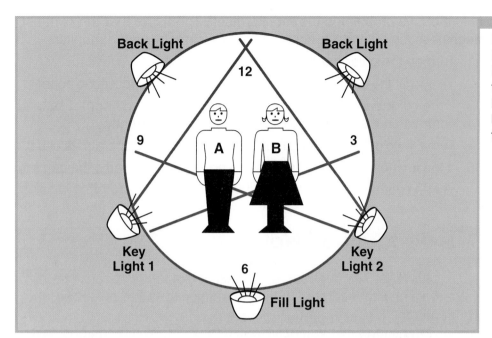

Figure 9-25
In cross-key lighting, Key Light 1 provides key lighting for person A and the fill light for person B. Key Light 2 provides key lighting for person B and the fill light for person A.

Figure 9-26
Limbo lighting is used when the talent or subject is in front of a completely indistinct background.

Lighting Check

Always check the lighting setup on a monitor with the contrast, brightness, color, and tint controls set correctly. If the shot does not look good on the monitor, stop shooting immediately. The cause of the poor image on the monitor must be determined before shooting continues. A likely culprit of this problem is the monitor itself. To ensure that the contrast, brightness, color, and tint controls are set correctly on the monitor:

1. Turn on the color bar generator in your camera.
2. Verify that the color bars are in the order they are supposed to appear.
3. If the color bars are incorrect, adjust the color, tint, brightness, and contrast on the monitor until the bars appear correctly.
4. Turn the color bar generator off and the camera will operate as usual.
5. If the images on the monitor still do not appear properly, the camera needs adjustment before shooting can continue.

Production Note

To check the contrast, brightness, color, and tint settings on a monitor with a camera that is not equipped with a color bar generator:
1. Find a tape that you have watched and know the images have good color.
2. Place the tape in the camera and play it.
3. Watch the monitor and check the colors.
4. If the colors on the monitor are incorrect, adjust the monitor settings until the colors are displayed correctly.

Adjusting any of the controls on a camera to improve the picture affects the audience's picture while watching the program. Viewers will then need to adjust the contrast, brightness, color, and tint controls on their own television sets to improve the picture. It is doubtful that you have ever needed to adjust these controls on the television at home while watching a network television program. This is because all programs adhere to industry-established standards regarding the color, tint, brightness, and contrast levels. The goal is to shoot a program in the correct lighting situation, so the viewing public can just sit back and watch your award-winning television program.

Wrapping Up

Unfortunately, many inexperienced television production personnel often consider lighting to be an afterthought. Proper lighting is extremely important. As part of an assignment, a student produced a commercial for a burglar alarm system. In the commercial, the burglar climbed into a house at night and triggered the burglar alarm. When viewing the commercial, it was difficult to miss the lack of a picture. There was only a black screen with sound. The student said that he intended the picture to be dark because it took place at night. He had very successfully produced a radio program, not a television program. Audiences have been trained to accept a slightly darker scene as "night," especially when shot with a dark blue filter on the camera. But, they will not accept a completely black screen as an artistic depiction of "night." If the viewer is unable to clearly see what the camera is shooting, they reach for the remote control and the program's effort to communicate fails.

Review Questions

Please answer the following questions on a separate sheet of paper. Do not write in this book.

1. Name the lighting instruments commonly used on a production studio set.

2. What items can be used to redirect or change the shape of light?

3. How is power supplied to the lighting instruments that hang from the studio ceiling?

4. How do different frequencies (colors) of light affect a recorded video image?

5. Explain three methods to reduce the intensity of production lighting.

6. What precautions can be taken to preserve the life of incandescent lamps?

7. List each of the instruments used in three-point lighting and explain the function of each.

8. What is limbo lighting?

Activities

1. Look around your home and identify the light created by the following instruments as either hard light or soft light:
   - The tabletop lighting instruments in your living room.
   - The instrument that illuminates your desk.
   - The lighting fixture in your bathroom.
   - The lighting instrument over your kitchen table.
   - The lighting instrument over the stove in your kitchen.
   - The instrument that generally lights your bedroom.

2. Research the experiments and discoveries of Lord Kelvin. Choose one of his accomplishments (other than the Kelvin Color Temperature Scale) and write a report on it. Be prepared to present this information in class.

Chapter 10
Studio and Remote Shooting

Objectives

After completing this chapter, you will be able to:

- Describe specific characteristics of both studio and remote shooting.
- Name the types of monitors set up in the control room and state the function of each.
- Explain the differences between the two types of remote shooting.
- List the items to be evaluated during a location survey.
- Cite advantages and challenges of both studio and remote shooting.

Introduction

Studio shooting may be the method that students most commonly associate with television production. Shooting in a studio environment may not, however, be the most effective location for every type of program. There are advantages and disadvantages to both studio shooting and shooting at a remote location. This chapter examines some of these issues in order to help you determine which is more appropriate for particular production types.

The Production Meeting

Whether the shoot takes place in a studio or at a remote location, a *production meeting* must take place before shooting can begin. During the production meeting, the director lays out the program's main message to the entire crew. The director/producer assigns each task involved in the production to members of the crew. The success of the entire project depends on the completion of each task. Responsibility and dependability are requirements of every member of the production team.

At this meeting, the director distributes a tentative production schedule. The crew members review their commitment calendars and arrange schedules to meet the production schedule, **Figure 10-1**. Flexibility is very beneficial when putting a production schedule together. Through the course of the production meeting, a rough production schedule is completed. The director takes all the notes and compiles them into one master calendar. This calendar indicates who is needed, on which day, at what time, at which location, for which scene, and what they need to bring, wear, and do when they are there. The schedule is printed and distributed to the crew. Last-minute corrections are made and the entire schedule is finalized.

Figure 10-1

The production meeting results in a production calendar that serves as the roadmap for completing the entire program.

Studio Shooting

A shoot in a studio occurs in a controlled environment where outside conditions and sounds do not affect the shooting schedule. All the necessary equipment and supplies are readily accessible and, usually, do not require any major set up. The set, lighting, and cameras are planned and positioned according to the program and production requirements.

The Studio Environment

At first glance, a studio may seem to be an intimidating space. Each feature of the studio and each piece of equipment is purposely constructed and placed to ensure a quality production, **Figure 10-2**.

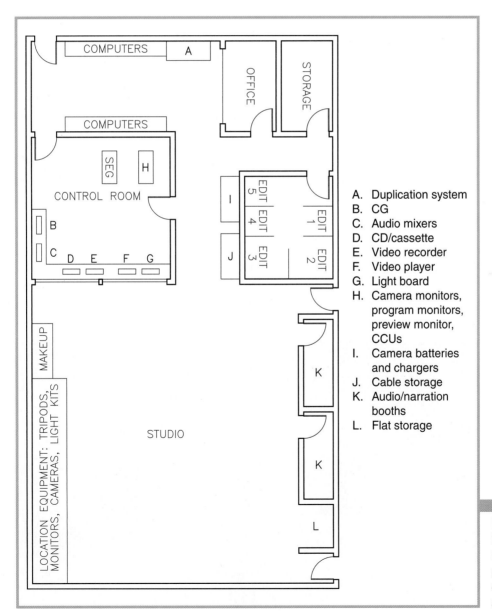

A. Duplication system
B. CG
C. Audio mixers
D. CD/cassette
E. Video recorder
F. Video player
G. Light board
H. Camera monitors, program monitors, preview monitor, CCUs
I. Camera batteries and chargers
J. Cable storage
K. Audio/narration booths
L. Flat storage

Figure 10-2
Each area of the studio is designed and organized to make the production process as efficient and effective as possible.

The Ceiling

The television production studio is usually a large room with a high ceiling. In most cases, 10′ is a *minimum* requirement. With a lower ceiling, the lighting grid hangs too low. This results in the instruments themselves appearing in shots. Additionally, if the talent walks near an instrument that is hung too low, their head glows. The heat generated by the instruments also becomes significant if the ceiling is not high enough to help the heat dissipate.

The Walls

The studio walls should be treated with any number of substances that are designed to do two things:

- Keep sound within the studio from bouncing around the room, **Figure 10-3**.
- Keep unwanted outside sounds from entering the studio.

> **! Safety Note**
>
> Local fire laws are an important consideration when deciding on sound treatment materials. The decision of the local fire marshall always prevails in a dispute over suitable materials.

Along the walls of the studio are various places to plug microphone cables into jacks, **Figure 10-4**. These jacks are hardwired to the audio console in the control room.

Curtains

The studio walls should, ideally, be covered on all four sides with a curtain. In truth, most studios curtain only two or three walls. Having all four walls curtained provides even more flexibility, **Figure 10-5**. The

Figure 10-3
The sound deadening material on the walls of the controlled studio environment prevents unwanted outside sound from entering the studio. This material also prevents sounds from echoing inside the large open space of a studio.

Figure 10-4
Studio microphones
plug into these studio
wall-mounted jacks,
which are connected to
the audio mixer in the
control room.

curtain color is entirely up to studio management. Black curtains are integral to limbo lighting, but bring down the contrast ratio in all other situations. White curtains also create a limbo effect, but invariably bring up the contrast ratio. Gray curtains of varying shades are most often used. A gray curtain should be selected to match a shade in the middle of the gray scale. (See figure 8-5 in Chapter 8, *Image Display*.) Cobalt blue or emerald green curtains are also sometimes used. Some studios have curtains of varying colors hanging from multiple tracks in the ceiling. This arrangement provides maximum flexibility.

Figure 10-5
The studio curtain can
be pulled tight or left
loose to hang in folds.

Production Note

Never touch the front of a studio curtain with bare hands. Oil from the skin transfers to the curtain and attracts dirt. If a curtain must be grabbed to pull along a track, it should only be grasped from the back side. Studio curtains are quite expensive. Avoid puncturing, snagging, or ripping the cloth. The repair bill may be as staggering as the cost of a complete replacement.

The Floor

The studio floor should be as even as possible to allow studio cameras to smoothly move across in dolly, truck, and arc movements. The floors should be maintained without using a high-gloss polish or wax. Maintaining a nonreflective floor surface is critical in the effort to control the lighting in the studio. A highly reflective floor bounces light all over the set.

Scenery Units

Flat: A scenery unit that is usually a simple wood frame with a painted plywood shell.

The scenery unit most commonly used on a television studio is called a *flat*. A flat is usually a 4′ × 8′ frame constructed with 2″ × 4″ or 1″ × 3″ boards and braced in the center. 4′ × 8′ sheets of plywood are attached to the skeleton. Flats are found in almost any theater department. These flats may be placed beside each other and painted to

Figure 10-6
A flat rack allows scenery flats to be stored like books in a bookcase.

create the appearance of a wall. The joint space between the units can be concealed, before painting, with either masking tape or drywall tape. Storage for scenery units and other props should be located near the studio floor, **Figure 10-6**.

Cameras

A studio has several cameras permanently located within the room. Any camera that is part of a studio system should be kept in the studio environment at all times. Ideally, studio cameras should be identical in brand, model, and age. When cutting between camera shots, there is little to no variation in color balance or video signal quality when extremely similar cameras are used within the studio.

The Control Room

The *control room* contains several monitors and the special effects generator, **Figure 10-7**. In smaller facilities, the control room also houses the audio mixer, all of the sound equipment, video recorders, the CG, CCUs, and even the light board. The director is stationed in the control room during a shoot and communicates with the control room and studio production teams via headsets. A very noticeable aspect of a control room is the number of television monitors in the dimly lit room. The director is positioned at or near the special effects generator and faces the wall of monitors.

Control room: A room in the studio containing several monitors and the special effects generator. In smaller facilities, the control room also houses the audio mixer, all of the sound equipment, video recorders, the CG, CCUs, and even the light board.

Figure 10-7
A control room is the location of the major equipment used to process a studio shoot.

Camera monitor: A monitor that displays the image shot by the corresponding camera.

Program monitor: A monitor that displays the image going to the recorder.

Preview monitor: A monitor that allows the director to set up an effect on the SEG before the audience sees it.

Confidence monitor: A monitor connected to the output of the VCR. Seeing the image on this monitor ensures that the video recorder received the signal.

The control room contains at least one monitor for each camera in the studio, **Figure 10-8**. Each monitor displays the image that its corresponding camera is shooting. Therefore, a three-camera studio has one *camera monitor* for Camera 1, another for Camera 2, and a third for Camera 3. A *program monitor* displays the image going to the recorder. There may also be a *preview monitor*, which allows the director to set up an effect before the audience sees it. A *confidence monitor* is connected to the output of the VCR. Seeing the image on the confidence monitor ensures that the video recorder received the signal. However, the confidence monitor is not an indicator that the image was actually recorded. Playback is the only sure way to know that the signal was recorded. Since the CG is located in the control room, there may also be a corresponding CG monitor in the grouping.

Production Note

Even though the director is stationed in the control room, headsets are still used to communicate with the control room staff. There are several sources of background noise in the control room: audio of the program, chatter of control room staff and observers, and commands being relayed from the studio floor to the control room. The headphones used have multiple channels. Everyone wears headphones to filter the noise and hear only the information that applies to them.

Audio booth: A room in the studio that contains all of the equipment capable of adding sound to the program.

Audio console: A console that includes many different pieces of audio gear, including the microphone mixer, audio cassette players, CD players, and turntables.

The Audio Booth

In smaller production facilities, the control room and audio booth are combined into one large control room. In larger facilities, the *audio booth* is a separate room that contains the *audio console*. This console includes many different pieces of audio gear, including the microphone mixer, audio cassette players, CD players, and turntables. Any equipment capable of adding sound to the program is located in the audio booth, **Figure 10-9**.

Master control room: A room in a production facility where all the hardware is located, including video recorders and other equipment needed to improve and process the video and audio signals.

Master Control Room

The *master control room* is where all the hardware is located. The video recorders and other equipment needed to improve and process the video and audio signals are housed in the master control room. In larger facilities, the master control room is not located near the control room. This equipment is usually placed in a separate room because it creates a fair amount of noise and heat. In smaller studio facilities, the control room, audio booth, and master control are combined into one large control room.

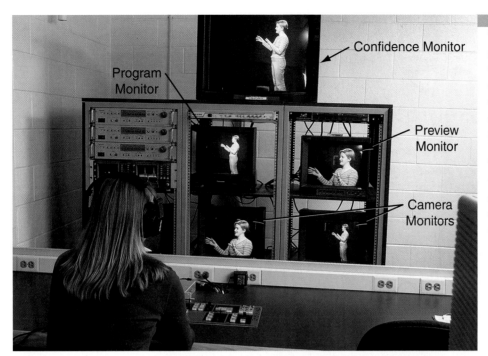

Figure 10-8
The director calls the shots for the program by watching the individual camera monitors. The camera monitors are on the bottom row, with program and preview monitors above them. The final output going to videotape is displayed on the large top monitor, called a "confidence monitor."

Figure 10-9
The audio console includes the audio mixer(s), amplifier, CD players, and audio cassette decks.

Specialized Areas

Studio facilities usually have a carpentry shop—an area where the sets can be built and painted. Dressing rooms and make-up areas are located near the studio. The requisite number of offices and conference rooms are also part of the facility. *Editing suites* are cubicles or small rooms where the program is put through post-production processing, **Figure 10-10**. Post-production processes performed in editing suites

Editing suite: A cubicle or small room where the program is put through post-production processing, such as video and audio editing, voice-over, music and sound effects recording, and graphics recording.

include: video and audio editing, voice-over, music and sound effects recording, and graphics recording. Individual studios may have many other types of specialized rooms or areas on the premises.

Remote Shooting

Remote shoot: Any production shooting that takes place outside of the studio.

A *remote shoot* is any shoot that takes place outside of the studio. A remote shoot has its own set of features and details, just like the studio shoot.

Types of Remote Shoots

Remote shoots are divided into two categories:

- Electronic News Gathering (ENG)
- Electronic Field Production (EFP)

Electronic news gathering (ENG): The process of shooting information, events, or activity that would have happened whether a reporting/production team was there with a camera or not.

ENG

Electronic news gathering (ENG) is the process of shooting information, events, or activity that would have happened whether a reporting/production team was there with a camera or not. For example, a major car crash on the local freeway covered by a news crew is ENG.

Figure 10-10
An editing suite is a cubicle or small room where the program material is put through postproduction processing.

The crew arrived fifteen minutes after the crash and, obviously, did not shoot the crash itself. The crash cannot be staged again to be captured on tape. If a news crew arrives 30 minutes late for a parade, the parade officials will not back everyone up and start again. In the ENG environment, the camera is an observer of an event that would happen whether the camera is there or not. There is no possibility for a second take. Another unique characteristic of ENG is that only two crew members are necessary for a shoot—a reporter and a camera operator.

EFP

Electronic field production (EFP) is the opposite of ENG. In EFP, the video crew and production staff are in total control of the event. If the director is not satisfied with the way the cars crashed in a particular scene, additional cars can be acquired and the stunt drivers can redo the scene. Depending on the scope and details of the scene, restaging it may not be financially feasible. Purchasing an additional building, for example, to rig with explosives and demolish is not likely to be within budget constraints. In EFP, however, the director often calls for an additional take.

EFP is much more expensive than ENG, but it is also dramatically more effective. Where ENG offers only a single viewpoint of an event, scenes in EFP may be reshot until the director is satisfied and several camera angles can be acquired. All the footage is edited together to create a scene that draws the attention and interest of the audience. In EFP, extra expense is allotted to performers, technicians, producers, directors, staff members, and all other production members. If the director calls a "Take 2," everyone must be paid for their additional time and services.

Electronic field production (EFP): A shoot in which the video crew and production staff are in total control of the events and action.

Location: Any place, other than the studio, where production shooting is planned.

Location survey: An assessment of a proposed shoot location that includes placement of cameras and lights, available power supply, equipment necessary, and accommodations needed for the talent and crew.

The Location Survey

A *location* is any place, other than the studio, where production shooting is planned. Anytime the shoot takes place on location, a *location survey* is required before the shoot date, **Figure 10-11**. The day of the shoot is too late to complete a location survey.

To avoid a trespassing charge, the first order of business must be getting the property owner's permission to shoot on the selected location. If ownership is unknown, refer to the appropriate real estate records. These are usually a matter of public record.

Location Survey Check List

☑ Permission from property owner.

☑ Availability of electrical power supply.

☑ Placement of cameras.

☑ Placement of lighting instruments.

☑ Note the natural sunlight present at the location.

☑ Note noises that are part of the environment during various times of the day.

☑ Availability of necessary facilities.

☑ Equipment necessary for the shoot.

☑ The number of crew members necessary on location.

Figure 10-11
Important items to consider when performing a location survey.

After securing permission to be on the property, go to the location and determine the placement/positioning of cameras, lights, and other equipment. Always be mindful of electrical power supply issues. If using electricity, the owner must grant permission to plug into the property's outlets.

Consider the lighting situations at that location. Keep in mind the position of the sun during each part of the day. Assess how the sunlight will affect the shooting schedule. The production equipment cannot be set up to shoot into the sun, but if the sun is directly at the operator's back, the talent will squint at the camera.

Make a point to perform the location survey on the same day of the week and time of day that the shoot is scheduled. Note the various noises that are part of the environment, such as traffic and low-flying aircraft.

Other considerations for a location include:

● Are necessary facilities, like rest rooms, water, and food, readily available?

● Where will the electrical, camera and audio cables be run?

● What kinds of microphones are needed?

● How much cable is necessary?

● How many crew members are necessary for the production on location?

Comparing Studio and Remote Shooting

Both studio and remote shooting are effective in gathering footage for a program. The type of program being produced is a large factor in deciding whether studio or remote shooting should be used. In addition, the specific advantages and disadvantages associated with both studio and remote shooting must be considered.

Advantages of the Studio Shoot

● Arrangements for on-site transportation, food, and lodging are not necessary.

● The forces of nature rarely affect the inside of a studio; it never rains in a TV studio.

● All equipment and supplies are easily accessible. If, for example, a cable goes bad, it is readily replaced with back stock.

● Major set up of equipment is usually not required. Equipment is already wired into a full system, including a switcher/special effects generator.

- Control of the people within the studio environment; a person mistakenly walking through the background of a shot is not a concern.
- Precise control of the lighting situation; the sun does not cast shadows that move as time passes inside a studio.
- Extraneous sounds do not enter the studio to interrupt the shooting schedule.
- Proper use of the video switcher greatly reduces editing time—the program is essentially edited while being shot.

Disadvantages of the Studio Shoot

- Building a set can be expensive and time consuming.
- The ambient sound of "the great outdoors" is difficult to recreate in a sound-treated studio.
- Recreating an outdoor feeling in the studio presents serious lighting concerns. As the sun moves during the course of the day, the shadows it casts also move.
- The equipment necessary for a full-scale studio production is extensive and expensive. This is primarily because the video equipment must be linked together with the signal from each matched to the others.
- A shoot in the studio usually requires more personnel than a remote shoot. In addition to the talent and the director, the minimum staff required for a studio shoot includes: up to three camera operators, a floor manager, an audio engineer, video engineer, technical director, and lighting director, **Figure 10-12**.

Figure 10-12
Many technical team members are necessary for a studio shoot.

Advantages of a Remote Shoot

● In most cases, it is not necessary to build a set. The location is usually chosen because the set already exists.

● Natural light can often be used.

● Everything about an existing set is realistic. This supports the illusion of reality created in the program.

● A remote shoot usually requires less equipment overall than a studio shoot.

● A remote shoot usually involves fewer crew members.

Disadvantages of a Remote Shoot

● Murphy's Law, "If anything can go wrong, it will," is a constant threat in location shooting.

● Inevitably, something goes wrong with the equipment. Therefore, plan for that eventuality. Bring spares of everything, extra cables, adapters, etc., if possible.

● Inclement weather may completely halt production, **Figure 10-13**. Pay attention to weather forecasts and always have an alternate plan.

Figure 10-13
An unexpected change in the weather can make a selected location unusable and cause a remote shoot to be cancelled.

- In a remote interior location, power supply for equipment and lights may be insufficient. Always check for circuit limitations.

- Permission from the property owner must be granted before setting foot on the location selected for the shoot.

- If something breaks or is forgotten at the studio, there is significant downtime while someone travels back to get it.

- The terrain is often not suitable for simple dollying, trucking, or arcing. Special track must be installed to perform these camera moves.

- All equipment must be transported to and from the location and must be repeatedly set up and torn down. This increases wear and tear on the equipment and, in turn, contributes to equipment failure.

- In order to get varying camera angles, a single camera must shoot each scene several times from different angles. This also requires numerous hours in the editing room, cutting together a cohesive and interesting program.

Wrapping Up

When deciding whether to shoot in the studio or on a remote location, carefully consider the program type and the benefits and risks that each environment presents. A remote location offers the excitement of the real world. The studio offers a stable and controlled production environment. Programs in a studio can usually be produced in much less time than those shot remotely. A studio shoot utilizes the camera switcher, which can save hours in the editing room. On location, a single camera must shoot something multiple times to get various angles. Each option must be weighed carefully before deciding to shoot in the studio or on a remote location.

Review Questions

Please answer the following questions on a separate sheet of paper. Do not write in this book.

1. What topics are addressed in the production meeting?
2. Explain the special features of studio walls.
3. Name each of the television monitors found in the control room and state the function of each.
4. What do the letters "ENG" stand for? What does the term mean?
5. What are the unique characteristics of EFP?
6. List the items that should be evaluated during a location survey.
7. What are the disadvantages of a studio shoot?
8. What are the advantages of a remote shoot?

Activities

1. Research the fire laws and regulations in your area. List all that are applicable to the construction and use of a television production set.
2. Perform a location survey for shooting an interview. For this activity, assume that the interview is with someone you know and will be shot at their place of work.

Important Terms

Crab Dolly
Film-Style Shooting
Multi-Camera Shooting
Nickel Cadmium (NiCad)
Single-Camera Shooting
Windscreen

Objectives

After completing this chapter, you will be able to:

● Explain the options available to solve lighting problems when shooting outdoors.

● List general safety precautions related to the handling of cameras and batteries.

● Define both of the remote shooting techniques.

Introduction

Shooting outside of the studio was almost unheard of in the early days of television. The size and weight of the equipment, cabling, and power requirements prevented remote shooting. Any remote work was done on film and transferred to videotape once back at the studio. For many years, all news footage was shot on film and transferred to tape. The disadvantage of using film, especially for news, is the considerable time needed to develop and print film, before it could be transferred to tape and used on a newscast. This process did not make it possible to immediately release a story to the public.

Remote shooting is actually the majority of production work done today by many television production facilities. Much of the location footage seen on television today is now shot on videotape. A few network television dramas still use film, but the number is steadily declining because of changes in technology.

Television technology is progressing rapidly. Bulky cameras attached to large recorders have given way to relatively small, self-contained camcorders. The most sophisticated camcorders are now being replaced by very small cameras that have built-in transmitters to send a radio signal to the recorder, **Figure 11-1**. The footage from political convention floors is recorded using cameras with transmitters. Cameras on a convention center floor cannot trail cables through the crowds, causing tripping hazards along their path. Even more sophisticated examples of this technology are the cameras built into headgear, such as football helmets, and even smaller units that can be placed into the frame of eyeglasses, **Figure 11-2**.

Camera Mounts

Extensive camera movement is not usually seen in many of the programs shot on location. Dolly shots are more realistic than a zoom, but the camera movement required with a dolly on location is very difficult to accomplish. On location, the ground is usually not smooth and level. While using a dolly is possible, both a larger budget and additional equipment are necessary.

Transmitter

Figure 11-1

A camcorder may be equipped with a small transmitter that sends the video signal to the receiver without using wires.

Figure 11-2
Current technology has produced tiny camera devices that were once depicted as "futuristic" equipment in science fiction films.

Several companies manufacture a type of track, similar to railroad track, that is relatively lightweight and portable. Once the track is assembled, a four-wheeled cart, called a ***crab dolly***, is set in place. The camera, along with the operator in some cases, is placed on the crab dolly to capture the movement shots, **Figure 11-3**. The crab dolly may be pushed or pulled along the track by a grip. The advantage of

Crab dolly: A four-wheeled cart that travels on a lightweight track and enables the camera to smoothly capture movement shots while being pushed or pulled along the track.

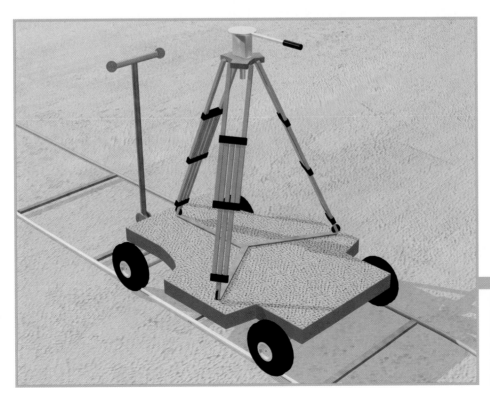

Figure 11-3
On a location shoot, using a crab dolly on its track makes smooth dolly and truck movements possible on uneven terrain.

this track system is that smooth dolly, truck, and arc movements may be accomplished in the field. The disadvantages of the track system, unfortunately, drive up the costs of a remote shoot. They include:

- The time consumed by constructing and leveling the track and cart.
- The cost of the equipment.
- The additional personnel needed to assemble and operate the track system.
- The movement of the camera is restricted to the path of the track. If a shot is changed, production is delayed to reposition the track.

Since the development of camera stabilization systems, **Figure 11-4**, a decreasing number of location shoots require the track system. A camera stabilization system can be rented or purchased. In either case, a trained operator must be hired.

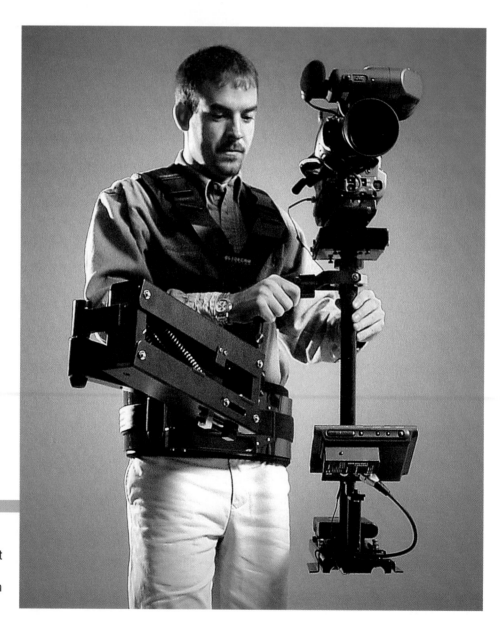

Figure 11-4
The Glidecam is a body mounted camera stabilization system that facilitates very smooth camerawork. (Glidecam Industries, Inc.)

Production Note

A camera stabilization system is an expensive investment for any production studio, let alone for a classroom. It is not likely that this type of equipment will be readily available while learning the processes of television production, or even when initially entering the industry. Remote shooting must be accomplished using either tripod-mounted cameras or hand-held cameras. With time and experience, you may come to work for a company that utilizes the track system or a stabilization system. The experience gained by that time will help in tackling the special challenges each system presents.

Lighting for a Remote Shoot

Lighting is always a serious issue for remote shooting. If something is not sufficiently lit in the studio, additional instruments are added and aimed. This is not the case at a remote location. Shooting inside someone's home, for example, does not afford the luxury of unlimited power supply, ventilation, ceiling height, or a convenient grid and raceway. Any windows in the home provide additional challenges.

As an example, consider that a shoot is scheduled in the living room of a house for 1:00 p.m. through 4:00 p.m. The lamps in the living room cannot be used because they are not the correct color temperature and will produce an orange tint. The crew must bring white (32K) lights. The windows in the living room let in sunlight, which casts blue light on the shot even with the additional lighting instruments. Solutions to these lighting problems include:

- Change the color of the sunlight by attaching a gel (85N6 or 85N9) to the inside of the window. This removes the excess color temperature, so that the light coming through the window is essentially white on the inside of the room. The camera can then be white balanced.

- Place gels on the additional lighting instruments to bring the color temperature up to match the sunlight. Then white balance the camera.

- Cover the window with a light-blocking object, such as a black or blue plastic tarp, available at any hardware store. Close the curtains on the window to create a neat appearance. Turn on the TV lighting instruments and white balance the camera.

- Shoot at night. At night, however, any exposed window turns into a mirror unless covered. Turn on the TV lighting instruments and white balance the camera.

In smaller budget productions, the last two options are most often used. Any lights brought to the location must have mounts, such as a light stand or large spring-loaded clips that attach to a door, bookcase, or table.

Audio

On remote indoor shoots, microphones must be placed very close to the talent. Lapel mics, mics on booms, or mics hidden on the set are ideal. If the mics are too far away or are attached to the camera itself, the talent sounds as if they are speaking from the bottom of a well.

When shooting outside, using the wrong type of mic or incorrectly placing a mic may cause the audio of the environment to completely overpower the talent. If the talent is standing in a forest, for example, the birds chirping may be louder on the tape than the talent's voice. When shooting outside, a lapel mic is the best option if a directional boom mic is not used.

Production Note

Always check the audio levels on the recorder to ensure that the mic signal is being picked up at an appropriate level. For analog, the reading should fall between −3 and +3. For digital systems, the audio level should be approximately −20.

Windscreen: A covering, usually foam, placed over a mic to reduce the rumble or flapping sound created when wind blows across the mic.

When shooting outdoors, the wind creates another obstacle. Using a *windscreen* is an effective solution. A windscreen is a covering, usually foam or furry fabric, placed over the mic. See **Figure 11-5**. It reduces the rumble or flapping sound created when wind blows across the mic. The size of the windscreen is directly related to the amount of wind in

Figure 11-5
A windscreen completely surrounds the microphone and is designed to lessen or eliminate the sound of air blowing across the mic.

the environment. A news reporter standing outside during a hurricane uses a more substantial windscreen than the reporter in the middle of a field on an average spring day.

Production Note

Do not confuse a windscreen with a mic mouse. The mic mouse sits on a hard surface, like a floor or table, and accentuates the pick-up pattern of a hand-held mic.

Power

Plan for power sources when shooting on location. The electrical circuits in most homes are either 15 or 20 amps. Plugging too many lighting instruments into one circuit may trip the circuit breaker or blow a fuse in the house. Electrical professionals use a technical, complex formula to determine the amount of amps a lighting instrument draws. A simplified formula is not as accurate, but works very well for television production purposes, **Figure 11-6**. This formula is safe because it always overestimates the amount of power drawn by an instrument. To use the formula:

- Check the wattage of the lamp to be used. For this example, assume the lamp is 650 watts.
- Divide the wattage value by 100 (move the decimal point two places to the left). The result is 6.50 amps.

This means that three 6.50 amp instruments may be connected on a 20 amp circuit. According to the formula, all three combined draw 19.5 amps. In actuality, slightly fewer amps are drawn. The formula provides a safety margin.

Converting Watts to Amps for

Location Shooting

Watts = 650

Move decimal two places to left:

Amps = 6.5

Figure 11-6
This simple conversion provides a safe over-estimation of the power requirements.

Batteries

Plugging a cord into the wall outlet is the most convenient power option. However, remote shooting does not often involve conveniently placed wall outlets. Therefore, the videographer must rely on battery power. There are many different types of batteries used for cameras. The most common type is a *Nickel Cadmium* battery, usually called a *NiCad*. These are rechargeable, but may take as long to recharge as they take to discharge. Buying a charger with two sets of batteries allows the camera to run uninterrupted. The operator must remember to change batteries when one begins to get low on power. Lithium Ion (Li-ion) and Nickel Metal Hydride (NiMH) batteries are becoming more popular and are also rechargeable, **Figure 11-7**.

Nickel Cadmium (NiCad): A type of rechargeable battery commonly used to power cameras.

General Cautions

- Do not drop batteries. The cells inside can break, severely reducing the life of the battery.
- Batteries discharge very quickly in the cold.
- Do not completely discharge batteries. Always leave a small amount of power in the battery before removing it and placing it on the charger. Pay strict attention to battery level indicators on the battery or in the viewfinder of the camera.
- Most professional batteries perform better if they are placed on the plugged-in charger whenever they are not in use.
- Do not *ever* leave batteries in the trunk or on the seat of a car parked in the hot sun. *Batteries can rupture when heated.*

Figure 11-7
All the various types of rechargeable batteries available must be handled with care.

Production Note

Always carefully check the charging instructions provided with any type of battery. While most professional batteries should be placed on a charger when not in use, this does not apply to *all* professional, prosumer, and consumer grade batteries. Some types of batteries may actually be damaged if they are continuously left on the charger.

Cold Temperatures and Batteries

Because batteries discharge so quickly in the cold, precautions should be taken to keep the batteries warm. Some solutions that are effective when on location include:

- Wear a belt with your pants and a shirt that is tucked in. Place the batteries inside the shirt, next to your skin. Your body temperature keeps the batteries warm.
- Wrap the camera in a blanket to keep the cold out of it for as long as possible.
- Take frequent breaks inside a warm environment to help prolong the life of the battery.

Condensation

Circuit boards inside cameras, recorders, and camcorders are so minute that even a single drop of moisture can short them out. That short causes the equipment to require servicing before it can be used again. Condensation is a problem because many of the internal components of the equipment are metal and portable equipment is exposed to a wide variety of environments. Remote shooting environments have a wide range of humidity and temperature levels. When equipment is stored in a cool air-conditioned environment and is then taken outside into humid summer weather, condensation forms on the inner components and on the camera lens. If shooting is planned in these kinds of conditions, the camera should be powered off and placed in the environment an hour or more before it is needed. This allows the equipment to acclimate to the humidity and temperature levels. Condensation still forms inside the camera, but evaporates as the camera warms to the temperature of the environment.

Most cameras and camcorders have a special circuit that senses condensation before it shorts out the equipment. This sensor overrides the power switch and shuts the power off completely. W hen this happens, many people panic thinking that the camera just stopped working for no apparent reason. The equipment is not operable again until the condensation evaporates. When attempting to turn the equipment back on after this override, the phrase "Dew," "Auto Shut-Off," or

"Self-Protect Mode" is momentarily displayed in the camera's viewfinder, **Figure 11-8**. This may cause further confusion because the camera may appear to be working again, but then shuts down. If this happens, do not be alarmed. This is the way the camera protects itself against the condensation inside.

To speed up evaporation:

1. Turn the camcorder on.
2. Press the "Eject Tape" button. The door opens and the camera, once again, turns itself off.
3. Use a blow dryer set on "cool" to blow air into the open panel, **Figure 11-9**.

Condensation can also form on the lens. Like the mirror in a steamy bathroom, wiping the lens with lens paper does not prevent the condensation from reforming. The moisture must evaporate and leave the affected area. As the lens acclimates to the temperature of a room, the moisture will evaporate. Once the moisture has completely evaporated, the lens may be used again.

Remote Shooting Techniques

There are two methods used when shooting on location:

● Multi-Camera Shooting
● Single-Camera Shooting

Figure 11-8
When this message is displayed in the view-finder, condensation has developed inside the camera body. Once the moisture evaporates, the camera will operate normally.

Figure 11-9
A blow dryer may be used to circulate cool air into the camcorder body to speed up evaporation.

Multi-Camera Shooting

Multi-camera shooting is exactly what its name implies—shooting with multiple cameras. This is accomplished in one of two ways:

- A separate recorder is used for each camera while shooting. A scene is shot from different positions and angles by several cameras at the same time. A multi-camera appearance can then be created in the editing room during post-production. This technique requires less shooting time than other options, but greatly increases the amount of time spent in the editing room. Using this kind of shooting is dependent on the production budget and the time performers are available, compared to the time available for work in the editing room. Extra personnel and equipment are also necessary to have multiple cameras running at the same time.

- Another form of multi-camera shooting is accomplished by using a truck that provides a mobile control room, **Figure 11-10**. Even though the crew parks the truck as close as possible to the shoot location, hundreds of feet of cable are run to the cameras shooting on location. When a network covers a professional football game, for example, the truck is parked outside the stadium and the cameras are located inside the stadium. The director and, often, the announcers are outside in the truck. In this case, the game pictured behind the announcers is a simple chromakey background wall.

Multi-camera shooting: A technique of remote shooting where multiple cameras are used.

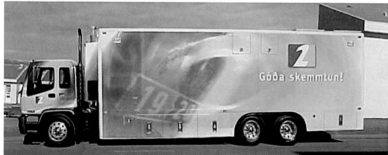

Figure 11-10
The mobile truck is essentially a control room on wheels.

Single-Camera Shooting

Single-camera shooting: A technique of remote shooting that involves only one camera and is most often used for event recording.

Single-camera shooting involves only one camera and is the least difficult type of shooting, **Figure 11-11**. The only setup required is to set the camera on a tripod, turn it on, and cue the performer(s). After the scene is over, the camera can be moved, set up again, and turned on to capture another scene. This type of shooting is not suitable for entertainment television programs, because it is not interesting and does not keep the audience's attention. On prime-time television programs, the average camera shot lasts seven seconds. Unless the picture on the screen is extremely compelling in action or dialog, the audience tends to look away when shots last longer than seven seconds.

Figure 11-11
Single-camera shooting is easy to set up, but results in uninteresting images.

Single-camera shooting is most often used for event recording. A videographer of this type is usually hired by a client to shoot a concert, play, speech, or wedding. The client is not interested in what is normally considered entertainment television, with many cuts and effects. They merely want an event recorded as it happens, without all the production aspects of entertainment television.

Film-Style Shooting

Film-style shooting is a unique subcategory of single-camera shooting. In film-style shooting, only one camera is used and it is moved very frequently. While there are many methods to this style of shooting, the following example is one procedure for using film-style shooting.

1. A master shot is recorded of the entire scene. The master shot is a relatively long shot of all the action in a scene.

2. After the master shot is completed, the entire scene is shot several more times from different positions and camera angles.

3. Certain smaller segments of the scene are then restaged to get specific close-ups of key actions.

4. Cutaways are then shot, but may also be shot before the entire process starts. See Chapter 13, *Production Staging and Interacting with Talent* for more information on cutaways.

Each of the different shots recorded in film-style shooting are edited together, and the finished scene looks as if it was originally shot with many cameras. The finished product is far more interesting than a single-camera, single-shot production, because the cut rate is much higher. The disadvantage of film-style shooting is having the talent perform each take of the scene with the exact same action and dialog. Without this exact repetition, the program cannot be edited together properly. Also, the editing process of film-style shooting is considerably more complex.

Film-style shooting: A type of single-camera shooting in which a scene is shot many times with the camera moving to a different position each time to capture the scene from various angles. The finished scene is edited together to look like it was shot with several cameras.

Wrapping Up

Remote shooting is very enticing because it eliminates the need to construct a set. On the other hand, remote shoots have their own collection of quirks. The real key to successful television production is extensive and detailed pre-production planning, in conjunction with strategy and planning throughout the process.

Review Questions

Please answer the following questions on a separate sheet of paper. Do not write in this book.

1. What is a crab dolly? When is it most often used?
2. What are the challenges of planning the audio for a location shoot?
3. What is the formula presented to estimate the power requirements of an instrument? Why is this imprecise formula safe to use?
4. List three precautions that apply to the use and care of camera batteries.
5. What is the built-in safety feature that protects a camera from condensation?
6. How are the various camera angles captured when using film-style shooting?

Activities

1. Visit an electronics or other specialty equipment store and locate the rechargeable batteries section of the store. Review the recharging instructions on several types and brands of batteries. Note the cautions on each package and the differences in the directions provided.
2. Research the various camera stabilization systems available. Make a spreadsheet comparing the features and prices of several systems.

Important Terms

Cyclorama (Cyc)
Moiré
Props
Set Decorator
Set Design
Set Dresser
Set Dressing

Objectives

After completing this chapter, you will be able to:

- Identify factors to be considered when selecting furniture for a production.

- Describe how an item that appears to be set dressing becomes a prop.

- Explain how the pattern on various set materials affects the video image.

Set Dressing: All the visual and design elements on a set, such as rugs, lamps, wall coverings, curtains, and room accent accessories.

Set Dresser: The person responsible for selecting the furniture, wall and window coverings, accent accessories, and all the other design elements that complete a program's set. Also called a *set decorator*.

Introduction

An interior decorator working in a house selects the furniture, wall treatments, curtains and drapes, accent accessories, and many other design and visual elements to make the rooms appealing and to meet the needs of the homeowner. In the television industry, all of the design and visual elements chosen for a set are considered **set dressing**. The **set dresser**, or **set decorator**, is responsible for selecting the furniture, wall and window coverings, accent accessories, and all the other design elements that complete a program's set. In making these decisions, the set dresser must consider the contrast ratio (see Chapter 8, *Image Display*) of the items chosen, as well as accurately create the director's vision of the set. This chapter discusses the various design and visual elements of set design and presents related techniques and professional tips.

Creating the Set Design

Set Design: A scale drawing of the set, as viewed from above, that illustrates the location of furniture, walls, doors, and windows.

The **set design** is a sketch of the set, as viewed from above, drawn to scale, **Figure 12-1**. The set designer lays out the location of walls, doors, and windows on the set. Then, the set dresser adds the location of furniture and larger decorator items. The director uses the design when rehearsing the program with the actors and talent while the set is under construction. The set design notes the location of major pieces on the set, but does not necessarily indicate the placement of accent and decorative items.

Production Note

To help the performers get accustomed to the amount of space available once the set is completed, the set design is used to mark the floor of the rehearsal space. Regular masking tape is commonly used to indicate where the walls and doors will be located on the finished set. Masking tape is quite inexpensive and readily available, but it leaves a sticky residue on the floor if left in place for very long. Set marking tape, or spiking tape, is brightly colored, leaves no sticky residue, and is available from any theatrical supply company.

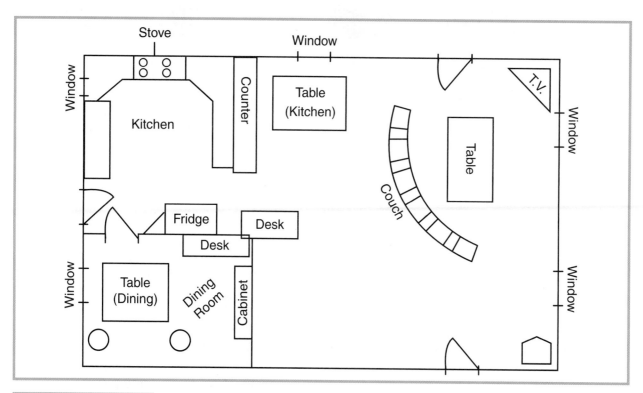

Figure 12-1

A set design resembles the floor plan of a model home.

Furniture

When selecting furniture for a set, consider that the talent should be able to get into and out of furniture gracefully. The furniture needs to be solid and firm and the seat cannot be lower than the talent's knees, **Figure 12-2**. If the chair is too low, the talent must either bounce out of the seat or roll out on one side or the other. The problem is that the center of gravity is not correct and does not allow a fluid movement into and out of the chair or sofa.

Talent is forced to slouch when sitting naturally in a low chair. Slouching is not only unattractive, but the talent's diaphragm is compressed. This makes it very difficult, if not impossible, to clearly

Figure 12-2

A chair that places the talent's midsection lower than their knees looks very unattractive and poses a problem in gracefully rising from the chair.

project his or her voice. Also, the talent's eyes are positioned lower than the camera lens when seated in a low chair. This forces a high angle camera shot, looking down on the talent.

Never use chairs that swivel or rock on a set. The talent has a tendency to swivel back and forth or to rock. Talent moving in this manner creates a shot that is unpleasant to the audience. Chairs that swivel or rock also tend to squeak, which is a distracting, unintentional sound in a scene.

Be aware of any shiny surfaces, such as chrome or brass fittings, on furniture and other items on the set. Shiny surfaces may cause unattractive or distracting light hits, **Figure 12-3**. These reflections are very distracting to the audience and interrupt the viewer's attention from the message of the program.

Some solutions to keep reflections off shiny surfaces include:

- Lightly apply crème makeup on the surface to dull the shine.
- Spray the area with hair spray.
- Apply dulling spray, which is available at any good camera shop.

Figure 12-3
The shiny chrome arms on this chair will produce distracting light hits. Adding dulling spray, or another treatment, reduces or eliminates this problem. Another issue is that this is a swivel chair. The talent is likely to swivel back and forth while seated, which is distracting the viewers.

Visualize This

While light hits are usually considered to be negative program attributes, they can also be used artistically within a program. Hundreds of light hits are produced if, for example, you shoot the surface of a lake under bright sunlight. These light hits create the appearance of a sparkling clear, inviting body of water. When multiple light hits are a desired effect, a *star filter* may be attached to the front of a camera lens to cause each light hit to become a star, rather than simply bright, white spots. A star filter was employed for Figure 12-3.

Placement

In most homes, it is very common to see the furniture that people sit on (sofas, loveseats, and chairs) placed against the walls of a room. Placing this type of furniture in the middle of a room looks odd, unless the room is rather large. Think of the sets in various situation comedy shows that portray the living room in a home. On these sets, furniture may be placed against a wall, but none of the characters sit on those pieces of furniture. The furniture used by talent is placed in the middle of the room. This arrangement of furniture appears so natural on the television screen that it probably never stood out to you while watching.

With furniture arranged against the wall of a set, it is not possible to backlight the talent seated on the furniture. The purpose of backlighting is to separate the talent from the background. Without the appropriate backlight, the talent, as well as the entire image, appears flat and unrealistic. Additionally, backlighting the talent so close to a wall causes a shadow of the person to be cast on the wall. Several background lights are commonly used, which would create several shadows. It is not likely that you see multiple shadows on a wall behind someone in your home. If these shadows are present on a set that the audience sees, the illusion of reality of the living room will be broken. A standard rule in set design is to place the furniture used by the talent at least *six feet* away from any wall of the set. Furniture not used by the talent is considered set dressing and may be placed wherever the designer likes.

Props

Props are any of the items handled by the performers during a production, other than furniture. Just as there are exceptions to spelling rules in English class, television production principles are equally loaded with exceptions. A simple piece of furniture may become a prop if it is used in a way, the audience assumes, that it was not manufactured to be used. Examples of this may be a couch that is single-handedly hoisted into the air by a character with super strength, a bed that collapses when the talent gets into it, or a bookcase whose shelves give way with the weight of a single book.

Props: Any item handled by the performers during a production, other than furniture.

When selecting or creating props, it is not always necessary to attend to every last detail. The television camera is more forgiving to smaller sized props. For example, the phasers used in the Star Trek television series were a couple of pieces of wood glued together and painted a dark gray with a few pieces of colored plastic attached. Before spending a great deal of time and money on props, consider the cardinal rule of television: it does not *have* to be, it must only *appear* to be.

Flats, Curtains, and Backdrops

Scenery is whatever stops the distant view of the camera. In a studio setting, this includes flats, curtains, and backdrops. If a set is not supposed to reproduce a real-life environment, such as someone's living room, flats can be placed at odd angles, with gaps between them, or be painted in unusual colors and textures. The effect can be attractive and eye catching without upstaging the talent or subject matter of the program. Set designers must always consider contrast ratio and the limitations they place on other items in the picture when choosing a background color.

Background curtains may be loose, having the attractive folds found in living room curtains. The curtains may also be stretched tight and pulled to cover the walls and curves of the studio, forming a solid background color. This is called a **cyclorama**, or **cyc** (pronounced "sike," rhymes with "hike"), **Figure 12-4**. A cyc differs from a backdrop because a cyc is usually just one color and has no definition. On the other hand, a backdrop may have scenery painted on it. For a studio production set in London, as an example, someone may be contracted to paint a skyline of London on a backdrop that hangs behind the set. That way, if a shot ever moves off the set, the audience sees London in the distance. In modern studios, a backdrop is a rare thing indeed. Digital technology allows computer-generated backgrounds to be inserted into a picture that previously had no background at all. In this case, the only backdrop on the set is a blue wall behind the talent.

Cyclorama (Cyc): A background curtain on a set that is stretched tight and pulled to cover the walls and curves of the studio, forming a solid background color.

Visual Design Considerations

While choosing items for the set, the set dresser must be conscious of other factors that affect the visual appeal and realism of the set. Both the placement of items on the set and the patterns on set items have a great impact on the video image.

The 3-D Effect

A television screen is a two-dimensional piece of glass. The creative use of light and shadow, as previously discussed in Chapter 9, *Lighting*, creates a third dimension. Another technique in producing the illusion of

Figure 12-4
When a curtain is pulled tight around a set, it is called a cyc.

three-dimensionality is to place items in layers on the set, **Figure 12-5**. Items on the set should be placed in the front area of the set (closest to the cameras), in the middle of the set, and at the back of the set (furthest away from the cameras). The sets of most modern sitcoms use this layout by placing some item of furniture right in front of the camera. This may be a table, a chair with its back to the camera, a TV set, or any other item found in a home. With the talent placed in the middle of the set, objects layered in front of and behind the talent add great depth to the picture.

Patterns

Patterns are an issue in the areas of upholstery, wallpaper, curtains, and costumes. The current television systems produce a picture from colored dots arranged in rows on the screen (discussed further in Chapter 20, *Getting Technical–The Video Signal*). The rows, or lines, flicker on and off in such rapid succession that the human eye cannot detect the flicker. The odd lines light, then the even lines light, then the

Figure 12-5
Placing items in layers on the set helps to add a three-dimensional feel to the picture.

odd, then the even, and so on. As a result, any horizontal line or high-contrast patterns on the set appear, to the viewer's eye, to be jumping up and down. This effect may even cause a rainbow of colors to appear in the patterned area called **moiré** (pronounced "more-ray"), **Figure 12-6**. This is distracting to the viewers and can be avoided by carefully selecting the materials and patterns used on the set.

- Avoid bold horizontal and vertical lines.
- Avoid tightly woven, complex patterns of high-contrast lines, such as herringbone patterns.
- Avoid elaborately or thinly striped neckties and scarves.

Moiré: An effect caused by certain fabric patterns in which the television system reproduces the pattern with a rainbow of colors or moving lines displayed in the patterned area.

Figure 12-6
The rainbow effect caused by high-contrast patterns in a picture is called moiré.

Wrapping Up

Most of the principles of set construction in theater apply to television production. The important exceptions to the theatrical principles are color and contrast ratio. These two concepts weigh heavily in most every aspect of television production. Unlike an interior decorator working in someone's home, a set dresser must be aware of how the completed set will appear to the camera and on the final video image.

Review Questions

Please answer the following questions on a separate sheet of paper. Do not write in this book.

1. What are some considerations when selecting furniture for a production set?
2. What is a prop?
3. How does a cyc differ from a backdrop?
4. How does the set dresser contribute to creating the illusion of three-dimensionality on the television screen?
5. Explain how the responsibilities of an interior designer and a set dresser are different.

Activities

1. Visit a local fabric store. Choose some fabrics that would cause moiré on a television image. Bring a few samples to class for discussion.
2. Create a basic set design for an afternoon talk show. The designs should include furniture, camera placement, decorative items, and a faux window.

Chapter 13
Production Staging and Interacting with Talent

Objectives

After completing this chapter, you will be able to:

- Define *foreground*, *middle ground*, and *background*.
- Explain the function and importance of the vector line in camera staging.
- Differentiate between a jump cut and an error in continuity.
- Describe the staging for both two-person and three-person studio interviews.
- Differentiate between a dramatic aside and ad-libbing.
- List three things that production staff members must remember when working with non-professional talent.

Introduction

This chapter discusses the placement of furniture, props, and talent in front of the camera. The arrangement of items in a shot is called *staging*. In theater production, staging refers to the movement instructions given to the performers by the director. In television production, staging also applies to the placement and movement of cameras. This chapter presents guidelines and methods of effective staging for television production.

> **Staging:** The arrangement of items, such as furniture, props, and talent, in a shot.

Areas on a Set

The television screen is a relatively flat piece of glass. All images displayed on the screen are two-dimensional. An important goal in production is to attempt to create the illusion of three dimensions in order to increase the realism of television images. Purposeful use of the areas on the set—foreground, middle ground, and background—is an effective method in creating three-dimensionality on the television screen.

The *foreground* is the area between the talent and the camera. Placing items in the foreground of a shot is a simple and effective way to create three-dimensionality, **Figure 13-1**. Novice camera operators often make the mistake of ignoring the foreground area of a set when framing a shot. While leaving the foreground of a set empty creates additional space for camera movement, it does not help in creating the illusion of a three-dimensional image on the flat television screen. This is an important area for staging to create a realistic image for the viewer.

The *middle ground* is most commonly where the important items in a picture are positioned. This is the area in which the talent performs and the action of the program usually takes place.

The *background* of a picture is the material or object(s) behind the talent in a shot. The distance between the talent and the background, if properly lit, greatly contributes to creating three-dimensionality.

Foreground: The area on a set that lies between the talent and the camera.

Middle Ground: The area on a set where the most important items in a picture are usually positioned. This is the area in which the action of the program typically takes place.

Background: The material or object(s) on a set that are placed behind the talent in a shot.

Figure 13-1
The center of focus in this shot is the person at the desk. Notice that the person seated in the foreground helps create the illusion of three-dimensionality.

Talk the Talk

While the terms *background* and *scenery* may seem very similar, they are two different elements on a production set. For example, a glass window on the back wall of a set is background. The painting or photograph depicting the outdoors placed behind the window is scenery because it stops the distant view of the camera.

If the set depicts the interior of a living room, for example, a back wall and partial left and right walls would be constructed for the set. A couch facing the cameras may be placed in the middle ground. Using creative lighting in conjunction with the middle ground and background set, an acceptable illusion of depth may be created in the picture. However, by placing a coffee table or chair in the foreground, even more depth is added to the picture. Effective use of the foreground area helps heighten the impact of a dramatic program. Even most news programs have an anchor desk separating the talent from the cameras. The desk is placed in the foreground and enhances the three-dimensional illusion of the program.

Assistant Activity

- Watch four sitcoms that include scenes that take place in a home of one of the characters.
- List the foreground, middle ground, and background items that are common in most shots.
- Be prepared to discuss your findings in class.

Camera Staging

The placement and movement (dolly, truck, and arc) of cameras, particularly when using multiple cameras, is planned during the pre-production process of marking the script. This planning makes the most efficient use of the talent and staff's time and the production budget.

If using multiple cameras for a production, each camera is assigned a number. The industry convention is to number the cameras from the camera operator's point of view. Therefore, the camera on the operator's far left is camera 1 and the remaining cameras are numbered sequentially moving from left to right; camera 1 is on the left, camera 2 is in the middle, and camera 3 is on the right. The images from the cameras are displayed on monitors in the control room that are also arranged from left to right. The monitor corresponding to the video from camera 1 is on the left in the control room and the monitor for camera 3 is on the right.

Stage directions, however, are given from the performer's point of view, **Figure 13-2**. Imagine a weekly interview program that focuses on local musicians called "Musician's Corner." The studio segment of the program is a brief, informal interview with a different musician every week, one-on-one with the host of the program. The current segment of the program has the host, Michael, speaking with a saxophonist named Katharine. Michael is seated on Katharine's right. In this example, Michael is stage right of Katharine. From the camera and audience's point of view, he is on the left of Katharine. When referring to the position of people or items in front of the camera, the direction is communicated as stage direction. When referring to the items and people behind the cameras, the directions are given more naturally from the perspective of someone looking at the set.

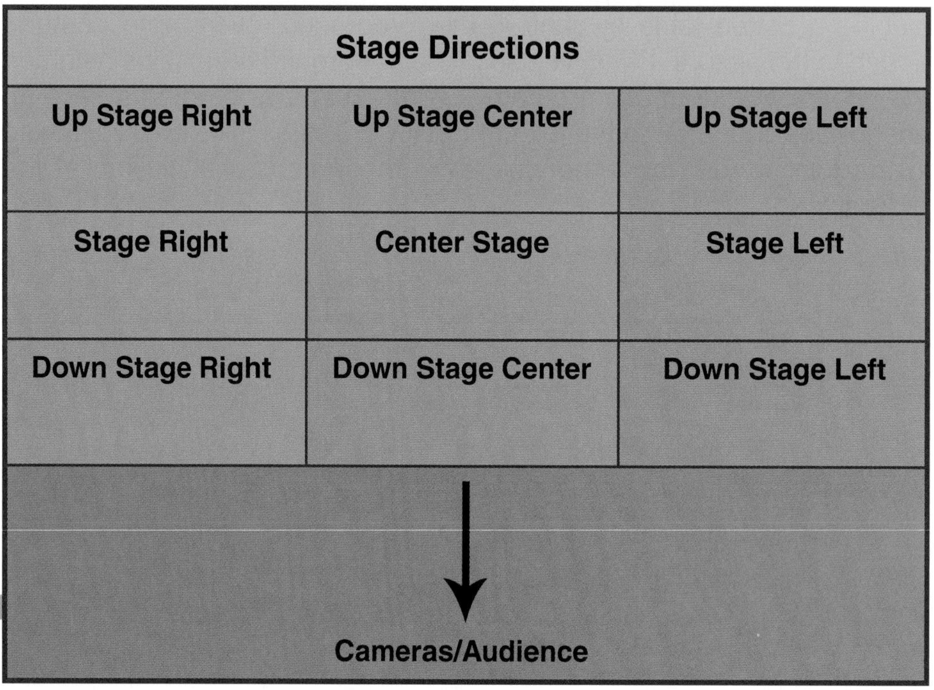

Stage Directions		
Up Stage Right	Up Stage Center	Up Stage Left
Stage Right	Center Stage	Stage Left
Down Stage Right	Down Stage Center	Down Stage Left
	Cameras/Audience	

Figure 13-2
Proper stage direction terms.

To shoot this interview, it may seem most logical to have camera 1 shoot Michael and camera 3 shoot Katharine. Camera 2 provides a two-shot of them both, **Figure 13-3**. This, however, is not the most appropriate camera placement. Because the interview is a conversation and the participants face each other, camera 1 and camera 3 would capture profile shots of Katharine and Michael. Profile shots create a very flat and confrontational feel to the program. Cross-camera shooting is the solution in this situation.

Cross-camera shooting is a technique where the camera on the left shoots the person on the right of the set and the camera on the right shoots the person on the left of the set, **Figure 13-4**. In the interview example, camera 1 shoots Katharine and camera 3 shoots Michael. Camera 2 remains available and positioned for the two-shot.

Cross-Camera Shooting: A two-camera shooting technique in which the camera on the left shoots the person on the right of the set and the camera on the right shoots the person on the left of the set.

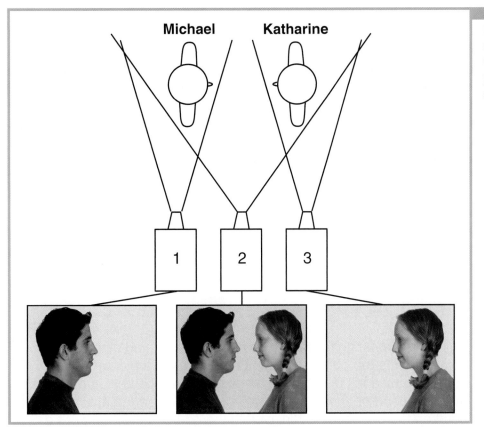

Figure 13-3
If camera 1 (on the left) shoots the talent on the left, the result is a profile shot that has no dimension.

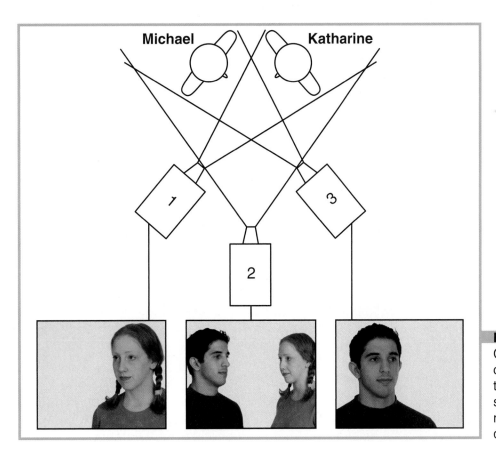

Figure 13-4
Changing the subject of cameras 1 and 3 to the talent on the opposite side of the set creates more realistic shots with dimension.

Vector Line

Vector Line: An imaginary line, parallel to the camera, which bisects a set into a foreground and a background. Also called a *camera line*.

A *vector line* is an imaginary, horizontal line that bisects a set into a foreground and a background. In the previous example, imagine a line drawn horizontally across the set, through the noses of both Michael and Katharine. The line drawn is the vector line of the set. It is extremely important that all cameras remain on the same side of the vector line during shooting. If the program cuts to the image of a camera on the opposite side of the vector line, all items in the picture are reversed, **Figure 13-5**. This is a grave production error.

For the "Musicians Corner" interview, Michael and Katharine are facing each other. Cameras 1 and 2 have two-shots with Michael on the left of the screen and Katharine on the right. If camera 3 crosses the vector line, Katharine will be on the left of the screen. This creates a terrible jump cut.

Visualize This

While preparing to shoot a basketball game, you place a camera at the top of the stands on both sides of the court to make sure that you don't miss any of the action in the game. Camera 1 is at center court on the home team's side and camera 2 is at center court on the opponent's side. During the game, a player makes a very long shot. The ball goes high in the air, traveling from screen left to screen right. Camera 1 has the shot. At the peak of the mid-air curve, you cut to the shot from camera 2. Because camera 2 is on the other side of the court, or vector line of camera 1, the ball now appears to be traveling from screen right to screen left. On the viewer's television screen, the ball appears to have magically reversed direction in the middle of the shot. This image is a major error on the part of the director and could have been avoided.

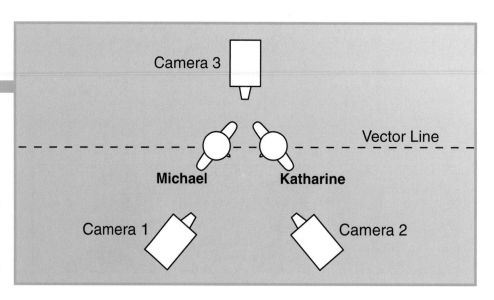

Figure 13-5
In the image captured by cameras 1 and 2, Michael is on the left side of the screen and Katharine is on the right. Camera 3, however, depicts Katharine on the left and Michael on the right. Because of this, cutting from camera 1 to 2 to 3 would create jump cuts.

The vector line extends all the way across the set from left to right. A camera may cross the line while it is hot and, essentially, take the audience with it as it crosses the line. If the audience crosses the vector line with the camera, the camera re-orients the vector line as it moves. Once it stops moving, the other cameras must be repositioned so that they are not on the wrong side of the new vector line. Because the placement of cameras on the set cannot be identical, each camera has its own vector line. The vector lines of all the cameras must complement each other so that no camera is on the wrong side of any other camera's vector line. In some facilities, the term *camera line* is used synonymously with vector line.

Creative use of the vector line may result in savings in the production budget. Suppose two scenes need to be shot of a train moving across the prairie. In one scene, the train is on its way to Arizona from Oklahoma and moving from screen right to screen left. In the other scene, the train is returning to Oklahoma from Arizona and is moving from screen left to screen right. Instead of setting up and shooting the scene twice, simply position a camera on either side of the railroad track. Make sure the two cameras do not shoot each other by hiding them or staggering them along the track. The train runs once and two scenes are accomplished with one take.

Cutaway: A shot that is not a key element in the action. It is commonly used to bridge what would otherwise be a jump cut.

Cutaways

A *cutaway* is a shot that is not a key element in the action. It is usually a close-up of different items found on the set, such as some inanimate object or a person in the background. When a cutaway is used, the audience should not feel that the shot is jarring or out of place. However, a cutaway shot should not include an integral action or moment in the scene. If the cutaway shot is not included in a scene, the audience should not feel as though some part of the scene is missing.

One of the most common uses of cutaways is to bridge what would otherwise be a jump cut. For example, cutting a shot of a teacher writing on the board to a shot of the teacher standing over a student offering assistance creates the illusion that the teacher "jumped" from the blackboard to the student. However, if a cutaway of a student looking forward, then writing studiously is placed between the two shots, no jump cut is created in the sequence.

Other uses of cutaways include:

- Adding interest to an otherwise slow-paced program.
- Showing the reaction of other characters to the events or dialog in a scene.
- Providing nod shots for an interview format program.
- Providing charts, graphs, text, or video to support or supplement the speaker.
- Covering audio editing of a long-winded speaker.

The Jump Cut

A *jump cut* is an error that is found far too often in television programs because it is a very easy mistake to make. A jump cut is sometimes, incorrectly, called an error in continuity. An *error in continuity* occurs when the finished product contains physically impossible actions or items, **Figure 13-6**. These two terms are not interchangeable, as the following examples demonstrate.

To illustrate a jump cut, consider that a three-shot has been set up in the studio, **Figure 13-7**. The staging has Chris, Renna, and Dave standing in a rough triangle facing each other. Chris is on screen left, Renna is in the center, and Dave is on screen right. Renna is the moderator interviewing both Chris and Dave.

- Camera 1 has a shot of Chris and Renna. In this shot, Chris is on screen left and Renna is on screen right.
- Camera 2 has a shot of all three people.
- Camera 3 has a shot of Renna and Dave. In this shot, Renna is on screen left and Dave is on screen right.

Figure 13-6
The change in this woman's earrings from one shot to the next is an example of an error in continuity. A—In the first over-the-shoulder shot, the woman is wearing small, star-shaped earrings. B—In the very next shot, the earrings are long and dangling.

If the director cuts from camera 1 to camera 3, Renna appears to "jump" across the screen from the right to the left. This movement is very jarring to the audience.

Errors in continuity occur during the editing process, such as when a hat disappears off someone's head from one scene to the next, wounds that look severe in one shot are almost healed the next shot, or a glass that is one-quarter full of soda in one camera angle is three-quarters full when the scene cuts to another camera angle.

Figure 13-7
In a jump cut, a performer appears to jump across the screen when the image displayed cuts from one camera to another.

Visualize This

Picture a scene of a man and a woman on a date. The woman is wearing a fancy scarf that is daintily arranged on her shoulders and clipped-on with an elaborate pin. The next take of the scene occurs the next day. What are the chances that the scarf can be arranged exactly as it was 24 hours ago with the pin placed in the same position as the previous day? What if the woman is wearing different earrings? Imagine the audience's confusion if the woman gets into a car wearing large hoop-style earrings and the scene cuts to a shot of her turning the key in the ignition wearing diamond stud earrings!

The audience rarely sees the plate while performers dine. The camera shoots the talent eating, but the plate is not usually in the picture while they are eating from it. Most often, the audience is shown before and after shots of the plate. If, for example, peas were on a plate, it would be very difficult to place each pea in the same position on the plate for every take. If the peas are not placed exactly as they were in the previous take, it would be comical to see them appear in another location on the plate.

In a scene that takes place in a restaurant, keeping track of the amount of liquid in each glass from take to take would be a very tedious job. For example, a woman in the scene is drinking soda from a glass that is 1/4 full. It would be very noticeable if the camera cut to a different angle of the woman drinking and the glass was 3/4 full of soda. This is an error in continuity that can easily occur when dealing with multiple takes of a scene.

On large shoots, a person in charge of continuity constantly snaps photographs of all the on-screen elements in a shot. The next time the scene is shot, everything is returned to its exact position.

Production Equipment in the Shot

In dramatic programming, it is not acceptable to see production equipment in a shot. The program's director tries to simulate real life, and production equipment does not surround most of us in everyday life. Watchful viewers may, from time to time, see a microphone on a boom accidentally dipping into the picture from the top of the screen or catch the shadow of a boom on the background flats. Microphones and cameras should never be seen in a completed dramatic program.

There is, however, an exception. If the dramatic program is set in an environment that naturally includes production equipment, seeing these items in a shot is acceptable. A television drama about a television station would surely have equipment present on the set. The equipment seen on screen is most likely props or set dressing, and not functioning equipment. If the audience sees production gear in non-dramatic programming, such as news programs, talk shows, and game shows, it is perfectly acceptable. Viewers are accustomed to seeing cameras, mics, and lights on programs of this type.

Talent Placement

All cultures have certain acceptable "bubbles" of personal space. In certain Far Eastern and some European countries, for example, having virtually no personal space is the cultural norm. Western cultures presume a larger "bubble" of personal space surrounding us. We are very comfortable in our bubble of personal space and become uncomfortable when others enter this space uninvited. This space is smaller, or almost nonexistent, with close friendships and romances. Mere acquaintances, however, are not usually welcome within our personal space.

When performing on television, people must be placed much closer to each other than is considered normal in Western culture. If performers were spaced apart as they are in real life, the distance would appear much greater on the television screen. Therefore, all performers on television must adjust their personal space to allow them to be very close to others, **Figure 13-8**. On any dramatic television program, notice just how close the performers actually are to each other. It appears so natural on the television screen that most viewers are unaware of it.

Figure 13-8
Personal space must be reduced in order to obtain acceptable television staging. A—Actors are positioned to create the appearance of realistic distance for conversation. B—In reality, the actors are much closer than is commonly considered comfortable in Western culture.

This lack of personal space is a bit of a shock to an actor performing and reciting lines in front of television cameras for the first time. It does not seem natural to be so close to another person while speaking.

Production Note

The director must resist the urge to take performers by the hand and appropriately place them on the set. It is considered amateur behavior for a director to touch the talent in this manner. Because the director is often out of the talent's direct line of sight, using hand gestures is not effective. The director must maneuver the talent into position using only verbal direction.

The ultimate goal is a good television picture. Everyone on the production team must contribute to this effort and realize that things that look or feel a bit unusual in real life, often make a good picture on camera.

Visualize This

When positioning seated talent to capture a tight two-shot, using only verbal commands can become challenging. The talent's knees seem to be in the way no matter how they move, **Figure A**. The solution is to remove personal space and have the talent tuck their inside feet under the chair behind their outside feet, **Figure B**. This allows their hips to move much closer together. In reality, the two students will look ridiculous, but in a medium close-up the audience will not know how contorted their bodies are. When properly positioned, place a table in front of the students with the corner of the table between them. This places the two participants on different, but adjoining, sides of the table, **Figure C**. The overall appearance is normal, but their feet are still contorted. The audience will not see what you do not show them on camera.

Figure A

Figure B

Figure C

Staging for a Two-Person Interview

When positioning Michael and Katharine for the "Musicians Corner" interview, they should not be placed facing each other. The front of each chair should be slightly angled toward each other, **Figure 13-9**. If the angled lines of the chairs were extended, they would form an inverted "V." This staging opens the area downstage of Michael and Katharine, making the audience feel like they are part of the conversation as well, **Figure 13-10**. If three people were standing and having a conversation in real life, the participants would be naturally positioned in some form of a triangle. This arrangement makes each person in the conversation feel involved.

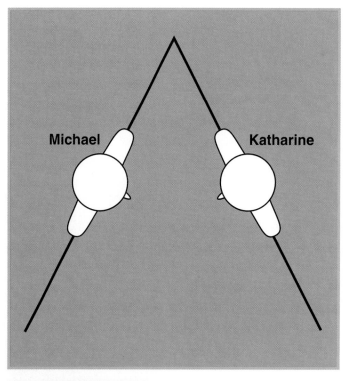

Figure 13-9
The angled placement of on-screen talent creates an inverted "V."

Figure 13-10
The inverted "V" staging leaves room for the audience to feel like they are a part of the conversation.

Think about almost every instance you have seen on television where people are seated around the dinner table at someone's home. To include the viewer as a participant at the table, all the actors are positioned around one-half of the dinner table, **Figure 13-11**. Until now, the placement of actors around a table probably never seemed odd to you. Leaving half the table empty creates the illusion that the audience can sit at the open side of the table, downstage, and see everyone at the table.

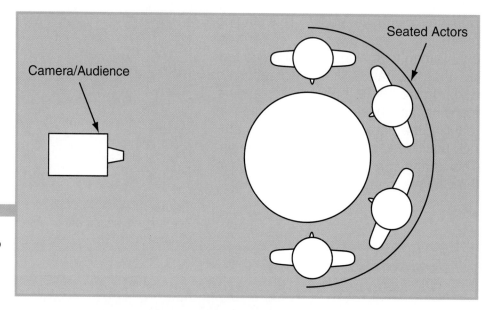

Figure 13-11
The downstage end of the table is left empty so that the camera (audience) is included as a participant at the table.

Staging for a Three-Person Interview

If a violinist named Agnes were to join Katharine and Michael, the chairs would be shifted to place Michael at the apex of the triangle with Agnes and Katharine on either side, **Figure 13-12**. The bottom of the triangle remains open for the audience. Camera 2 now has a one-shot of Michael and a three-shot of all the participants. Cameras 1 and 3 can alternate between one-shots of Agnes or Katharine and two-shots that include Michael.

Using the three-person interview scenario described above, cameras 1 and 3 can each capture a two-shot. Cutting between the two-shots, however, may create jump cuts because each of the two-shots contains one common person—Michael. Cutting between the two-shots results in Michael jumping from one side of the screen to the other. When marking the script in pre-production, camera shots must be thoroughly thought out to avoid jump cuts in the studio or in the editing room.

Figure 13-12
When three people are positioned in the inverted "V" arrangement, the middle person is usually at the apex of the triangle.

Dramatic Programming

In most dramatic programming, the talent cannot look directly at the camera. The exceptions to this are:

- If the camera is used as a subjective camera. Because the camera is shooting from the viewpoint of one of the program's characters, it is natural for other cast members to look directly at the character/camera.

- In the case of a dramatic aside. A *dramatic aside* occurs when a performer steps out of character, turns to the audience, and directly addresses the audience. Dramatic asides are not regularly used in television programming.

Ad-libbing is when talent begins speaking lines or performing actions that are not in the script or have not been rehearsed. Ad-libbing on a dramatic program can be a disaster. This may accidentally happen during a stage performance without great detriment to the production. The stage actor must eventually return to the script, so the other actors can proceed with their lines. On television, however, the script involves more than just the actor's dialog. The technical director follows the script exactly and uses certain words as cues to cut to shots from a different camera. If this particular word or line is not recited, the TD does not cut

Dramatic Aside: When a performer steps out of character and directly addresses the audience.

Ad-Libbing: When talent speaks lines or performs actions that are not in the script or have not been rehearsed.

to the scripted shot, **Figure 13-13**. Likewise, the camera operators are not able to follow the shot sheets if a performer deviates from the script. Once a script has been finalized during the camera rehearsal or dry run, it is in the best interest of the entire production for *everyone* to follow that script during the shoot.

Non-Dramatic Programming

In non-dramatic programming, such as game shows, news, documentaries, sports programs, and talk shows, talent may look at the camera at any time because addressing the audience is part of the very nature of the program. For example, a news anchor tells the audience about current events and, therefore, looks directly at the lens of the camera to speak to the audience. If the talent looks away from the camera in non-dramatic programs, the audience wonders what is happening and becomes distracted and frustrated.

Visualize This

Imagine watching the network news broadcast this evening and the anchor turns his attention to something on the ceiling of the studio. The news continues, but the camera does not tilt up to show you what he is looking at. Most likely, you will stop listening to the news being reported and wonder what the anchor is looking at.

Figure 13-13
The technical director and camera operators are caught unprepared when actors suddenly start speaking lines not in the script. They cannot follow action that has not been planned and rehearsed.

In nondramatic programming, the talent should directly address the audience/television camera. There are two exceptions to this rule:

● Talent may look down at their notes while addressing the audience.

● An anchor may look to the side at a co-anchor, but only if the co-anchor is included in a two-shot that immediately follows.

Unlike the talent in dramatic programs, the on-screen participants of nondramatic programs, such as news anchors and talk shows hosts, commonly read their lines from a teleprompter, **Figure 13-14**. A *teleprompter* is a computer screen positioned in front of the camera lens that displays dialog text in large letters. This allows the talent to look directly at the lens of the camera and read the text. The camera shoots right through the screen at the end of the lens, without seeing the dialog displayed. If the camera zooms in too closely on the talent, the audience can see the talent's eyes moving from left to right as they read the teleprompter. Because of this, the tightest shot of anchors on news programming is usually between a mid-shot and a medium close-up.

It is quite common to see a small pile of papers on the desk in front of news anchors. Those papers are usually props that provide something for the talent to grasp so their hands do not move around. Many people use their hands when they speak, but this is very distracting to a television audience. The audience commonly assumes that the papers are a script, so it does not appear to be out of place.

Ad-libbing is a more common occurrence in non-dramatic programming. In some formats, like talk shows, very few things are actually scripted. A comment from an audience member or show guest may provoke an unplanned course of discussion. This does not cause a great disruption, as in dramatic programming, because the talent is usually stationary. Additionally, an experienced TD can easily follow the conversation.

Teleprompter: A computer screen positioned in front of the camera lens that displays dialog text in large letters, which allows the talent to look directly at the lens of the camera and read the text.

Figure 13-14
A teleprompter allows the talent to look directly into the lens of the camera, at the viewing audience, while reading the program's script.

Staff and Talent Interaction

The interaction of production personnel and talent affects the success of the production process and is an important topic when learning television production. Every member of the production staff has the opportunity to interact with the program's talent at some point in the production process. Just as in other workplaces, professional behavior in a studio can be friendly, even jovial at times. When guests are present in the studio, however, more serious and professional behavior is necessary.

Managing Guest Talent

When guest talent enters a television studio, they are naturally uncomfortable. The environment is strange to them and they know very little about the activities of others around them. They see many strangers bustling around in semi-darkness and probably have some anxiety about being placed under bright lights in front of untold numbers of people. A nervous guest will not look good on camera and does not contribute to a successful production. To help guest talent relax:

● Prepare guest talent for the experience before they arrive at the studio, **Figure 13-15**. Explain what they should expect when they arrive, provide suggestions for clothing and makeup selection, and offer some information on what is expected from them during the production process.

● Designate a staff member to greet the guest upon arrival and be their friendly guide during the production process.

● The greeter should introduce the guest to the director, offer some refreshments, and keep them talking.

● A tour of the facility that includes a description of the various activities helps ease the guest's anxiety. For example, allowing them to observe the editing process may help distract them from their nervousness.

● The greeter may take the time to introduce the guest to some of the crew members. Everyone on the production team is responsible for making the talent comfortable to produce a good program.

● The greeter should try to answer all of the guest's questions.

● Guest talent should not be placed under the studio lights until the program is ready to begin. Under the bright lights, they are not able to see anything in the studio. They can only hear the surrounding activity and will wonder what is happening. Keep the talent informed to ease their anxiety.

Talent Information Sheet

In preparing for your television appearance, you have probably thought of several questions that you would like answered before you arrive at the television studio. This information sheet should answer many of those questions and offer useful tips on performing and looking your best on the television screen.

Common Questions

What can I expect when I get to the studio?

When you enter the studio, it may seem like all the activity around you is organized chaos. "Hurry up and wait" may seem to be the theme of the day. While you should arrive completely prepared for your part in the program, the television crew will probably have to make on the spot adjustments for your unique performance. Expect there to be some last minute lighting changes and adjustment of set pieces. Bear with the activity of the studio staff, as their goal is to make you look your best!

What do I wear?

When deciding what to wear for your television appearance, there are several things to consider:

- The colors black, white, and red are not flattering in large quantities on television. If you must wear black or white, do not wear a great amount of either color and do not wear them side-by-side, such as a white shirt and black suit.
- If your complexion is dark, do not wear light-colored clothing. Light colors will make you look even darker and may silhouette you. If you have a very light complexion, however, avoid dark clothing. Dark colors will cause your skin to shine with a science-fiction type of glow.
- The colors you wear should be near the middle of the spectrum, such as light gray and pastel tones rather than white and dark gray, and dark blue, brown, or dark green rather than black. If you have an olive complexion, however, avoid wearing green.
- Avoid extreme contrasts between items of clothing and between your clothing and the set backgrounds. Avoid small, busy patterns, such as herringbone, and vertical or horizontal thin stripes. These patterns will appear to vibrate in rainbows of color on the television screen. Horizontal stripes also make you appear considerably heavier than you actually are.
- Both men and women should wear a button-up item of clothing, like a shirt, jacket, or vest. These articles of clothing allow a clip-on mic to be clipped to an edge of the clothing. Mics should not be placed at the neck of a pullover article of clothing.
- Do not wear skin-tight clothing. The TV camera adds the appearance of about ten pounds onto a person. This additional "weight" will be unattractive in skin-tight clothing.
- Do not wear a shirt with insignias or writing printed on it. The writing is most likely not in a size or font that is readable to the audience. Additionally, wearing a particular logo or company insignia on the program may create complicated copyright issues.
- Avoid wearing short sleeves. Elbows are not pretty on television.
- Clothing should be pressed. Wrinkles in clothing are magnified by the television camera.

Is makeup used on both men and women?

Yes, makeup is applied to both men and women who appear in a television program. In addition to your face, makeup must be applied to your neck, ears, and perhaps even your hands. People with extremely pale complexions need to have a darker shade of base makeup applied. Most men do not need more than a base layer applied. Teenagers usually appear better on-camera if they have translucent powder applied to take away an oily shine.

(Continued)

Figure 13-15

Providing program guests with information before they arrive at the studio helps to ease some of their anxiety and answers many common questions. This talent information sheet provides many helpful tips for guest talent.

Should I apply more facial makeup than I usually wear?

No. Heavy makeup is only needed in theater. If you wear eyeliner, do not line all the way around your eyes. Using this much eyeliner gives you a beady-eyed, villainous look and diminishes the effect of the most expressive feature on your face. Also, avoid both glossy and very red shades of lipstick. Remember that red is one of the colors that is not flattering on television. Lipstick with too much gloss produces light reflections visible on the television screen that are very distracting to the viewers.

Should I wear larger pieces of jewelry so they can be seen on television?

Not necessarily. Avoid large, shiny metallic pieces of jewelry. These pieces reflect light back into the camera, which creates a distraction for the viewer. Large dangling earrings wiggle with the natural movement of your head and body while you speak, which is very distracting on television. Large jewelry also gives nervous hands something to fiddle with, which is an undesirable action on camera.

Where do I look when I'm in front of the camera?

In an interview or talk show type of program, for example, you should look at the people you are talking to, just as you would in real life. If you are acting in a scene, look at your fellow actors and completely ignore the cameras. If you are giving a campaign speech or delivering news, look directly at the lens of the camera—that is where your audience is.

General Guidelines

The following items are general guidelines to keep in mind while you are at the television studio and while giving your performance during the program. Following these simple rules will help the taping process run more smoothly.

Please be quiet in the studio!

This is a common rule in any television studio. The technical crew will be very busy with last minute details, such as setting mic levels. They need to be able to hear each other. Any questions you have should be directed to the floor manager.

Watch your step!

It is very likely that there will be wiring run along the floor. Be aware that these wires may be in your walking path so you do not trip and fall. Please do not stand or step on the wires and cables. They break rather easily, which will cause a delay in the program for repairs.

If you make a mistake during your performance, do not yell, "Cut!"

Try not to let your facial expression or actions show that you have made a mistake. Do not roll your eyes, make a disgusted face, or giggle. The studio staff can sometimes fix errors with editing. If necessary, they will call "Cut" and back everyone up to begin again just before the mistake occurred. The staff cannot, however, fix a mistake in the editing room if you suddenly change your behavior, persona, actions, or if you make sudden sounds.

Pay attention to the floor manager.

The floor manager is in charge of starting and stopping action in the studio. Be attentive to what he says and follow his direction.

If the floor manager says "Cut," it means that taping has been stopped by the director. This is usually due to an error somewhere. If it was something you did, you will be told. Otherwise, it may have been a technical error on the production side of the cameras. Please do not ask what happened. The production staff does not have time right at that moment to explain. If you ask later, they will be glad to tell you. Until that time, you should remain quiet and in position. Listen for the floor manager to let you know at which point you should begin again. Return to that spot physically and verbally. Quietly wait for the floor manager to give you the cue to start again.

Use the microphone properly.

If possible, the mic cord will be run under your clothing and clipped to a lapel. Never put the mic right next to your mouth and speak into it. Do not blow into the mic or tap it. Be careful not to roll over the mic cord or get the cord caught in the wheels of a chair or stool. When asked to do a sound check, do not be shy. Just speak normally. Speaking in a normal voice will give the technician an accurate audio level reading. A helpful suggestion is to recite what you are going to say when the tape starts rolling.

Figure 13-15

(Continued)

Working with Non-Professional Talent

Production personnel may often work with non-professional talent and must be prepared to react and compensate for their actions. The cameraperson must be especially alert when working with non-professional talent. Non-professional talent may move unpredictably, such as a sudden move left or right, in ways no professional would. If the cameraperson is not alert or the shot is too tight, the talent may completely leave the frame before the cameraperson has time to react, **Figure 13-16**. To compensate for this, the camera operator should never have a shot tighter than a medium close-up of non-professional talent standing in a shot.

Professional talent always provides a cue to the camera operators when they are about to move. In the standing position, the talent shifts their weight to one foot and turns their body in the direction they are about to move before actually moving. This gives the camera operator time to adjust and follow them. From a seated position, a professional leans forward, perhaps placing their hands on the desk to push up, and smoothly rises from the chair. Experienced talent will not abruptly spring from the chair, like a jack-in-the-box.

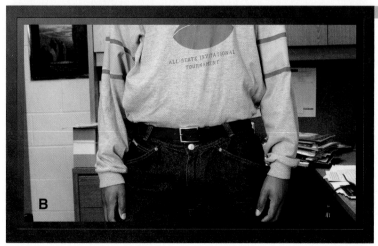

Figure 13-16
Camera operators must always be alert to sudden movements made by non-professional talent while on screen. A—As long as the talent follows the script, the camera operator can maintain a good shot. B—If the talent makes an unplanned movement, the resulting image is worthless to the production.

Headphone Etiquette

In the studio, the floor manager and camera operators wear headphones to communicate with the director and other control room personnel. During production, no one wearing headphones should laugh at any time. In a studio setting where the talent is not able to see the staff, sudden laughter from an unknown source is very unsettling to an already nervous guest. Their first thought is usually, "They are laughing at me." Even though this is probably not the case, the guest is already extremely self-conscious in an unfamiliar environment.

The volume of the headphones is also a consideration. Some operators have the volume of their headphones set so loud that others can actually hear what the director is saying. This sound is not usually picked up by the mics, but talent can hear it. The barely audible sound of someone speaking is very distracting to talent, especially to non-professional talent. Ensure that headphone volume controls are set appropriately for the studio environment.

Wrapping Up

Most of the previous chapters have focused on explaining the equipment used and the responsibilities of personnel on a production. This chapter addresses what to do with the people and objects in front of the camera. The placement of visual elements in the picture is called staging. Correctly staging a set adds to the visual appeal and realism of a program. Successfully managing guest talent and keeping them relaxed during production also improves the visual appeal of a program. When talent is nervous or anxious they may fidget, sweat, or shake while on the set. This is not the best portrayal of the talent on the television screen. Even if all other production guidelines are followed, neglecting staging techniques and guidelines will result in a program that resembles a common home video.

Review Questions

Please answer the following questions on a separate sheet of paper. Do not write in this book.

1. Define foreground, middle ground, and background.
2. In a dramatic program, production equipment should not be seen in a shot. What is the exception to this?
3. What is cross-camera shooting? What problem does it solve?
4. What is the problem created when a camera shot crosses the vector line? What is the exception to this rule?
5. What is a cutaway? How is it most commonly used?
6. What is the difference between a jump cut and an error in continuity?
7. How does the concept of personal space change when performing on television?
8. Which production staff members are affected when a television actor begins ad-libbing?
9. List six things that studio or production personnel can do to help guest talent relax before shooting begins.
10. What must camera operators (specifically) be prepared for when working with non-professional talent?

Activities

1. Create an illustration that depicts the best placement of talent and equipment on a set for an interview program with an interviewer and two guests.

2. Research some of the differences that exist between stage acting and television acting. Summarize some of the differences and be prepared to discuss them in class. (Hint: Some topics may involve gestures, projection, movement, and memorization of lines.)

3. While watching any half-hour sitcom, pay particular attention to any jump cuts or errors in continuity. Note each instance that you find and be prepared to discuss them in class.

4. The following activity should provide practice in giving stage direction and help you understand the concept of personal space related to a television production set.

   1. Choose two students to stand in front of a camera. Give one a microphone as a prop.

   2. Select another student to operate the camera.

   3. Designate one student from the class as the director.

   4. The director and the rest of the class must turn their backs on the talent and watch a studio monitor only. The only person allowed to look directly at the talent is the camera operator.

   5. Using only correct terminology and commands, the director must move the talent and camera operator into position for a tight two-shot that is appropriate for an interview.

   6. The student director should obtain the best possible staging of the two individuals and announce, "I'm finished."

   7. A critique should follow that includes the instruction by the director and the actions and understanding of the camera operator and talent.

   8. All students should take a turn as the director, camera operator, and talent positions in this exercise.

   9. Vary this exercise by using three on-camera individuals or by having the talent seated in chairs on the set.

Chapter 14 Directing

Objectives

After completing this chapter, you will be able to:

- Name each type of script breakdown and cite the information included in each.

- Identify the director's responsibilities in each phase of production.

- Explain the importance of marking the script when shooting on location.

- List qualities common to good directors.

Introduction

This chapter focuses on some of the director's activities and responsibilities when shooting. Some of the issues discussed apply to both studio and remote shoots, and others apply only to one type of shoot. Directing is the most exciting, high-profile job in the television industry. It is also one of the most difficult because the director is involved in each phase of the production. Before any shooting can take place, a tremendous amount of pre-production work and planning must be completed. During production shooting, the director must coordinate the activities of the crew and talent, determine when sufficient takes have been recorded, and keep an organized account of the scenes and transitions. Even in the editing room, during post-production, the director works to ensure that the best possible program is produced.

The Director's Role in Pre-Production

During the pre-production phase, the director's responsibilities include script breakdowns, marking the script, auditions, and pre-production meetings with the staff and crew. Organization is the absolute key to directing. It is not possible to be a successful director with poor organizational skills. A director must be willing and able to make things happen, either by doing things independently or by delegating authority to competent coworkers. The director needs to understand that the responsibilities of the entire production cannot be accomplished by one person. Taking on too much only results in mediocrity. Television production is a team activity.

Script Breakdowns

Before script breakdowns can begin:

- The program proposal must be approved by the executive producer.
- The outline must be approved.
- The script must be written.
- Locations must be scouted.

Script Breakdown: The process of analyzing a program's script from many different perspectives.

A *script breakdown* is the process of analyzing the script from many different perspectives. This process results in a production that is well organized and efficient. Once each type of breakdown has been completed, the director can confidently answer production questions and develop a realistic production schedule. The pros develop many different types of breakdowns as part of their pre-production procedure.

Prop List: A list of each prop needed for a production.

Prop Plot: A listing of all the props used in a program sorted by scene.

Figure 14-1
A prop list is essentially a shopping list of props for the production.

Prop List
Pens
Paper
Coffee Mug
Date Book
Contract
Letter Opener
Desk Phone
Cell Phone
Place Setting (2)
Salt and Pepper Shakers
Napkins
Silverware Settings (2)
Small Vase with Flowers
Sugar and Cream Dispenser
Water Skis
Tow Rope
Life Jackets (4)
Cooler

Prop List

A *prop list* is developed by reading through the script and keeping a list of each prop that is referenced. The director should visualize how the shots are to be staged and note any additional props necessary. The completed prop list becomes the shopping list used to obtain all the props for the production, **Figure 14-1**.

Prop Plot

Immediately upon completion of the prop list, the *prop plot* should be developed. The prop plot is a more involved list of all the props, sorted by each scene of the program, **Figure 14-2**. If a prop is needed for more than one scene, it is listed once for each applicable scene. The prop plot is used to access the props once they are obtained.

Visualize This

To help in understanding the importance of a prop plot, consider that all the props have been acquired for a large production and packed into two tractor-trailer trucks. The day for shooting Scene 38 arrives. The props needed for that scene include general office supplies and a treasure map. The shoot location is four miles from the studio. It is not practical to drive two tractor-trailer trucks to the location, in addition to the necessary equipment, crew, talent, etc. By reviewing the prop plot, only the props needed for Scene 38 can be gathered and transported.

Prop Plot

Scene 4

Pens
Paper
Coffee Mug
Date Book
Contract
Letter Opener
Desk Phone
Cell Phone

Scene 5

Contract
Cell Phone
Place Setting (2)
Salt and Pepper Shakers
Napkins
Silverware Settings (2)
Small Vase with Flowers
Sugar and Cream Dispenser

Scene 6

Cell Phone
Water Skis
Tow Rope
Life Jackets (4)
Cooler

Figure 14-2
A prop plot sorts the prop list by scene number.

Location Breakdown

A *location breakdown* is a list of each location included in the program. Next to each location are the scene numbers that take place at that location, **Figure 14-3**. Organizing the information in this way further assists the director and crew in scheduling resources and general time management.

Location Breakdown:
A list of each location included in the program with the corresponding scene numbers that take place at that location.

Location Breakdown

Park:

Scenes 3, 9, 17, 30, 49

Apartment:

Scenes 5, 14, 28, 35, 36, 37

Office:

Scenes 1, 4, 10, 13, 20

Figure 14-3
All of the scenes to be shot at each location are listed on a location breakdown.

Cast Breakdown by Scene: A listing of the program's cast members that indicates the scene numbers in which they appear.

Figure 14-4
A cast breakdown by scene lists each cast member with the scenes in which they appear.

Cast Breakdown by Scene

John: 2, 5, 6, 7, 12, 14

Mary: 2, 4, 5, 6, 9, 10

Eric: 1, 3, 15

Alex: 1, 3, 15

Susan: 4, 8, 10, 11

Extras: 13, 15

Scene Breakdown by Cast: A listing of each scene number in a program with all the cast members needed for each scene.

Scene Breakdown by Cast

1	–	Eric, Alex
2	–	John, Mary
3	–	Eric, Alex
4	–	Mary, Susan
5	–	John, Mary
6	–	John, Mary
7	–	John
8	–	Susan
9	–	Mary
10	–	Mary, Susan
11	–	Susan
12	–	John
13	–	Extras
14	–	John
15	–	Eric, Alex, Extras

Figure 14-5
A scene breakdown by cast is a listing of each scene number with all of the cast members appearing in that scene.

Equipment Breakdown: A list of each scene in a program with all the equipment needed to shoot each scene.

Cast Breakdown by Scene

The *cast breakdown by scene* is very similar to a location breakdown, **Figure 14-4**. A cast breakdown lists cast members in the left column on a page, with the scenes in which they appear in the right column of the page.

Scene Breakdown by Cast

The *scene breakdown by cast* is a listing of each scene number in the left-hand column of a page, with all the cast members needed for that scene in the right-hand column, **Figure 14-5**. The cast receives a copy of the cast breakdown by scene so they know where they need to be. The production staff, primarily the director, assistant director, makeup artist, and costumer, uses the scene breakdown by cast to ensure that all of the necessary cast is present when shooting each scene. The production assistant typically uses the scene breakdown by cast to contact the performers to remind them when and where to be for the next day's shoot.

Equipment Breakdown

An *equipment breakdown* lists each scene with all the equipment needed to shoot that scene, **Figure 14-6**. The equipment breakdown benefits the production in several ways:

● Organizing the equipment in this manner makes it very unlikely that something will be forgotten when shooting outside of the studio. Gathering equipment without a checklist increases the chances of crucial items being left behind.

● This checklist alleviates the possible confusion that occurs when more than one person packs the gear. Each person may assume that the other packed a certain item or two. While setting up equipment on location, 50 miles from the studio, is an unfortunate time to discover that both people thought the other had packed an essential piece of equipment, such as the camera.

● An equipment breakdown ensures that unnecessary equipment is not transported to a location and that excess crew members are not scheduled for the shoot.

Production Note

Students frequently ask if all these breakdowns are really necessary.

1. Performing all the breakdowns forces you to look at the script analytically. You become extremely familiar with the production, can answer any questions posed by the cast and crew without hesitation, and will gain respect for your leadership.

2. When directing your first production, the value of these breakdowns will become crystal clear. Without them, you will be directing a disorganized mess and will risk losing the confidence of your crew. The breakdowns add to the meticulous organization required by the director of any production.

Equipment Breakdown for Scene 12:

- ☑ 2 Camcorders
- ☑ 2 Tripods
- ☐ 2 Power supplies (for cameras)
- ☐ 8 Mic cables
- ☐ 2 Lapel mics
- ☐ 2 Boundary mics
- ☑ 4-input Mic mixer
- ☐ 4 Light kits
- ☐ 4 Extension power cables
- ☐ 2 Multiple outlet strips
- ☑ 2 Monitors
- ☐ 2 Male BNC to male BNC cables
- ☐ 2 Double male RCA to male RCA cables
- ☑ Videotape
- ☐ Duct tape
- ☐ Tool kit
- ☑ Lens cleaning paper
- ☐ 4 Camera batteries
- ☐ 2 Battery chargers

Figure 14-6
Listed in this breakdown is all the equipment needed for a two-camera, film style shoot.

Marking the Script

If a production is planned using film-style shooting (see Chapter 11, *Remote Shooting*), the director must carefully mark the script with scene and cut numbers to help later in the editing room. For example, if Scene 3 of a program is set for shooting, each planned cut of the scene needs to be labeled 3a, 3b, 3c, 3d, and so on. These labels are written into the shooting script, prior to shooting the scene. This ensures that a shot is not accidentally omitted, whether shooting in the studio or on location. Returning to the set days or weeks later to record a shot that was omitted may be unreasonably expensive.

Camera Shots

The director often enters all the camera shots on the shooting script, instead of the scriptwriter. The script is clearly marked with abbreviations understood by all the crew members. A detailed and complete camera script aids in a smooth production shoot.

Shots should vary considerably, using both horizontal and vertical angles and a great variety of shot sizes. Novice directors often place cameras at uninteresting angles, such as directly in front of talent at eye level. Using a wide variety of angles and sizes keeps the audience interested, even if the program's subject matter is relatively mundane. Cutaways and reaction shots should be noted on the camera script, in addition to the primary action shots.

Set Design

After both the director and the producer approve the set design, it should be studied in detail, **Figure 14-7**. The director visualizes where the cameras can be placed and where the action will take place. Many

Figure 14-7
The director studies the set design to determine placement of cameras and talent, and how to coordinate the movements of both.

sets are built with removable walls to allow room for specific camera positioning. If alterations to the set are necessary, it is much easier and more efficient to make changes to the plan, than it is to make changes after the set has been built.

The director is the final authority on the colors used on the set, because the individual designers may not be in communication with each other. Therefore, the director needs to consider the colors with respect to makeup, costumes, set pieces, furniture, and lighting. Each of these elements factor into the contrast ratio and contribute to the visual quality of the production.

Auditions

Whether the program is a drama, comedy, game show, documentary, or a news program, the director needs to make decisions about the talent in front of the camera. This process is called the *audition*. During an audition, the director watches and listens to a prospective performer and decides if the performer is capable of portraying the role he is casting. The director must try to be extremely objective when auditioning talent.

For the initial audition, directors often listen to the quality of the talent's voice without visually observing the talent. The talent may be asked to read an excerpt from the script or to recite a prepared monologue. During a visual audition, the director may test the talent's ability to follow stage directions in addition to another reading from the script, **Figure 14-8**. Unlike performance theater, the director should not be in the same room as the talent for the audition. The director should watch the aspiring cast member on a monitor in the control room, much the same way that the audience will see him/her.

Audition: The process in which a director makes casting decisions for a program by watching and listening to prospective performers.

Figure 14-8
When auditioning talent, the director should view the audition on a monitor in the control room, rather than in the studio.

Production Note

One of the biggest mistakes made in this process is casting a good friend. A friend is less likely to follow direction, because of the familiar relationship outside of the studio. This may lead to arguments, resulting in the loss of a friendship.

Directors sometimes forget that they are "stuck" with their casting decisions. Once shooting begins, a cast member can be fired if necessary. However, each scene that person was in must be re-shot with the replacement performer.

Pre-Production Meeting

A pre-production meeting includes every member of the staff. At this meeting, the expectations of each member of the crew are discussed and everyone involved develops a production schedule/calendar. Because so many different schedules are combined in the production process, a commitment to the production calendar is taken very seriously. Neglecting a scheduled commitment is a horribly irresponsible act and is not likely to be forgotten.

The equipment needed for shoots must be scheduled. The director must make arrangements for the necessary equipment to be available at the scheduled time. This requires reserving equipment well ahead of time. Most studios have equipment schedules that allow equipment to be reserved up to two weeks in advance of the shoot date.

In the meantime, the director holds rehearsals with the cast. As the cast becomes more proficient with the script, the crew begins to attend rehearsals. The cast and crew need to know what is going to happen in a scene before it happens, to make sure a camera is there to record the shot. This requires tremendous coordination between the director, camera operators, technical director, and the talent.

The Director's Role in Production

Before a studio shoot begins, the camera script is reviewed (remote shoots are discussed in Chapter 11, *Remote Shooting*). The final camera directions are noted in the left column of the script. The transitional devices for the beginning of the scene and the end of the scene are also indicated. A variety of shots from many angles are included, using dollies instead of zooms wherever possible.

The **dry run**, or **camera rehearsal**, includes only the talent, technical director, audio engineer, camera operators, and the director. Costumes and makeup are not worn, and tape is not run. To save money and keep the heat down, the studio lighting instruments are not turned on. The talent goes through the scenes, as the camera operators are given directions.

Dry Run: A practice session of scenes in a program that includes the talent, technical director, audio engineer, camera operators, and director. Also called a **camera rehearsal**.

Figure 14-9
A dry run, or camera rehearsal, is necessary to coordinate the technical production staff with the movements of the performers.

All shots are rehearsed, along with the audio cues, while the technical director practices with the camera switching. When the director is satisfied with everyone's performance, he calls for the actual shoot to begin, **Figure 14-9**. While the performers get into costume and makeup, the crew readies the set, lights, and other equipment.

During the shoot, it is important that the director always use correct terminology. The correct use of terms fosters the crew's confidence in the director. Using the correct terminology is also the most efficient method of communicating. Many directors memorize a start-up sequence of commands to get the program started smoothly, **Figure 14-10**. Aspiring directors should memorize a standard start-up dialog. On the day of a shoot, novice directors often get nervous or stressed and may forget a crucial command, such as "roll tape." Committing a start-up sequence to memory decreases the likelihood of this happening.

Start-up Sequence

DIRECTOR: Studio ready?
FLOOR MANAGER: Ready.
DIRECTOR: Standby.
FLOOR MANAGER: Standby.
DIRECTOR: Audio ready?
AUDIO ENGINEER: Ready.
DIRECTOR: Video ready?
VTR OPERATOR: Ready.
DIRECTOR: CG ready?
CG OPERATOR: Ready.
DIRECTOR: Standby control room.
DIRECTOR: Roll tape.
VTR OPERATOR: (begins tape recording) Tape rolling.
DIRECTOR: Countdown.
FLOOR MANAGER: 10, 9, 8, 7, 6, (5–0 are counted off with his fingers. His hand is in front of the talent with the first line).
(When the FM gets to 2, the Director speaks again).
DIRECTOR: Fade up on (camera) 1.
DIRECTOR: Audio up.
FLOOR MANAGER: (gesture for zero).
DIRECTOR: Bring in title.
DIRECTOR: Lose title.

Figure 14-10
An example of a director's start-up sequence of commands.

Shooting for the Edit

Shooting for the Edit: The process in which a director plans exactly how each scene in a program will transition from the scenes that immediately precede and follow it. Production shooting then follows the director's plan.

The director must plan exactly how the scene being shot will transition from the scene that immediately precedes and follows it. This process is called *shooting for the edit*. Before shooting Scene 9, for example, the director needs to know how Scene 8 ends (fade, cut, dissolve, or other effect), as well as the direction of the action in Scene 8. This information dictates the beginning of the shoot for Scene 9. The two scenes must be edited together later without jarring the audience. The director must also be concerned with how Scene 9 leads into Scene 10. Planning these transitions would be easily accomplished if the scenes were shot in the order they appear in the finished program. This, however, is not the reality of television production shooting.

It is very likely that scenes will not be shot in the order the audience sees in the final program. Therefore, before the first day of shooting, the director needs to mark the entire script with notes as to how each scene transitions out of the previous scene and into the next scene. The screen direction of the action and camerawork should also be noted at the beginning and end of each scene. With this information marked for every scene, the director can confidently shoot the scenes in any order and know that, if the script notations are followed, the scene will be smoothly edited into the program.

Another aspect of shooting for the edit is considering four basic rules regarding action on the screen. Breaking any of these rules is guaranteed to jar the audience, which, depending on the nature of the program, is usually a negative program attribute. The following rules apply to the processes in the editing room:

- A stationary camera shot should not immediately precede a moving camera shot.
- A moving camera shot should not immediately precede a stationary camera shot.
- An edit can be made from a stationary camera shot to another stationary camera shot.
- An edit can be made from a moving camera shot to another moving camera shot.

Multiple Takes

Take: A term that identifies each time an individual scene is shot.

Each time a scene is shot, it is called a *take*. Multiple takes of scenes may be planned to capture different angles. Multiple takes may also be necessary due to a mistake made by the talent or crew, which causes the director to yell "Cut!" Each scene should be retaken until three "good" takes are recorded. It is better to have the choice between several good takes, than to come up short in the editing room. Never move on to another scene until the takes of the current scene are acceptable. When shooting a scene is complete, rewind the tape and view the shots and takes of the scene. This additional time is well justified when compared to the alternative: gathering all the crew, talent, sets, props, and equipment for a re-shoot weeks after the initial shoot.

When multiple takes of a single scene are shot, the *slate* becomes particularly important. The slate is a board or page that is held in front of the camera to note the scene number, the take number, and several other pieces of information about the scene being shot. The slate can be as elaborate as a clapboard or as simple as a piece of paper, **Figure 14-11**. If, for example, mistakes are made five times in Scene 5, the sixth take is slated as "Scene 5, Take 6." The slate is held in front of the camera for at least 10 seconds, but usually not more than 15 seconds. The countdown then begins to initiate action on the set and to cue the performers.

A *take log*, or *shot log*, is a written list of each scene and take number that have been shot and recorded on a particular tape, **Figure 14-12**. When the performance of a scene is acceptable to the director, the take

Slate: A board or page that is held in front of the camera noting the scene number, the take number, and several other pieces of information about the scene being shot.

Take Log: A written list of each scene and take number that have been shot and recorded on a particular tape. Also called a *shot log*.

Figure 14-11
The slate can be a simple notation that indicates the scene and take numbers. It is placed or held in front of the camera for about 10 seconds and can save hours in the editing room.

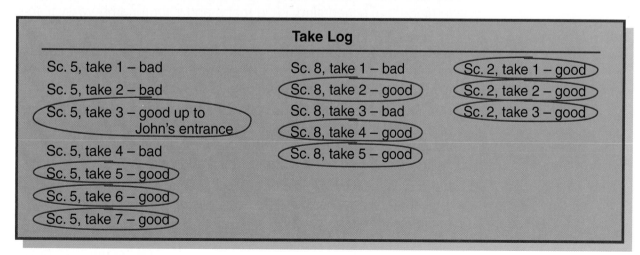

Take Log

Sc. 5, take 1 – bad	Sc. 8, take 1 – bad	Sc. 2, take 1 – good
Sc. 5, take 2 – bad	Sc. 8, take 2 – good	Sc. 2, take 2 – good
Sc. 5, take 3 – good up to John's entrance	Sc. 8, take 3 – bad	Sc. 2, take 3 – good
Sc. 5, take 4 – bad	Sc. 8, take 4 – good	
Sc. 5, take 5 – good	Sc. 8, take 5 – good	
Sc. 5, take 6 – good		
Sc. 5, take 7 – good		

Figure 14-12
The director develops a take log to decrease the amount of time spent in the editing room.

is circled on the log. Later in the production process, the director can scan directly to the beginning of the good take; instead of reviewing each preceding bad take.

Post-Production

After the shooting is complete, post-production begins. The processes during post-production include: editing, adding background music, scene transitions, sound effects, some special effects, and titles. Post-production is most commonly referred to as "post."

Keep in mind that very few aspects of a program can be satisfactorily fixed in post. Accepting a substandard shot with the belief that it can be fixed in post-production is a terrible mistake. Fixing substandard shots is nearly impossible with analog post processes. While digital processes offer more tools to fix a shot, it may become so time-consuming that the cost is not within the budget. The best solution is to plan and shoot the scenes correctly during production.

Starting Something You Can Actually Finish

- Keep the program short; a dynamic 5–7 minutes vs. boring 30 minutes.
- Keep it simple. The more complex the program, the greater the chance for mechanical or human failure.
- A small crew reduces complications; more people equals higher probability for failure.
- Have a realistic vision of the program that is proportional to the budget. Scale the production for success, not disappointment.
- Be a professional. Treat people with respect, provide plenty of reminders of scheduling, have maps and phone numbers available for everyone.
- Be organized and do not waste anyone's time. Have lists of everything, breakdowns of everything, props, locations, camera shots, equipment, eating locations, restrooms, etc.
- Keep contact information for clients and each member of the cast and crew to facilitate quick and efficient communication. This information should include address, home phone, business phone, cell phone, pager number, and e-mail addresses.
- Keep an eye on the big picture. Do not spend excessive time getting one small scene perfect, while sacrificing the time necessary to complete the entire show.

Being an Effective Director

Good directors commonly possess certain characteristics:

- A good director understands that he/she is not the dictator of the production.

- A good director takes the initiative to do whatever is necessary to successfully complete the program.

- A good director knows the capabilities of the equipment and strives to make the most of available resources, instead of complaining about what is lacking or not available.

- A good director maintains an even temper in front of the cast or crew. Showing anger or bursts of emotion causes others to lose faith in the director's abilities.

- A good director gives only constructive criticism when instructing the talent or crew.

- A director is part artist and part technician. The best directors work their way up through the production team and know the job responsibilities of each production crew member.

- A good director uses the knowledge of and experience with various staff positions to develop effective interpersonal relations between the director and the production staff.

- A good director delegates tasks, rather than trying to do everything personally.

- A good director is highly organized, almost to a fault.

- A good director realizes that making final decisions is his responsibility.

Wrapping Up

The best directors have come up through the ranks and have held almost every production staff position on the way. All of that experience is called upon throughout the production process. Professional directors work in the business for years before directing their first program.

Student directors attend courses in the psychology of presentation, which address methods in making the audience "feel" things and the responsibilities related to using those methods. A director can influence attitudes, emotions, and actions of the audience using visual media. Classes in the ethics of visual media instruct student directors on how to be unbiased in the presentation of information, as well as being totally biased and manipulative. Having a well-rounded education in geography, history, and political science is beneficial for a director.

Throughout your education, really watch television programs and film productions to analyze what the professionals do and how they do it. Examine how a director makes a particular scene exciting. Turning down the audio helps in staying attentive to the production aspects of the program, without becoming involved in the plot of the program.

As a student learning television production, you will begin to develop your own style as you direct more programs. Meanwhile, work as often as possible in all of the technical positions. Experience in each position is beneficial for success with future projects and responsibilities.

Questions for Review

Please answer the following questions on a separate sheet of paper. Do not write in this book.

1. List some of the director's responsibilities for each phase of production: pre-production, production, and post-production.

2. What steps must be completed before script breakdowns can begin?

3. List each type of script breakdown and note the information contained in each.

4. What is the director's role in the audition process?

5. Which members of the production are involved in a camera rehearsal?

6. What is "shooting for the edit?"

7. Identify five characteristics of effective directors.

Activities

1. Tape an episode of your favorite television show. Create a prop plot for one scene in the program. Include a description of the events and activities in the scene.

2. A slate can be as elaborate or as simple as the resources available. Create a reusable slate, using only items found in your home.

3. Research the Directors Guild of America. Summarize important facts and initiatives of the organization.

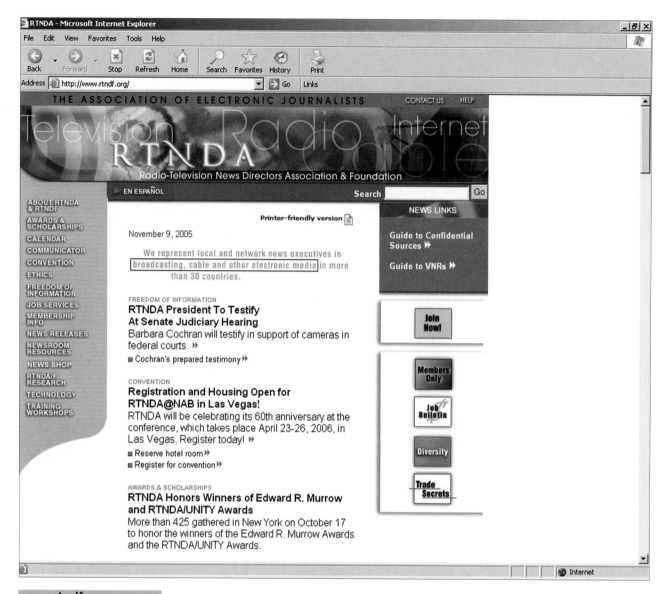

www.rtndf.org.
Web site of the Radio-Television News Directors Association and Foundation.
The RTNDA (assoication) sets standards for and provides programs that encourage
excellence in electronic journalism. The RTNDF (foundation) offers development
and educational opportunities for journalism professionals and educators.

Important Terms

Base
Blending
Character Makeup
Crème Makeup
Foundation
Highlight
Pancake Makeup
Prosthetics
Shadow
Spirit Gum
Straight Makeup

Objectives

After completing this chapter, you will be able to:

- Explain why the use of makeup is necessary on television.
- Differentiate between character makeup and straight makeup.
- List the materials and products used for each layer of makeup application.
- Cite common considerations when selecting the costumes for a production.

Introduction

Makeup is the collection of various cosmetics and materials that are applied to the skin. These cosmetics are necessary for all studio productions on both male and female talent. Wearing makeup is the norm for television. Even news anchors, although not considered actors, wear makeup when on camera. This chapter introduces different kinds of makeup products, the uses of each, and some application tips.

Why Is Makeup Necessary on Television?

Performers placed under bright 32K white light look gray, pasty, flat, and unattractive without makeup. When using digital video, images are so sharp that even the slightest imperfection on the skin is greatly magnified on television. Skin blemishes, dark circles under the eyes, acne, rashes, bruises, five o'clock shadows, and wrinkles that are insignificant in real life, appear magnified on television.

While many performers may resist wearing makeup, they need to understand its necessity. A capable lighting designer lights the performers evenly and brightly. Being evenly lit means that practically all shadows are removed from the talent's appearance because light comes from all directions around the performer. A face without shadows does not appear to have any depth; it looks flat. A face without depth, when displayed on a television screen, appears blemished and flat and seems to be a part of a horror film, rather than a professional television production. Most people performing on television, whether portraying a character or being themselves, want to be as attractive as possible. Sometimes the simplest way to convince a performer to wear makeup is to roll a bit of tape to let them see how they look without it, **Figure 15-1**. The resistance usually melts after seeing themselves on camera without makeup.

Figure 15-1
The even, bright white light in a television studio causes a face without makeup to lose all depth and dimension.

Stage Makeup

Students in television production classes often have some exposure to stage makeup in drama classes or theater production. Stage makeup is worn for three reasons:

- To make the actor look attractive under very bright stage lights.
- To help the actor portray a character by creating a "look" that is more appropriate for that character.
- To add three-dimensionality to the actor's face by replacing natural shadows that are removed by the bright lights.

Stage makeup is usually applied rather heavily so people in the audience can see the exaggerated facial expressions, regardless of their location within the theater. If the actor were to move into the audience, however, the makeup would appear garish and overdone, **Figure 15-2**.

Television Makeup

Television makeup is used for the same three reasons as theatrical stage makeup. The application for television, however, is much more subtle. All of the aspects and techniques of stage makeup are used for television, but the makeup is not applied as heavily. The talent on television should, most often, not appear to be wearing makeup at all. The goal is to create a natural appearance from a distance of 8 to 12 feet, which is the average distance between a television set and viewers at home.

Figure 15-2
Stage makeup techniques are not appropriate for television. Stage makeup is too heavy and exaggerated.

Makeup Styles

Fundamentally, there are two styles of makeup: painted and natural. Both styles are perfectly acceptable, depending on the type of program and the director's goals for the program.

When makeup is applied in a painted style, the audience can clearly see that the performer is wearing makeup, **Figure 15-3**. For example, an actress playing a woman who lived in the 1960s would be made-up with dark eyeliner, long dark eyelashes, and layers of blue eye shadow. This was the trend in fashion makeup in that era and is appropriate for a realistic portrayal of the character.

Makeup applied in a natural style simply enhances a person's facial features, but does not draw attention to the makeup applied. Female performers often do their makeup for television in a completely natural style and add cosmetics based on their character's wardrobe, personality, or situation. It may seem odd to spend time applying natural makeup if the purpose is to appear as though no makeup was used at all. Consider the alternative: If a natural style of makeup is not applied, the television image presents an unhealthy, unattractive, and unnatural picture.

Application Techniques

Character Makeup: Makeup application technique used to make a performer look like someone or something other than the performer's own persona.

Prosthetic: A cosmetic appliance, usually made of foam or putty, which may be glued to the skin with special adhesives.

Spirit Gum: A type of adhesive commonly used to apply prosthetic items.

Character makeup application is used to make a performer look like someone or something other than the performer's own persona, **Figure 15-4**. For example, the performer can be made to appear older or younger, as a different race, or an alien from another world. A myriad of special effects makeup and injuries are categorized with character makeup, including cuts, bruises, scars, and warts.

Special-effect makeup for television creates or exaggerates physical features on performers. Examples include noses, wounds, swelling, and warts. These items are prosthetic devices that are added to a performer's appearance based on the character they portray or the action in a scene. A *prosthetic* is an appliance, usually made of foam or putty, which may be glued to the skin with special adhesives. The adhesive most commonly used to apply prosthetic items is *spirit gum*. Spirit gum is as thin as water and is applied with a brush. To attach a prosthetic using spirit gum:

1. Brush the spirit gum onto the skin in the area where the appliance is to be attached. Let the adhesive set for a few moments.

2. When the spirit gum is no longer shiny, gently tap it with your fingertip. If it is tacky and strings of adhesive attach to your finger, the gum is ready for adhesion.

3. Clean any adhesive off your fingers.

4. Attach the prosthetic item with gentle, even pressure.

! Safety Note

Do not use spirit gum around the eyes. Irritation, rash, or inflammation can occur when the chemicals in the adhesive come into contact with the sensitive skin around the eyes.

Figure 15-3
The painted look for television is an accepted style of makeup design. A character wearing the painted look obviously appears to be wearing makeup, which is usually not applicable to male actors.

Figure 15-4
Character makeup is designed to make a person look like someone or something other than the performer's own persona.

To remove the prosthetic, as well as any adhesive on your hands, use spirit gum remover. The remover chemically dissolves the gum on contact. To apply the spirit gum remover, dip a cotton ball or makeup brush into the remover and gently work it into the edges of the prosthetic appliance. This dissolves the gum and allows the appliance to be detached from the skin with ease.

The goal of *straight makeup* application is to make people look like themselves under the bright television lights, **Figure 15-5**. This application technique corrects or hides blemishes, makes the complexion more even, and helps people generally look attractive on television.

Makeup Products

When choosing the type of makeup to use, there are two types to choose from: theatrical and over-the-counter. If economy is a concern, use theatrical makeup. It is far less expensive than consumer cosmetics. Over-the-counter makeup is packaged in smaller quantities than the theatrical varieties and will need to be purchased more frequently. Additionally, the amount of powder and fragrances used in over-the-counter cosmetics irritates and dries the skin. However, if convenience is a major concern, the corner store is more accessible for some people than a professional makeup supply center.

Makeup is available in two forms, **Figure 15-6**:

- Crème Makeup
- Pancake Makeup.

Crème Makeup

Crème makeup is an oil-based product that easily blends with other colors. As additional layers of makeup are applied, colors can be mixed together to create a more natural progression from one shade to another. Today's oil-based makeup is far removed from the greasy products of yesteryear. There is a stigma that oil-based makeup compounds problems with skin that is already oily. On the contrary, the natural human oil and the oil in the makeup mix and do not clog the pores of the skin if removed properly.

Pancake Makeup

Pancake makeup is a water-soluble, pressed powder makeup foundation that is pressed into a compact container. Pancake makeup once was the most common type of makeup used by most television and film performers, but that is no longer the case. Pancake makeup can clog the pores of the skin and cause breakouts. Additionally, pancake makeup does not blend well with other colors. Once the color is applied, it remains at the applied intensity until removal. Therefore, a very light

Figure 15-5
The natural look enhances facial features under the bright lights without drawing attention to the fact that the performer is wearing makeup.

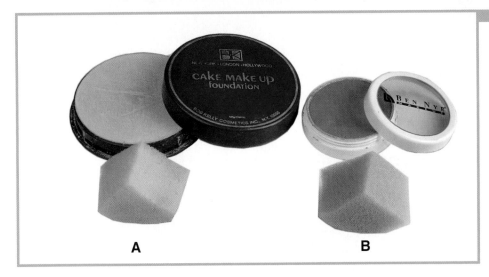

A   B

Figure 15-6
The makeup applied to on-screen talent is available in two forms: pancake and crème. A—Pancake makeup is a powder that must be applied with a moistened sponge. B—Crème makeup can be applied lightly with a sponge.

touch is required to apply this kind of makeup. Any additional layers of color must also be powder-based. When pancake and crème products are mixed, a sticky goop results.

Makeup Application

Several layers of makeup are required to create a realistic appearance on camera. This is true for both character and straight makeup applications. Makeup should be applied under lighting conditions that closely reproduce the lighting on the studio set or shoot location.

First Makeup Layer

The first layer of makeup applied usually covers the entire face, neck, ears, back of the hands, and bald spot, if present. This layer is called *base*, or *foundation*, **Figure 15-7**. Base is best applied with a slightly moistened cosmetic sponge. These dense foam sponges are available at most retail outlets in the cosmetics section and come in a wedge shape. Cosmetic sponges are very effective for applying base on everyone except males who are old enough to shave. The beard stubble on a man's face shreds the sponges and leaves bits of foam all over their face. Use a different kind of sponge on adult men, such as a natural sea sponge or one made of polyester. If base is applied properly, the performers should not feel the makeup on their faces at all. If they feel this layer of makeup, it was applied too heavily.

No Makeup

Base Layer Applied

Figure 15-7
The difference between a bare face and a performer wearing a layer of base.

Production Note

To simplify the process, use the same kind of sponge to apply makeup on everyone. This way, there is no need to keep a supply of both cosmetic and sea sponge or polyester sponges on hand for each production. However, performers should each have their own set of sponges. Polyester and sea sponges can be cleaned after each use with soap and hot water.

Second Makeup Layer

Highlight and shadow are applied after the base makeup. The bright studio lights remove all the shadows on the face and makeup is necessary to replace these shadows. When applied, highlight and shadow should be blended. *Blending* involves brushing the makeup with the fingers or a brush until the makeup applied seems to merge into the surrounding areas, **Figure 15-8**. There should be no definitive line or separation between areas with only base makeup and areas with additional colors or layers applied.

Shadow makeup is three or four shades darker than the surrounding area. Anywhere shadow is placed makes that area appear to *sink into* the plane of the face. Shadow is most commonly placed:

- Above the eyes, but below the brow.
- Below or to one side of the nose.
- Below the chin.
- In the temple area for an aged appearance.
- On the cheek, below the cheekbone.

Blending: Incorporating applied makeup into the areas surrounding it by brushing the makeup with the fingers or a brush.

Shadow: Makeup that is three or four shades darker than the base makeup applied.

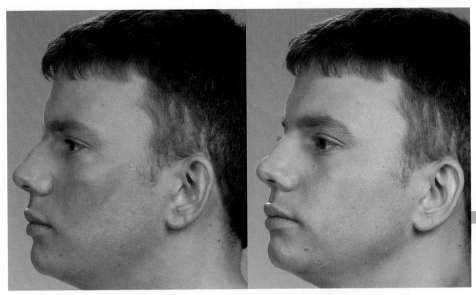

Initial Application   **Blended into the Area**

Figure 15-6
Once applied, cheek shadow is blended to create depth on the talent's face.

Cheek shadow, sometimes called rouge, should not be placed directly on the cheekbones. This creates the appearance that the cheekbones are crushed or damaged. To determine the proper placement of cheek shadow:

1. Look at a mirror and use a light-colored eyebrow pencil to place a tiny dot halfway between the outside corner of the eye and the actual opening of the ear.
2. Turn and look straight ahead, directly into the mirror.
3. Place your fingers in the center of the cheek and gently press.
4. Continue gently pressing and slowly walk your fingers up the cheek until a bone is felt. This is the bottom edge of the cheekbone.
5. Continue walking your fingers up the face to the top of the cheekbone. This is located just below the depression of the eye socket.
6. Look straight ahead and place a dot one-quarter of the way up from the bottom of the cheekbone and position it directly in line with the pupil of the eye.
7. Imagine a line between the pupil and the second dot on the cheekbone. Continue that line down until it is even with the outside corner of the mouth. Place the third dot in this location.
8. Connect the three dots to create a rough triangle shape with a slight curve on the top-side, **Figure 15-9**. This is the area, and roughly the shape, to apply the cheek shadow.

Highlight is makeup that is three or four shades lighter than the surrounding area, **Figure 15-10**. Highlight is usually applied to:

● The bridge of the nose.
● The bone just above the eye, below the eyebrow.

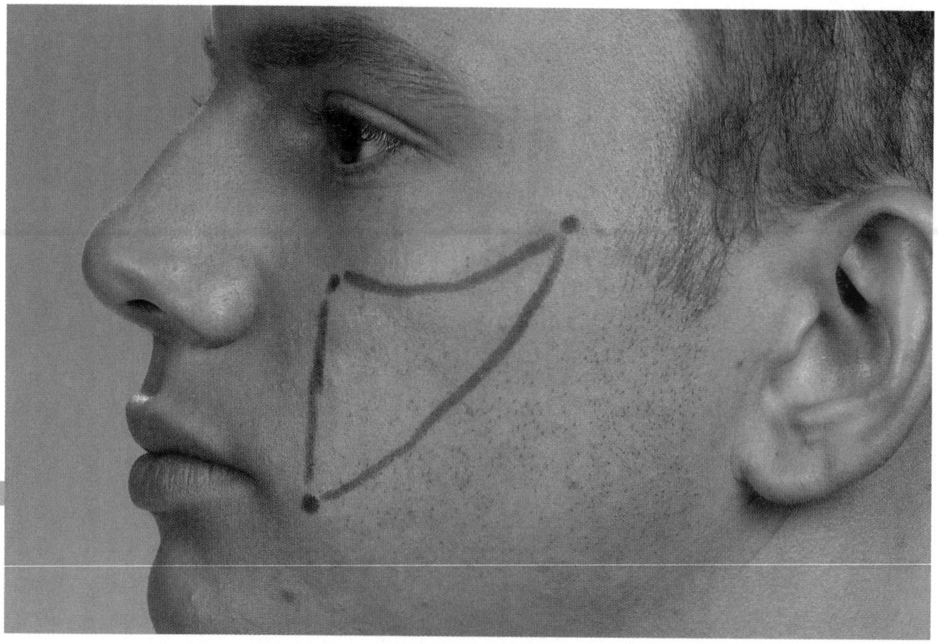

Highlight: Makeup that is three or four shades lighter than the area to which it is applied.

Figure 15-9
Connecting the dots creates a triangular placement template for cheek shadow.

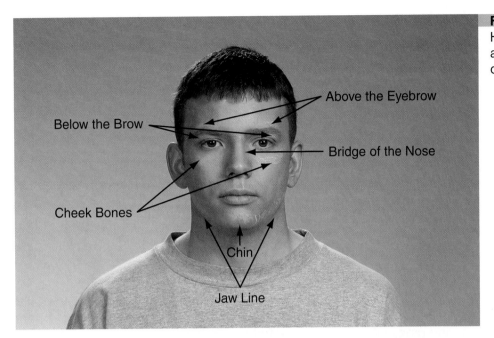

Figure 15-10
Highlight is placed on areas that should stand out on the face.

● Above the eyebrow, on the bony ridge across the forehead.

The chin and the jaw line to give the appearance of strength (usually used for men).

● The cheekbones.

Applying highlight to the bone just above the eye, below the eyebrow, is necessary on both men and women. When highlight is applied to this area on men, it should be subtle and particularly well blended. If applied too heavily or improperly blended, it is apparent that the talent is wearing eye makeup.

Highlight should be applied to the bony ridge across the eyebrow on men who do not have a strong brow line. Accentuating this area with highlight gives the appearance of a stronger, more masculine individual. If a man already has a prominent brow ridge, accentuating this area makes him appear brutish and savage. To accentuate this area on a woman creates a rather unattractive appearance. Always keep in mind that the makeup applied to talent should help the performer portray exactly the type of character necessary for the betterment of the program.

Third Makeup Layer

After the crèmes of various shades have been applied, the entire face must be powdered. The object of powdering crème makeup is to dull its shine and to set the makeup. Remember that crème makeup is oil based and naturally has a slight shine. Setting makeup with translucent powder keeps it from easily smearing. The powder used must be translucent makeup powder. Never use baby or talcum powder. These powders are white and change all the shadows and highlights that were strategically placed on the face.

To apply the translucent makeup powder:

1. Place a powder puff on the powder and work some powder into the puff with your fingers.
2. Gently pat the powder on the face, **Figure 15-11**. Do not rub the powder onto the face.
3. Use a makeup powder brush to gently brush off any excess.

> ## Production Note
>
> A bald spot, or a completely bald head, almost always needs to be powdered to avoid reflecting large light hits.

Fourth Makeup Layer

Lipstick should be applied after powdering. Glossy lipstick should not be used because it causes light hits that are very distracting. Talent wearing glossy lipstick appears to have sequins glued to their lips.

Eyeliner rarely is used on men or children. Women should wear eyeliner only if it should be obvious that they are wearing makeup. It does not look natural and television amplifies the intensity of eyeliner.

Mascara thickens and lengthens eyelashes. Men should never use mascara unless they are extremely blonde and their eyelashes are not visible without it.

> ## Production Note
>
> A single tube of mascara should never be used on multiple people. Mascara should never be shared with another person. It is a fertile breeding ground for bacteria. Eye diseases such as conjunctivitis, or "pinkeye," are highly contagious and could affect the entire cast if mascara is shared. Even if only one person uses mascara, the product should be discarded and replaced once a month.

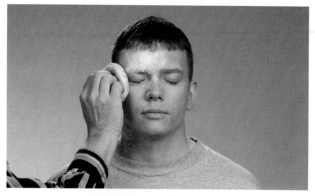
Initial Application

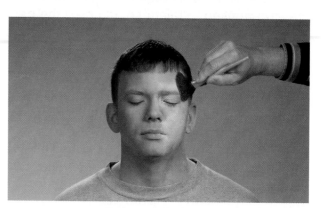
Remove Excess

Figure 15-11
The powder is applied with a powder puff and the excess is removed with a powder brush.

Makeup Removal

Cold cream used to be the most common product to remove makeup and is still used, though much less frequently. The disadvantage of using cold cream is that it is very messy. It must be slathered on the face and wiped off with a great many tissues. The face must then be washed with hot water and soap. Neglecting to wash with hot water and soap practically guarantees a skin breakout by the next day. Makeup remover is an alternative that accomplishes the same task, but often with the same degree of messiness. Makeup remover is an oil that is rather expensive at cosmetic stores. Presently, most people in the performing arts remove makeup with baby wipes, which are readily available and cost effective, **Figure 15-12**. Additionally, some brands offer fragrance-free wipes and many contain moisturizers, like aloe. Using two or three wipes removes all traces of makeup without the mess of other products. Regardless of the removal product used, the talent should always wash their face with soap and warm water after removing the layers of makeup.

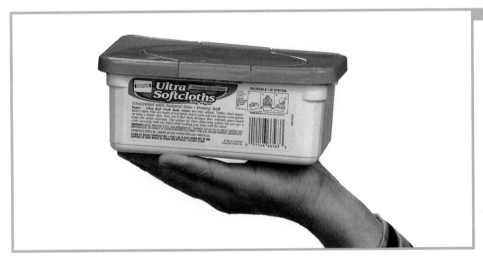

Figure 15-12
Unscented baby wipes effectively remove makeup and are inexpensive. They are more convenient and much less messy than cold cream.

Makeup Application Considerations

Each production brings a unique set of challenges for a makeup artist. The action in the production, the characters involved, and the characteristics of individual performers are all considerations for a makeup artist.

Eyes

Before applying makeup on another person, always ask if they wear contact lenses and if the lenses are "hard" or "soft." The response determines which application techniques to use and the ease with which makeup can be applied around their eyes.

If the person wears hard lenses, it is recommended that a novice makeup artist not apply their makeup. Extra care needs to be taken to prevent hurting the person's eyes. Hard contact lenses are just that–hard. If a novice makeup artist presses too hard when applying makeup to the eyelids, the edge of the contact lens can scratch the cornea of the eyeball underneath the lid. In this situation, there are two alternatives:

● Coach the person to apply their own makeup, **Figure 15-13**.

● Obtain assistance from another makeup artist experienced in dealing with performers wearing hard lenses.

Soft contact lenses, on the other hand, are soft and do not have hard edges. Performers who wear soft lenses pose no additional challenge in applying their makeup. When applying makeup, you will inevitably be working near the talent's eyes. Those who wear contacts are more comfortable when others work around their eyes, because they deal with their contacts daily. These people are well aware that working around the eyes is not a source of pain or discomfort.

Those who do not wear contacts are more likely to be squeamish when others work near their eyes. Female performers may be more comfortable, as they are more likely to apply their own eye makeup on

Figure 15-13
In some cases, it may be easier to coach someone in applying their own makeup, rather than trying to apply the makeup yourself.

a regular basis. Men and children are not used to anything being near their eyes and may react with unintentional resistance. They may blink, tear, or move away from you when trying to apply makeup near their eyes. The best solution is to be patient and rely on your personality. An effective technique is to distract them by talking constantly with them. Because it is more difficult to trust a stranger, another option is to coach them in applying their own makeup.

Talent who wear glasses may present unique difficulties. The glass lenses or the frames themselves can produce unattractive light hits. The simplest solution is to have the talent remove their glasses. If this is not possible due to poor vision or a trait of that particular character, the glasses can be tilted slightly downward. This directs the light reflection to the floor. Another option is to move or re-aim the lighting instruments in the studio, which is a more time consuming task.

Skin Sensitivity or Allergies

Because the Food and Drug Administration has not officially defined the term "hypo-allergenic," it is not accurate to rely on the "hypoallergenic" label on some products. Commonly, products labeled "hypo-allergenic" contain all the same ingredients as those without the label. The difference is the omission of fragrance. Fragrance is a common allergen that is added to consumer cosmetics, but not included in theatrical makeup. If a person is allergic to lanolin or wool, they should not wear crème makeup and must use pancake makeup. However, most people can wear theatrical crème makeup without problems.

Men and Makeup

Males frequently resist the very concept of wearing makeup. It is not generally viewed as a masculine attribute in our society. This is ironic because most of the men who are seen by the public as the most masculine wear makeup. Actors, politicians, and sports figures all wear makeup on television, when in a studio environment. Recall the appearance of any professional athlete in a locker room or on the sidelines speaking with a newscaster after coming off of the playing field. The appearance of this same athlete is drastically different when seen giving a studio interview or in promotional product spots. This is because studio makeup has been applied to ensure the best quality camera image of the athlete.

Costume Selection

Selecting the costumes for a program is dependent on many existing factors: plot, setting, set dressing, program format, lighting arrangement, and many others. The look of the costume design for the production cannot be determined without accounting for all these factors. In dramatic programs, for example, the plot and setting dictate the costuming for the program. The type and style of costumes used in a Western set in the late 1800s would be very different from the type of costuming used in a science fiction program set in the year 3005.

The actual program set and set dressing must also be considered when selecting the costumes. The patterns and colors used on the set and in the set dressing must be coordinated with the talent's costuming. Both striking clashes and perfect matching of colors and patterns should be avoided. Clashes of color or pattern can be so distracting to the audience that the message of the program is completely lost. When the colors or patterns used on the set and the costumes match, the talent and background may blend together causing the talent to disappear from the shot.

Lighting is another consideration in costume selection. If the lighting designer uses colored gels in the lighting instruments, for example, the colored light will change the appearance of the costume. Including the lighting designer's plans in the selection process helps to avoid problems with costuming that meets all the other needs of the program.

The following items should be considered when selecting costumes for a production:

- Avoid extreme contrasts between individual items of clothing, between clothing and skin tone, and between clothing and the background. Always remember the limitations of contrast ratio.

- Avoid the color white unless the set and other costumes are light in color.

- Avoid the color black unless the set and other costumes are dark in color.

- Costume colors should not match the background color. When these colors match, the depth created between the performer and the background is lost.

- Avoid the color red, if possible. Red is the most difficult color to accurately process, for both the television camera and the home viewer's television set.

- Be aware of the chromakey color (Chapter 18, *Electronic Special Effects*), if used in a production. The talent should not wear a color that matches or is very similar to the chromakey color.

- Avoid flashy jewelry because the pieces of jewelry produce distracting light hits.

- Avoid vertical or horizontal thin stripes and small, busy patterns, such as herringbone. These patterns appear to vibrate in rainbows of color called moiré.

Planning for Productions

If a scene is scheduled for shooting over a period of a few days, both the costuming and makeup on the talent must not change from one day of shooting to the next. All of the footage shot for the scene is likely to be edited down to a scene that lasts mere minutes. To ensure consistency:

1. Take photographs of the talent on the first day after their makeup and costuming is complete.

2. The brands and colors of makeup should be written on a makeup chart specific to that performer, **Figure 15-14**. The makeup chart also includes the placement and application techniques for the products used.

3. Create a chart that records which articles of clothing each performer wears and the scenes in which the clothing is worn.

Mistakes, however, occur. For instance, an actor has a large wound of a certain shape on his face in one shot and in the very next shot of the same scene, the wound is smaller and shaped differently. In a third shot, the wound is larger and returns to its original shape. This error in continuity may occur because the first and third shots were taken on a different day than the second shot. The makeup artist did not accurately duplicate the wound on both days. A makeup chart helps prevent errors in makeup continuity. On each consecutive day of shooting, the makeup artist uses the photographs and the makeup chart to duplicate the makeup application. The same applies to costumes used in a production. If a scene began with a male actor's shirttail tucked into his pants, but the scene ends with the shirttail untucked, the shirttail must be retucked if the scene is shot a second time. Costuming records and photographs are reviewed before additional takes of the same scene are shot.

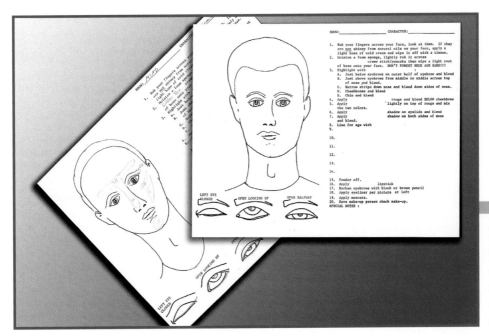

Figure 15-14
A makeup chart ensures that the talent's makeup is applied the same way for every day of shooting. This avoids creating errors in continuity.

Wrapping Up

Much practice is necessary in order to become competent with makeup application and design techniques. Television makeup is almost identical to theatrical makeup, except in the amount and intensity of application. Subtle application is the rule. To gain some practical experience, volunteer to help with makeup for the next theatrical production in your school. A variety of theatrical makeup books are also available through local libraries and bookstores.

Review Questions

Please answer the following questions on a separate sheet of paper. Do not write in this book.

1. Why is makeup necessary on television talent?
2. What is the one distinct difference between stage makeup and television makeup?
3. What are the advantages of crème makeup over pancake makeup?
4. List the cosmetic products used in each of the four layers of makeup application.
5. What are the options available for makeup removal? Which option is recommended?
6. What are some of the considerations a makeup artist must weigh for each production?
7. List some of the cautions related to costume selection.
8. How are errors in continuity related to costuming and makeup application avoided in a production?

Activities

1. Create a spreadsheet comparing the prices of comparable items of professional makeup and over-the-counter retail makeup products. Compare items such as base/foundation, cheek shadow, eye makeup, and brushed-on powders. Include the product type and brand in the spreadsheet information.
2. Make a pictorial display of images depicting both character and straight makeup applications using ads and layouts in current periodicals and local publications.

Important Terms

Background Music
Broadcasting Rights
Cablecasting Rights
Foreground Music
Recording Rights
Re-Recording Rights
Synchronization Rights

Chapter 16
Music

Objectives

After completing this chapter, you will be able to:

- List the guidelines and corresponding exceptions for using background music in a production.
- Describe the permissions that must be obtained to use copyrighted music in a production.
- Cite the permissions that must be obtained to use original music in a production.
- Identify the types of contracts available when choosing to use a music library.

Introduction

The vast majority of programs utilize music to some extent because without it, the audience feels that the program is missing something. To use music in a production, the appropriate permissions must be secured. Even though some music may be free when used for educational purposes, this is never a safe assumption. Always verify permission with the rights holder before using music in a production. Copyright laws are established by the government, as provided in the United States Constitution, **Figure 16-1**. Violations are dealt with harshly in the court systems. This chapter presents general items to consider when selecting music for a production. It does not offer legal advice and nothing contained in this chapter should be construed as legal advice.

Figure 16-1
The United States Constitution provides Congress with the power to make and enforce copyright laws.

The Congress shall have Power... To promote the Progress of Science and useful Arts, by securing for limited Times to Authors and Inventors the exclusive Right to their respective Writings and Discoveries.

The Constitution of The United States of America, Article I, Section 8 (Clause 8)

Production Note

When working in the industry, the director is involved in choosing the music used in a production and works closely with the composer in making decisions about original music. The production company's attorneys are responsible for acquiring the permissions necessary and handling the corresponding contracts.

Background Music: Music in a program that helps to relay or emphasize the program's message by increasing its emotional impact.

Foreground Music: Music in a program that is the subject of the production.

Using Music in a Production

Music used in any type of program can be placed into one of two categories: background music and foreground music. *Background music* helps relay or emphasize the message of a program by increasing its emotional impact. A common example is the use of exciting or intense music during a chase scene. *Foreground music* is the subject of the production. In a music video, for example, music is the primary element and the video is secondary.

Production Note

Regardless of the type of music selected, you must secure permission to use the music in your production. Your local school district should be able to inform you of its policies on the use of copyrighted music.

Guidelines for Using Background Music

The following is a list of general guidelines regarding the use of background music in television productions:

- Avoid music that is widely recognized. When the audience hears a piece of music they recognize, they begin to reminisce about the things they associate with the song, such as special events, particular people, or childhood memories. This is nice for the audience, but while they are recalling these moments, they are not watching and paying attention to the program.

- Avoid music containing lyrics during a dialog scene. The audience will find it difficult to separate the lyrics from the dialog while the talent is speaking.

- Use music only to enhance a mood. Music should not be placed in a program merely because "it is a really good song" or someone "just wanted to put it somewhere in the program." Sometimes, no music is best.

- Do not use catchy or busy music during a dialog scene. Once again, if the music distracts attention from the dialog, you will be making the audience work too hard.

- Do not mix styles of music within a program. In other words, do not include heavy metal, rock and roll, country, opera, classical and blues all within the same program. A wide array of styles within a single program produces an amateur–sounding audio track.

Exceptions to the Rules

As with almost any set of guidelines or rules, there are exceptions. Breaking the rules is not something that teachers usually encourage, but there are often valid reasons for doing so. The following are examples:

- Using music that is widely recognized. Recognizable music is sometimes required in a program. The famous nostalgic music used in the classic movie *American Graffiti* reinforced the program's era setting and increased the impact of action in the program.

- Playing music with lyrics during a dialog scene. If a scene takes place in a nightclub, for example, it is very unlikely that the music playing would be exclusively instrumental music. Vocals accompany most popular music. In this situation, the audio engineer's challenge is to keep the music levels far below the level of the talent's dialog.

- Using music for reasons other than mood enhancement. Breaking this rule often produces effects that are jarring to the audience, but also demands their attention. For example, playing the *Blue Danube* waltz in the background of a scene that depicts a bombing run during World War II, makes the effects of the bombs even more horrifying.

- Using catchy or busy music during a dialog scene. Depending on the environment in which a scene is set, having a myriad of background sounds may be necessary to create a convincingly real setting. If the scene takes place on the midway of a carnival or on a beach boardwalk during the summer, the environment is naturally full of many different sounds, including music. Omitting these sounds is an error that leaves the audience questioning the realism of the setting.

● Mixing styles of music within a program. Various styles of music may be used with a program to be consistent with the action and setting of particular scenes. In a documentary about an opera star, it is expected that opera music be in the background of most scenes. In a scene that portrays the opera star having dinner in a country-western themed restaurant, the most appropriate background music is country-western style music. To have opera music playing in this type of restaurant would be laughably wrong.

Sources of Music

The music used in productions may come from various sources:
● Professional and commercial recordings
● Unrecorded sheet music
● Original music
● Music in the public domain
● Music libraries

Using any of these sources requires that specific permissions be obtained *before* the music is placed in the program, **Figure 16-2**.

Figure 16-2
It may not be possible to use your favorite piece of music in a production. The proper permission must be obtained from the rights holders.

Recorded and Copyrighted Music

If it is absolutely necessary to use copyrighted music from a record, CD, tape, or from a video recording of a live concert, you must:

- Contact the record company listed on the record, CD, or tape. (A tape you record at a live concert is not a legal recording.)
- Request "master rights" from the record company for each piece of their music you would like to use.

If the videotape is to be shown anywhere other than in your own school, such as on a local cable system, you must contact the record company and request master rights.

It is not recommended that amateurs attempt to get permission from major recording artists for use of their music on student projects. The process is lengthy and can be discouraging. The result, most often, is a resounding "no" or a very high usage fee that may be equal to a month of college tuition, **Figure 16-3**.

Sheet Music

If the music you want to use is published in sheet music form, but not already recorded (such as the music used in a school band concert that will be shown on cable), you must obtain permission from the sheet music publisher. Occasionally, permission may be obtained by contacting the American Society of Composers, Authors, and Publishers (ASCAP) or Broadcast Music, Inc. (BMI). Contact information for both ASCAP and BMI may be found on the Internet. If the music is not listed with either ASCAP or BMI, you must contact the publisher directly.

Music Usage Fees

- There is no standard in the amount charged to use a piece of copyright music.

- The fees are often set by the agency or the artists themselves.

- The fee may depend on the particular television station's market (size of the potential viewing audience).

- If a program is "for profit" (has commercials), "not for profit," or public access programming affects the fee amount.

- Because rights cannot be granted to multiple people at the same time, the artist or agency may wait for a party that is willing to pay more for usage rights.

Figure 16-3
The fees charged for using copyrighted music are dependent on various factors.

Original Music

A faster route, involving less red tape, would be to contact local musicians who have their own original music. Obtain their permission to use their original music in the production. Most local artists love the free publicity of having their music included in a television program and, in some cases, will not charge you for recording it. It is still important to get that permission in writing!

You need:

- *Recording Rights.* Permission to record the music if it is from a live performance.
- *Re-Recording Rights.* Permission to copy the music from a CD or cassette tape onto videotape.
- *Synchronization Rights.* Permission to place video in synchronization with the music.
- *Broadcasting Rights.* Permission to broadcast the music to the public.
- *Cablecasting Rights.* Permission to cablecast the music to the public.

It is important to note that you can only use the local band's original music in the production. The band's rendition of a copyrighted song cannot be used. Their version of a copyrighted song is sometimes called a "cover." This version of the song requires that re-recording rights be obtained from the record company, in addition to the other rights listed above.

Recording Rights: Permission to record music from a live performance.

Re-Recording Rights: Permission to copy music from a CD or cassette tape onto videotape.

Synchronization Rights: Permission to place video in synchronization with a piece of music.

Broadcasting Rights: Permission to broadcast a piece of music to the public.

Cablecasting Rights: Permission to cablecast a piece of music to the public.

Assistant Activity

Choose a popular song that would be appropriate for use in a production that is broadcast locally. Research the necessary permissions and fees involved in using that song. Record each step of the process, including names, dates, and the information provided to you.

Music in the Public Domain

Using music in the public domain for your program is another possibility. Just because music is in the public domain, however, does not mean that it may automatically be used in a production. Any recording purchased at a music store has been recorded by an organization that, most likely, copyrighted their performance of the music. For example, Beethoven's Fifth Symphony is a piece of music in the public domain that may be perfect for your production. On the CD you purchased, the piece is performed by the London Philharmonic Orchestra. This recording is copyrighted by the London Philharmonic Orchestra and cannot be used without their permission.

To use Beethoven's Fifth Symphony in your production, ask a local orchestra or your high school or college band to perform the music and give you permission to use their recording of it. Use the guidelines previously described for getting permission from a local band when using music performed by a local orchestra or high school or college band.

Music Libraries

Another effective and less complicated way to get music for your programs is to use the services of a music library. There are a variety of companies that own large libraries containing many kinds and styles of music that can be purchased by a studio facility, **Figure 16-4**. These companies use several types of contracts with their clients:

- With a "buy-out" contract, the studio facility is free to use the music as often as they like without additional fees, once the music is purchased.

- "Needle-drop" is a term left over from the days of vinyl records. In a "needle-drop" contract, every time a piece of music is recorded for a program (drop the phonograph needle on a record), a fee is paid to the music library company.

- When using a "lease" contract, a flat fee is paid for unlimited use of a specified number of CDs in the library. As long as the lease is paid up, you may use the music in the library. When you stop paying on the lease contract, however, you must return all the CDs and can no longer use music from the library in any new videos.

Figure 16-4
There are dozens of music libraries available for purchase. Once the music is purchased, depending on the contract, the user is free to use the music at any time.

Wrapping Up

The message of this chapter is very simple: original music that you create can be freely used in your video productions. Any other type of music requires permission from the creators and/or their agents to be used in programs.

The process of getting the appropriate permission(s) is complicated and is subject to change with any alteration to the existing copyright laws. Under no circumstances should the content of this chapter be construed as legal advice. Examples of the complexities in legally using copyrighted music are presented. As previously mentioned, the simplest course of action is to make your own music locally.

Review Questions

Please answer the following questions on a separate sheet of paper. Do not write in this book.

1. What is the purpose of background music?
2. What are the five caveats of using background music in a television production?
3. What permissions must be obtained to use original music in a production?
4. What types of contracts are available for the use of music libraries?

Activities

1. Go to the Public Domain Information Project Web site and review the various songs considered to be "in the public domain." Make a list of song titles that you were surprised to see included on the Web site.
2. Investigate what a copyright protects and what it does not. Create an outline summarizing the information you discover.

Objectives

After completing this chapter, you will be able to:

● Explain the main function of a video switcher.

● Name some of the effects that are possible when using a special effects generator (SEG).

● Define the terms "bus" and "bank" in relation to a SEG.

● List the steps involved in using the cut bar on a SEG to cut between different camera shots.

Chapter 17

Video Switchers and Special Effects Generators

Introduction

When entering the control room of a professional television studio, the most interesting and intimidating piece of equipment in the room is the video switcher. Large video switchers have row after row of lighted buttons, levers, and knobs that look terribly confusing. The video switcher is the "brains" of the operation. A SEG is the next generation of a basic switcher, with the basic switcher functions in addition to the capability of producing many video effects commonly seen in television programs.

The Video Switcher

Video switcher:
Piece of equipment
to which all video
sources in a studio are
connected. A switcher
allows the operator
to select one signal
from various video
inputs and output the
selected signal to the
video recorder for
recording. Also called
a *switcher*.

All of the video sources in the studio are connected to the *video switcher*, or switcher, **Figure 17-1**. This piece of equipment allows the operator to select one signal from various video inputs, for example camera 1, camera 2, camera 3, CG, or VCR 1, and output the selected signal to the video recorder for recording, **Figure 17-2**. Video switchers can be inexpensive; under $50 in many consumer electronics stores. A switcher operates much the same as many common household items:

- The remote control for a television set allows the operator to select from all the inputs going to the television set, such as the various channels of programming, VCR, DVD player, and video game console. It is not normally possible to have two of the inputs on the screen simultaneously.

- Most cars have radios with buttons that are programmed with preset stations. When different buttons are selected, the radio tunes in the corresponding radio station. Pressing two buttons at the same time does not allow the listener to hear two stations at the same time.

- The receiver component of most stereo systems has a knob or individual buttons labeled AUX, FM, AM, TAPE, CD, and PHONO. Selection allows the signal from one component of the system to be heard through the speakers. The song playing on an FM radio station and a song on a CD cannot be simultaneously heard on an individual stereo.

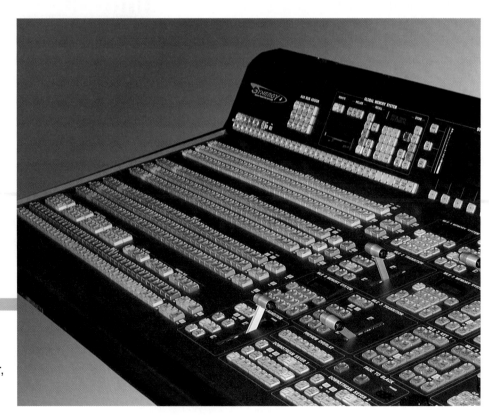

Figure 17-1
Initially, a large video switcher can be very intimidating. It works just like a small switcher, except it allows more video inputs.

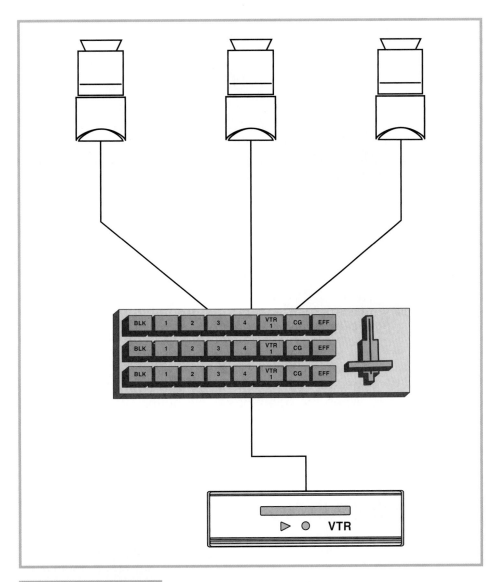

Figure 17-2
Any of the various inputs connected to a video switcher may
be selected and sent to the VTR.

Video Switcher Controls

Like the household items previously described, a video switcher
performs one function at a time. All the video inputs are plugged into
the switcher. At least one row of buttons on the switcher control panel
is marked with numbers that represent one of the inputs. A word or
abbreviation may also be used to mark buttons on the control panel,
Figure 17-3. Some switchers come with extra, preprinted buttons that
can be placed on the panel after removing a numbered button. For
example, a small studio with 3 cameras and 1 CG may remove the
camera "4" button and replace it with a "CG" button. This simplifies the
selections for the operator. When the CG button is selected, the VCR
receives the output of the CG.

Figure 17-3
Each button on the control panel of a video switcher is marked to indicate the corresponding signal or function.

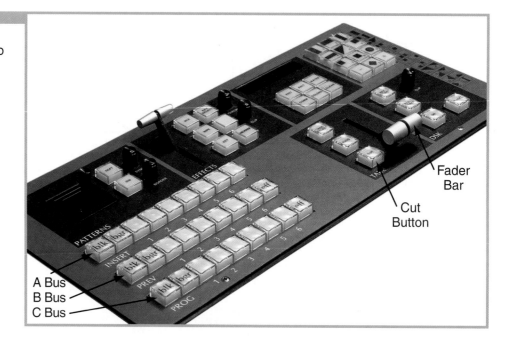

Fader Bar

Cut Button

A Bus
B Bus
C Bus

One cable connected to the output of the switcher runs to the video input of the VTR. When the operator selects button "2" on the control panel, the signal coming from camera 2 is sent to the VTR for recording. When the button for camera 3 is pressed, the image switches from camera 2 to the image from camera 3.

Production Note

At first glance, the difference between an analog switcher and a digital switcher is not obvious. A digital switcher has the same capabilities as an analog switcher. The main difference between the two is that a digital switcher can perform digital video effects, discussed in Chapter 18, *Electronic Special Effects*.

Video Switcher Operation

Technical director (TD): A member of the production team whose primary job function is to follow the camera script or verbal commands from the director and operate the video switcher accordingly.

The operation of the switcher is the primary job function of the *technical director*, or *TD*. The TD follows the camera script, prepared by the director, or verbal commands directly from the director. The camera operators follow the orders of the director and the TD selects the camera shots by skillful operation of the switcher. In some smaller operations, the director may also function as the TD.

Connected to the switcher is a video monitor for each input signal, as well as a monitor for the output signal, **Figure 17-4**. Each monitor is labeled with the signal it represents. The TD watches the monitors and constantly evaluates the images from each camera to determine which

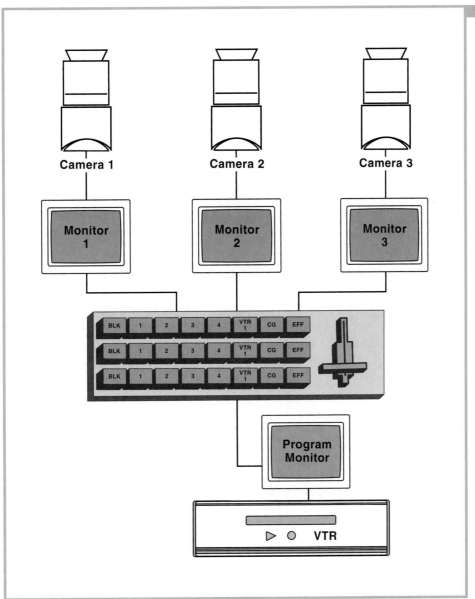

Figure 17-4
The control room system has a camera monitor for each camera signal, as well as a program monitor that displays the signal being recorded.

Cut: An instantaneous picture change that occurs on screen. Used synonymously with *take* in this context.

Glitch: A momentary "trashing" of the video signal (such as a roll, tear, or briefly appearing noise).

signal is sent to the recorder. The video switcher only switches from one input to another input. The result on the screen is an instantaneous picture change called a *cut*. With most switchers, a cut is accompanied by a momentary "trashing" of the video signal (such as a roll, tear, or briefly appearing noise) called a *glitch*. Glitches are not acceptable on professionally produced programs.

Talk the Talk

A *take*, in this context, is an instantaneous picture change and is synonymous with "cut." The director may say, "Cut to Camera 2" or he may say, "Take 2."

The output of the switcher is called the "program" and is viewed on the program monitor. This is the output that goes to the VCR for recording. The image on the program monitor is always identical to the image on one of the input monitors. The monitors are generally placed in a horizontal row, reading from left to right. The program monitor is usually placed on top of the row of input monitors.

Visualize This

To understand the importance of correctly using a switcher, consider that many people fall asleep when they are bored. When students become disinterested in a classroom activity or discussion, for example, they begin to feel drowsy and their eyelids get heavy. To help perk up, looking at different elements in the environment provides stimulus to the brain. If History class gets boring during a lecture, you might cast your eyes around the room looking at your book, fellow students, your fingernails, a pen, doodles in your notes, or the teacher's hairstyle. Looking at anything changes the picture in your mind, or switches to a different camera image. The audio of your mind-movie remains the same, but visually, you make the movie more interesting. This process is the same as production switching. The moment the audience decides that a program does not provide sufficient visual stimulus, they turn away from the television screen and the director fails in his mission.

A special effects generator (SEG) has the capability of producing various video effects, in addition to the functionality of a video switcher. Any SEG is also a video switcher, but any video switcher is not necessarily a SEG.

Production switcher: The general, technical name used for either a video switcher or a special effects generator.

Special effects generator (SEG): A piece of production equipment that performs clean cuts, fades, dissolves, wipes, and various keys in addition to the basic functions of a video switcher.

Talk the Talk

"*Production switcher*" is the general, technical name used for either a video switcher or a special effects generator. Because very few video switchers are found in television production facilities, some people call the SEG a switcher. This is not the proper name for the machine, but is increasingly more accepted as a reference to a SEG.

The Special Effects Generator (SEG)

A *special effects generator*, or *SEG*, is a device used in the television production industry that is based on the principles of the video switcher. Like a video switcher, a SEG allows the operator to select one signal from the various video inputs available for processing and recording. Additionally, a SEG performs clean cuts, fades, dissolves, wipes, and various keys. Compared to the simple cut created by a switcher, these effects are much more appealing to the program viewers.

Talk the Talk

The term *SEG* is pronounced like "egg" with an *S* at the beginning. This piece of equipment is also commonly referred to by simply saying the three letters "S-E-G." Either way of referring to a SEG is perfectly acceptable.

- *Fade.* The video image slowly appears from a solid-colored screen. Or, the video image slowly disintegrates from an image to a solid-colored screen. The color of the screen is usually black, but can be any color of the director's choosing if this option is available on the SEG. Some SEGs only offer black as a screen color for a fade.
  - *Fade In.* The viewer sees a black screen and the image appears, **Figure 17-5**. This effect is usually used for the beginning of a program or scene, and corresponds directly to the concept of opening the curtain on a stage performance. A fade may also be used when a character wakes up, while shooting with the subjective camera technique. The appearance is almost as if the set was completely unlit, and the lighting instruments are slowly brought up. An *up from black* effect is the same as the fade in.
  - *Fade Out.* As the viewer sees the scene of a program end, the image slowly goes to a black screen. This effect is usually used at the end of a scene or program, and corresponds directly to the concept of closing the curtain on a stage performance. Another use of fade out may be when a character goes to sleep, passes out, or dies while using subjective camera. A *fade to black* effect is the same as fade out.

Fade: A visual effect where the video image either slowly appears from a solid-colored screen or slowly disintegrates from an image to a solid-colored screen.

Fade in: A video effect where a totally dark picture transitions into a fully visible picture. Also called *up from black*.

Fade out: A video effect where the image slowly goes to a black screen as a scene of a program ends. Also called *fade to black*.

Figure 17-5
A totally dark picture transitions into a fully visible picture when using a fade in. A fade out is the reverse.

Dissolve: A video effect where one picture slowly disintegrates while another image slowly appears. Also called a *lap dissolve*.

● *Dissolve.* One picture slowly disintegrates while another slowly appears, **Figure 17-6**. During a dissolve, the screen is never black. The dissolve is a visual statement to the audience, meaning "you are now seeing another place, during the same time," or "meanwhile." It is also used to show a time passage in the program. For example, a cook puts a cake in the oven and sets the timer for 35 minutes. The audience does not want to stare at an oven timer for 35 minutes. Therefore, they see a dissolve to the same oven timer 35 minutes later. In this case, 35 "real time" minutes have passed in 3 seconds of "screen time." This effect is called a *lap dissolve* in the film industry because, originally, two pieces of film would have to overlap to produce a dissolve.

Visualize This

Many students confuse the terms "fade" and "dissolve," using them interchangeably. To help differentiate the two terms, consider that the original color of cotton is white. The white cotton is dyed blue before making blue jeans. As blue jeans are worn and washed, the blue color slowly washes out, or *fades*, revealing the original white color of the cotton. When the applied color fades, the natural color begins to show through. The "natural" color of the television screen is black. Therefore, when colorful images on the television are removed, the screen returns to black. When a television image is removed from the screen, or is washed out, the screen fades to black.

Wipe: A video effect where a line, or multiple lines, moves across the screen and replaces one picture with another.

● *Wipe.* A line, or multiple lines, moves across the screen, replacing one picture with another. If the line is stopped at some point as it moves across the screen, a split screen is created (discussed in Chapter 18, *Electronic Special Effects*). A split screen occurs when the line, or lines, of a wipe stop moving part of the way across the screen, dividing the screen into two or more sections.

Figure 17-6
In a dissolve, one image slowly becomes another image. At no time is the screen black.

- **Key.** A portion of the picture is electronically removed and replaced with another image (discussed in Chapter 18, *Electronic Special Effects*).

Key: A video effect where a portion of the picture is electronically removed and replaced with another image.

Components of a SEG

A *bus* is a row of buttons on the control panel of a SEG. Most SEGs have at least three buses, with a minimum of 5 buttons per bus. Some SEGs, however, may have more than 30 buttons on a bus. Each button accesses a different video input and is clearly labeled. If there are 10 cameras, for example, ten of the buttons are labeled 1 through 10. Other buttons may be available for additional VCRs, CG, and BLACK. The more video inputs on a SEG, the more buttons are required to access each at any time. The buses are identical, with the possible exception of an additional button on the right end, **Figure 17-7**.

Bus: A row of buttons on the control panel of a SEG that access different functions.

Figure 17-7
Each of three buses are identical, with Black, 1, 2, 3, 4, VTR 1, CG, and EFF buttons.

Production Note

Do not let the great number of buttons on larger SEGs intimidate you. A SEG that has additional video inputs requires more buttons to access those inputs. The additional buttons are simply more of the same buttons and functions you will become familiar with on a smaller SEG.

A SEG sits flat on a countertop and the TD operates it while seated. Most commonly, the bus closest to the TD is labeled *Program Bus*. Any signal button pressed on the program bus goes directly to the output of the SEG and to the VCR for recording. The other two buses are electronically connected to each other. In order to dissolve, two pictures must be on screen at the same time. Since multiple buttons cannot be pressed at once on a single bus, the two buses are connected to allow the display of two images. When two buses are electronically connected to each other, they are called a *bank*.

Bank: Two buses on the control panel of a SEG that are electronically connected to each other.

Next to each bank is a *fader lever*, also referred to as a *fader bar* or *fader handle*, **Figure 17-8**. A fader lever is usually a T-shaped handle that can be moved forward and backward. The further the bar is moved in one direction, the stronger the signal coming from the bus in that direction. Using this instrument, the signal from each bus in the bank can be manipulated. To begin a dissolve, one signal can be at 90% strength with 10% of the other signal. To perform the dissolve, gradually move the fader lever (80/20%, 70/30%, 60/40%, 50/50%, and so on) until complete.

Fader lever: A control on a SEG, usually a T-shaped handle, that controls the strength of that signal coming from each bus. Also called a *fader bar* or *fader handle*.

Figure 17-8
The fader lever can be moved forward and backward. As it moves, it diminishes one signal and increases another signal.

To differentiate between the buses, the industry convention is to assign a letter of the alphabet to each bus. The bus farthest away from the TD is called "A" bus, **Figure 17-9**. Each bus that follows is sequentially assigned a letter. For example, the program bus on a SEG with 7 buses would be G bus. The program bus is typically the bus closest to the TD and, therefore, the last bus on the panel. Buses are referred to by the letter assigned.

Assistant Activity

Review the explanation of how letters are assigned when labeling buses. Using **Figure 17-3** as a guide, sketch the control panel of a SEG and close the book when you are finished. Label each of the buses and identify the program bus and mix bank. Check your work using the previous sections in the text and the corresponding figures.

Figure 17-9
Each bus is assigned a letter, beginning with the row farthest from the TD.

To illustrate a dissolve:

1. Imagine that button 3 has been pressed on the program bus, C bus in this case, and the audience is watching the image coming from camera 3.

2. To set up a dissolve, push the fader lever all the way up, so it is pointing at A bus.

3. Press 1 on A bus and 2 on B bus.

4. Press the EFFECTS button on the far right of C bus and the output jumps up to the mix bank, **Figure 17-10**. The output goes to A bus in the mix bank because the fader lever is pushed all the way up to A bus.

5. The audience watching the image from camera 3, simply sees a cut to camera 1. The audience never knows that they are now watching a signal coming from the mix bank.

6. Dissolve from camera 1 to camera 2 by moving the fader lever from the up position to the down position, pointing at B bus.

Figure 17-10
If camera 1 is selected, or "punched up," on A bus and camera 2 is punched up on B bus, what happens when the fader lever is pulled down to the lower position?

If the fader lever is stopped halfway through a dissolve, the images from camera 1 and camera 2 are both displayed on the screen at 50% strength. As a result, they are both semitransparent and look "ghostly." This effect is called a superimposition. The image in the middle of the series in **Figure 17-6** is a superimposition. If the "BLACK" button were selected on B bus in step 3 above, a dissolve to black would have been produced. From the audience's perspective, a dissolve to black appears the same as a fade to black.

Banks

Mix bank: A single bank on an SEG that contains the cut, fade, and dissolve effects.

Effects bank: A bank on a SEG that allows each signal to be processed individually.

Delegation control: A switch or button on the control panel of a SEG that toggles the A bank or B bank from one function to another. For example, the delegation control can switch the A bank from operating as a mix bank to an effects bank.

The cut, fade, and dissolve are the simplest effects a SEG can produce. All three of these effects are contained in a single bank called the *mix bank*. Like the ingredients combined in a kitchen mixer, the inputs on the SEG cannot be separated and processed individually once they have been mixed. An *effects bank*, however, allows each signal to be processed individually. The TD can set up various keys and wipes on the effects bank (discussed in Chapter 18, *Electronic Special Effects*).

A SEG with both a mix bank and an effects bank has at least 5 buses; A and B may be the mix bank, with C and D as the effects bank, and E as the program bus. Large SEGs may have 4 mix banks and 4 effects banks, totaling 17 buses. Even these are nothing more than multiples of the same functions found on a three-bus SEG.

The most economical SEGs have only three buses, but are still capable of both mixing and producing effects. A small SEG accomplishes this by allowing bus A and B to be *either* a mix bus, an effects bus, a key bank, or a DVE bank (discussed in Chapter 18, *Electronics Special Effects*). A switch or button, called a *delegation control*, simply toggles the functionality of the A or B bank, **Figure 17-11**.

Black Video

Black video: A bona-fide video signal that has no lightness.

Black video is a bona fide video signal that has no lightness. When the "BLACK" button on the SEG is pressed, the output is a purely black signal. The black button is not an input on the SEG. Black is generated by the SEG itself. The black output may be used at the beginning or end of the program, making either end neater than just displaying video noise at the beginning and end of the program. This may also be used within a program. If, for example, a character loses consciousness, selecting this button represents the world going "dark."

Only when light is applied to the screen is an image visible, because the natural color of the television screen is black. When the SEG outputs a black signal, it is an actual signal with no light. During a program, the director may want the screen to go black. By turning off the SEG, the VCR is not actually recording a black signal; it is recording nothing. "Nothing" video is also black in color, but the tape may have major glitches on it.

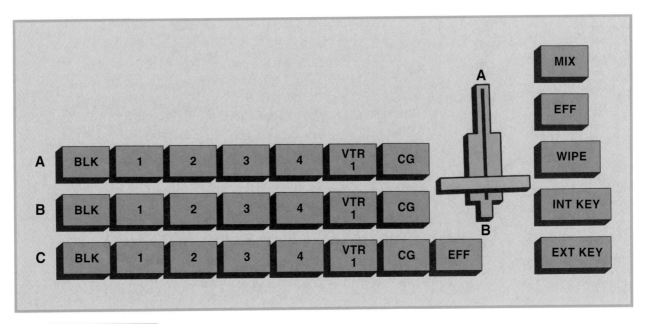

Figure 17-11
A delegation switch or button allows the A/B bank to perform either mix or effects. Once "effects" is selected as the function of A/B, some switchers present the option of indicating which kind of effect should be processed.

To record a clean black screen, the black must be created on the SEG. Black video is very important to the successful operation of a television production facility. "Nothing" video looks black, but can cause problems on a videotape. Other methods of placing a black signal onto a video- tape are discussed in Chapter 19, *Video Editing*.

Visualize This

A human being's eyes are like a video camera and the signal going up the optic nerve to the brain is like the video signal going to a television screen. Imagine that you are exploring a deep cave that extends far into the earth. You turn off your flashlight and are suddenly in total darkness. Does this mean that your eyes have stopped functioning and that you are blind? Of course not. Your eyes are functioning perfectly, but there is no light for your eyes to pick up an image to send to your brain. Likewise, black video is a perfectly good video signal that simply lacks any light.

Preview Monitor

The preview monitor is connected to the output of the mix bank, **Figure 17-12**. The purpose of the preview monitor is to allow the TD to set up an effect on the mix bank (A bus and B bus). The TD can see the

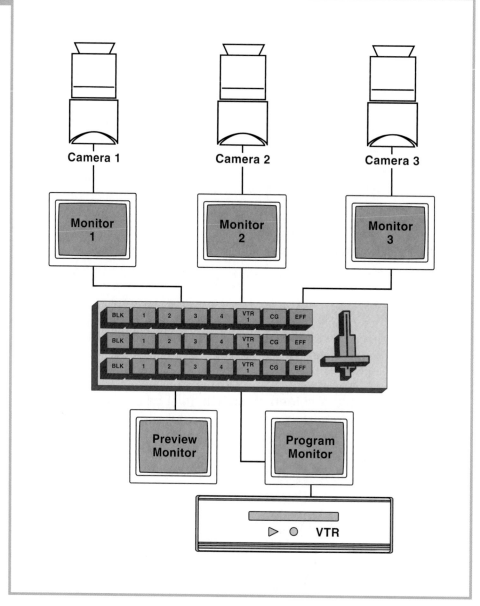

effect on the preview monitor before pressing the EFFECTS button on C bus, which sends it out to the viewers. For example, while the audience watches camera 3 on the C bus, the TD sets up a split screen between cameras 1 and 2 and watches it on the preview monitor. When it looks the way he wants, the EFFECTS button on C bus is pressed and the audience instantly sees the split screen already created.

Cut Bar

A *cut bar*, or *cut button*, is a convenient accessory on many SEGs. A cut bar is a selection on a SEG that provides a quick way of cutting between the input selected on one bus and the input selected on the other bus in the bank. If shooting a 2-person interview with two cameras,

Cut bar: A feature on a SEG that provides a quick way of cutting between the input selected on one bus and the input selected on another bus in the bank. Also called a *cut button*.

each camera is on a different person during the taping. The entire interview consists of cutting from one camera to the other as the two people speak to each other.

Using the SEG controls, **Figure 17-13**, the TD may simply alternate pressing button 1 and button 2 on C bus. This motion can become monotonous after a short time, which may lead to mistakes. Pressing the wrong button may send the audience the interviewer's face as the interviewee speaks. This is probably not the desired image. The cut bar eliminates this mistake. To use the cut bar in this scenario:

1. Select the EFFECTS button on C bus.

2. Press camera 1 on A bus and camera 2 on B bus.

3. Begin the interview on B bus. The fader lever should be down, pointing at B bus.

4. To change cameras, simply press the cut bar or cut button.

5. The first time it is pressed, the output of the SEG switches from B bus to A bus. This creates a cut from camera 2 to camera 1.

6. Press the cut bar again to cut the output from camera 1 back to camera 2.

7. Repeat steps 5 and 6 as many times as necessary during the program.

Figure 17-13
The cut button on a SEG allows a simple switch from one camera to another and back again, by pressing just one button instead of two.

Wrapping Up

The vast number of SEGs available offer many variations on the basic features presented in this chapter. Whether a SEG has 3 inputs or 33 inputs, almost all SEGs operate on the same basic principles.

Most TDs switch when instructed to do so by the director. Over time, and with experience, many TDs develop a talent for the sequences and timing of images. They can often predict the director's instructions.

Review Questions

Please answer the following questions on a separate sheet of paper. Do not write in this book.

1. What is the difference between a video switcher and a SEG?
2. How do you differentiate between a fade and a dissolve?
3. What is a bus?
4. What is the function of a bank?
5. What is the difference between a mix bank and an effects bank?
6. How is black video used in a production?

Activities

1. Tape about 5 minutes of television and watch the tape with the sound turned off. Notice the camera switches. Determine why the switch was made at each point and make note of the reason.
2. Research various brands and models of SEGs. Summarize the options available on five different models and compare the purchase price of each.

Important Terms

Chromakey
Chrominance
Circle Wipe
Clip Control
Colorizer
Corner Insert
Corner Wipe
Digital Video Effect (DVE)
Edge Mode
External Key
Horizontal Wipe
Internal Key
Key
Key Camera
Key Level Control
Lower Third Key
Lower Third Super
Luminance
Luminance Key
Matte Key
Pixel
Shadow Mode
Split Screen
Superimposition (Super)
Transitional Device
Vertical Wipe

Objectives

After completing this chapter, you will be able to:

- Explain the difference between a mix bank and an effects bank.
- Differentiate between a superimposition and a key.
- Describe the importance of pixels to DVEs.

Introduction

Students learning about television production are often tempted to add "cool" effects that hold no real purpose to the overall goals of their program. Special effects in a program that do not serve a purpose and do not support the program become nothing more than gimmicks and are a big mistake in a production. The audience stops paying attention and the message of the program is lost. Effects are very seductive, but they should only be used when a special effect supports the program and its message.

Electronic special effects can be divided into two types:

- Analog Special Effects
- Digital Video Effects (DVE)

Analog Special Effects

Many analog special effects are built into the SEG. These types of effects are commonly seen in programs and include wipes, superimpositions, and keys.

Wipes

The wipe is a line that moves across the screen, replacing one picture with another. Common types of wipes are *horizontal wipes*, a vertical line moving across the screen horizontally, and *vertical wipes*, a horizontal line moving across the screen vertically. A vertical wipe looks similar to a window shade being raised or lowered. Analog wipes involve a line moving across the screen, revealing a picture that is "behind" the image being wiped off the screen. No part of either image is moved in any way; each is either removed or revealed by the line. A wipe can take many different forms, depending on the wipe effects built into the SEG, **Figure 18-1**.

A wipe is accomplished in much the same way as a mix. One camera signal is selected on one bus and another camera signal is selected on the other bus. Moving the fader handle determines the progress of the line across the screen.

Horizontal wipe: A video effect where a vertical line moves across the screen horizontally, replacing one picture with another.

Vertical wipe: A video effect where a horizontal line moves across the screen vertically, replacing one picture with another.

Production Note

It is important to note that an *analog* wipe involves a line moving across the screen that reveals an image "behind" the image being removed from the screen. Imagine a teacher erasing the writing on a blackboard. As the words are erased, they are not moved or pushed off the blackboard. The chalk writing is removed by the eraser and the blackboard surface is revealed. An analog wipe is much like this example because no part of either image is moved in any way. The images are either removed or revealed by the moving line. A *digital* wipe can do anything an analog wipe can do and much more. As discussed later in this chapter, a digital wipe can make an image "move."

Transitional device: An effect that is used as a means of getting from one scene to another.

Split screen: A wipe that is stopped part of the way through its move, dividing the screen into two or more parts.

Wipes are usually used as a means of getting from one scene to another, or as a *transitional device*. A wipe that is stopped part of the way through its move and divides the screen into two or more parts is called a *split screen*. This effect is used most often to portray a telephone conversation, **Figure 18-2**. Each person is shown on one-half of the screen as they speak to each other on the telephone. Split screens are also used for interviews on news programs when the participants are in different locations. Showing both interviewees on the screen allows the audience to see the conversational interaction during the interview.

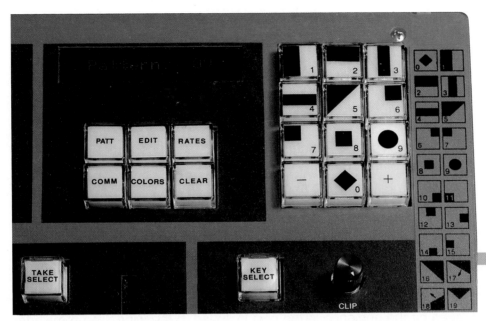

Figure 18-1
Some of the most common wipes are indicated on this chart.

Figure 18-2
A wipe is a line that moves across the screen, replacing one picture with another. If the wipe is stopped at some point mid-screen, a split screen is created.

Circle wipe: A video effect where a circle grows or shrinks, replacing one picture with another.

Corner wipe: A video effect where a small image is positioned in any corner, usually the upper right or left corner, of the full screen image. Two sides of the smaller image touch the actual frame of the larger picture.

Corner insert: A video effect where a small image is positioned in any corner, usually the upper right or left corner, of the full screen image. All four sides of the smaller image rest inside the frame of the larger picture.

The *circle wipe* is a circle that grows or shrinks to replace one picture with another. A SEG with the capability of a circle wipe often has a joystick to control the position of the circle on the screen.

The *corner wipe* is seen on many smaller news broadcasts where an image related to a story is displayed over the studio anchor's left or right shoulder. Achieving this effect requires two cameras or sources of video:

- Camera A shoots a picture of the story and positions it in the upper quarter of the screen.
- Camera B shoots the anchor.

When the wipe is performed, the image from camera A appears over the newscaster's shoulder. In the corner wipe, two sides of the smaller picture touch the actual frame of the larger picture, **Figure 18-3**. The corner wipe appears only in the upper corner of the full screen image that is shot by camera B. This is an important consideration when framing a picture for a corner wipe. The only portion of the picture shot by camera A seen by the audience is the part included in the wipe. The remainder of the picture from camera A may actually be poorly framed. The main concern is the portion of the image being wiped. To properly frame the shots, the camera operator must know which corner is going to be wiped before the image is shot.

A *corner insert* is a different kind of wipe that is similar to the corner wipe. All four sides of the corner insert image rest fully inside the frame of the larger picture, **Figure 18-4**. This resembles the "picture-in-picture" feature on some television sets.

Figure 18-3
In a corner wipe, two of the four edges touch the edges of the large picture frame.

Figure 18-4
None of the four edges
of the inserted picture
touch any of the edges
of the background frame
in a corner insert.

**Superimposition
(super):** A video effect
where the images or
the output from two
different sources are
placed on screen at the
same time. Each image
is less than 100% of its
original intensity, but
when combined, the
result is 100% of the
intensity possible on
the television screen.

Lower third super:
A video effect created
when an image or
text is displayed in
the lower third of
the screen using a
superimposition.

Superimpositions

A *superimposition*, or *super*, places images or the output from two different sources on screen at the same time. Each image is less than 100% of its original intensity, but when combined, the result is 100% of the intensity possible on the television screen. For example, one image is the picture of an athlete and the other is the athlete's name created on a character generator (CG). The director wants the athlete's name to appear on the screen, so the audience can read his name as they hear what he has to say, **Figure 18-5**. When a name, or other text, is placed in the lower third of the screen with a superimposition, the effect is called a *lower third super*. This is a commonly used effect.

Figure 18-5
Both images mixed in a superimposition are somewhat
transparent.

Suppose that the player's jersey is red and the CG letters are white. With the superimposition effect, both images are less than 100% of their original intensity and have a ghostly, see-through appearance. The image of the athlete is not quite as bright as it would be without the super, because there is less of the image presented. The white CG letters are less intense than pure white, and allow some of the red color of the jersey to bleed through. The final picture is an athlete wearing a red jersey with pink letters spelling out his name on the screen. This is, most likely, not the image the director intended.

Keys

The *key* is an effect similar to a superimposition, except that both images are displayed at 100% of their original intensity. For years, using the lower third super effect meant dealing with the color compromises described in the previous section. Newer technology has solved this problem by creating the key. A key visually cuts a hole in the original background picture and fills the hole with the desired text or image. When this effect is positioned in the lower third of the screen, it is called a *lower third key*.

Key: A video effect where the images or the output from two different sources are displayed on screen at the same time. Each image is displayed with 100% of its original intensity.

Lower third key: A video effect created when an image or text is displayed in the lower third of the screen using a key effect.

Visualize This

Using the example for superimpositions, imagine a still photograph of the athlete. Cut the letters spelling the athlete's name right out of the photograph; literally cut holes in the shape of each letter right out of the photograph. Place the photograph over a piece of white paper. The letters can clearly be seen. Each image, the player and the white letters, is 100% of the possible intensity, **Figure 18-6**. Visually, this is the result of a key.

Internal key: A video effect that is a mixture of two images. One image provides the shape that is cut out of the other (background) picture. White fills the shape that is cut out. Also called a *luminance key*.

Luminance: The brightness or lightness of the video picture.

Key camera: The camera used to shoot the object providing the shape to be cut into the background picture when creating an internal key effect.

Internal Key

The *internal key*, or *luminance key*, is a mixture of two images. The example above, of the athlete and the lower third key, is actually an internal key. It operates on the *luminance* coming from the key camera. Luminance is the brightness or lightness of the video picture. Whenever a key is activated, at least two cameras must be in operation. One camera provides the background, such as the athlete in the previous example. The other camera, called the *key camera*, provides the shape of the hole cut into the background picture. The key camera always shoots a high contrast image, such as white letters on a black background.

Production Note

When setting-up to key graphics or letters, as in the football player example, a CG is usually used as the key source. When using an image shot with a camera as the key, as in the basketball and tennis ball example in the following section, a camera is the key source.

Figure 18-6
The key permits both the background image and the keyed image to be visible at 100% intensity.

An internal key operates by taking the area of highest luminance in the key camera's image and uses it as a pattern to be cut out in the background camera's image. Once the hole is cut, it is filled with the keyed luminance and, in this example, the resulting image is solid, pure white letters on the player's jersey, **Figure 18-6**.

If a key is attempted with a normal picture as the keyed source, the luminance key takes the area of the highest luminance and sends it into the SEG. A hole is then cut in the background image. If the key image is a brown surface with a white chair on it, the white chair has the highest luminance in the picture. The luminance of the white chair is sent to the SEG and a shape matching the chair is cut out of the player's image. The combined picture does not look like a 3-dimensional white chair sitting on the player's body, **Figure 18-7**. The shading and detail in the picture of the chair is not sent to the SEG, just the luminance. Therefore, only the shape of the white chair is included in the key.

 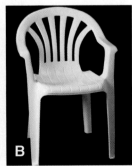 

Figure 18-7
A luminance key cuts the shape of the keyed object out of the background picture and places white in the space, or hole, that is created. A—Background image. B—Keyed object. C—Luminance key.

If a yellow tennis ball and an orange basketball are placed on the ground in front of the white chair, the image now has four colors: white, yellow, orange, and brown. Placing these colors in order of luminance, from highest to lowest, they appear as:

- White
- Yellow
- Orange
- Brown

Clip control: A knob on the control panel of a SEG that allows the operator to adjust the amount of luminance that is sent to the SEG. Also called *key level control*.

Many SEGs also have a *clip control*, sometimes called a *key level control*, **Figure 18-8**. By adjusting the clip control, the amount of luminance sent to the SEG can be adjusted, increased or decreased. In the previous example, the key level control may be adjusted to allow the luminance of the chair, yellow tennis ball, and orange basketball to go to SEG. The background image of the athlete now has cutout shapes of the chair, tennis ball, and basketball—all of which are white, **Figure 18-9**. The tennis ball is not yellow and the basketball is not orange because this type of key only deals with luminance. The luminance key takes the items sent to the SEG, cuts the hole in the background picture, and fills the hole with white. A luminance key operates with white light, not colors. A chromakey works with colors. A luminance key is much easier to operate than chromakey. Luminance, or internal key, is a much less expensive module to incorporate into a SEG.

Figure 18-8
The clip control allows the operator to adjust the amount of luminance sent to the SEG.

Figure 18-9
The luminance key allows objects of different shapes and colors into the background picture, but the objects are always featureless and colored white.

Matte key

The matte key is usually an add-on option to the internal key. If shooting a program about snowboarding with the opening titles displayed against the side of a mountain, white letters are not visible on a snow-covered hill. By using the matte key, the luminance of the letters can be adjusted to be seen against the white snow, **Figure 18-10**. Where an internal key fills the key cutout only with white, a *matte key* allows the operator to adjust the fill color to any shade of gray, from light gray to black. After the cutout is created, a control knob or lever is manipulated to control the key's luminance.

Matte key: An add-on option to the internal key that allows the operator to fill the key cutout with any shade of gray, from light gray to black, instead of simply white.

Figure 18-10
The matte key turns the white of a luminance key into any shade of gray the operator desires.

Colorizer

The *colorizer* is another add-on feature to an internal key. It operates similarly to the matte key, but allows the white key fill color to be changed to any color, **Figure 18-11**. Adding color to a key shape does not add the shading and detail that it lacks. It is as if holes have been cut out of a photograph and it is placed on top of colored paper. The key shape or lettering is still flat, or one-dimensional.

Colorizer: An add-on feature to the internal key that allows the operator to fill the key cutout with any color, instead of simply white.

Studio Rules Of Operation

Figure 18-11
A colorizer allows the luminance of the keyed image to be changed from white to any appropriate color.

Shadow and edge mode

Edge mode and *shadow mode* are two more add-ons for an internal key. The edge mode places a border around the keyed image. Additional controls allow the operator to adjust the thickness and color of the border. The shadow mode places a drop shadow around two sides of the image. The edge and shadow often provide needed clarity to the keyed image by offering a degree of separation from the background image, **Figure 18-12**.

Edge mode: An add-on feature to the internal key that places a border around the keyed image.

Shadow mode: An add-on feature to the internal key that places a drop shadow around two sides of the keyed image.

Figure 18-12
Edge and shadow modes further separate a keyed image from the background image. This separation helps the viewer to more clearly understand the total image.

External Key

The *external key* is a mixture of three images: the background image, the key source (shape of the cutout), and the key fill. The key fill is a unique component to this effect. The key fill is the image or pattern that fills the key cutout.

If shooting an instructional program on masonry construction techniques, imagine that the opening title is "Brick is Back." The letters are keyed on top of the studio blue curtain and should appear as if they are constructed out of brick. The colorizer on a luminance key provides red letters, but does not make the letters look as if they are made of brick. Use an external key instead. To make the letters look like brick:

1. The background shot is on tape input 1 on the SEG.
2. Input 2 of the SEG is the CG, or camera, pointed at a black card with white letters spelling out "Brick is Back."
3. Input 3 is the shot of a brick wall.
4. Activate the external key.
5. The background image now has "Brick is Back" cut out and the letters are filled with the brick pattern from input 3 on the SEG, **Figure 18-13**.

The advantage of using an external key camera is the addition of texture, rather than flat filled letters. The fill camera can shoot a brick wall, fire, grass, people, or any object, and the letters can be filled with the image. In the example of the white chair, the cutout can be filled with the image of that same chair and will include all of the detail and shading. However, lining up the two cameras to fill the same image is very difficult.

External key: A video effect that is a mixture of three images: the background image, the key source (shape of the cutout), and the key fill. The image or pattern that fills the key cutout shape is the key fill.

Background

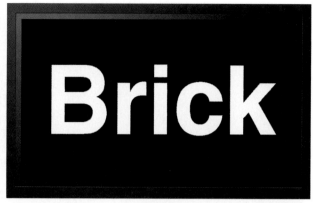

Key

Fill

External Key

Figure 18-13
The external key is a mixture of three cameras: the background camera, the key camera, and the fill camera. (Jack Klasey)

Chromakey

Chromakey: A type of key effect where a specific color can be blocked from the key camera's input.

Chrominance: The color portion of the video signal, which includes the hue and color saturation.

Chromakey operates with specific colors, or *chrominance*, and can be set for any color. Chrominance is the color portion of the video signal, where luminance is the brightness quality of the signal. Chromakey is frequently used on television, most often during the weather report on the local evening news. The audience sees the weathercaster standing in front of various maps, pointing out current and future weather activity. In the studio, however, the crew sees the weathercaster standing in front of a completely blue or green background; there is no map behind him.

The chromakey circuitry allows the SEG to tell itself not to "see" a particular color. In this case, the blue or green of the background is not used on the key camera's input. Therefore, the SEG now uses everything except items that are blue. The SEG sends an image with holes cut in it, eliminating everything that is blue, to the effects circuitry. The SEG has another camera pointed at a background source, which, in the weather-caster example, is the output of a computer-generated weather map. The chromakey circuit places the image in the background source camera, with the map, wherever there is a hole. So, the blue background behind the weathercaster is completely replaced by the map, **Figure 18-14**.

Figure 18-14
Using a keyed image allows a background to be inserted behind the talent, without constructing an elaborate backdrop.

If the weathercaster has blue eyes or stripes in his tie that match the background, the viewers at home see right through his eyes or tie and see the map. This effect is eliminated by colored contact lenses and wardrobe personnel who are on their toes.

The chromakey circuit does not necessarily key all shades of blue or green. The SEG can be tuned or adjusted to key any color desired by the production company. More expensive chromakey modules can fine-tune the color to a very specific shade of blue. Less expensive chromakeys may key only broad shades of blue that encompass many hues. Lighting the blue background is also critical. It should be very evenly lit, so that no area is brighter or darker than other areas.

Blue is most commonly used because no race of humans on the planet has blue pigment in their skin. Therefore, people look natural on the mixed picture. Green is the second most common color for chromakey. However, people with olive complexions do not look very healthy if all the green is removed from their skin tone.

Pixel: One of the millions of little dots that make up the picture on a television screen, in a photograph, or any other type of image display medium.

Pixels and Digital Video

The picture on a television screen is actually made up of millions of little dots, called *pixels*, **Figure 18-15**. A picture printed in the newspaper is also composed of these little dots, but has many fewer than a glossy magazine picture. Therefore, the magazine picture is much sharper than the newspaper picture. The magazine has many, many more dots that are much smaller and packed more closely together. A greater number of dots packed closely together results in a clearer picture. The pixels that make up a television picture are even smaller and more numerous.

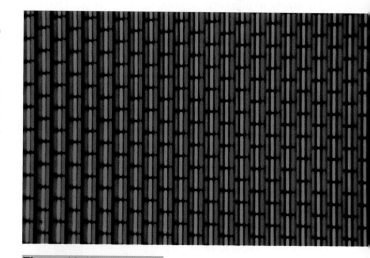

Figure 18-15
The television picture is made up of an incredible number of little dots, or pixels.

Digital television systems utilize at least twice the number of pixels than analog television, which is why digital televisions provide a tremendously sharper picture than an analog television.

Recall exercises in math class on graphing points on the x-axis and y-axis. Each point graphed has coordinates that designate its location on the graph. Each pixel on the television screen also has coordinates, or an address, on an x- and y-axis. It is possible to pick a point and carefully count columns and rows to determine the exact address of that point on the television screen.

Since the images are composed of dots, locating the dots and controlling where they appear allows us to control the picture completely. Imagine a black capital letter *T*, almost as tall as the television screen, against a white background, **Figure 18-16**. The address of the pixel on the very tip of the left arm of the *T* is (50, 500). This means that the pixel is in the 50th column of pixels from the left edge of the screen, and 500 rows up from the bottom of the screen. Knowing the exact address allows a computer to take that pixel and place it, for example, at (50, 25). The program can then take the pixel normally at (50, 25), and place it at (50, 500). This move essentially replaces a black dot with its exact counterpart from the bottom half of the screen. If this were performed repeatedly, the upper left end of the *T* would be moved to the bottom of the TV screen. One pixel at a time, the *T* can be turned upside-down. Millions of mathematical calculations are performed in order to turn that *T* upside-down, but computers complete this operation in a fraction of a second. On screen, it appears as a smooth "morph" from a right-side-up *T* to an up-side-down *T*.

Digital video effect (DVE): Video effects that are created using digital technology and the ability to alter an image by manipulating each individual pixel.

Digital Video Effects

Digital video effects, or *DVE*, are video effects created using digital technology and the ability to alter an image by manipulating each individual pixel. DVE can produce nearly limitless additional spectacular effects. The previous example of morphing is one of the most well-known examples of DVE. In fact, morphing is so commonplace that consumers

Figure 18-16
Controlling each pixel of a picture allows individual pixels to be moved around, which can affect the entire picture.

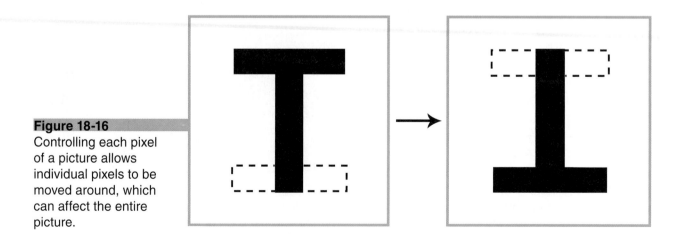

can now buy a computer program for less than $400.00, which morphs snapshots from one into the next. When this technology was first used in music videos, it cost hundreds of thousands of dollars.

Using DVE, an image on the screen can be stretched, twisted, scrunched, rolled up into a ball, and spun out of the frame of the picture, **Figure 18-17**. It can be torn, rotated, wiggled, changed into a runny liquid, made to slither across the screen like a snake, or any other motion that the budget and imagination allows. DVEs are purchased in packages, or bundles, and installed on digital SEGs. The number of effects is entirely dependent upon the available budget. If a desired effect does not already exist, someone can be paid to create it.

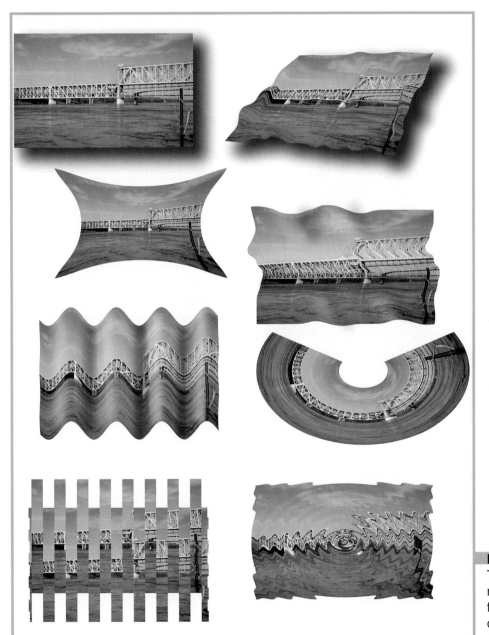

Figure 18-17
There are an infinite number of possibilities for the use of DVEs, depending on the program's budget.

Production Note

Digital video effects have had a profound effect on the film industry. Many special effects are far too expensive or impossible to create using the film medium. However, DVE technology provides complete control of all the pixels that make up a picture, making anything possible in digital video. Because of this, the film industry has begun utilizing the capabilities of high definition digital video when creating visual effects.

The first film to successfully use digital video effects to a notable extent was *Terminator 2: Judgment Day* in 1991. The realism created on the screen stunned many film and television industry professionals. In this film, viewers saw images that they knew could not be real, yet the images did not appear fake or unrealistic in any way. This movie marked the beginning of a trend in film making where anything the director envisions, no matter how fantastic or impossible, can become an on-screen reality.

George Lucas was one of the first high-profile film directors to choose to work exclusively in high definition digital video. He waited to shoot *Star Wars–Episode I, The Phantom Menace* (1999) until the available technology could transform the image in his mind into a realistic computer generated effect.

The video technology now exists to combine reality and fantasy seamlessly into an image and convert it onto film. This, of course, depends on the production budget and the ability to hire digital effects artists and computer graphics specialists to make the director's vision come true. The future of digital video technology holds great possibilities. Viewers can be certain that the effects they see in films and television programs will continue to blur the line between reality and computer-generated as digital technology evolves.

Wrapping Up

Even some technical experts cannot easily determine if an image is real or generated by a computer. This is a factor in why "eyewitness" video is considered very suspect in most courtrooms. The next step in this technology is 3D television. There is no way to predict what we will be watching on television at home in the future.

Special effects are amazing and great fun to experiment with. However, all video professionals must remember that, if not used to further the message or plot of the program, special effects should not be used at all. If special effects are overused or wasted, they become mundane annoyances and the trademark of inept and amateur videographers.

Review Questions

Please answer the following questions on a separate sheet of paper. Do not write in this book.

1. List each type of wipe discussed in the chapter and note the unique characteristics of each.
2. What are the challenges in using superimpositions?
3. What is luminance? How does it function in creating an internal key?
4. Explain what each of the following options add to the functionality of an internal key: matte key, colorizer, shadow mode, and edge mode.
5. Which three elements does the external key combine?
6. How does a chromakey operate?
7. Which image is comprised of more pixels: a picture in the newspaper, a picture in a magazine ad, or the television picture?

Activities

1. While watching television, make note of each time you notice the use of a key. Try to determine if the image is an internal key, an external key, or if other options were used to produce the image. Be prepared to discuss your findings in class.
2. What effects can you apply to an image on your computer at home? Bring some examples into class.

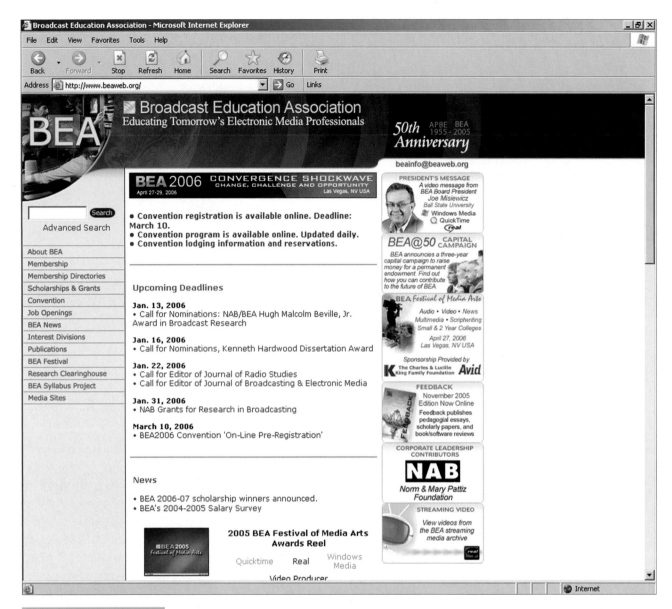

www.beaweb.org.
The Broadcast Education Association provides a link between electronic media educators and industry professionals in an effort to enhance the education of future radio and television professionals.

Important Terms

Assemble Edit Mode
Assemble Edit
    Technique
Audio Delay Edit
Backspace
Bin
Control Track Editing
Control Track
    Logic (CTL)
Crash Bang Editing
Cut Rate
Distribution
    Amplifier (DA)
Dub
Dup
Editing
Edit Controller
Edit Decision List (EDL)
Edit Points
Edit Through Black
Edit Transition

Edit Trim
Insert Edit Mode
Insert Edit Technique
Kiss Black
Linear Editing System
Lock-up Time
Matched Cut
Matched Dissolve
Mode
Nonlinear Editing
    System (NLE)
Pace
Pre-Roll
Processing Amplifier
    (Proc Amp)
Source VCR
Technique
Time Base Corrector
    (TBC)
Time Coding
Video Delay Edit

Objectives

After completing this chapter, you will be able to:

- Define "edit transition."
- Describe how generational losses occur on videotapes.
- List each step involved in nonlinear editing and those involved in linear editing.
- Explain the importance of the control track to the editing process.
- Differentiate between assemble edit mode and insert edit mode.
- Cite the advantages and challenges of using nonlinear editing systems.
- List the advantages and challenges of using linear editing systems.

Introduction

Because television program scenes are not shot in order, they must be rearranged, or edited into the correct order. Errors must be removed; any footage that is unwanted must be edited out. Editing is a very complex process with important ethical issues. It is unethical to fundamentally change a program or person's intended message. Advances in editing technology have made it relatively simple to manipulate the spoken word. An individual video editor has an awesome responsibility and power over the thoughts of the viewers. This chapter presents the basic concepts and skills necessary to begin using professional editing systems.

Editing Systems

Editing: The process of selecting the good portions of raw video footage and combining them into a coherent, sequential, and complete television program. Editing also includes post-production additions of music and sound effects, as well as effects used as scene transitions.

Linear editing system: Video editing equipment that is based on videotape. The raw footage is placed in a source VCR and the "good" takes of the program footage are copied, in the order the audience will see them, to a tape in the record VCR.

Source VCR: A VCR into which raw camera footage is placed for linear editing.

Editing is the process of selecting the good portions of raw video footage and combining them into a coherent, sequential, and complete television program. Editing also includes the post-production addition of music and sound effects, as well as video effects used as scene transitions. There are two types of systems used for video editing:

● Linear Editing Systems
● Nonlinear Editing Systems

Linear Editing Systems

Linear editing systems are based on videotape. The raw footage is placed on a playback VCR, or *source VCR*, with a blank videotape in the record VCR. The good takes of the program footage are copied to the second VCR in the order the audience will see it. Using this process, the program is assembled in a straight line, or "linear" fashion.

Linear editing systems have been in use for several decades. This system requires a minimum of 5 pieces of equipment:

● Source VCR
● Record VCR
● Edit controller to operate both VCRs
● Monitor for the source VCR
● Monitor for the record VCR

These five pieces of equipment are placed in close proximity to each other in the editing booth, **Figure 19-1**. This provides the operator with easy access to each piece of equipment from a seated position. If the VCRs are placed on top of each other, the source VCR is positioned on top.

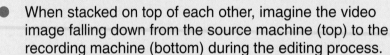

Visualize This

To help you remember how the VCRs are positioned:

● When stacked on top of each other, imagine the video image falling down from the source machine (top) to the recording machine (bottom) during the editing process.

● If the machines are placed beside each other, the source VCR is placed on the left-hand side with the recorder on the right. Our society is accustomed to information flowing from left to right, in the same manner we read and write.

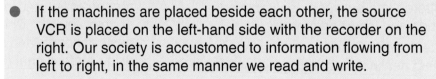

Simple linear editors can only perform cuts when editing. Cuts-only editing is appropriate for certain types of program editing. Suppose a client has requested that a lecturer's presentation be recorded. The client would like titles added before and after the program. Editing the titles on

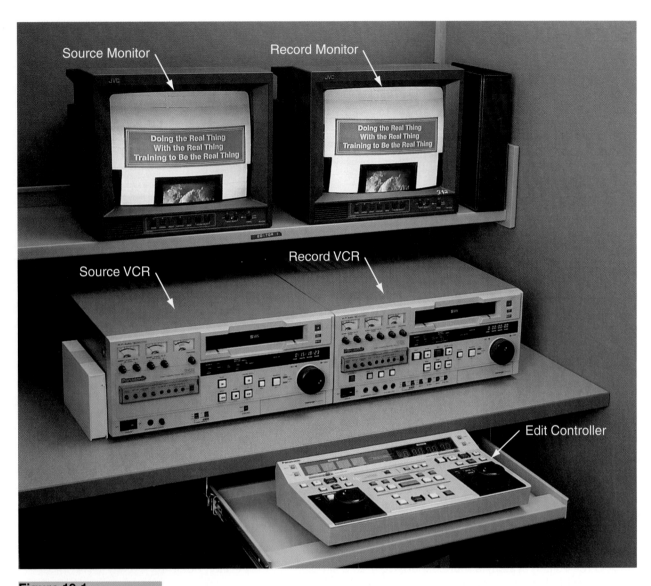

Figure 19-1

A linear editing system has a minimum of five components.

a program in this situation takes mere minutes with a linear editor, but requires hours to accomplish with a nonlinear editor. To use a nonlinear editor, the entire event must first be digitized (usually in real-time) onto a hard drive. The titles can then be added and the completed event is off-loaded (again, usually in real-time) back to tape for duplication.

A-B Roll Editing

A-B roll editing is a type of linear editing that is a level up from a simple cuts-only editor. The equipment for this system is more expensive, with several additional pieces required, **Figure 19-2**.

- Source VCR (A-roll deck)
- Second source VCR (B-roll deck)
- Record VCR

Preview
Monitor A

Preview
Monitor B

AJ-D960
Studio DVCPRO50
Recorder

Deck A

Deck B

AJ-D940
DVCPRO50
Slow Motion Player

Program/
Record
Monitor

Record Deck

Remote Control
For The A Deck

AJ-A95
VTR RS422 Remote Controller

Remote Control
For The B Deck
and The Record Deck

AJ-D950A
Studio DVCPRO50
Recorder

Figure 19-2
An A-B roll editing system is more expensive than a simple cuts-only editor, but it
makes use of all the transitions possible on a SEG during the editing process.

- Monitor for the source VCR (A-roll monitor)
- Monitor for the second source VCR (B-roll monitor)
- Monitor for the record VCR
- SEG
- Edit controller that operates three decks

On an A-B roll system, both source units are connected to the SEG.
The output of the SEG is connected to the edit recorder. Using this
system, any effect the SEG is capable of producing (fades, dissolves,
wipes) can be used as a transitional device on the editor.

Crash Bang Editing

Crash bang editing is a kind of nonprofessional linear editing that
is accomplished without a video editor. The video out and audio out on
one consumer VCR is connected to the video in and audio in on another

**Crash bang
editing:** A type of
nonprofessional
linear editing that is
accomplished using
only two consumer
VCRs, neither of which
is a video editor.

consumer VCR. Crash bang editing usually results in several seconds of glitch at each point on the finished tape where an edit occurs. This type of editing also significantly decreases the video quality on the edited tape. Each of these factors makes the finished tape unacceptable at any professional facility.

Nonlinear Editing Systems

Nonlinear editing systems (NLE) are based on digital technology and use high-capacity computer hard drives to store and process video and audio, **Figure 19-3**. The taped raw footage is converted to a digital format and copied to the computer's hard drive. Scenes can then be properly arranged, with special effects and transitions added during the process. Once the program is complete, the video and audio can be recorded onto a blank videotape.

Arranging scenes on a NLE is similar to the cut and paste or drag and drop functions of a computer word processing program. Instead of moving text within a document, scenes are arranged on a timeline.

Nonlinear editing system (NLE): Video editing equipment that is based on digital technology and uses high-capacity computer hard drives to store and process video and audio. The taped raw footage is converted to a digital format, copied to a computer's hard drive, and may then be arranged and otherwise manipulated.

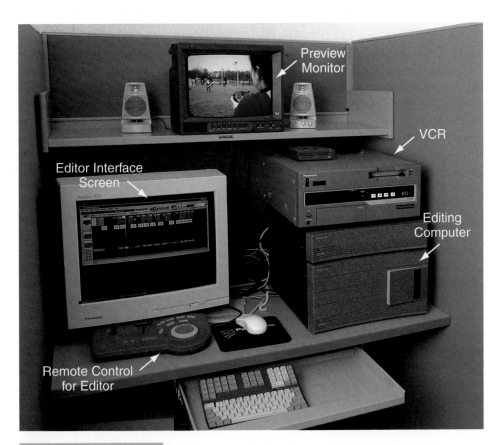

Figure 19-3

The capability of a nonlinear editing system depends on the hard drive capacity of the computer used. The camera footage is uploaded onto the hard drive, all the program components are manipulated, and the completed program is downloaded back to tape.

There are many different brands of nonlinear editing systems on the market, each offering different features. The basic functionality of each brand is the same, but the processing options vary.

Program Editing Basics

Some editing processes and concepts are the same, whether a linear editing system or a nonlinear editing system is used in program editing. Understanding and effectively utilizing concepts such as screen time vs. real-time and editing action sequences add to the production values of a program. This, in turn, strengthens the delivery of the program's message.

Previewing the Raw Tapes

The editing process begins with previewing all the footage shot. While previewing the raw footage, note exactly which takes of each scene should be used in the finished product and where the takes are located on the tape. This list of scene and take numbers becomes an *edit decision list (EDL)*. To indicate the location of the "good" takes, make note of the time code or control track counter mark at the beginning and end of each desired take while reviewing, **Figure 19-4**. Creating an accurate EDL saves hours of expensive time in an editing suite because the good takes of each scene can be quickly located.

The take log developed while shooting notes the number of takes that were recorded per scene and, if accurately recorded, can be used as the foundation of an EDL. An accurate and detailed take log saves time spent in creating the EDL. Remember that the head recorded before each take displays the slate and countdown. Even during high-speed scanning, the slate is noticeable on the monitor and assists you in locating the "good" takes of each scene recorded.

Edit decision list (EDL): A list that notes which take of each scene should be used in the final program and the location of each take on the raw footage tape.

Edit Decision List (EDL)		
In Point	**Out Point**	**Scene Number or Description**
00:05:10:21	00:07:22:10	Scene 7, Take 3
00:12:13:24	00:14:03:12	Scene 3, Take 2
00:21:17:02	00:25:09:14	Scene 6, Take 4

Figure 19-4
An EDL notes the location and a brief description of the good takes contained on each raw footage tape.

Production Note

Many schools, as well as professional production companies, require that an EDL be prepared before using an available video editor. This ensures the efficient use of costly editing equipment for editing purposes only—not for reviewing raw footage. Before previewing the raw footage to create an EDL, copy the raw footage onto a VHS videotape. The deck used to play the raw footage should have a "MONITOR OUT" video selection, which places the control track or time code display in a small black window on the screen of the VHS copy. This inexpensive VHS copy can be played on any VHS player. The tape may be stopped and started, rewound and fast-forwarded many times as the take log is adapted to become an EDL. Subjecting the raw footage to this type of activity would stretch the master tape and damage the signal.

Screen Time

One main goal of successful editing is to create the illusion that the audience has missed nothing in the sequence of action. In editing a program, the "real time" of the footage shot must be changed to reflect the available "screen time" in order to keep the audience's attention. Consider a cooking program's host demonstrating how to make choco-late chip cookies. The cookies go into the oven and the camera shoots them baking for the entire 10 minutes of cooking time. Shooting through the window of the oven for the entire baking time does not create action that keeps an audience's interest. Too often, directors feel that every frame of video shot is "too good to lose" and are unwilling to part with anything. The result can be 20 minutes of torturous programming that would have been quite interesting if it had been cut to five minutes. In the cooking program example, 10 minutes of real-time can be cut to 20 seconds of screen-time by editing the shots as follows:

1. Shot of cookies in the oven.
2. Cut to a shot of a timer set to 10 minutes.
3. Dissolve to the timer's alarm sounding 10 minutes later.
4. Cut to a shot of the baked cookies being removed from the oven.

Editing and Action

An edit must occur between two shots within a scene and also between two scenes in a program in a way that connects them together. Careful consideration should be given when deciding where and *when* an edit should be performed. All shots have a 10 second tail, so *when* during the tail should the edit be made? All shots also have a 10 second head recorded that includes the countdown and slate. *When* during the head should the edit be made? Guidelines for video cuts and editing, **Figure 19-5**, include:

- If shot A includes a moving object/action or is taken by a camera that is moving or zooming, shot B should also include an action shot or camera movement for continuity.
- An edit should not take place between a still shot, or a shot without action, and a moving or action shot.
- An edit should not take place between an action (moving) shot and a still (nonaction) shot.
- Edits can occur between two still, or nonaction, shots.

Audio considerations when editing include:

- If the audio track is the primary focus, the pauses between talent's lines must be a natural length of time.
- When the response to an interview question runs long and is more than can be used, the response is edited. This edit may create a jump cut. To correct this, keep the audio flowing and insert a nod shot or cutaway of the interviewer.

Breaking these rules is acceptable only if the producer or director actually intends to jar the audience. Any time a conventional rule is broken, there should be a purposeful reason for doing so that supports the program and its message.

The Matched Cut and Matched Dissolve

Matched cut: A type of edit in which a similar action, concept, item, or a combination of these is placed on either side of a cut.

The *matched cut* is a very creative type of edit that places a similar action, concept, item, or a combination of these on either side of a cut. The following are examples of match cuts:

- A historical drama portrays a prisoner about to have his head removed on a guillotine. The camera watches the blade fall in a close-up and the program cuts to a butcher swinging a meat cleaver onto a piece of beef. The same kind of action occurs on both sides of the edit.

Editing Shots		
	Yes	No
Action to Action	✓	
Action to Still		✓
Still to Still	✓	
Still to Action		✓

Figure 19-5
Guidelines for video cuts and editing between action and still shots.

● A man leaves his home, gets in a car, and drives off screen right. The program cuts to the car driving into the frame from screen left, as the man arrives at his workplace 15 miles from home. The same item (man and car) and same action (driving) occur on either side of the edit.

A *matched dissolve* is another type of creative edit that uses a similar action, concept, item, or combination of these to transition from one scene to the next. Instead of a cut between the scenes, a dissolve is used to tie the scenes together. A typical cooking show provides excellent examples of matched dissolves:

1. A cake is placed in an oven.

2. The oven closes and the camera zooms to a clock reading "1:15 p.m."

3. The shot dissolves to same clock 20 minutes later, reading "1:35 p.m."

The same concept (time) and same item (clock) occur on either side of the dissolve.

> **Matched dissolve:** A type of edit in which a similar action, concept, item, or a combination of these is placed on either side of a dissolve.

Editing Transitions

In English class, a "poor transition" means the ending of one paragraph does not flow well into the beginning of the next paragraph. Video editing is like writing a paper—as each scene must transition into the next scene. An *edit transition* refers to the way one scene ends and the next scene begins: fading Scene 6 out, for example, while fading Scene 7 in. The transition can be a fade, dissolve, wipe, special effect, or a digital video effect. Regardless of the method used in the edit transition, the action, plot, and theme must all transition smoothly from one scene to the next. If they do not, the audience is left confused. In the television world, a confused audience is very likely to reach for the remote and change channels.

Even on the simplest linear editor, called a "cuts-only" editor, all editing transitions do not necessarily look like cuts. It is possible, for example, to edit a fade out and fade in if the appropriate script marking is done before shooting. If the director has marked that Scene 6 should fade out and Scene 7 fades in, the scene can be shot with a fade out or fade in. Some camcorders have an automatic fade feature. If this feature is not available, shoot a fade out by smoothly closing the iris of the camera. Since the end of Scene 6 fades to black and the beginning of Scene 7 fades in, the edit between the scenes can be made while the screen is black. A cut from black to black is not noticeable to the audience. This kind of edit is called an *edit through black*, or *kiss black*.

To create the illusion of moving in and out of a flashback, a shot can be brought into and out of focus. While the picture is out of focus, the cut to another out of focus shot is nearly invisible to the audience. Again, the scenes must be shot using rack focus, or pull focus, on the camera while the scene is being taped.

The frequency of cuts or edits, per minute, during a program is the *pace*, or *cut rate*. The pace of most prime time television programs averages one cut every 7 seconds. Always strive to keep a program moving to retain the audience's interest.

> **Edit transition:** The way in which one scene ends and the next scene begins.
>
> **Edit through black:** An edit in which a cut is made during the black that appears on screen between a fade out and a fade in. Also called *kiss black*.
>
> **Pace:** The frequency of cuts or edits, per minute, during a program. Also referred to as *cut rate*.

Videotape Generation Losses

A generation is each duplication of the original camera footage. Generations are noted sequentially. Raw footage straight from the camera to tape is the first generation. If the footage is placed in an editor and edited, the edited version is second generation. If the edited tape is placed into a duplication system to make 20 copies, each of the copies made is a third generation. Using the duplication system to make many copies of a master tape is called dubbing, or duping, tapes. A copy of the master tape is a *dub*, or a *dup*.

Dub: A copy of the master videotape. Also called a *dup*.

🎤 Talk the Talk

The letter "u" in the term *dup* is long and is pronounced "dupe."

Time base corrector (TBC): A machine that corrects any quality related imperfections in the video and audio signals caused by mechanical errors associated with the VCR's functionality.

Processing amplifier (proc amp): A machine that corrects some color and brightness problems in the video signal passing through it. This piece of equipment is commonly used when recording and/or duplicating videotapes.

The quality of the picture decreases with each generation of videotape. While most types of videotape experience generational losses, the losses are greatest with VHS. Currently, only digital tapes can be duplicated without significant deterioration in quality. The speed at which a tape is recorded is a factor in duplication. The more slowly the tape moves, the greater the picture quality loss on the copy, **Figure 19-6**. Other factors that affect the quality of the copied tape include:

- The quality of the tape.
- The quality of the VCRs.
- Use of a time base corrector, processing amplifier, distribution amplifier, or any combination of these.

A *time base corrector (TBC)* is a machine that corrects mechanical errors, due to age or use, related to the operation of a VCR. A TBC strips any quality related imperfections out of the signal and leaves only pure audio and video in the signal. This piece of equipment compensates for any deterioration in VCR functionality by giving the signal a virtual face-lift! A *processing amplifier (proc amp)* corrects some color and brightness problems in the video signal as it passes through. It is commonly

Figure 19-6
The approximate video generation loss expected when copying tapes at different speeds.

Approximate Video Generation Signal Loss		
Copy From Speed	**Copy To Speed**	**Picture Quality Loss**
VHS SP (2 hr. speed)	VHS SP	10%
VHS SP	VHS LP (4 hr. speed)	25%
VHS SP	VHS EP/SLP (6 hr. speed)	50%

used in videotape recording and duplication systems. A *distribution amplifier (DA)* is used when a signal must be split and sent to multiple outputs. A DA amplifies the signal before it is split and sent so each output receives nearly 100% of the original signal. If the original signal was simply split and sent, each output would receive only a portion of the signal. For example, if a signal is split and sent to five outputs, each may receive only 20% of the original signal (20 x 5 = 100%).

Distribution amplifier (DA): A machine used when a signal must be split and sent to multiple outputs. The signal is amplified before it is split so that each output receives nearly 100% of the original signal.

Linear Editing

Even with the availability of digital technology, linear editing continues to be quite prevalent in the television production industry. It is a standard process that may be applied to almost every production format.

The *edit controller*, **Figure 19-7**, is a remote console that controls the editing and operating functions of both the source and record VCRs. Using the edit controller, the operator may mark edit points, preview and perform an edit, adjust the flow of an edited scene, and review an edit once completed.

Edit controller: A remote console that controls the editing and operation functions of both the source and record VCRs.

The Control Track and Time Coding

A control track pulse indicates the beginning of every frame recorded on a videotape (30 frames/pulses per second). Control track pulses are counted sequentially on a counter that is visible on the outside of

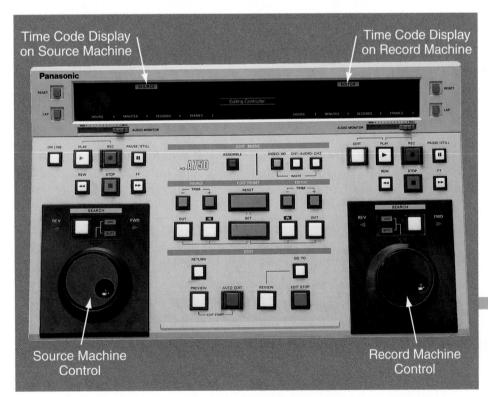

Figure 19-7
An edit controller operates both the source and record VCRs, in addition to regulating the editing functions.

Control track editing: A method of linear editing where the editing system uses the inaudible control track pulses as reference point for setting, locating, and using edit points.

Control track logic (CTL): The most common and least expensive type of linear editing system available.

Time coding: A system of assigning each frame of a video a specific number, like an address.

the VCR. This counter should be set to zero at the beginning of each new tape that is inserted. In ***control track editing***, the editing system uses the inaudible control track pulses as reference points for setting, locating, and using edit points. The control track is vital to control track logic editing. ***Control track logic (CTL)*** is the most common and least expensive type of linear editing system available.

The control track is automatically recorded onto the raw footage tape while shooting and must be uninterrupted. The videotape in the record VCR must also have an existing control track recorded. Since a completely blank tape contains only video noise, this tape must be "blacked" to record the control track before editing begins.

To ensure that the control track is uninterrupted on raw footage, the "stop" button on the recorder should not be pressed from the moment the camera begins shooting a scene, including the slate, through the end of the scene's tail. The control track is broken if the "stop" button is pressed, even if only for a brief moment. If the editing system comes to a break in the control track while editing, the entire system stops. The scene cannot be edited and the tape itself cannot be "fixed." Without an uninterrupted control track, the scene must be reshot to be included on the edit master tape. An individual raw footage tape may have 20 or more different scenes recorded on it. Because of this, the control track is broken many times on the tape between the scenes. *Within* each of the scenes, however, there must be no break in the control track.

Time coding is a system of assigning each frame of a video a specific number, like an address, **Figure 19-8**. To use time code editing, the camera must have a circuit that records time code onto the tape while shooting. The time code is recorded on an area of the tape that does not affect the picture. The editing system must also have a circuit that reads time code. Time code editing is far more precise than CTL editing, if all the necessary equipment is enabled with time code capability.

Blacking the Tape

Blacking a videotape is the process of recording a control track onto a blank tape. This should be the first step taken in the linear editing process. The black signal recorded onto the tape must run, uninterrupted, for the entire length of the program to be recorded. If the tape

Time Code

01:17:32:12

A shot marked with this time code is located exactly one hour, seventeen minutes, thirty-two seconds, and twelve frames from the beginning of the tape.

Figure 19-8
The time code indicates the exact location of a shot on the tape.

runs out of control track before program editing is completed, the system refuses to edit further. The tape must be re-blacked and the editing process must begin again.

Methods for blacking a tape include:

- Place the lens cap on the camera lens and record a black image onto the tape.
- Close the iris on the camera and record a black image onto the tape.
- Press the BLACK button on the SEG with the tape in the studio recorder to record black onto the tape.
- Record the output from the black burst on a time base corrector.
- Copy a blacked videotape.

The signal on the "blacked" tape does not need to be black. It can be any video signal that is recorded at the highest possible speed (SP). Any type of recording works to place a control track on the tape. Since the screen appears before the program begins and after it concludes on the completed tape, a black screen looks more professional.

Production Note

Copying the edited program, up to the broken control track, onto another fully blacked tape is not a valid solution to finish editing. The edited video copied onto the new tape from the previously edited tape is a generation down in quality. The final product would have two dramatically different picture qualities and, therefore, be unacceptable.

Marking the Edit Points

Edit points are specific locations on the videotape where an edit should begin and where it should end. When using a linear editing system, at least two edit points must be entered on the edit controller; one edit point (in or out) for each VCR. Three points are most commonly entered. The operator may enter two edit-in points and one edit-out point, or two edit-out points and one edit-in point, for a successful edit. It is not necessary to enter all four points. After the first three points are entered, the system calculates the fourth edit point. To mark the edit points:

1. Identify the good take of one scene, as marked on the EDL.
2. On the source deck, forward the tape through the head and count-down, to the point just before the actual scene begins.
3. Locate the exact point where the edit should begin.
4. Steps 4–8 are a part of the process called "setting the edit points." Select the button on the controller that marks the "Edit-In" point on the source deck, **Figure 19-9**.

Edit points: Specific locations on the videotape where an edit should begin and end.

Figure 19-9
The edit points, edit-in and edit-out, are set on both the source and record VCRs.

5. Roll through the scene to locate the exact point the scene should end, before the tail is over.
6. Select the buttons on the controller that set the "Edit-Out" point on the source deck.
7. On the record deck, locate a point on the blacked tape to start the edit.
8. Select the buttons on the controller to mark the "Edit-In" point on the record deck.

> ## Production Note
>
> Never use the first two minutes of a videocassette. Always begin shooting or editing after rolling at least two minutes of the beginning of the tape. If the tape should break, it usually happens at the very beginning, or lead, of the tape. Not using the first two minutes of the tape allows repair space, if needed.

Backspace and Pre-Roll

To preview or perform an edit once the edit points have been established, the editing system performs two functions:

- Backspace
- Pre-Roll

Both the source and record machines rewind to the edit-in point previously marked in the scene. The system counts the control track pulses for approximately 5–7 seconds as the tape automatically rewinds past the marked edit-in point, or ***backspaces***. Rewinding the tape past

Backspace: When both the source and record machines automatically rewind the tape to a point about 5 to 7 seconds before the marked edit-in point.

the edit-in point allows both machines to get a "running start" before reaching the edit-in point. The number of seconds of backspacing varies from one equipment manufacturer to another. Some models allow the user to determine the length of the backspace. The 20 second head originally put on the tape allows the machine to count control track pulses in the backing up process. If the control track is broken, the machine cannot backspace the required number of seconds. The system stops and does not continue the editing process if the tape cannot be backspaced far enough over uninterrupted control track pulses.

Once both machines have reached the appropriate backspace point, each automatically moves the tape forward, or **_pre-rolls_** the tape. Pre-rolling continues until the edit-in point is reached.

When the PLAY button is pressed on a VCR, several seconds pass before the picture appears on the screen. This delay occurs because:

● The tape must be threaded around the heads.

● The tape must be moving at the correct speed before a stable picture can be seen.

The time it takes, after pressing PLAY, for the machine to get the tape up to speed and produce a stable picture is called **_lock-up time_**. Due to lock-up time, the machines must backspace the tapes to a point before the scene begins. This ensures that the tape is up to speed and producing a stable picture by the time the scene begins. It is similar to the running start a high jumper takes before making the leap.

Pre-roll: Rolling the tape in the source and record machines forward until reaching the edit-in point—automatically performed after backspacing is complete.

Lock-up time: The amount of time it takes, after pressing PLAY, for the machine to get the tape up to speed and produce a stable picture.

Previewing an Edit

After the edit points have been selected, preview the edit to ensure that the audio and video match up properly with the end of the previous edit. The PREVIEW button on the controller, see **Figure 19-10**, rolls the tape in both machines back to the backspace point, places both machines in pre-roll, and the image on the record monitor switches to the new scene at the edit point. Nothing is recorded to tape during the

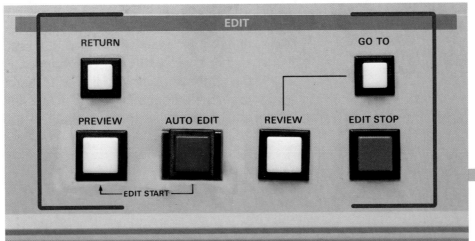

Figure 19-10
The "Edit" portion of the controller includes the edit and preview function buttons.

preview. Previewing the edit allows the operator to make certain that the audio levels are properly adjusted for recording and that the edited scene flows correctly from the previous scene.

In the flow of a conversation between two people, for example, there is a natural pause between the words spoken by each individual. If the pause is too long or too short, the conversation sounds unrealistic. If the edit points are set a bit too soon or too late in the dialog, the completed edit of the conversation sounds odd. If the flow between scenes is not correct:

● Reenter the edit-in points and preview the edit again.
● Move the edit points using the edit trim button on the controller, if available.

Edit trim: A linear editing system feature that allows the operator to move edit points forward or backward one frame at a time.

The *edit trim* feature, **Figure 19-11**, moves the edit point one frame at a time. The two edit trim buttons are marked + (plus) and – (minus). The + button moves the edit point forward one frame every time the button is pressed and the – button moves the edit point one frame back each time the button is pressed. Preview the adjustments to ensure the edit flows properly. Do not perform the edit until the audio recording levels and flow between scenes are exactly as they should be in the final product.

Perform Edit

Once all aspects of the preview edit are correct, select the PERFORM EDIT button to backspace and pre-roll the tapes once again. When the record VCR reaches the edit-in point, it automatically switches to record mode and the new scene is recorded onto the edit master tape. The PERFORM EDIT button may be labeled "Edit Start" or "Auto Edit," **Figure 19-10**, on various edit controller models.

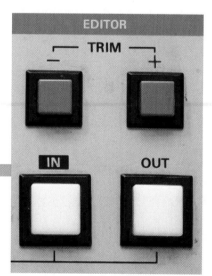

Figure 19-11
The edit trim feature allows the operator to fine tune edit points by moving an edit point forward or backward one frame at a time.

Review Edit

When the editing system reaches the edit-out point, it halts processing. Before continuing on to the next scene, check the result of the previous edit. Select the REVIEW EDIT button on the controller to rewind the edit master tape to the beginning of the scene just edited to review the sequence. If the edited scene is satisfactory, continue to the next scene.

Linear Editing Methods

While the functionality of linear editing systems is constant, how the system features are used to complete an editing task may vary. Common methods used in linear editing include:

● Assemble Editing
● Insert Editing

Assemble Editing and Insert Editing

Assemble editing mode, insert editing mode, assemble editing technique, and insert editing technique are four distinctly different linear editing concepts. These terms must be clearly understood to be successful in the editing room.

Mode refers to a function available on the editing system. When the corresponding button is pressed, the system operates in the specified mode. A *technique* is the manner in which a person performs a task or completes a procedure. The operator of an editing system may have a particular technique in completing a task.

Mode: A function available on editing system equipment; an available operation on a piece of equipment.

Technique: The manner in which a person performs a task or completes a procedure.

Visualize This

Compare *mode* to the gearshift on a car with the available functions of "Drive" and "Reverse." *Mode* is a function of a machine. Compare *technique* with driving safely or driving recklessly. *Technique*, in this case, is a person's method of driving.

The edit controller typically has 4 buttons placed in a row, labeled "Assemble," "Video," "Audio 1," and "Audio 2," **Figure 19-12**. The last three buttons listed are grouped within an "Insert" category. Selecting the ASSEMBLE button sets the system in assemble edit mode. Choosing the VIDEO, AUDIO 1, or AUDIO 2 button sets the editing system into insert edit mode.

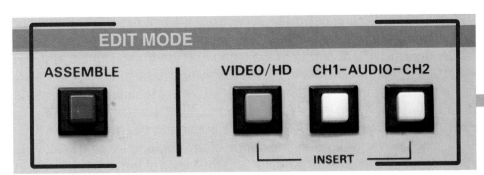

Figure 19-12
The operator may choose to edit in the assemble mode or the insert mode.

Assemble Edit Mode

The *assemble edit mode* allows for quick editing. It is not necessary to use a blacked tape in the recorder when in assemble edit mode, which saves overall editing time. Because of this, however, the control track is broken on the edited master tape with each edit performed. Each edit lays down a completely new control track onto the tape. The trade-off for a time savings is a high chance of creating a glitch in playback because of the broken control track.

Using assemble edit mode, it is not possible to go back at a later time to insert music effects or cutaways to bridge an edit. Assemble edit mode is designed to quickly connect Scene 2, for example, to the end of Scene 1 and Scene 3 to the end of Scene 2. The entire program must be built, or assembled, in order.

Insert Edit Mode

Insert edit mode, VIDEO, AUDIO 1, and AUDIO 2 buttons, requires that the edit master videotape have a control track signal on it; the tape must be blacked. With the control track on the tape, additional video or audio may be added later in the editing process without causing glitches.

Assemble Edit and Insert Edit Techniques

The *assemble edit technique* is a method of editing where the scenes of a program are edited in the order they will be seen in the finished program, while the editing system is set in insert edit *mode*. Because the editing system is set to insert edit mode, the videotape in the record VCR has an existing control track recorded. This eliminates the problems created with glitches. The assemble edit technique is the recommended method of linear editing.

Using the *insert edit technique*, video or audio can be inserted on top of existing video and audio tracks. The existing audio or video is erased in the process, but no glitches are created. The existing audio or video tracks do not shift to make room for the inserted material; they are written over. When laying background audio tracks using the insert edit technique, the music can be adjusted to end at a certain moment or part of the scene by marking one in point and two out points.

Video and Audio Delay Edits

If a program is edited using the insert mode with the assemble technique, it is possible to separate the video and the audio signals and edit each at different times. Consider the following scene:

Maria and Janet are sitting in Janet's office. Maria asks, "What time is your husband flying in?" Janet responds, "He'll be landing at 5:00 this afternoon." Cut to a shot of the airplane landing at the airport.

Using a video delay edit, the sound of the airplane landing is audible when Janet says the word "landing" and the video of the airplane is cut in after the word "afternoon." A *video delay edit* cuts to the audio portion of the next scene before the corresponding video of the new scene is

---

Assemble edit mode: A linear editing process in which using a blacked tape in the recorder is not necessary. Assemble edit mode saves in overall editing time, but is more likely to create glitches because the control track is broken on the edited master tape with each edit performed.

Insert edit mode: A linear editing process that requires a control track signal be recorded on the edit master videotape. With a control track on the tape, additional video or audio may be added later in the editing process without causing glitches.

Assemble edit technique: A method of editing where scenes are edited in the order they will be seen in the finished program while the editing system is set in insert edit *mode*.

Insert edit technique: A method of linear editing where either video or audio may be inserted on top of existing video and audio tracks. Any existing audio or video is erased in the process, but no glitches are created.

Video delay edit: An edit that cuts to the audio portion of the next scene before the corresponding video of the new scene is seen by the audience.

seen by the audience, **Figure 19-13**. An *audio delay edit* cuts to the video portion of the next scene before the corresponding audio is heard by the audience. In the example above, the video image of an airplane would cut in on the word "landing" while we hear Janet complete her line, "at 5:00 this afternoon." The audio of the plane landing then cuts into the scene.

> **Audio delay edit:** An edit that cuts to the video portion of the next scene before the corresponding audio of the new scene is heard by the audience.

Nonlinear Editing

A great advantage of using a nonlinear editing (NLE) system is the efficiency that digital technology offers. The overall editing time is less and a great variety of effects are available, compared to a linear editing system. Once the EDL is finalized and all the applicable raw footage tapes are accessible, editing with a nonlinear editing system can begin. Steps in the nonlinear editing process include:

- Uploading and digitizing the recorded footage.
- Creating a timeline of scenes.
- Applying effects and transitions.
- Offloading the completed program.

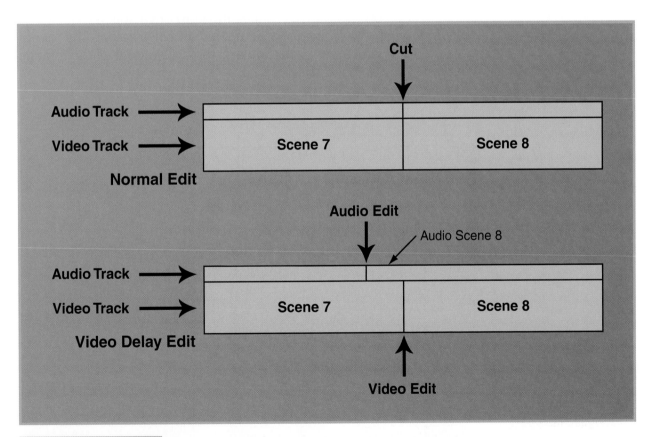

Figure 19-13
A video delay edit or an audio delay edit can make an otherwise plain cut appear more interesting.

Uploading and Digitizing

Uploading raw footage to a NLE computer hard drive is usually a real-time copying process, during which the video and audio are digitized. Converting the taped audio and video footage to a digital format allows individual images, scenes, and audio tracks to be manipulated and edited using the features and technology available on the system. The images can be viewed as they are transferred to the hard drive. As the beginning of each new scene is displayed, the NLE operator presses a button to mark it as a new scene. As footage is loaded onto the NLE, a frame of each video clip is displayed as a thumbnail icon. All of the thumbnail icons are contained in a folder known as a *bin* and may be viewed in a window on the computer screen, **Figure 19-14**. If there are 45 scenes or video clips of a program loaded onto the hard drive of an NLE, the bin will contain 45 thumbnail icons. On some NLEs, both bins and clips can be given a short descriptive name to reflect its contents. Bins may be named for the corresponding program and clips may be named to reflect the scene footage, such as "Scene 4, Take 3."

NLE systems require computers with high capacity hard drives that have a great amount of available memory. Depending on the size of the production, there may be insufficient memory available to upload all the footage. Using an EDL reduces the hard drive space required for the program footage. The editor can upload and digitize only the "good" takes with the corresponding heads and tails, instead of all the footage recorded for a particular shot.

Bin: A folder on an NLE computer that contains all of the footage for a program that has been loaded onto the hard drive. A thumbnail icon of a frame of each video clip contained in the bin may be viewed in a window on the computer monitor.

Figure 19-14
The first frame of each scene is displayed to help identify the footage contained in the bin.

Timeline Creation

The digitized scenes are then arranged along a timeline in the order they will appear in the finished program, **Figure 19-15**. NLE systems offer the ease of clicking on a scene, dragging it to the desired place on the timeline, and dropping the scene into the sequence. If another scene or effect is inserted at a later time, the existing material shifts along the timeline to make room. The previous work is not copied over.

When the scenes are all in order, they are trimmed to flow naturally. The order of the scenes, effects, or audio can be adjusted, previewed, and moved again until correctly placed.

Effects and Transitions

NLEs are equipped with built-in special effects, DVEs, and editing transitions, **Figure 19-16**. A transition may be selected from a menu and set to last for a specific amount of time. Completing a program can

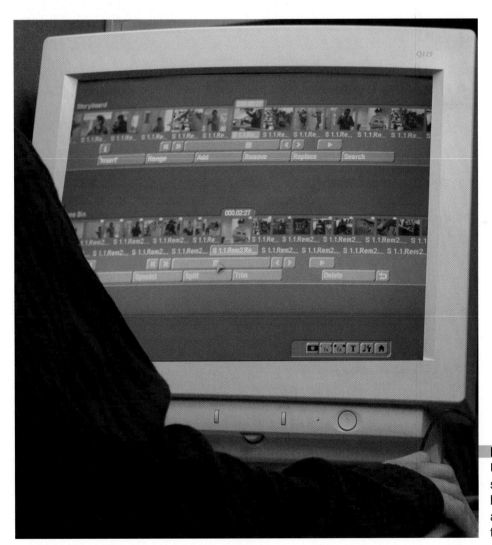

Figure 19-15
Using a nonlinear editing system, the timeline can be rearranged as easily as clicking and dragging the scene icon.

Figure 19-16
Selecting the transition from one shot to another is as simple as pressing a button.

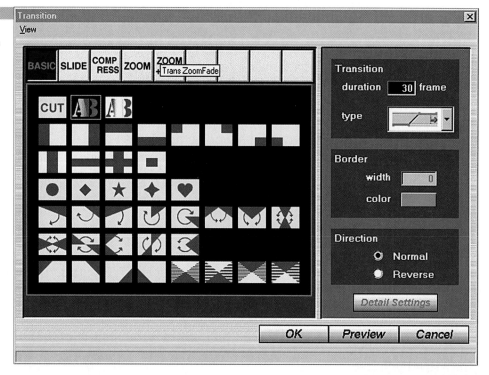

be accomplished in a relatively short amount of time. The duration of the editing process is dependent on the editor's knowledge of the NLE processes and the rendering capabilities of the system. The best way to become proficient in operating a NLE is to practice on the system as often as possible.

Offloading

Once the program is complete, it can be offloaded back to tape for duplication and distribution, or may be aired directly from the hard drive without any loss in quality. Offloading an edited program to tape is usually a real-time process. A deck must be connected to the output of the editor and placed in record mode. The program can then be played from the editor and recorded onto tape.

Wrapping Up

Editing is one of the most exciting positions on the production team. Both linear and nonlinear editing systems present advantages and challenges that must be considered before beginning the process of program editing, **Figure 19-17**. Novice editors should practice with cuts-only, regardless of the type of editing system available. Learn to

	Advantages	Disadvantages
Linear Editing Systems	With the raw footage tape and a tape for the edited program in hand, editing can begin immediately.	An edited tape is, at best, a copy of the raw footage. Copying a tape in an analog system always results in a lower quality product than the original raw footage. By using high quality tapes and adding a TBC and ProcAmp, the quality loss can be significantly reduced.
	The videotapes can be reinserted into the recording machines from session to session, allowing the operator to resume editing exactly where the previous session ended.	After a sequence of several edits is performed, the operator can replay the sequence to verify the flow. If shots need to be removed or replaced, the replacement material must be exactly the same length as the shot being removed. Otherwise, the entire sequence must be re-edited from the "changed" point forward.
	Because the tapes are portable and should remain in the editor's care at all times, no one can accidentally damage or erase the tapes.	Most linear editors can make only cuts as edits. A-B roll editing systems and other similar systems, however, provide some limited effects.
Nonlinear Editing Systems	A great advantage of nonlinear editing systems is accessibility. With the video on a computer's hard drive, any point in the video can be instantly accessed without the hassle of scanning a tape forward and backward.	Raw footage must be copied, usually in real-time, onto the hard drive. This is a time-intensive portion of the process.
	Editing usually occurs more rapidly compared to linear editing systems.	Video tracks require large amounts of hard drive space. An EDL helps keep the amount of video in-check by noting only the usable takes of each scene.
	The operator can perform several edits and play back a sequence. If part of the edited sequence is not suitable, a shot can be easily deleted and another inserted in its place.	It is difficult to share an NLE with another operator. Both must be careful not to accidentally damage or delete the other's files or to use too much of the hard drive space. Some NLE systems provide password protection for program bins.
	There is no picture quality loss due to increased generations of video because the editing is performed on a computer hard drive. Therefore, the picture quality is essentially as high as that on the original raw footage. A vast array of effects can be added to the edited program.	Once editing is complete, the program must be copied back to tape, usually in real-time.

Figure 19-17
A comparison of the advantages and disadvantages in using nonlinear editing systems and linear editing systems.

tell a simple story without flashy special effects and practice until the results are acceptable. The features and functions of more elaborate editing systems will become familiar with experience. Technology promises to continually provide changes and improvements to video editing systems. To be successful, you must learn to make the best use of new technology and adapt to the changes created.

Review Questions

Please answer the following questions on a separate sheet of paper. Do not write in this book.

1. What are the electronic components required for a linear editing system?

2. What is the added advantage of using an A-B roll system?

3. What information is included on an EDL? When is the EDL created?

4. What is the difference between real-time and screen time?

5. What is an edit transition?

6. What is a video generation?

7. Explain the importance of blacking the videotape when using a linear editing system.

8. What are the benefits of using insert edit mode over assemble edit mode?

9. How are control track editing and time code editing different?

10. What is the main difference between nonlinear editing and linear editing systems?

11. Which system (linear or nonlinear) uses bins during the editing process? What is the function of a bin?

12. What are the disadvantages of using a nonlinear editing system?

Activities

1. Watch a few prime time television programs. Make a list of all the matched cuts you notice. Be prepared to describe the matched cuts in class.

2. Compare the cut rates of two different types of programs. Is the cut rate of one faster or slower than the other? Does the cut rate serve a particular purpose in either program?

Chapter 20
Getting Technical— The Video Signal

Objectives

After completing this chapter, you will be able to:

- Describe how the television picture is produced.
- Name and define each of the video scanning signals.
- Explain the importance of sync to video equipment during production.
- Describe how the imminent changes in video technology will affect both current and new video equipment.

Introduction

Even though current television technology is being tremendously impacted by the digital revolution, the television system most common throughout the country is analog. This chapter provides a rather simple overview of the technical aspects of the analog video signal and is designed as a general perspective for the average production personnel. A basic understanding of the video signal is helpful when troubleshooting problems during a program shoot.

This chapter is not intended to be an introduction to video engineering. A video engineer is intimately acquainted with the intricacies of the television signal from an electronics perspective. Students with an aptitude for electronics may find a rewarding career as a video engineer.

How the Television Picture Is Made

If you were to saw the picture tube of a television set in half lengthwise, we could see that the inside of the front piece of glass is coated with phosphors. When a phosphor is struck by an electron, it glows for a fraction of a second. The cathode is positioned in the back of the picture tube and "fires" a ray, or beam, of electrons through the tube, **Figure 20-1**. When the electrons hit the back of the television screen, they produce a glowing dot. Wire coils wrapped around the back of the tube serve as electromagnets that vary their magnetic strength to "steer" the beam of electrons. The trajectory of the beam can then be bent after being fired to hit the entire phosphor-coated surface, instead of just the very center of the screen. The electromagnet, in essence, changes the course of the electron beam from a straight pitch to the screen, to a "curve ball."

Production Note

Move close to the television screen and notice that each picture is actually made up of glowing dots. You now know that the dots glow on the screen because of the electrons hitting the surface inside the tube. Now try to imagine just how many dots there are in one picture!

A closer inspection of the television screen reveals that the glowing dots are arranged in horizontal lines. There are 525 lines of dots on the television screen, but only 486 of those lines are visible. The remaining lines are at the very top and bottom of the screen. If you have ever seen the picture "roll," the image visually scrolls up or down, on a television screen, the black bar between each rolling picture contains the 39 lines that are not normally visible on the screen. Those 39 lines are black,

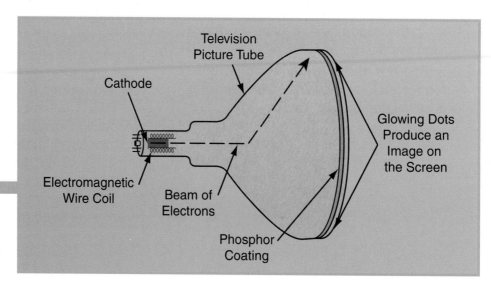

Figure 20-1
The cathode "fires" a ray of electrons at the phosphor-coated television screen, which produces glowing dots.

having no luminance, but they contain much information about how the television set creates the image. This information is relevant to the responsibilities of a video engineer and will be addressed in advanced television production courses.

Developing the Technology

During the early development of television systems, electrons were sprayed on the back of the screen, also coated with phosphors, to create a picture from the resulting glowing dots. There were understandable limitations to this technology. The pioneers of television determined that the standard used in this country would be to spray each individual line horizontally until all 525 lines were sprayed. The beam would then return to the top of the screen and begin again. This system is very much like typing a paper on a typewriter. The typewriter "sprays" the letters across the page until it reaches the end of the right edge of the page, returns to the left edge on the next line to begin spraying again to the end of the right edge, returns to the left edge of the next line, and so on.

By the time the cathode ray sprayed the bottom line of the television screen, the top of the screen had already dimmed out to black. Remember that the phosphor glows for only a fraction of a second. No matter what they tried, the television pioneers could not get the beam to move fast enough to go all the way to the bottom of the screen and return to the top to respray before the top line dimmed out. There were just too many dots that needed to be fired.

It was then decided to try spraying every other line with the cathode ray. This would allow the beam of electrons to reach the bottom of the screen in half the time. It could then return to the top of the screen and spray the lines it skipped on the first pass. In other words, the first pass would spray all the odd lines (1, 3, 5, 7) and the second pass would spray the even lines (2, 4, 6, 8). This concept of alternately firing odd and even lines is called *interlace*, **Figure 20-2**. After some experimentation, it was determined that the new set of lines was sprayed just before the first set dimmed out. This gave the illusion of a continuous picture. It

Interlace: The process of firing all the odd lines on the television screen with the cathode ray in one pass and returning to the top of the screen to fire all the even lines in the second pass of the cathode ray.

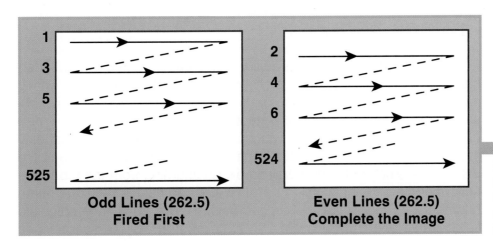

**Odd Lines (262.5)
Fired First**

**Even Lines (262.5)
Complete the Image**

Figure 20-2
Interlace is the process of firing all the odd lines and returning to the top of the screen to fire all the even lines.

was, in fact, two pictures that "jumped" up and down so quickly that they appeared to be one. The picture clarity did suffer, unfortunately, with this process. The television pioneers decided that half of the lines produced an acceptable picture quality and made it the national standard. This standard came to be known by the initials of the committee that created it: NTSC (National Television Standards Committee).

Video Scanning Signals

In addition to the video signal, several other signals travel to the cathode to control the movement of the cathode ray.

The *horizontal sync pulse* is a signal sent with the video signal and tells the cathode that the ray of electrons has reached the end of a line. Imagine that you are writing a paper. The horizontal sync pulse is much like the realization that you are at the end of a line and need to start a new line. Otherwise, you will be writing off the edge of the paper.

Horizontal blanking is the signal that stops the cathode from firing electrons. When writing a paper, this is the realization that you are at the end of the line and now must take your pen off the paper.

Horizontal retrace is the signal that tells the cathode to re-aim the ray at the left edge of the screen and begin spraying again. When writing, this signal tells you to move the pen back to the left margin of the paper in order to begin writing on a new line.

The *vertical sync pulse* is a signal that alerts the cathode that the last line of the screen has been sprayed. When writing a paper, this is when you realize that you have reached the bottom of the page.

The *vertical blanking* signal turns off the cathode ray when it reaches the bottom of the screen. This signal stops you from writing before you write off the bottom of the page.

The *vertical retrace* signal returns the cathode ray position to the top of the screen to begin firing again. This is similar to moving to the next page when writing a paper, and moving the pen to the top left corner of the page to begin writing again.

Frames and Fields

The entire process seems a bit tedious, but is not difficult to understand. The interlace process simply breaks the logical method of writing into 6 individual steps. We each perform the 6 steps when we write, but we do not actually think about the steps as we do them. The amazing part of this process is the speed at which it must occur. Remember that only every other line is fired in a single pass of the cathode ray. One entire pass of the electron beam, spraying every other line from the top to the bottom of the screen, is called a *field*. After one field is fired, the beam returns to the top to fire the second field, **Figure 20-3**. Two complete fields create one *frame*. There are 60 fields of 262.5 lines per second

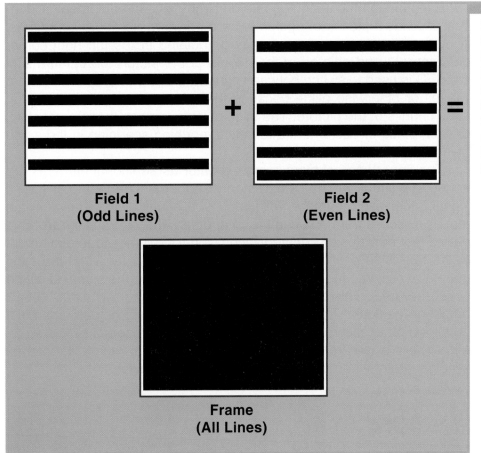

**Field 1
(Odd Lines)**

**Field 2
(Even Lines)**

**Frame
(All Lines)**

Figure 20-3
Each pass of the cathode ray "sprays" half of the lines on the television screen with electrons, which creates a field. Two consecutive fields completes the spraying of every line on the screen and creates a frame.

or 30 frames of 525 lines per second. This amounts to 15,750 lines fired every second! Each field is slightly different than the preceding field. The slight change in odd to even fields, along with the rapid flashing of the fields, provides the illusion of motion pictures. This amazing technology is more than 50 years old and currently remains the standard for television in this country.

Sync

If the picture tube is like an amazingly fast ray gun that fires electrons, then the television camera can be compared to an amazingly fast vacuum cleaner wand that sucks up the electrons to be fired later at the phosphors on the screen. This preposterous analogy works in describing the sync signal. If the "vacuum wand" in the camera is pointed at the upper-right corner of the image, how does the "ray gun" in the television set know to aim itself at the upper-right corner of the screen? If the cathode ray were aimed at a different place on the screen, the television screen would display a collection of multicolored dots resembling confetti. The sync pulse is the means by which the cathode ray in the television picture tube is tied to video camera's "vacuum wand."

Even though the scanning rate on each piece of equipment is identical, individual pieces of equipment are powered up at different times. Therefore, the "vacuum wand" may be pointed at the top right corner on camera 1 and pointed at the middle of the picture on camera 2. If the SEG is used to switch between camera 1 and camera 2, the picture will roll or otherwise glitch because the cathode ray is forced to skip large chunks of the picture. The sync pulse overrides the internal clock of each piece of equipment and sets everything scanning in the same place at the same time.

The importance of sync is even greater as additional cameras are added to a shoot. All the cameras on a shoot must be tied to one sync signal, otherwise the image will jump or be briefly distorted every time the TD switches from one camera to another. The *sync generator* is a device that provides a synchronization signal to all the video equipment in the television production facility. In small studio facilities, the sync generator built into the SEG is often used to provide the signal to all the necessary gear. This output signal is usually labeled "sync out," "black burst," or "genlock." The sync generators built into some cameras must be turned off to allow the camera to "listen" to the external sync source. *Genlock* is a feature that allows the equipment to ignore its internal sync generator when an external sync signal is applied.

Sync generator: A device that provides a synchronization signal to all the video equipment in the television production facility.

Genlock: A feature that allows a piece of video equipment to ignore its internal sync generator when an external sync signal is applied.

Visualize This

Imagine a marching band without a drum section to keep the beat while marching in a parade. After the band stops playing, it would not take long for the band members to get out of step with each other. When the drum beat, like the sync pulse, is added, everyone gets back in step very quickly.

Waveform Monitor and Vectorscope

The waveform monitor and vectorscope are two pieces of testing equipment that allow an engineer to examine the quality and strength of the video signal. The *waveform monitor*, **Figure 20-4**, measures every aspect of an image, as well as the brightness and darkness of the video signal. The *vectorscope*, **Figure 20-5**, graphically measures the way the colors are structured in the signal. Color bars are a series of colors, including black, white, and gray, on a chart which can be shot by a camera or may be internally generated by the camera, SEG, CCU, or several other pieces of gear. See **Figure 20-6**. The purpose of color bars is to verify that all cameras on a shoot are "seeing" the same shade of a color when all are pointed at the same object. The output from two or more cameras can be simultaneously brought into the waveform monitor and vectorscope. This allows the operator to adjust the CCU for each camera to match the output to an industry standard. The colors

Waveform monitor: A piece of testing equipment that measures every aspect of an image, including the brightness and darkness of the video signal.

Vectorscope: A piece of testing equipment that graphically measures the way the colors are structured in the video signal.

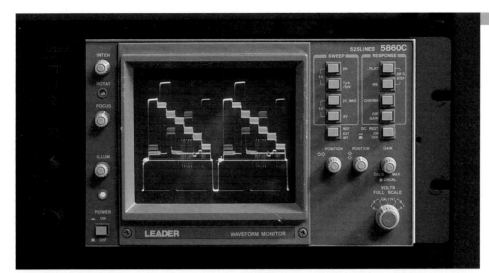

Figure 20-4
The waveform monitor measures every aspect of the television signal except color strength.

Figure 20-5
The vectorscope graphically measures a signal's color strength and adherence to industry standard settings.

on the color bar chart should be memorized. The colors, displayed from left to right, are:

- White
- Yellow
- Cyan (a light blue)
- Green
- Magenta
- Red
- Blue (navy blue)
- Black

When the color bar chart is activated on a camera, the specified colors should appear on the monitor. If the colors do

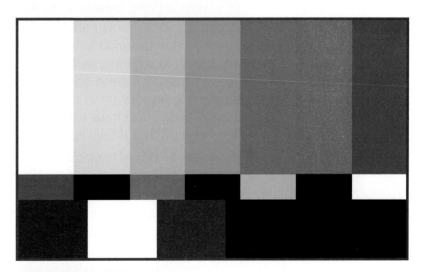

Figure 20-6
The bars are used to provide an industry-wide standard for color reproduction.

not appear in order, it is likely that the monitor's color or tint settings need adjustment. It is important to make the necessary adjustments before beginning the shoot, otherwise colors in the program will be skewed on the monitor. You may assume the camera is not functioning properly and delay or cancel the shoot unnecessarily.

Preparing for the Future

The Federal Communications Commission decreed that all television stations in the country must cease broadcasting an analog signal and begin broadcasting digital signals, based on the guidelines and timeframe they provided. This sounds like a very good change, and it is, for the most part. Unfortunately, every piece of analog-based television equipment in production houses, studios, cable systems, and private homes must be replaced. This means that every television set in your home will eventually have to be replaced by a digital television. Those people who do not purchase a new (digital) television set will have the opportunity to purchase a conversion box. The conversion box will be setup near the television to convert the digital broadcast signals into the old-fashioned analog signal. Once people see the incredible quality of a digital picture, however, the analog TV picture will be less and less desired.

Video Format

Letterbox: A video display format that allows a program originally shot using a wide screen film or video format (16:9 aspect ratio) to be displayed on a normal, 4:3 aspect ratio analog television.

Many broadcast programs are now in letterbox format. ***Letterbox*** means that the original program was shot in a wide screen film or video format (16:9 aspect ratio) instead of the normal analog television 4:3 aspect ratio, **Figure 20-7**. In order to squeeze a very wide picture onto an almost square screen without distorting the image, the top of the screen is pushed down and the bottom of the screen is pulled up. This leaves a short but wide image. The 16:9 format will be the norm after the conversion to digital broadcast signals. Most electronics and television stores currently have a variety of 16:9 format digital televisions. Some people find a program in letterbox format annoying to watch. Does the change to digital signals mean that after the conversion is complete, the picture on all digital televisions will be letterboxed?

- **Yes.** The digital television screen is already in the 16:9 format. When you first see a digital television screen, you will immediately notice the rectangular shape.

- **No.** The shape of the television matches the shape of the picture. Therefore, the television picture will not *appear* to be letterboxed at all. There will not be a black bar at the top and bottom of the screen because the entire television screen itself is shaped differently.

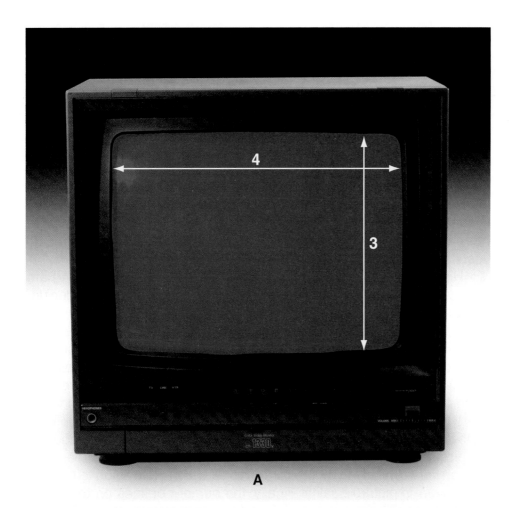

A

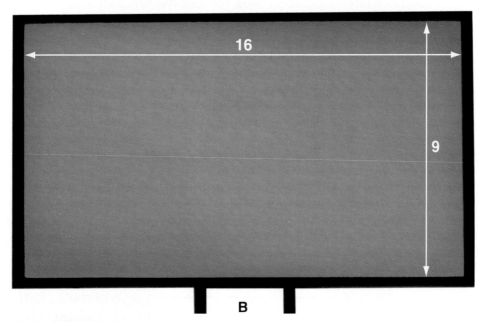

B

Figure 20-7

A—A letterboxed image would appear considerably smaller on a 4:3 format television. B—Notice that the 16:9 format television is in the shape of a letterboxed image.

Those choosing to keep 4:3 aspect ratio analog television sets will not only have to purchase the converter box, but will also be viewing 100% letterbox images. Even though some digital televisions are available in 4:3 aspect ratio, purchasing these TVs is not a wise investment!

Home Video Equipment

The 525 line interlaced, 4:3 aspect ratio television technology is over 50 years old. It is easy to see how much technology changed in the last 50 years. Consider how much the computer industry has changed in just the last 2 years, or the last few weeks. The point is, technology has clearly taken us far beyond the best possible solution developed 50 years ago.

High definition, digital 16:9 aspect ratio television sets (HDTV) are now available in consumer markets. They do seem expensive, but considering inflation, they are not much more expensive than new color television sets for the average American home were in 1959. The technology that will become the standard in the future is still not settled. However, interlaced television is no longer the requirement. Television sets are now produced that use progressive scan technology. With *progressive scan technology*, the monitor's cathode ray moves fast enough to fire every line on the screen, instead of every other line, before the top lines on the screen fade out, **Figure 20-8**. This technology effectively doubles the picture sharpness and clarity. Moreover, 16:9 television screens are shaped very similarly to 35 mm film. This allows the television to rival the film theater in picture quality. Finally, the number of lines on the television screen has been increased. New formats available include 720 and 1080 lines interlaced (720i and 1080i) and 720 and 1080 lines progressive (720p and 1080p).

With television stations broadcasting a digital signal, your old analog VCR will continue to play analog tapes on an analog television, but will not record digital signals off the air. New digital VCRs are now on the market that have this capability. It is not necessary to replace existing DVD players, as long as the model has a digital output. Many DVD players have only an analog output.

Progressive scan technology: The process of firing every line on the television screen in one pass instead of every other line. The cathode ray moves fast enough to complete firing every line on the screen before the lines at the top of the screen begin to fade.

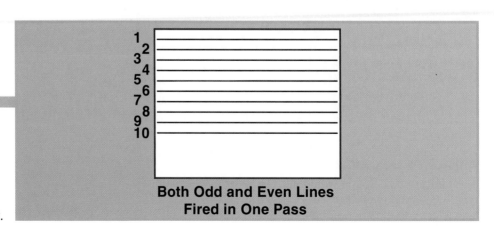

Figure 20-8
Progressive scan technology allows the beam of electrons to move rapidly enough to scan every line on the screen and return to the top line before it has dimmed out.

Wrapping Up

Upon completion of the FCC's mandated digital conversion, the newer digital 16:9 television formats will become a unified standard of television technology. This milestone marks a new video age. A comprehensive knowledge of upcoming technology is vital to success in the television industry and can be found in articles published in the various trade magazines. The technology is changing too rapidly to commit information to the pages of a textbook.

Review Questions

Please answer the following questions on a separate sheet of paper. Do not write in this book.

1. Explain how the picture on the television screen is produced.
2. How many lines are there on the television screen? How many are visible?
3. What is interlace?
4. What is the difference between horizontal sync pulse and vertical sync pulse?
5. What is a field? How many fields are completed every second?
6. How do the waveform monitor and the vectorscope function in verifying a quality video signal?

Activities

1. Research the development of the cathode used in television picture tubes. Report on other methods and devices that were created for the same purpose.
2. Search the Federal Communications Commission Web site for facts about digital broadcasting. Make note of any items related to the conversion that may specifically affect you or your family. Be prepared to share this information with the class.

Congratulations!

You have successfully completed this text! Hopefully, you have created a dictionary of terms that can be used as a reference throughout your career. You have learned an entirely new language and should be practicing its usage every day.

This is not the end of your course of study to enter and succeed in the television production industry. You are now armed with enough basic information about the entire system to launch into many different directions of study. Never stop learning about new gear and technologies. Believe me, the technology will not stop changing because you finally master it. Technology always marches onward. It is your job to try to ride the crest of that wave as much and as long as possible. Remember that knowledge, enthusiasm, hard work, networking, "talking the talk," flexibility, and responsibility are the keys to entry and longevity in this industry. Good luck to you!

Acknowledgements

The publisher would like to acknowledge the following companies and individuals for their contributions to the illustrations and photos used within this text:

Chuck Pharis Video
Glidecam Industries, Inc.
Jack Klasey
Mole-Richardson Co.
National Association of Broadcasters
Popless Voice Screens
RCA
Vinten Broadcast Limited

Dedication

The greatest acknowledgements in completing this book must be reserved for the most important people in my life. My daughter, Katie, and my son, Michael, had to share me with this book for over two years and did not complain. My wife, Agnes, is the reason you are reading this book. She inspired me to write it, she stepped into the "Dad" duties around the house while I was writing it, she edited the grammar and spelling, she motivated me to continue with the project when I was tired and wanted to quit, and she encouraged me to seek a publisher so the text would be available to other teachers looking for just this type of text.

Thank you to everyone involved in the creation of this text.

Glossary

½″ tape: A reel format videotape found only in low-end, industrial equipment.

¼″ connector: A connector that is ¼″ in diameter and single-pronged, with a little indentation near the end of the prong. This type of connector is commonly found on the cord used with large stereo headphones. Also called a *phone connector.*

1″ tape: A reel format videotape available in three formats: Type A, Type B, and Type C. Type C was the most common format.

16:9 aspect ratio: The aspect ratio of a television that is 16 units wide by 9 units high.

2″ tape: A reel format videotape used on older machines called quadruplex recorders.

¾″ tape: A videotape format that has been surpassed by current technology. Also called *U-Matic.*

3200° Kelvin: The temperature of white light in degrees Kelvin. Also noted as *3200°K* or "32K" when spoken.

4:3 aspect ratio: The aspect ratio of a television that is 4 units wide by 3 units high.

8mm: A videotape format designed for consumer camcorders and is named for the width of the tape.

A

Actors: Individuals who participate in a drama or comedy program, performing as someone or something other than themselves.

Ad: A television advertisement for a product or service. Also called a *spot.*

AD: See *assistant director.*

Ad-lib: When talent speaks lines or performs actions that are not in the script or have not been rehearsed.

Adapter: A device that changes the type, or connector end, of an existing connector.

Affiliate: A broadcast station that has aligned itself with a particular network. The network provides a certain number of hours of daily programming. The affiliate is responsible for providing the remainder of programming to fill the daily schedule.

AGC: See *automatic gain control.*

Aperture: The opening, adjusted by the iris, through which light passes into the lens.

Arc: Moving the camera in a curved truck around the set, while the camera remains fixed on the main object in the shot. The main subject never leaves the frame of the picture.

Arc left: Rolling the camera, tripod, and dolly in a circle to the left (clockwise) around the subject of a shot.

Arc right: Rolling the camera, tripod, and dolly in a circle to the right (counterclockwise) around the subject of a shot.

Artifacts: Rectangular distortions that are seen on the screen on digital video formats.

Aspect ratio: The relationship of the width of the television screen to the height of the television screen, as in 4:3 or 16:9.

Assemble edit mode: A linear editing process in which using a blacked tape in the recorder is not necessary. Assemble edit mode saves in overall editing time, but is more likely to create glitches because the control track is broken on the edited master tape with each edit performed.

Assemble edit technique: A method of editing where scenes are edited in the order they will be seen in the finished program while the editing system is set in insert edit *mode.*

Assistant director (AD): Person who provides general assistance around the studio or production facility. The AD is commonly hired to fill a variety of positions when key personnel are sick, out of town, working on another project, or otherwise unavailable. In many facilities, the assistant director position is synonymous with the production assistant position.

Audio: The portion of a program that you can hear. Audio includes narration, spoken lines, sound effects, and background music.

Audio booth: A room in the studio that contains all of the equipment capable of adding sound to the program.

Audio console: A console that includes many different pieces of audio gear, including the microphone mixer, audio cassette players, CD players, and turntables.

Audio delay edit: An edit that cuts to the video portion of the next scene before the corresponding audio of the new scene is heard by the audience.

Audio engineer: The person responsible for the audio/sound quality on the production and related equipment.

Audio mixer: A piece of equipment that takes the sounds from a variety of sources, such as mics, a CD player, or tape player, and combines them into a single sound signal that is sent to the recorder.

Audition: The process in which a director makes casting decisions for a program by watching and listening to prospective performers.

Auto-focus: A common feature on consumer cameras that keeps only the center of the picture in focus.

Auto-iris circuit: A feature on many consumer and professional cameras that automatically examines the light levels coming into the camera and adjusts the iris according to generic standards of a "good" picture.

Automatic gain control (AGC): A circuit found on most consumer video cameras that controls the audio level during the recording process.

B

Back light: The lighting instrument placed above and behind, at the twelve o'clock position, the talent or object in a shot to separate the talent or object from the background.

Background: The material or object(s) on a set that are placed behind the talent in a shot.

Background light: A lighting instrument that is pointed at the background of a set.

Background music: Music in a program that helps to relay or emphasize the program's message by increasing its emotional impact.

Background sound: The noise that is normally associated with a particular location.

Backspace: When both the source and record machines automatically rewind the tape to a point about 5 to 7 seconds before the marked edit-in point.

Bank: Two buses on the control panel of a SEG that are electronically connected to each other.

Barndoors: Fully moveable black metal flaps attached to the front of a lighting instrument, used to block or reshape the light.

Barrel adapter: A type of adapter that has the same type of connector and connector end on both sides.

Base: The first layer of makeup applied—usually covers the entire face, neck, ears, back of the hands, and bald spot, if present. Also called *foundation*.

Beta SX: A ½″ videotape that uses digital MPEG compression.

Betacam: A ½″ format, broadcast-quality videotape.

Betacam SP: A ½″ videotape format that used to be the best format for professional television use, but digital video formats are challenging this format in professional markets.

Betamax: A ½″ videotape format developed as a consumer medium. It is, for the most part, extinct.

Big talking face (BTF): A program format in which the talent speaks and the camera shoots almost entirely in a medium close-up. Also called *lecture* and *talking head*.

Bin: A window on the computer monitor that displays the first frame of the video clips to be edited.

Black video: A bona-fide video signal that has no luminance.

Blending: Incorporating applied makeup into the areas surrounding it by brushing the makeup with the fingers or a brush.

BNC connector: A type of connector commonly used in television production. The female and male versions lock together securely with a simple ¼-turn twist.

Boom: A pole that is held over the set with a microphone attached to the end of the pole. Any type of mic may be attached to the end of the boom.

Bounce lighting: A lighting technique where a lighting instrument is not pointed directly at the subject of the shot, but the light is bounced off another object, such as a ceiling, wall, or the ground.

Boundary mic: A microphone used to pick up sound on a stage or in a large room and is most commonly a condenser type. Boundary mics work on the principle that sound is reflected off hard surfaces and are usually placed on a table, floor, or wall.

Broadcast: The television signal travels through the air from one antenna to another antenna.

Broadcasting rights: Permission to broadcast a piece of music to the public.

BTF: See *big talking face.*

Bus: A row of buttons on the control panel of a SEG that access different functions.

C

Cable end connector: A connector found on the end of a length of cable.

Cablecasting rights: Permission to cablecast a piece of music to the public.

Camcorder: A portable camera/recorder combination.

Camera control unit (CCU): A piece of equipment that controls various attributes of the video signal sent from the camera and is usually placed in the control room or the master control room. Also called a *remote control unit (RCU).*

Camera head: The portion of the video camera that contains all the electronics needed to convert the reflection of light from the subject into an electronic signal.

Camera line: An imaginary line, parallel to the camera, which bisects a set into a foreground and a background. Also called a *vector line.*

Camera monitor: A monitor that displays the image shot by the corresponding camera.

Camera operator: The person who runs the piece of equipment that captures the video images of the program.

Camera rehearsal: A practice session of scenes in a program that includes the talent, technical director, audio engineer, camera operators, and director. Also called a *dry run.*

Cardioid mic: A mic with a pick-up pattern that captures sound from primarily one direction. Also called a *uni-directional mic* or *directional mic.*

Cast: The collective name given to all the talent participating in a production.

Cast breakdown by scene: A listing of the program's cast members that indicates the scene numbers in which they appear.

C-clamp: A clamp in the shape of a *C,* used to attach lighting instruments to the grid.

CCD: See *charge coupled device.*

CCTV: See *closed circuit television.*

CCU: See *camera control unit.*

CG: See *character generator.*

CG operator: The person who creates the titles for the program using a character generator.

Character generator (CG): Device that creates (generates) letters (characters), primarily for titles.

Character makeup: Makeup application technique used to make a performer look like someone or something other than the performer's own persona.

Charge coupled device (CCD): A dime-sized component of the camera head into which light enters and is converted into an electronic signal. The signal exits on the opposite side of the CCD and enters the rest of the camera.

Chassis mount connector: A connector that is built into a piece of equipment.

Chromakey: A type of key effect where a specific color can be blocked from the key camera's input.

Chrominance: The color portion of the video signal, which includes the hue and color saturation.

Circle wipe: A video effect where a circle grows or shrinks, replacing one picture with another.

Clip control: A knob on the control panel of a SEG that allows the operator to adjust the amount of luminance that is sent to the SEG. Also called *key level control.*

Closed circuit television (CCTV): Television where the signal is sent through wires and serves only an extremely small, private predetermined area.

Close-up (CU): A shot that captures a subject from the top of the head to just below the shoulders. Also called a *narrow angle shot.*

Colorizer: An add-on feature to the internal key that allows the operator to fill the key cutout with any color, instead of simply white.

Commercial broadcast television: This type of television production facility is "for-profit." The television signal is sent via a transmitter tower through the air and is free for anyone with an antenna to receive it.

Concert style: A type of music video in which the audience sees the band perform the music that is heard.

Condenser mic: A type of mic that requires an external power supply (usually a battery) to operate. Also called an *electret condenser mic.*

Confidence monitor: A monitor connected to the output of the VCR. Seeing the image on this monitor ensures that the video recorder received the signal.

Connectors: Metal devices that attach cables to equipment or to other cables.

Content specialist: A person who works with the scriptwriter and is considered to be an expert in the program's subject matter.

Contrast ratio: The relationship between the brightest object and the darkest object in the television picture.

Control room: A room in the studio containing several monitors and the special effects generator. In smaller facilities, the control room also houses the audio mixer, all of the sound equipment, video recorders, the CG, CCUs, and even the light board.

Control track: A series of inaudible pulses recorded onto a tape that regulates the speed of the tape in playback.

Control track editing: A method of linear editing where the editing system uses the inaudible control track pulses as reference points for setting, locating, and using edit points.

Control track logic (CTL): The most common and least expensive type of linear editing system available.

Convertible camera: A camera with a variety of accessory packages available to make it operational in a studio, as a portable field camera, or both.

Corner insert: A video effect where a small image is positioned in any corner, usually the upper right or left corner, of the full screen image. All four sides of the smaller image rest inside the frame of the larger picture.

Corner wipe: A video effect where a small image is positioned in any corner, usually the upper right or left corner, of the full screen image. Two sides of the smaller image touch the actual frame of the larger picture.

Crab dolly: A four-wheeled cart that travels on a lightweight track and enables the camera to smoothly capture movement shots while being pushed or pulled along the track.

Crash bang editing: A type of nonprofessional linear editing that is accomplished using only two consumer VCRs, neither of which is a video editor.

Crawl: Words that appear either at the top or the bottom of the screen and move from the right edge of the screen to the left, without interrupting the program in progress.

Credits: The written material presented before and/or after a program listing the names and job titles of the people involved in the program's production.

Crème makeup: An oil-based makeup product that easily blends with other colors.

Crew: Production personnel that are not normally seen by the camera and generally includes equipment operators.

Cross-camera shooting: A two-camera shooting technique in which the camera on the left shoots the person on the right of the set and the camera on the right shoots the person on the left of the set.

Cross-key lighting: A lighting technique that combines aspects of both three-point and four-point lighting, with the added ability to cover more than one person or object in the lighting spread.

CTL: See *control track logic.*

CU: See *close-up.*

Cue: A signal that implies something specific is to happen.

Cut: An instantaneous picture change that occurs on screen. Used synonymously with *take* in this context.

Cut bar: A feature on a SEG that provides a quick way of cutting between the input selected on one bus and the input selected on another bus in the bank. Also called a *cut button.*

Cut button: A feature on a SEG that provides a quick way of cutting between the input selected on one bus and the input selected on another bus in the bank. Also called a *cut bar.*

Cut rate: The frequency of cuts or edits, per minute, during a program. Also referred to as *pace.*

Cutaway: A shot that is not a key element in the action. It is commonly used to bridge what would otherwise be a jump cut.

Cyc: See *cyclorama.*

Cyclorama (Cyc): A background curtain on a set that is stretched tight and pulled to cover the walls and curves of the studio, forming a solid background color.

D

D-9: A ½″ digital videotape format that is broadcast quality. Also called *Digital S*.

DA: See *distribution amplifier*.

Delegation control: A switch or button on the control panel of a SEG that toggles the A bank or B bank from one function to another. For example, the delegation control can switch the A bank from operating as a mix bank to an effects bank.

Depth of field (DOF): The distance between the minimum object distance and the furthest point from the camera a subject can be positioned while remaining in focus.

Diaphragm: A thin surface inside the mic which vibrates when hit by sound waves in the air. The vibration moves a tiny wire back and forth through a magnetic field creating an electrical signal. Also called a *generating element*.

Diffusion device: A device that is placed in front of a lighting instrument to reduce and soften the intensity of light without altering the color temperature.

Digi-Beta: See *digital betacam*.

Digital Betacam (Digi-Beta): A ½″ videotape with higher quality than Betacam SP and the capability of recording of digital signals instead of analog signals.

Digital S: A ½″ digital videotape format that is broadcast quality. Also known as *D-9*.

Digital video effect (DVE): Video effects that are created using digital technology and the ability to alter an image by manipulating each individual pixel.

Dimmer: A device attached to the power control of a lighting instrument that can reduce or increase the amount of electricity that flows to the lamp.

DIN connector: A term that refers to any type of connector with 4 or more holes/pins.

Directional mic: A mic with a pick-up pattern that captures sound from primarily one direction. Also called a *uni-directional mic* or *cardioid mic*.

Director: The person who is in charge of the creative aspects of the program and interacts with the entire staff.

Dissolve: A video effect where one picture slowly disintegrates while another image slowly appears. Also called a *lap dissolve*.

Distribution amplifier (DA): A machine used when a signal must be split and sent to multiple outputs. The signal is amplified before it is split so that each output receives nearly 100% of the original signal.

Docking: The process of attaching the camera head and recorder together to make one larger "camcorder."

Documentary: A program format that is essentially a research paper for television. The audio in the program is on-camera and/or off-camera narration. The video footage used in the program is determined by the topic research and should support the audio of the program.

DOF: See *depth of field*.

Dolly: *1 (noun)*—A three-wheeled cart onto which the feet of a tripod are mounted. A dolly allows smooth camera movements to be performed. *2 (verb)*—Physically moving the camera, its tripod, and dolly perpendicularly toward or away from the set.

Dolly in: Smoothly pushing the camera directly forward toward the set.

Dolly out: Pulling the camera backward while facing the set.

Drama: A program format that includes both dramas and comedies and requires actors to portray someone or something other than themselves.

Dramatic aside: When a performer steps out of character and directly addresses the audience.

Dropout: A tiny white dot seen on the television screen when the medium has fallen off an analog videotape and the video head passes over an "empty spot" on the tape.

Dry run: A practice session of scenes in a program that includes the talent, technical director, audio engineer, camera operators, and director. Also called a *camera rehearsal*.

Dub: A copy of the master videotape. Also called a *dup*.

Dubbing: The process of copying the recorded material on a tape.

Dup: A copy of the master videotape. Also called a *dub*.

DVCam: A 6mm digital format that is proprietary for Sony Corporation.

DVCPRO: A 6mm, metal particle tape used as a professional digital video format.

DVCPRO50: A 6mm digital format with even higher quality than DVCPRO.

DVE: See *digital video effect*.

Dynamic mic: A very rugged, virtually indestructible type of mic that has good sound reproduction ability.

E

ECU: See *extreme close-up.*

Edge mode: An add-on feature to the internal key that places a border around the keyed image.

Edit controller: A remote console that controls the editing and operation functions of both the source and record VCRs.

Edit decision list (EDL): A list that notes which take of each scene should be used in the final program and the location of each take on the raw footage tape.

Edit points: Specific locations on the videotape where an edit should begin and end.

Edit through black: An edit in which a cut is made during the black that appears on screen between a fade out and a fade in. Also called *kiss black.*

Edit transition: The way in which one scene ends and the next scene begins.

Edit trim: A linear editing system feature that allows the operator to move edit points forward or backward one frame at a time.

Editing: The process of selecting the good portions of raw video footage and combining them into a coherent, sequential, and complete television program. Editing also includes post-production additions of music and sound effects, as well as effects used as scene transitions.

Editing suite: A cubicle or small room where the program is put through post-production processing, such as video and audio editing, voice-over, music and sound effects recording, and graphics recording.

Editor: The person responsible for putting the various pieces of the entire program together. The editor removes all the mistakes and bad takes, leaving only the best version of each scene, and arranges the individual scenes into the proper order.

EDL: See *edit decision list.*

Educational television: Television that aims to inform the public about various topics. This includes television programming that supports classroom studies and replays classroom sessions.

Effects bank: A bank on a SEG that allows each signal to be processed individually.

EFP: See *electronic field production.*

Electret condenser mic: A type of mic that requires an external power supply (usually a battery) to operate. Also called a *condenser mic.*

Electronic field production (EFP): A shoot in which the video crew and production staff are in total control of the events and action.

Electronic news gathering (ENG): The process of shooting information, events, or activity that would have happened whether a reporting/production team was there with a camera or not.

ELS: See *extreme long shot.*

ENG: See *electronic news gathering.*

EP: See *executive producer.*

Equipment breakdown: A list of each scene in a program with all the equipment needed to shoot each scene.

Error in continuity: An error that occurs during editing where a sequence of shots in the finished product contains physically impossible actions or items.

Essential area: The area of an image or shot that must be seen on any television set, regardless of aspect ratio or age, and must include all the words in a graphic.

Establishing shot: A specific type of extreme long shot used to tell the audience where and when the program takes place.

Executive producer (EP): The person, or people, who provides the funding necessary to produce the program.

External key: A video effect that is a mixture of three images: the background image, the key source (shape of the cutout), and the key fill. The image or pattern that fills the key cutout shape is the key fill.

Extreme close-up (ECU/XCU): A shot of an object that is so magnified that only a specific part of the object fills the screen.

Extreme long shot (ELS/XLS): The biggest shot a camera can capture of the subject matter. Also called a *wide angle shot.*

F

F-connector: A type of connector that carries an RF signal and is commonly found on the back of consumer VCRs.

Fade: A visual effect where the video image either slowly appears from a solid-colored screen or slowly disintegrates from an image to a solid-colored screen.

Fade in: A video effect where a totally dark picture transitions into a fully visible picture. Also called *up from black*.

Fade out: A video effect where the image slowly goes to a black screen as a scene of a program ends. Also called *fade to black*.

Fade to black: A video effect where the image slowly goes to a black screen as a scene of a program ends. Also called *fade out*.

Fader bar: A control on a SEG, usually a T-shaped handle, that controls the strength of that signal coming from each bus. Also called a *fader lever* or *fader handle*.

Fader handle: A control on a SEG, usually a T-shaped handle, that controls the strength of that signal coming from each bus. Also called a *fader bar* or *fader lever*.

Fader lever: A control on a SEG, usually a T-shaped handle, that controls the strength of that signal coming from each bus. Also called a *fader bar* or *fader handle*.

Feedback: A high-pitched squeal that occurs when a microphone picks up the sound coming from a speaker that is carrying that microphone's signal.

Female connector: A connector with one or more holes designed to receive the pins of a male connector. Also called a *jack*.

Field: One entire pass of the electron beam, spraying every other line from the top to the bottom of the screen.

Fill light: The lighting instrument that is placed opposite the key light to provide illumination on the other side of the talent's face or object in the shot.

Film chain: A device that facilitates the transfer of film images onto videotape. Film chains are used, for example, to transfer theatrical motion pictures to videotape for purchase or rental. Also called a *multiplexer, telecine,* or *film island*.

Film island: A device that facilitates the transfer of film images onto videotape. Film islands are used, for example, to transfer theatrical motion pictures to videotape for purchase or rental. Also called a *multiplexer, film chain,* or *telecine*.

Film-style shooting: A type of single-camera shooting in which a scene is shot many times with the camera moving to a different position each time to capture the scene from various angles. The finished scene is edited together to look like it was shot with several cameras.

Flag: A flexible metal rod with a clip and a flat piece of metal attached to the end. A flag is positioned between a light source and a reflective surface on the set to eliminate light hits.

Flat: A scenery unit that is usually a simple wood frame with a painted plywood shell.

Flood light: A soft light instrument that provides general lighting in a large area.

Floor manager: The person who is the director's "eyes and ears" in the studio. The floor manager relays the director's commands to the studio personnel.

Floor stand: A tripod or quadripod (4 legs) with a long vertical pole to which a lighting instrument is clamped.

Fluid head: A mounting assembly on some tripods that stabilizes the camera using the pressure between two pieces of metal and a thick fluid that provides additional resistance to movement.

Focal length: The distance (measured in millimeters) from the optical center, or focal point, of the lens assembly to the back of the lens assembly.

Focal point: The physical location within the lens assembly where an image is inverted. Also called *optical center*.

Focus: *1 (adjective)*—The state of an image when the lines of contrast appear as sharp as possible; "in focus." *2 (verb)*—The act of rotating the focus ring on a camera lens until the lines of contrast in the image are as sharp as possible.

Foreground: The area on a set that lies between the talent and the camera.

Foreground music: Music in a program that is the subject of the production.

Format script: A program script that is very brief and used for programs in which the order of events is predetermined and the sequence of each episode is consistent.

Foundation: The first layer of makeup applied—usually covers the entire face, neck, ears, back of the hands, and bald spot, if present. Also called *base*.

Four point lighting: A lighting technique that uses four lighting instruments for each person or object photographed: two key lights and two fill lights. The two key lights are positioned diagonally opposite each other, and the two fill lights are placed in the remaining two corners.

Four shot: A shot that captures four items.

Fps: The rate at which individual pictures are displayed in a motion picture and on television, expressed as frames per second.

Frame: *1*—The actual edge of the video picture; the edge of the picture on all four sides. *2*—Two consecutive passes of the cathode ray, spraying every line on the television screen with electrons. Two complete fields complete one frame.

Framing: Involves placing items in the camera's frame by operating the camera and tripod.

Fresnel: A hard light instrument that is lightweight and easily focused.

Friction head: A mounting assembly on some tripods that stabilizes the camera using the pressure created when two pieces of metal are squeezed together by a screw.

F-stop: A camera setting that determines the amount of light passing through the aperture of the lens by controlling the size of the iris.

G

Gaffer: The lighting director's assistant, who often does the actual hauling of heavy instruments up and down ladders.

Gain: The strength of an audio or video signal.

Gel: A heat resistant, thick plastic sheet placed in front of a lighting instrument to turn the white light from a lamp into a colored light.

Generating element: A thin surface inside the mic which vibrates when hit by sound waves in the air. The vibration moves a tiny wire back and forth through a magnetic field creating an electrical signal. Also called a *diaphragm*.

Genlock: A feature that allows a piece of video equipment to ignore its internal sync generator when an external sync signal is applied.

Glitch: A momentary "trashing" of the video signal (such as a roll, tear, or briefly appearing noise).

Graphic artist: The person responsible for all the artwork required for the production. This includes computer graphics, traditional works of art, charts, and graphs.

Graphics: All of the "artwork" seen in a program, including the paintings that hang on the walls of a set, the opening and closing program titles, computer graphics, charts, graphs, and any other electronic representation that may be part of a visual presentation.

Great depth of field: When a camera's depth of field is as large as possible, but also keeps all the items in the image in focus while zooming.

Grid: A pipe system that hangs from the studio ceiling and supports the lighting instruments.

Grip: A person who moves the equipment, scenery, and props on a studio set.

Group shot: A shot that incorporates any number of items above four.

H

Hand-held mic: A mic that is designed to be held in the hand, rather than placed on a boom or clipped to clothing.

Hard light: A type of illumination used in the studio that creates sharp, distinct, and very dark shadows.

Head: A 15 second "lead-in" recorded onto tape at the beginning of every take.

Head room: The space from the top of a person's head to the top of the television screen.

Helical scan: The pattern in which a video signal is placed onto a videotape. The videotape is wrapped around the video head and, because the head is slanted, the video signal is recorded diagonally on the tape. Also called *slant track*.

Hi8: An 8mm videotape that is higher in quality and uses a different recording system than 8mm.

High angle shot: Shooting talent with the camera high in the air, pointing down at an angle.

High impedance (HiZ): A type of mic that is typically inexpensive, low-quality, and cannot tolerate cable lengths longer than 8′.

Highlight: Makeup that is three or four shades lighter than the area to which it is applied.

HiZ: See *high impedance*.

Home video: Videotaped records of family events and activities taken by someone using a consumer camcorder.

Horizontal blanking: The signal that stops the cathode from firing electrons.

Horizontal retrace: The signal that tells the cathode to re-aim the ray at the left edge of the screen and begin spraying again.

Horizontal sync pulse: A signal sent with the video signal that tells the cathode that the ray has reached the end of a line.

Horizontal wipe: A video effect where a vertical line moves across the screen horizontally, replacing one picture with another.

Hot: *1*—A term used to describe an image or shot that is very bright. *2*—The state of a video camera when the image captured by the camera is being recorded.

Hypercardiod mic: A directional mic with a narrower and longer pick-up pattern than a cardioid mic.

I

Industrial television: Television that communicates relevant information to a specific audience, such as job training videos.

Input: A port or connection on a VCR through which a signal enters the VCR, such as the "audio in."

Insert edit mode: A linear editing process that requires a control track signal be recorded on the edit master videotape. With a control track on the tape, additional video or audio may be added later in the editing process without causing glitches.

Insert edit technique: A method of linear editing where either video or audio may be inserted on top of existing video and audio tracks. Any existing audio or video is erased in the process, but no glitches are created.

Interlace: The process of firing all the odd lines on the television screen with the cathode ray in one pass and returning to the top of the screen to fire all the even lines in the second pass of the cathode ray.

Internal key: A video effect that is a mixture of two images. One image provides the shape that is cut out of the other (background) picture. White fills the shape that is cut out. Also called a *luminance key.*

Interview: A program format that involves a conversation between an interviewer and an interviewee.

Iris: A component of a lens that is comprised of blades that physically expand and contract, adjusting the aperture size.

J

Jack: A connector with one or more holes designed to receive the pins of a male connector. Also called a *female connector.*

Jump cut: A sequence of shots that constitutes and error in editing. This error occurs during production when cutting between camera shots and results in an on-screen object or character appearing to jump from one side of the screen to the other.

K

Kelvin color temperature scale: A scale developed by the scientist Lord Kelvin that measures color temperatures of light in degrees Kelvin.

Key: A video effect where a portion of one picture is electronically removed and replaced with another image. Both images are displayed at 100% of the original intensity.

Key camera: The camera used to shoot the object providing the shape to be cut into the background picture when creating an internal key effect.

Key level control: A knob on the control panel of a SEG that allows the operator to adjust the amount of luminance that is sent to the SEG. Also called *clip control.*

Key light: The lighting instrument that provides the main source of illumination on the person or object in a shot.

Kiss black: An edit in which a cut is made during the black that appears on screen between a fade out and a fade in. Also called *edit through black.*

L

Lamp: The part of a lighting instrument that glows when electricity is supplied.

Lap dissolve: A video effect where one picture slowly disintegrates while another image slowly appears. Also called a *dissolve.*

Lapel mic: The smallest type of mic that can be worn by talent and is attached to clothing at or near the breastbone with a small clip or pin. Sometimes referred to as a "lav."

Large-scale video production companies: Facilities with sufficient staff and equipment to produce multi-camera, large-budget programming for broadcast networks or cable networks.

Lav: See *lavaliere microphone.*

Lavaliere (lav) microphone: A small mic that hangs from a cord around the talent's neck. A lav mic used to be the only type of mic that could be attached to people.

Lecture: A program format in which the talent speaks and the camera shoots almost entirely in a medium close-up. Also called *big talking face (BTF)* and *talking head.*

Lecture/Demonstration: A program format that provides action and makes use of props in addition to lecture. Examples of this format include cooking shows, how-to shows, and infomercials.

Lens: An assembly of several glass discs placed in a tube attached to the front of a camera.

Letterbox: A video display format that allows a program originally shot using a wide screen film or video format (16:9 aspect ratio) to be displayed on a normal, 4:3 aspect ratio analog television.

Light hit: A white spot or star shaped reflection of a lighting instrument or sunlight off a highly reflective surface on the set.

Light plot: A diagram developed by the lighting designer that indicates the placement of lighting instruments on the set of a program.

Lighting director: The person who decides the placement of lighting instruments, the appropriate color of light to use, and which lamps should be used in the instruments.

Lighting instrument: The device into which a lamp is installed to provide illumination on a set.

Limbo lighting: A lighting technique in which the background of the set is lit to create the illusion of a solid-colored, indistinct background.

Line level: The level of audio between pieces of audio equipment. For example, the level of audio going from the output of a CD player to the input on an amplifier.

Linear editing system: Video editing equipment that is based on videotape. The raw footage is placed in a source VCR and the "good" takes of the program footage are copied, in the order the audience will see them, to a tape in the record VCR.

Local origination: Programming made in a specific geographic area, to be shown to the public in that same geographic area.

Location: Any place, other than the studio, where production shooting is planned.

Location breakdown: A list of each location included in the program with the corresponding scene numbers that take place at that location.

Location survey: An assessment of a proposed shoot location that includes placement of cameras and lights, available power supply, equipment necessary, and accommodations needed for the talent and crew.

Lock-up time: The amount of time it takes, after pressing PLAY, for the machine to get the tape up to speed and produce a stable picture.

Long shot (LS): A shot that captures a subject from the top of the head to the bottom of the feet and does not include many of the surrounding details.

Low angle shot: A shot created by placing the camera anywhere from slightly to greatly below the eye level of the talent and pointing it upward.

Low impedance (LoZ): A type of mic that is costly, high-quality, and can tolerate long cable lengths.

Lower third key: A video effect created when an image or text is displayed in the lower third of the screen using a key effect.

Lower third super: A video effect created when an image or text is displayed in the lower third of the screen using a superimposition.

LoZ: See *low impedance.*

LS: See *long shot.*

Luminance: The brightness or lightness of the video picture.

Luminance key: A video effect that is a mixture of two images. One image provides the shape that is cut out of the other (background) picture. White fills the shape that is cut out. Also called an *internal key.*

M

Macro: A lens setting that allows the operator to focus on an object that is very close to the camera, almost touching the lens.

Magazine: A program format comprised of feature packages that address a single story.

Maintenance engineer: The person who keeps all the production equipment functioning at its optimum performance level.

Makeup: Any of the cosmetics applied to a performer's skin to change or enhance their appearance.

Makeup artist: The person responsible for applying cosmetics to the talent's face and body, giving them the intended appearance in front of the camera.

Male connector: A connector with one or more pins that are designed to fit into the holes of a female connector. Also called a *plug.*

Master control room: A room in a production facility where all the hardware is located, including video recorders and other equipment needed to improve and process the video and audio signals.

Matched cut: A type of edit in which a similar action, concept, item, or a combination of these is placed on either side of a cut.

Matched dissolve: A type of edit in which a similar action, concept, item, or a combination of these is placed on either side of a dissolve.

Matte key: An add-on option to the internal key that allows the operator to fill the key cutout with any shade of gray, from light gray to black, instead of simply white.

MCU: See *medium close-up.*

Medium close-up (MCU): A shot that frames a subject from the top of the head to a line just below the chest.

Medium long shot (MLS): A shot that includes the top of a subject's head to a line just above or just below the knee.

Medium shot (MS): A shot that captures a subject from the top of the head to a line just above or below the belt or waistline. Also called a *mid shot.*

Mic: See *microphone.*

Mic level: The level of audio that comes from a microphone. It is designed to be sent to the "mic in" on a recorder or mixer.

Mic mixer: A piece of equipment that combines only the microphone signals into a single sound signal.

Mic mouse: A device made of acoustical foam in the shape of a half-cylinder that turns a hand-held microphone into a boundary mic. A mic is placed inside the foam and the entire assembly is placed on the floor or desktop.

Microphone (Mic): The piece of equipment that picks up sounds in the air and sends them down a wire to the mixer or recorder.

Mid shot: A shot that captures a subject from the top of the head to a line just above or below the belt or waistline. Also called a *medium shot.*

Middle ground: The area on a set where the most important items in a picture are usually positioned. This is the area in which the action of the program typically takes place.

Mini connector: A connector that is 1/8″ in diameter and single-pronged. It is most commonly found on headsets used with portable CD players.

Mini-DV: A metal evaporated tape, 6mm digital video format used by many industrial video producers.

Minimum object distance (MOD): The closest an object can be to the camera and still be in focus.

Mix bank: A single bank on an SEG that contains the cut, fade, and dissolve effects.

MLS: See *medium long shot.*

MOD: See *minimum object distance.*

Mode: A function available on editing system equipment; an available operation on a piece of equipment.

Moiré: An effect caused by certain fabric patterns in which the television system reproduces the pattern with a rainbow of colors or moving lines displayed in the patterned area.

Monitor: A television set that can receive only pure video and audio signals.

Monitor/Receiver: A hybrid television that can receive pure video and audio signals, as well as RF signals.

Montage: A production device that allows a gradual change in a relationship or a lengthy time passage to occur in a very short amount of screen time by showing a series of silent shots accompanied by music.

MS: See *medium shot.*

Multi-camera shooting: A technique of remote shooting where multiple cameras are used.

Multiplexer: A device that facilitates the transfer of film images onto videotape. Multiplexers are used, for example, to transfer theatrical motion pictures to videotape for purchase or rental. Also called a *telecine, film chain,* or *film island.*

Music video: A program format that serves to promote a band, a new song, or an album.

N

Narrow angle shot: A shot that captures the top of the head to just below the shoulders. Also called a *close-up.*

Nat sound: See *natural sound.*

Natural sound (Nat sound): The sound present in a room, or at a location, before human occupation. Also called *room tone.*

Network: A corporation that bundles a collection of programs (sports, news, and entertainment) and makes the program bundles available exclusively to its affiliates. Generally, networks produce some of their own programming, but do not produce all of their own programs.

NiCad: See *nickel cadmium.*

Nickel cadmium (NiCad): A type of rechargeable battery commonly used to power cameras.

NLE: See *nonlinear editing system.*

Nod shots: A cutaway shot often used in interview programs and usually recorded after the interviewee has left the set. In a nod shot, the interviewer does not say anything, but simply "nods" naturally as if listening to the answer to a question.

Nonlinear editing system (NLE): Video editing equipment that is based on digital technology and uses high-capacity computer hard drives to store and process video and audio. The taped raw footage is converted to a digital format, copied to a computer's hard drive, and may then be arranged and otherwise manipulated.

Nose room: The space from the tip of a person's nose to the side edge of the frame.

O

Off-camera narrator: Talent who provides program narration, but is not seen by the viewer. Also called *voiceover*.

Omni-directional mic: A mic with a pick-up pattern that captures sound from nearly every direction equally well.

On-camera narrator: Talent who provides program narration while being seen by the camera.

Optical center: The physical location within the lens assembly where an image is inverted. Also called the *focal point*.

OSS: See *over-the-shoulder shot*.

Outline script: A program script that usually has a word-for-word introduction and conclusion, but an outline for the body of the script.

Output: A port or connection on a VCR, such as the "video out," through which the signal leaves the deck and travels to another piece of equipment.

Over-the-shoulder shot (OSS): A shot in which the back side of one person's head and shoulder are in the foreground of the shot, while a full-face shot of the other person in the conversation is in the background.

P

PA: See *production assistant*.

Pace: The frequency of cuts or edits, per minute, during a program. Also referred to as *cut rate*.

Pan: Moving only the camera to scan the set horizontally, while the dolly and tripod remain stationary.

Pan handle: A rod attached to the back of the tripod head that allows the camera operator to move the tripod head while standing behind the tripod.

Pan left: Moving the camera head to the left to scan the set, while the dolly and tripod remain stationary.

Pan right: Moving the camera head to the right to scan the set, while the dolly and tripod remain stationary.

Pancake makeup: A pressed powder makeup foundation that is water-soluble.

Panel discussion: A program format that presents a group of people gathered to discuss topics of interest. Daytime talk shows are an example of this format.

Parabolic reflector mic: A very sensitive mic that looks like a satellite dish with handles and is designed to pick up sounds at a distance.

Pedestal: Raising or lowering the camera on the pedestal column of a tripod. The tripod and dolly remain stationary.

Pedestal column: A column in the center of a tripod used to raise or lower the camera.

Pedestal control: A crank on the side of the pedestal column that twists a gear to raise and lower the pedestal column.

Pedestal down: Lowering the camera on the pedestal of a tripod. The tripod and dolly remain stationary.

Pedestal up: Raising the camera on the pedestal of a tripod. The tripod and dolly remain stationary.

Phone connector: A connector that is ¼″ in diameter and single-pronged, with a little indentation near the end of the prong. This type of connector is commonly found on the cord used with large stereo headphones. Also called a *¼″ connector*.

Phono connector: A connector commonly found on the back of quality home entertainment system components. The female phono connector is usually a chassis-mounted connector. The male phono connector is usually a cable end connector with a single, center prong surrounded by a shorter crown. Also called a *RCA connector*.

Pick-up pattern: A term that describes how well a mic hears sounds from various directions.

Pixel: One of the millions of little dots that make up the picture on a television screen, in a photograph, or any other type of image display medium.

PL259 connector: A connector that is similar to the F-connector, but much larger. The male end has a single prong with a large nut to tighten.

Plug: A connector with one or more pins that are designed to fit into the holes of a jack. Also called a *male connector*.

Pop filter: A barrier made of shaped wire covered with a piece of nylon that is placed between a sensitive mic and the talent to avoid damage to the diaphragm of the mic from the talent's breath.

Pop the contrast ratio: When the brightness or darkness of objects in a shot exceeds the contrast ratio limitations of video.

Post-production: Any of the activities performed after a program has been shot. This includes music beds, editing, audio overdubs, titles, and duplication.

Pot: See *potentiometer.*

Potentiometer (Pot): A knob or a slider that controls the strength of signals coming into the mixer.

Power level: The audio level from the output on an amplifier to the speaker.

Pre-focus: A three-step process to focus a zoom lens. 1) Zoom in on the furthest object on the set that must be in focus in the shot. 2) Focus the camera on that object. 3) Zoom the lens back out.

Pre-production: Any activity on a program that occurs prior to the time that the cameras begin rolling. This includes production meetings, set construction, costume design, music composition, scriptwriting, and location surveys.

Pre-roll: Rolling the tape in the source and record machines forward until reaching the edit-in point—automatically performed after backspacing is complete.

Preview monitor: A monitor that allows the technical director to set up an effect on the SEG before the audience sees it.

Proc amp: See *processing amplifier.*

Processing amplifier (proc amp): A machine that corrects some color and brightness problems in the video signal passing through it. This piece of equipment is commonly used when recording and/or duplicating videotapes.

Producer: The person who purchases materials and services necessary for the creation of a finished program.

Production: The actual shooting of the program.

Production assistant (PA): The person who provides general assistance around the studio or production facility. In most facilities, the PA is hired to fill a variety of positions when key personnel are sick, out of town, working on another project, or otherwise unavailable.

Production manager: The person who handles the business portion of the production by negotiating the fees for goods, services, and other contracts and by determining the staffing requirements based on the needs of each production.

Production meeting: A meeting with the entire crew in which the director lays out the program's main message and either the director or producer assigns each task involved in the production to members of the crew.

Production switcher: The general, technical name used for either a video switcher or a special effects generator.

Production switching: The process of cutting between cameras.

Production team: Everyone involved in the production, both staff and talent.

Production values: The general aesthetics of the show.

Profile shot: A shot in which the talent's face is displayed in profile.

Program monitor: A monitor that displays the image going to the recorder.

Program proposal: A document created by the scriptwriter that contains general information about the program, including the basic idea, applicable format, message to be imparted to the audience, the intended audience, budget considerations, shooting location considerations, and rough shooting schedule.

Progressive scan technology: The process of firing every line on the television screen in one pass, instead of every other line. The cathode ray moves fast enough to complete firing every line on the screen before the lines at the top of the screen begin to fade.

Prop: Any item handled by the performers during a production, other than furniture.

Prop list: A list of each prop needed for a production.

Prop plot: A listing of all the props used in a program sorted by scene.

Prosthetic: A cosmetic appliance, usually made of foam or putty, which may be glued to the skin with special adhesives.

PSA: See *public service announcement.*

Public service announcement (PSA): A program that is 30 or 60 seconds in length and aims to inform the public or to convince the public to do (or not to do) something in the interest of common good.

Pull focus: The process of changing focus on a camera while that camera is hot. Also called *rack focus.*

Q

Quad: See *quadruplex.*

Quadruplex (Quad): A very large, older videotape recorder that uses 2″ tape.

R

Raceway: The electrical cables and outlets that hang beside the grid pipes or mounted to the ceiling above the grid to power lighting instruments on the grid.

Rack focus: The process of changing focus on a camera while that camera is hot. Also called *pull focus*.

RCA connector: A connector commonly found on the back of quality home entertainment system components. The female RCA connector is usually a chassis-mounted connector. The male RCA connector is usually a cable end connector with a single, center prong surrounded by a shorter crown. Also called a *phono connector*.

RCU: See *remote control unit*.

Reaction shot: A shot that captures one person's face reacting to what another person is saying or doing.

Receiver: A television set that can receive only RF signals.

Recording rights: Permission to record music from a live performance.

Remote control unit (RCU): A piece of equipment that controls various attributes of the video signal sent from the camera to the video tape recorder, and is usually placed in the control room or the master control room. Also called a *camera control unit (CCU)*.

Remote shoot: Any production shooting that takes place outside of the studio.

Re-recording rights: Permission to copy music from a CD or cassette tape onto videotape.

RF: Radio frequency signal that is a combination of both audio and video.

RF converter: A small module inside the VCR that combines pure video and audio into one radio frequency.

Ribbon mic: The most sensitive type of mic, primarily used in music recording studios. A thin ribbon of metal surrounded by a magnetic field serves as the generating element.

Roll: Titles in a program that move up the screen.

Room tone: The sound present in a room, or at a location, before human occupation. Also called *natural sound*.

Rule of thirds: A composition rule that divides the screen into thirds horizontally and vertically, like a tic-tac-toe grid placed over the picture on a television set. Almost all of the important information included in every shot is located at one of the four intersections of the horizontal and vertical lines.

S

Scene breakdown by cast: A listing of each scene number in a program with all the cast members needed for each scene.

Scenery: Anything placed on a set that stops the distant view of the camera. Outside the studio, scenery may be a building or the horizon.

Scoop: A common type of flood light with a half-spheroid shape that produces a great deal of light.

Scrim: A type of diffusion device that appears transparent or translucent when placed in front of a lighting instrument.

Script: An entire program committed to paper, including dialog, music, camera angles, stage direction, camera direction, and computer graphics (CG) notations.

Script breakdown: The process of analyzing a program's script from many different perspectives.

Scriptwriter: The person responsible for placing the entire production on paper.

SEG: See *special effects generator*.

Selective depth of field: A technique of *choosing* to have a shallow depth of field in a shot or scene.

Set decorator: The person responsible for selecting the furniture, wall and window coverings, accent accessories, and all the other design elements that complete a program's set. Also called a *set dresser*.

Set design: A scale drawing of the set, as viewed from above, that illustrates the location of furniture, walls, doors, and windows.

Set dresser: The person responsible for selecting the furniture, wall and window coverings, accent accessories, and all the other design elements that complete a program's set. Also called a *set decorator*.

Set dressing: All the visual and design elements on a set, such as rugs, lamps, wall coverings, curtains, and room accent accessories.

Shadow: Makeup that is three or four shades darker than the base makeup applied.

Shadow mode: An add-on feature to the internal key that places a drop shadow around two sides of the keyed image.

Shallow depth of field: A depth of field technique that moves the audience's attention to the one portion of the picture that is in focus.

Shooting for the edit: The process in which a director plans exactly how each scene in a program will transition from the scenes that immediately precede and follow it. Production shooting then follows the director's plan.

Shot: An individual picture taken by a camera during the process of shooting program footage.

Shot log: A written list of each scene and take number that have been shot and recorded on a particular tape. Also called a *take log*.

Shot sheet: A numerical listing of each shot to be captured by each camera in a multi-camera shoot. Shot sheets are developed specifically for each camera.

Shotgun mic: A directional mic with an extremely narrow pick-up pattern.

Single-camera shooting: A technique of remote shooting that involves only one camera and is most often used for event recording.

Slant track: The pattern in which a video signal is placed onto a videotape. The slanted pattern allows more information to be placed on the tape. Also called *helical scan*.

Slate: A board or page that is held in front of the camera noting the scene number, the take number, and several other pieces of information about the scene being shot.

Small-scale video production companies: Businesses with limited staff and equipment resources. They thrive on producing videos of private events, commercials for local businesses, home inventories for insurance purposes, seminars, legal depositions, and real estate videos.

Soft light: Type of illumination used in a studio that creates indistinct shadows.

Source VCR: A VCR into which raw camera footage is placed for linear editing.

Special effects: Anything the audience sees in a video picture that did not really happen in the way it appears on the screen.

Special effects generator (SEG): A piece of production equipment that performs clean cuts, fades, dissolves, wipes, and various keys in addition to the basic functions of a video switcher.

Spirit gum: A type of adhesive commonly used to apply prosthetic items.

Split screen: A wipe that is stopped part of the way through its move, dividing the screen into two or more parts.

Spotlight: A hard light instrument.

Staff: Production personnel that work behind the scenes and generally include management and designers.

Staging: The arrangement of items, such as furniture, props, and talent, in a shot.

Story style: A type of music video in which the audience hears the music, but does not see the band perform. Instead, actors act out a story line that is supported by the lyrics of the song.

Storyboards: Sketches that portray the way the image on television should look in the finished program.

Straight makeup: Makeup application technique used to correct or hide blemishes, make the complexion more even, and generally help people look attractive and like themselves under bright television lights.

Studio camera: A television camera placed on a tripod or studio pedestal for exclusive use within the studio.

Studio pedestal: A large, single column on wheels that supports the camera and is pneumatically or hydraulically controlled.

Subjective camera: A hand-held camera technique, in which the camera itself becomes the eye of one cast member. The viewers see the world through the eyes of that character.

Subscriber television: Fee-for-service programming where customers pay scheduled fees based on the selected programming package. The television signals are transported by satellite transmission or by underground cables.

Super: See *superimposition*.

Super VHS (S-VHS): A low-end, industrial ½″ videotape format that is superior to VHS.

Supercardioid mic: A directional mic with a narrower pick-up pattern than a hyper-cardioid mic.

Superimposition (super): A video effect where the images or the output from two different sources are placed on screen at the same time. Each image is less than 100% of its original intensity, but when combined, the result is 100% of the intensity possible on the television screen.

Surveillance television: A form of CCTV that is usually, but not always, used for security purposes. The cameras used in the system are always interconnected to a closed circuit television system.

S-VHS: See *super VHS*.

S-VHS connector: The consumer term for a Y/C connector.

Sync generator: A device that provides a synchronization signal to all the video equipment in the television production facility.

Synchronization rights: Permission to place video in synchronization with a piece of music.

Syndication: The process of making a specified number of program episodes available for "lease" to other networks or individual broadcast stations, after the current network's contract for the program expires.

T

Tail: A 10 second "lead-out" recorded onto videotape at the end of each scene.

Take: *1*—A term that identifies each time an individual scene is shot. *2*—An instantaneous picture change that occurs on screen. Used synonymously with *cut* in this context.

Take log: A written list of each scene and take number that have been shot and recorded on a particular tape. Also called a *shot log*.

Talent: Anyone seen by the camera, whether or not they have a speaking or any other significant role in the program, as well as individuals who provide only their vocal skills to the production.

Talking head: A program format in which the talent speaks and the camera shoots almost entirely in a medium close-up. Also called *big talking face (BTF)* and *lecture*.

Target: Photosensitive surface of a charge coupled device (CCD).

TBC: See *time base corrector*.

T-connector: A connector that is shaped like the capital letter *T* and is made entirely of metal (on the outside). The three ends of a T-connector are used to split one signal into two signals, or to combine two signals into one.

TD: See *technical director*.

Technical director (TD): A member of the production team whose primary job function is to follow the camera script or verbal commands from the director and operate the video switcher accordingly.

Technique: The manner in which a person performs a task or completes a procedure.

Telecine: A device that facilitates the transfer of film images onto videotape. Telecines are used, for example, to transfer theatrical motion pictures to videotape for purchase or rental. Also called a *multiplexer, film chain,* or *film island*.

Teleprompter: A computer screen reflected in a one-way mirror that is positioned in front of the camera lens and displays dialog text in large letters. This allows the talent to look directly at the lens of the camera and read the text.

Test record: The process of using the VTR to record audio and video signals before the session taping begins to ensure the equipment is functioning properly and to indicate any necessary adjustments.

Three point lighting: A common lighting technique that uses three lighting instruments for each person or object photographed: a key light, a fill light, and a back light.

Three shot: A shot that frames three items.

Tilt: Pointing only the front of the camera (lens) vertically up or down while the dolly and tripod remain stationary.

Tilt down: Pointing the camera lens down toward the ground, while the dolly and tripod remain stationary.

Tilt up: Pointing the camera lens up toward the ceiling, while the dolly and tripod remain stationary.

Time base corrector (TBC): A machine that corrects any quality related imperfections in the video and audio signals caused by mechanical errors associated with the VCR's functionality.

Time coding: A system of assigning each frame of a video a specific number, like an address.

Tracking control: A knob on a professional VCR that is used to manually adjust the tape tracking speed.

Transitional device: An effect that is used as a means of getting from one scene to another.

Tripod: A three-legged stand that supports a camera.

Tripod head: The assembly at the top of the pedestal column to which the camera attaches.

Truck: Moving the camera, its tripod, and dolly to the left or right in a motion that is parallel to the set.

Truck left: To move the camera, its tripod, and dolly sideways and to the left while continuing to face the set.

Truck right: To move the camera, its tripod, and dolly sideways and to the right while continuing to face the set.

Two shot: A shot that includes two items of primary importance.

U

U-Matic: A ¾″ videotape format that has been surpassed by current technology. Also called *¾″ tape*.

Uni-directional mic: A mic with a pick-up pattern that captures sound from primarily one direction. Also called a *directional mic* or *cardioid mic*.

Up from black: A video effect where a totally dark picture transitions into a fully visible picture. Also called *fade in*.

V

V.O.: See *voiceover*.

Variable focal length lens: A lens in which the optical center can vary its position within the lens assembly, varying the focal length measurement as well. Also called a *zoom lens*.

Vector line: An imaginary line, parallel to the camera, which bisects a set into a foreground and a background. Also called a *camera line*.

Vectorscope: A piece of testing equipment that graphically measures the way the colors are structured in the video signal.

Vertical blanking: The signal that turns off the cathode ray when it reaches the bottom of the screen.

Vertical retrace: The signal that returns the cathode ray position to the top of the screen to begin firing again.

Vertical sync pulse: A signal that alerts the cathode that the last line of the screen has been sprayed.

Vertical wipe: A video effect where a horizontal line moves across the screen vertically, replacing one picture with another.

VHS (Video Home System): A ½″ videotape format that emerged as the preferred standard for consumer VCRs.

VHS-C: A ½″ VHS videotape that is shorter than regular VHS and is, therefore, packaged in a compact cassette.

Video: The portion of the program you can see.

Video delay edit: An edit that cuts to the audio portion of the next scene before the corresponding video of the new scene is seen by the audience.

Video engineer: The person who manages the video equipment and is ultimately responsible for the technical quality of the video signal.

Video heads: The components inside a VCR that lay down the video signal onto a tape when in record mode. When a VCR is in playback mode, the video heads pick up the video signal from a tape.

Video noise: The black and white dots seen on a screen if the videotape is blank or if the heads are dirty.

Video switcher: Piece of equipment to which all video sources in a studio are connected. A switcher allows the operator to select one signal from various video inputs and output the selected signal to the video recorder for recording. Also called a *switcher*.

Viewfinder: A small video monitor attached to the camera that allows the camera operator to view the images in the shot.

Visualization: The ability to mentally picture the finished program.

Voice track: The audio portion of a program created through dialog or narration.

Voiceover (V.O.): Talent that provides program narration, but is not seen by the viewer. Also called *off-camera narration*.

Volume unit meter (VU meter): A meter on either an audio or mic mixer that indicates signal strength.

VTR interchange: The ability of a tape that was recorded on one machine to be played back on another machine.

VTR operator: The person in charge of recording the program onto videotape by correctly operating the VTR equipment.

VU meter: See *volume unit meter*.

W

WA: See *wide angle shot*.

Waveform monitor: A piece of testing equipment that measures every aspect of an image, including the brightness and darkness of the video signal.

White balance: A function on cameras that forces the camera to see an object as white, without regard to the type of light hitting it or the actual color of the object.

Wide angle shot (WA): The biggest shot a camera can capture of the subject matter.

Windscreen: A covering, usually foam, placed over a mic to reduce the rumble or flapping sound created when wind blows across the mic.

Wipe: A video effect where a line, or multiple lines, moves across the screen and replaces one picture with another.

Wireless mic: A mic that uses a short cable to connect the mic to a radio transmitter with an antenna, or the transmitter may be built into the mic itself. The transmitter wirelessly sends the signal to the receiver, which sends the mic signal through a cable to the recorder.

Word-for-word script: A program script in which every word spoken by the talent is written out.

X

XCU: See *extreme close-up*.

XLR connector: A connector for microphones that usually has 3-pins, but can have 4-pins, 5-pins, and other pin configurations. The male and female ends lock together with a hook.

XLS: See *extreme long shot*.

Y

Y/C: The professional name for the signal placed onto S-VHS videotape.

Y/C connector: A video input and output connector that is characterized by four tiny round pins and a rectangular plastic stabilizing pin.

Y-connector: A connector that has three wires with a connector on the end of each. All the wires are tied together in the middle. The three ends of a Y-connector are used to split one signal into two signals, or to combine two signals into one.

Z

Zebra stripes: A special function of some viewfinders that displays black and white diagonal stripes on any object in a shot that is too brightly lit.

Zoom in: The act of rotating a ring on the zoom lens so that the center of the picture appears to be moving toward the camera.

Zoom lens: The particular piece of glass within the lens assembly that moves forward and back, magnifying or shrinking the image accordingly. This individual lens is the focal point, or optical center, of the zoom lens assembly.

Zoom lenses: A camera lens assembly that is capable of magnifying an image merely by twisting one of the rings on the outside of the lens housing. Also called a *variable focal length lens*.

Zoom out: The act of rotating a ring on the zoom lens so that the center of the picture appears to be moving away from the camera.

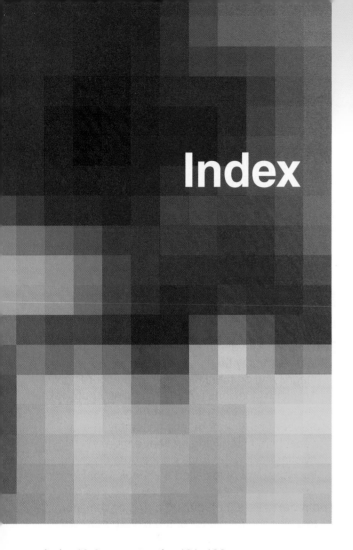

Index